330.9725 H27t
Hassig, Ross, 1945- 2267450
Trade, tribute, and
transportation

THE CIVILIZATION OF THE AMERICAN INDIAN SERIES

Trade, Tribute, and Transportation

Trade, Tribute, and Transportation

THE SIXTEENTH-CENTURY POLITICAL ECONOMY OF THE VALLEY OF MEXICO

By Ross Hassig

UNIVERSITY OF OKLAHOMA PRESS : NORMAN

By Ross Hassig

(Translator and editor, with J. Richard Andrews) Hernando Ruiz de Alarcón, *Treatise on the Heathen Superstitions and Customs That Today Live Among the Indians Native to This New Spain* (Norman, 1984)

Library of Congress Cataloging in Publication Data

Hassig, Ross, 1945–
Trade, tribute, and transportation.

(Civilization of the American Indian series; v. 171)
Includes bibliographies and index.
1. Aztecs—Economic conditions. 2. Indians of Mexico—Mexico, Valley of—Economic conditions. 3. Mexico, Valley of (Mexico)—Economic conditions. I. Title. II. Series.
F1219.76.E36H37 1985 330.9725'01'08997 84-25762
ISBN 0-8061-1911-X (alk. paper)

The paper in this book meets the guidelines for permanence and durability of the Committee on Production Guidelines for Book Longevity of the Council on Library Resources, Inc.

For My Parents,

Ronald and Janice Hassig

Acknowledgments

In thinking about acknowledgments during the preparation of this book, I amended it mentally many times as first one person and then another assisted my research. Now that the task is at hand, however, I find that space does not permit me to thank individually all the people and institutions who provided indispensable assistance—the anthropologists, historians, archivists, librarians, and researchers who have been invaluable. To an ethnohistorian these people are at the heart of the research. I want particularly to thank the staffs of the Archivo General de la Nación, the Archivo del Antiguo Ayuntamiento, the Archivo Histórico de Notarías, and the Biblioteca del Museo Nacional de Antropología. I am also grateful to the Organization of American States for supporting this study, to the Centro de Investigaciones Superiores del Instituto Nacional de Antropología e Historia for granting the affiliation that allowed me to accept the OAS grant, and to Stanford University for various grants and assistance.

My academic debts are numerous. I owe thanks to many members of the anthropology faculty at Stanford, especially George A. Collier, William H. Durham, James A. Fox, James L. Gibbs, Benjamin D. Paul, and G. William Skinner. I owe particular thanks to Philip L. Ritter and Claudio Lomnitz-Adler with whom I discussed many parts of this work; to Jule Kringel, who offered considerable encouragement; to Jim Fox for providing guidance, encouragement, and enthusiasm throughout the writing; and to G. William Skinner for redressing these excesses and for relentlessly forcing me to keep the significance of this work in its proper perspective.

I am indebted to Debi Higgs for reading and commenting on the complete manuscript, and to J. Richard Andrews for also reading and critiquing the manuscript, as well as providing much needed and appreciated assistance with Nahuatl. I would also like to thank Frederic Hicks for suggesting the citation form I have adopted, making the references to sources in multiple editions much more informative and helpful to others. Several rather long-standing debts are owed old friends, Dillon Fankhauser and Edwin LaQuay, who influenced me in choosing this profession. And last, I am also greatly indebted to my family, particularly my parents, for long-term and encouraging support.

ROSS HASSIG

New York City

Table of Contents

Illustrations and Maps

PLATES

FIGURES

MAPS

Trade, Tribute, and Transportation

CHAPTER 1

Introduction

When the Spaniards first entered central Mexico, they were not fully prepared for what they were to see. Here were no simple tribesmen such as they had encountered in the islands of the West Indies, but sophisticated civilizations with developed and flourishing urban traditions. Repeatedly the conquistadors marveled at the cities they found, comparing them favorably with those of their Spanish homeland and the other great centers of sixteenth-century Europe. They were greatly impressed by the first cities they encountered on their trek inland, such as Cempoala, Tlaxcala, and Cholula. But their astonishment knew no bounds on their arrival in the Aztec capital of Tenochtitlan. As Cortés wrote to the king:

This city has many squares where trading is done and markets are held continuously. There is also one square twice as big as that of Salamanca, with arcades all around, where more than sixty thousand people come each day to buy and sell, and where every kind of merchandise produced in these lands is found .... There are many sorts of spun cotton, in hanks of every color, and it seems like the silk market at Granada, except here there is a much greater quantity. ... There are, in all districts of this great city, many temples or houses for their idols. They are all very beautiful buildings. ... Amongst these temples there is one, the principal one, whose great size and magnificence no human tongue could describe, for it is so large that within the precincts, which are surrounded by a very high wall, a town of some five hundred inhabitants could easily be built. ... They are so well constructed in both their stone and woodwork that there can be none better in any place .... There are in the city many large and beautiful houses .... All these houses have very large and very good rooms and also very pleasant gardens of various sorts of flowers both on the upper and lower floors. . . . these people live like those in Spain, and in as much harmony and order as there, and considering that they are barbarous and so far from the knowledge of God and cut off from all civilized nations, it is truly remarkable to see what they have achieved in all things.[1]

Despite the grandeur of Tenochtitlan, the picture of the city at the apex of political and economic power is unduly static. Despite accounts of the lateness of the Aztec rise,[2] the most prevalent and forceful picture of pre-Hispanic Mexico is as the conquistadors found it; one receives the impression of the Aztec empire as a given rather than as a recent and developing entity. Tenochtitlan was founded in A.D. 1345, but it was not until 1428 that the Tepanec empire of Azcapotzalco was overthrown by the Triple Alliance of Tenochtitlan, Texcoco, and Tlacopan. The Valley of Mexico was not brought under unified dominance until the final defeat of Chalco in 1463, and Tenochtitlan became the dominant member of the Triple Alliance after 1473, when it subjugated its sister city, Tlatelolco.[3] Thus, central Mexico and the Valley of Mexico were undergoing considerable change as a result of the Aztec ascendency and the political and economic restructuring of the region that this rise entailed.

The complex urban system of Mexico is the focus of this book. Although there are many ways to approach the study of cities, the focus here is not on such issues as their internal layout, their political-economic-religious structuring, the psychological impact of urban living on the individual, or the general ethos of the society. Rather, the concern is with the growth and maintenance of the city in the context of its sustaining hinterland—the way hinterlands were acquired, controlled, and exploited in pre- and post-Conquest times.

Theories dealing with the rise and persistence of the urban form are many and varied.[4] Emerging from these diverse perspectives is the conclusion that urbanization is primarily a social revolution, not a technological one. Although many features have been examined and touted as crucial to urbanization—population size, density, and nucleation, the development of a state-level political organization, and the emergence of a class-based social structure—the key to urban growth is the acquisition and maintenance of control over the surrounding hinterland.

No population aggregation of any size (i.e., no city or town of consequence) exists as an independent entity: "Towns are intense food deficient points located within large areas where food production is in excess of local consumption."[5] No city is self-sufficient, and one of the most significant aspects of urbanization is the way the city provides for its own needs. These needs—primarily food, raw materials, and population—are supplied both from other cities and, more significantly, from the surrounding rural areas. Thus a major consequence of urbanization is not merely a symbiosis between town and country but an active restructuring of relationships between the city and the sustaining hinterland.

To provide for the systematic supply of necessities to its populace, cities alter the preexisting relationship (or the relationship that would obtain in the absence of a city) of rural production and producers to urban consumers and demand by creating an artificial dependency of rural areas on urban ones. While urban areas are always dependent upon rural areas, rural areas are not necessarily dependent upon urban areas. To ensure the flow of necessary commodities, cities seek to change this independent existence into a dependent one, most obviously by economic means, but also by political and sometimes religious means. Thus the pivotal problem for urbanization, the maintenance of the city's own existence, can be accomplished and sustained only through the systematic restructuring and perpetuation of a totally new set of dependency relationships. While this new relationship is not necessarily one-sided, in essence the countryside feeds the city, and the city feeds on the countryside.

The city is not an isolated phenomenon, but merely

the most evident feature of a symbiotic area.[6] Although their economic production has often been examined, cities are, in fact, inadequate producers, incapable of supplying enough food, people, or consumer demand. For these the surrounding hinterlands must be tapped.

The cities of Mesoamerica at the time of the Spanish conquest are not examples of pristine urbanization. They were not creations de novo but were the result of long traditions. Accordingly, much of the literature dealing with the inception of urbanism, though interesting, is of secondary relevance here. The significant focus is on Mesoamerican cities generally and on the Aztec capital of Tenochtitlan specifically and how these cities acquired and secured hinterlands necessary for their support and maintenance. And the same basic processes and constraints apply both before and after the Spanish conquest. Much scholarly concern has been directed at the degree of continuity or discontinuity between pre- and post-Columbian urban forms,[7] but the concerns have generally focused on such aspects as urban planning, architectural forms, and polities.

Urban development is shaped by political and economic systems. These systems are not completely different in each society. Although the way these systems are structured and organized may vary among societies, there are also constraints of a more general nature—such as transportation and the limitations imposed by the friction of distance—that affect these idiosyncratic political and economic systems. Urbanism is affected by general underlying factors that constrain all such developments. The pattern of political and economic systems depends on the relations between cities and their sustaining areas. Consequently, urbanism cannot be understood by examining the city in isolation, but requires a regional approach.

Four interrelated topics affecting the relationship between cities and hinterlands are examined: population, the agricultural potential of the land, consumption rates, and transportation efficiency. People must be fed. Consequently, the size of population concentrations is determined by the food available, which is in turn a function of the agricultural potential of the land. This productive potential is not, however, a simple given. Absolute productivity of the land does not establish the amounts of foodstuffs available to cities. Rather, both the amounts produced and the amounts flowing into the cities are determined by the efficiency of the system of transportation in use. Transportation systems affect urbanization, economic organization, and political systems in fundamental ways.

An analytical history can be approached in one of two ways. Each topic of the interrelated whole can be treated separately through time, the individual subjects being synthesized at the end. Or the various aspects can be interrelated functionally at the beginning, the complex whole being carried through time as a unit. Neither approach is wholly satisfactory, and although drawing on both, I emphasize the former course in the belief that it is easier to grasp the sequential changes of more narrowly defined bodies of data that may then be systematically related to form a coherent and comprehensive picture of sixteenth-century developments.

While it is feasible to detail specific changes after the Conquest (A.D. 1519–21), it is more difficult for pre-Columbian times owing to a lack of documentation of sufficient chronological depth and detail. Consequently, the picture of the pre-Conquest situation does not always possess the minute detail available for the post-Conquest era.

The primary data on which I rely are both published and unpublished. The published data consist of sixteenth- and seventeenth-century accounts of Mexican life and history, such as those of Bernardino de Sahagún and Diego Durán, and collections of documents of diverse content, such as the Colección de documentos inéditos . . . , Papeles de Nueva España, and Epistolario de Nueva España. The unpublished data have been drawn from the Archivo General de la Nación, the Archivo del Antiguo Ayuntamiento, and the Archivo Histórico de Notarías, all in Mexico City. Numerous archaeological reports from the Valley of Mexico also supply information of a primary nature.[8]

In reconstructing the economic and political life in the Valley of Mexico, published sources have furnished a fuller picture of events than have the archival data, although their descriptions tend to gloss over important, though mundane, events that bear significantly on the overall economic organization of indigenous society. Thus, while I have drawn on comprehensive accounts of sixteenth-century conditions, it is the archival materials that provide the record of events from which a fuller and more accurate representation of everyday life has been drawn.

PART ONE

The Pre-Columbian Era

CHAPTER 2

Economic Production in Central Mexico

THE ISSUE OF central Mexico's pre-Columbian population is intimately tied to the area's economic capacity and is much debated, although it is probably unresolvable. However, the crucial factors of interest focus on the carrying capacity of the area—land, crop complexes, and agricultural systems. These factors are not givens but vary according to the way society is organized to take advantage of them. Thus the general parameters of agriculture and its production must be examined and then placed in a context that explains what occurs where and why it permits or constrains overall urban growth.

PHYSICAL DESCRIPTION

The study of Middle America has always involved the area's division into regions of various sorts, usually along cultural or geographical lines. Culturally the primary division is embodied in the concept of Mesoamerica, which distinguishes the areas of high indigenous civilization from the areas of lower culture on both north and south. Within Mesoamerica the main division is between the Mayan and Mexican areas, with further divisions by additional cultural groups. Geographically, Mesoamerica begins at the desert north of the Valley of Mexico and extends through Guatemala and into parts of Honduras, El Salvador, Nicaragua, and Costa Rica on the south. Somewhat simplistically, the area is vertically divided into colder highlands *(tierra fría)*, intermediate temporate zones *(tierra templada)*, and tropical lowlands *(tierra caliente)*.[1]

Topographically, central Mexico is enormously va-

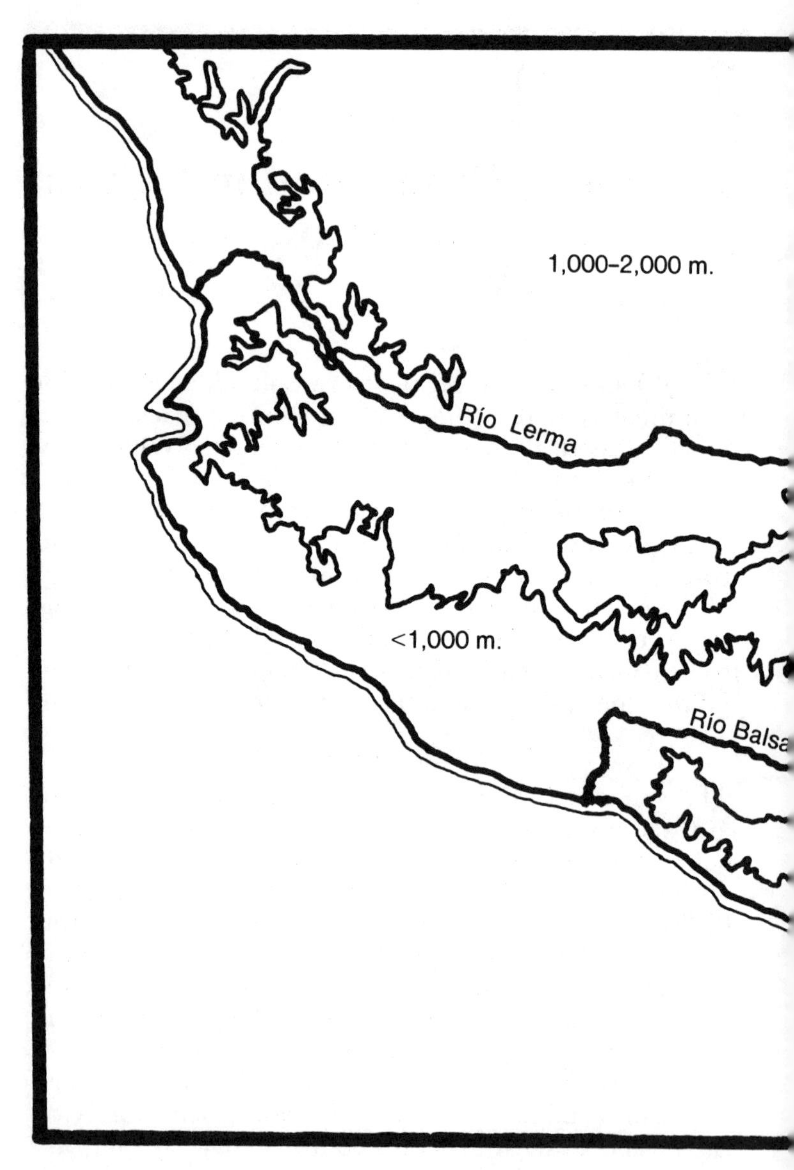

MAP 1. TOPOGRAPHY OF CENTRAL MEXICO. Contour lines demarcate *tierra caliente* (below 1,000 meters), *tierra templada* (between 1,000 and 2,000 meters), and *tierra fría* (above 2,000 meters).

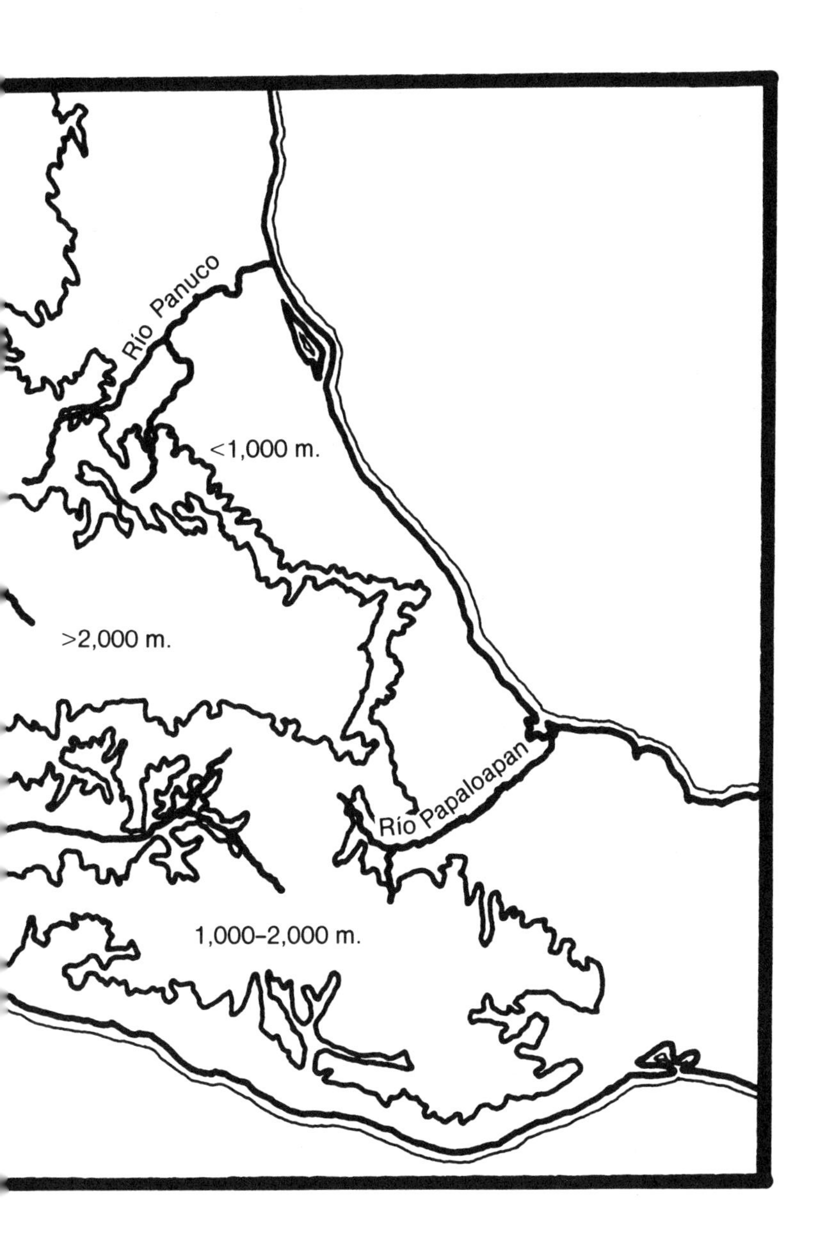
Río Panuco
<1,000 m.
>2,000 m.
Río Papaloapan
1,000–2,000 m.

ried. The high central plateau has several major valleys separated by mountain ranges and declines toward the sea on both coasts. Because of the sharp descent from the central plateau, central Mexico lacks large, slow-flowing rivers draining vast tracts of land. The four most significant rivers in the area are the Lerma, running from the region of Toluca northwest into the Pacific; the Balsas, running from Atlixco southwest to the Pacific; the Papaloapan, running from the southern highlands east to the Gulf; and the Pánuco, running from the region of the state of Mexico northeast to the Gulf (see map 1).

AGRICULTURE

Pre-Columbian agricultural practices were often highly developed. The indigenous peoples were acutely aware of variations in soil, rainfall, cultivation techniques, and crops. The Aztecs possessed a rather sophisticated system of soil classification (see table 2.1).

Table 2.1. Aztec Soil Classifications

Class	Description
Atoctli	Fertile alluvial soil
Cuauhtlalli	Humus or soil enriched by decayed trees
Tlalcoztli	Fine, fertile reddish-yellow soil
Xalatoctli	Sandy alluvial soil
Tlahzollalli	Soil enriched by decayed matter
Xallalli	Infertile sandy soil
Tezoquitl	Firm, clayey dark soil

The basic Aztec classification system divided soils into one of three types of earth material—rock, rocklike, and nonrock, depending on whether or not the material could be held in the hand and crushed. They also distinguished land by utility (see table 2.2). Furthermore, the Badianus Manuscript, an Aztec pictorial document, distinguishes soil varieties in a botanical spirit, according to the suitability of plants to specific soils, this ready identification being the dominant concept behind the creation of such classificatory schemes.[2]

Table 2.2. Aztec Land Utility Classifications

Class	Description
Tlalcohualli	Land that is bought or sold
Tlalmantli	Flatland, land that is neither hilly nor hollowed
Tlalhuitectli	Land that is worked down, packed
Tlalahuiac	Land to which fertilizer is added
Atlalli	Land that is irrigated

In general, the following was the method by which the Aztecs planted maize.[3] The best seed was selected, shelled, and soaked in water. After two or three days, when it was swollen, it was planted in worked soil. A hole was made, the grains were tossed in, and if there was no moisture, it was watered. The seeds were then covered with pulverized soil; after the seed sprouted, small hills were made around the shoots. Beans were also sown at that time. The maize was hilled twice more before it matured (see plate 1).

However, this planting description does not encompass the many agricultural systems in use in Mesoamerica. Based on planting practices, agricultural systems ranged from swidden, or slash-and-burn, agriculture through short-fallow to intensive-irrigation agriculture. Swidden cultivation was primarily practiced in the *tierra caliente* and in the humid regions of the *tierra templada.* Short-fallow cultivation was primary in the arid and subhumid regions of the *tierra templada* and in the *tierra fría.*[4]

Swidden cultivation, or slash and burn (*roza* in Mesoamerica), involves clearing a section of land and burning the brush. The soil is then seeded with a digging stick, or *coa,* and periodically weeded. The field is usually abandoned after two years because of declining productivity and increasing labor demands. Infield-outfield, or fallowing (*barbecho* in Mesoamerica), also begins with clearing

Plate 1. Maize planting (Sahagún 1979, 1:315r).

and burning the land. The planted field, or milpa, is cultivated in a manner similar to cultivation of swidden fields, the main difference being that the fallow periods in *barbecho* are much shorter.[5]

Relative productivity of the two systems is a complicated issue even for the present day, much less for the sixteenth century. Agricultural systems vary with population density. In a low-population situation, a long-fallow swidden system of extensive cultivation is employed, since the yield per unit of labor is the greatest. But with an increase in population density and consequent land scarcity, cultivators shift to short-fallow, and then intensive systems of cultivation. The shift from one system to the other appears to be a function of population pressure. Given sufficient land, cultivators practice swidden, shifting to more labor-intensive systems only when there is inadequate land to permit the use of the former.[6]

The estimated number of hectares (1 hectare = 10,000 square meters) necessary each year to support one family is 1.5 for swidden, 2.5 for infield-outfield, and 0.86 for irrigation agriculture. But since these systems require a cycle of use and fallowing, over a period of years, one family requires a total of 12 hectares for swidden, 6.5 for infield-outfield, and 0.86 for irrigation. The estimated ratio of land in use to land in reserve for infield-outfield ranges from 1 to 1 in unusually fertile soils, to a more common 1 to 2 or 1 to 3, whereas swidden ranges from 1 to 3 to 1 to 12. Highland practice ranged from cultivating an area for two to three years and then fallowing it for one year to cultivating it for one year and then fallowing it for two to three years, averaging a ratio of 1 to 3.[7] Irrigation agriculture, widely used in the sixteenth century,[8] was the most productive per unit of land, both yearly and throughout its cycle of cultivation. Although widely practiced, irrigation agriculture was, of course, practical only in areas with reliable water sources, such as in river valleys and near major lakes. As a result of these various systems of production, population density varied greatly throughout Mesoamerica, affecting the amount of surplus food produced and, consequently, the degree of urbanization.

Although the broad outlines are clear, specific agricultural practices and patterns for the sixteenth century are difficult to estimate with any precision. One modern estimate of the average crop yield in sixteenth-century Mexico is 30 fanegas (1 fanega = 46 kilograms) of maize produced per fanega planted and 24 to 1 for wheat on 1,000 square *brazas* of land (0.28 hectare; 1 *braza* = 1.67 meters). However, sixteenth-century sources indicate great variations in yield. In Veracruz, the ratio for maize was between 100 and 150 to 1, and in Metztitlan wheat had a 50-to-1 ratio. Other records show ratios of 200, 300, 400, and even 800 to 1. These figures yield ratios of harvested to sown grain but do not address the issues of harvest to land or harvest to labor. Nor are they given in relation to types of land or systems of cultivation, which greatly alter the yield ratios, and particularly glaring is the omission of spatial variation in agricultural productivity. Nevertheless, despite the problem of the accuracy of modern estimates of the productivity of sixteenth-century agricultural practices, they are helpful in understanding specific practices or regional variations, although substantially lower yields have been recorded for communally worked tribute lands in the Valley of Mexico during the 1530s and 1540s.[9]

Several problems intrude on issues of pre-Columbian agricultural systems. Many analyses are bound up with the issue of actual and potential population levels of given areas. From these two points arguments have flowed both ways. Estimated population is used to calculate how much land was under cultivation, which includes the problems of productivity of soils, agricultural systems, and crops. Estimated agricultural production is used to calculate areal carrying capacity, which includes assumptions about levels of individual consumption. In short, the problem of reconstructing pre-Columbian agricultural systems is fraught with unresolved difficulties, such as:

1. What systems of cultivation were being used and where?
2. How much land was being cultivated?
3. Was there continual cropping of the same plot, and if not, how much land was required in fallow per unit in production?
4. How productive per hectare was each agricultural system in use?
5. How productive were pre-Columbian crops?
6. What were the labor expenditures per unit of land and per unit of yield?
7. How much production was required to support one family?

To assess the adequacy of agricultural production, rates of consumption must be known. Based on the Tehuacan Valley excavations, Callen has reconstructed the general outlines of Mexican diet, indicating a progressive shift from meat and wild plants to domesticated crops. In 6500 B.C. the Mesoamerican diet was 50 percent hunted trapped meat, 49 percent wild plants, and 1 percent cultivated plants, whereas by A.D. 1120 it consisted of 17 percent meat, 75 percent cultivated plants, and 8 percent wild plants.[10] In the pre-Columbian period diet varied by social class, but the differences were primarily in elaboration, both commoners and nobles consuming the same basic foods.[11] Modern estimates of sixteenth-century Aztec consumption are varied: 200 to 250 kilograms per person per year, 200 kilograms per person per year, 8 pounds per day per family of five. Estimates of modern consumption are also varied: 3,200 calories per person per day, 1,500 kilograms per year per family of five, many estimates being based on the study of nutrition among Maya peasants in Yucatan.[12]

Maize was found to be the main ingredient of contemporary Maya diet, comprising an average 73 percent of the total 2,565 calories consumed per day by adult males. However, data derived from modern Maya consumption practices may not be completely applicable to sixteenth-century central Mexican practices. First, some changes in diet have occurred owing to the introduction of European crops and animals, and, second, projections based on Maya examples are not entirely appropriate. Theoretically, Aztecs and Mayas should differ by approximately five centimeters in height owing to environmental conditions, according to Bergmann's rule.[13] This is borne out by skeletal studies that place the average height in the central altiplano of Mexico at 163 centimeters for men and 150 centimeters for women, while in the Maya area, it was 159 centimeters for men and 148 centimeters for women. Thus Maya studies may be instructive for food proportions and dietary practices, but they cannot easily yield consumption rates for other areas of Mexico. To assess pre-Conquest Aztec consumption, the available sixteenth-century data must be examined.

References to Indian consumption are few for the sixteenth-century, but four available examples show a basic conformity. First, the daily ration for adult male laborers on public works was one *cuartillo* of maize per day (48 *cuartillos* per fanega of 100 Castilian pounds, which were equivalent to 460 grams each, totaling 46 kilograms), or 950 grams of maize (3,800 calories). Thus the annual adult male consumption would be 7.6 fanegas (349.6 kilograms) per year, and that of a family averaging 4.5 members would be 25 fanegas (1,150 kilograms) per year.[14] Second, an ordinance of 1536 required Indians working in the mines to be fed on a par with the slaves—one *cuartillo* of maize, chili, and beans per laborer per day.[15] Dry maize contains 4 calories per gram, beans 3.9 to 4.1 calories per gram, depending on type, and chili 5.3 calories per gram. Neither the type of beans nor the proportions of the foods are specified, so a precise caloric content is unattainable, but it would likely have been on a par with maize alone—3,800 calories. Third, an ordinance of 1579 ordered Indians working in the *obrajes* (textile mills) to be fed a total of 2 pounds of bread (tortillas, tamales, or wheat bread) per day, during three meals, plus a piece of meat at the midday meal or beans on meatless days, and at night, three or four chilis (a minimum caloric value of 3,800).[16] Fourth, an ordinance of 1587 required Indian laborers to be paid half a real per day plus food of at least ten tortillas, weighing one and a half pounds (at least 2,850 calories).[17]

Considering the close coincidence of the first three ration requirements, as well as the phrasing of the fourth as a minimum, the one-*cuartillo* estimate appears to be reasonable both for the work involved and as a statement of sixteenth-century practice. This does not mean that standard was adhered to in practice. Rather, one *cuartillo* was recognized as a reasonable standard of adult male consumption, and I shall accordingly use it and the estimates of 7.6 fanegas per year per adult male and 25 fanegas per year per family of 4.5.[18] Thus the background, however tentative, has been laid for assessing the difficulty of supplying urban centers with sufficient foodstuffs for their populace.[19]

URBAN FOOD SUPPLY

Urban growth and maintenance are dependent upon the quantities of goods available to the city. A city's population can grow only to the extent that a dependable supply of foodstuffs is made available to it. But this supply is not a given; rather, it is determined by two basic factors, production and transportation.

An increase in productivity can frequently be achieved for a given land area by means of intensification, such as multicropping, irrigation, altering of crop complexes, and fertilization. However, productivity can be calculated in two different ways, either per unit of land or per unit of labor. Whether a particular agricultural practice increases overall productivity depends, in part, on how much land is available. The cost of a given commodity will vary, not simply as a matter of supply and demand but according to the production techniques employed to produce it (see fig. 2.1). A 50 percent labor increase to achieve a 25 percent

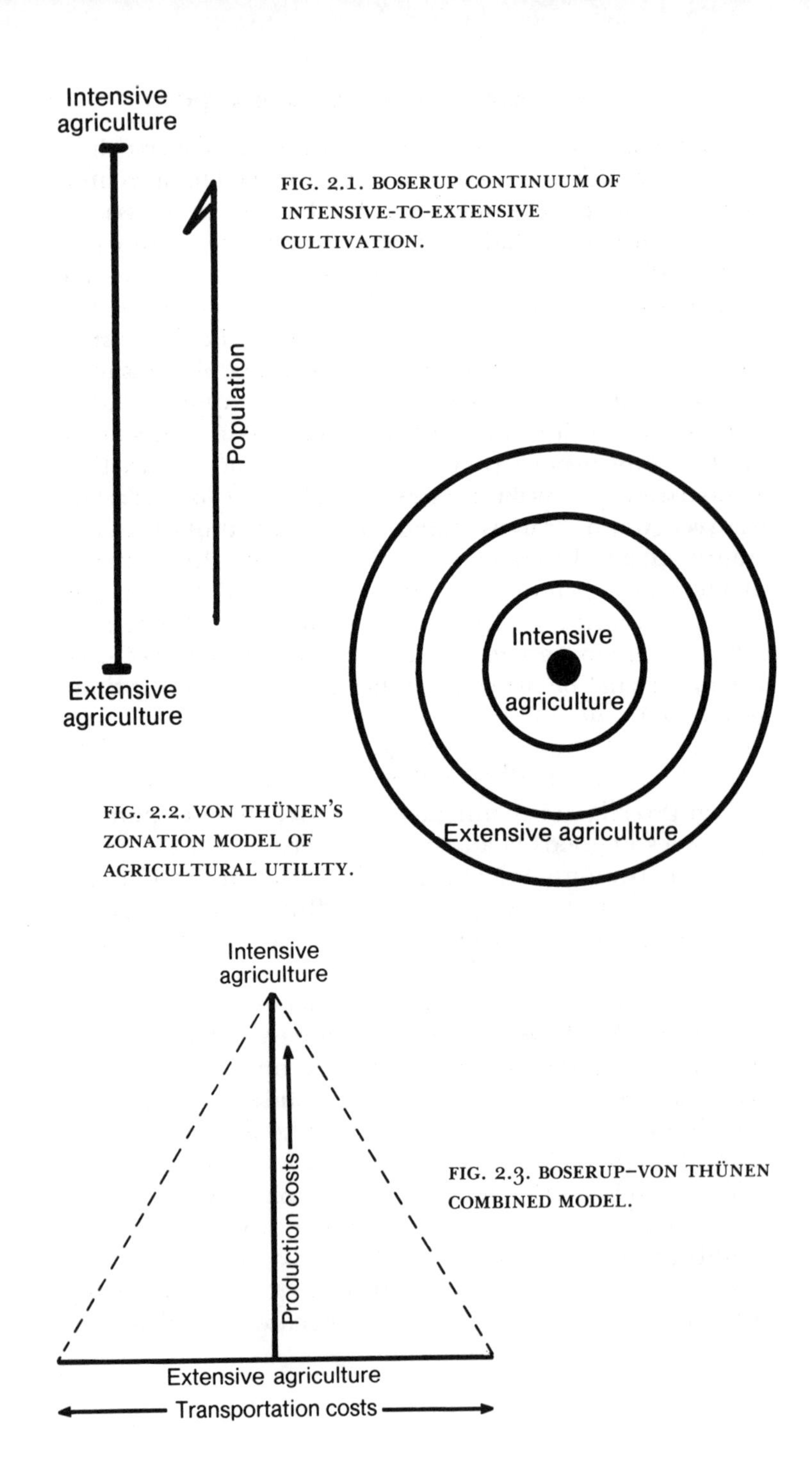

FIG. 2.1. BOSERUP CONTINUUM OF INTENSIVE-TO-EXTENSIVE CULTIVATION.

FIG. 2.2. VON THÜNEN'S ZONATION MODEL OF AGRICULTURAL UTILITY.

FIG. 2.3. BOSERUP–VON THÜNEN COMBINED MODEL.

production increase is acceptable when there is no additional land, but it is grossly inefficient when land is plentiful, since the same 50 percent labor increase addressed to additional land would yield a 50 percent production increase.

A second factor affecting the cost of commodities is the transportation system. Where production is close to the consuming center, the cost of bringing goods to market is low, so production costs may be higher without rendering the product uncompetitively expensive. Thus more intensive (and expensive) forms of cultivation are feasible. Consequently, if arable land is limited, increasing demand forces a shift from more extensive to more intensive forms of cultivation. This shift yields higher returns in raw goods but at higher production costs. Therefore, each area may increase its production by resorting to agricultural intensification up to the level at which transportation costs render additional intensification impractical—intensification is forced at the center while only extensive cultivation is practical at the periphery. What leads to this characteristic von Thünen pattern is the demand for goods at the center and the increased production necessary to meet it, up to the point where costs exceed the selling price.

Product demand and product competition help set market values. Value does not increase simply as production and transport expenses rise; rather, it is the cost of production that is flexible. Thus increased distance from the market center does not cause market values to rise but rather forces a decline in production costs. Axiomatically, the cost of producing a uniformly available commodity must decrease with distance from the market to compensate for the increase in transportation costs to remain economically competitive, or profits must drop with distance. How quickly the increasing transport costs force production costs to decline depends on the efficiency of the transportation system. But the net result is that, with distance, transport costs steadily erode the production-site value of commodities, resulting in an agricultural pattern in which the most intensive forms of cultivation are employed closest to the city (since their production costs may be highest but must bear the lowest transport costs) and the less intensive forms are employed on a declining gradient with distance from the city (since their lower costs of production permit their transport for greater distances).[20] This, however, varies by commodity (see fig. 2.2).

Boserup[21] views the type of agricultural system used as a function of the man-land ratio, which determines the degree of agricultural intensity. But what is essentially a temporal continuum for Boserup is spatial for von Thünen.[22] An examination of von Thünen demonstrates that, while the Boserup continuum can theoretically be applied to any given location, the actual extent to which a locale can undergo agricultural intensification is not totally flexible but depends on its location vis-à-vis its market. Given the increasing percentage of the total product cost that transportation entails, extensive cultivation alone is feasible for market at the periphery of the urban support area, whereas at the core the entire range is possible. The wedding of these two perspectives generates a model of maximal land use in relation to market (see fig. 2.3). With urban population growth more intensive agricultural systems displace less intensive ones in a ripple effect beginning at the center and proceeding toward the periphery. However, what can be produced and where is not a constant but varies by commodity.

Commodity Ranges

Each commodity has its own range, the feasible distance from which it can be transported and remain commercially viable. While a simple distinction between local trade and long-distance elite trade has been extensively used in discussing Mesoamerican trade, it is a false dichotomy. How far a commodity can economically travel depends on its bulk relative to its value and the efficiency of the transportation system. High bulk and low value shorten the distance a commodity is likely to travel, whereas low bulk

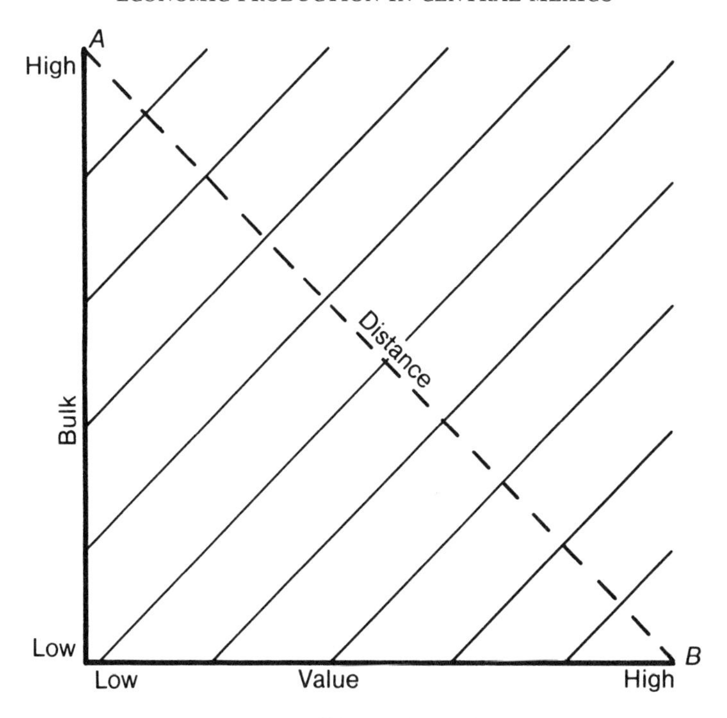

FIG. 2.4. TRADE MODEL. Feasible trade varies by bulk and value of the commodity in question. High-bulk/low-value goods *(A)*, such as maize, travel the shortest distance: low-bulk/high-value goods *(B)*, such as quetzal feathers, travel the longest. All other variations on these values fall in between.

and high value lengthen it. Consequently, high-bulk–low-value goods travel the shortest distance because the cost of transport rapidly consumes a large proportion of the overall value in relation to the bulk, and low-bulk–high-value goods travel the farthest for the reverse reasons (see fig. 2.4). For example, the range of maize would be relatively small, since each league would add considerable cost to a relatively cheap commodity, whereas the range of gold would be great, since the cost of transport would be a relatively minor part of that commodity's overall cost. While

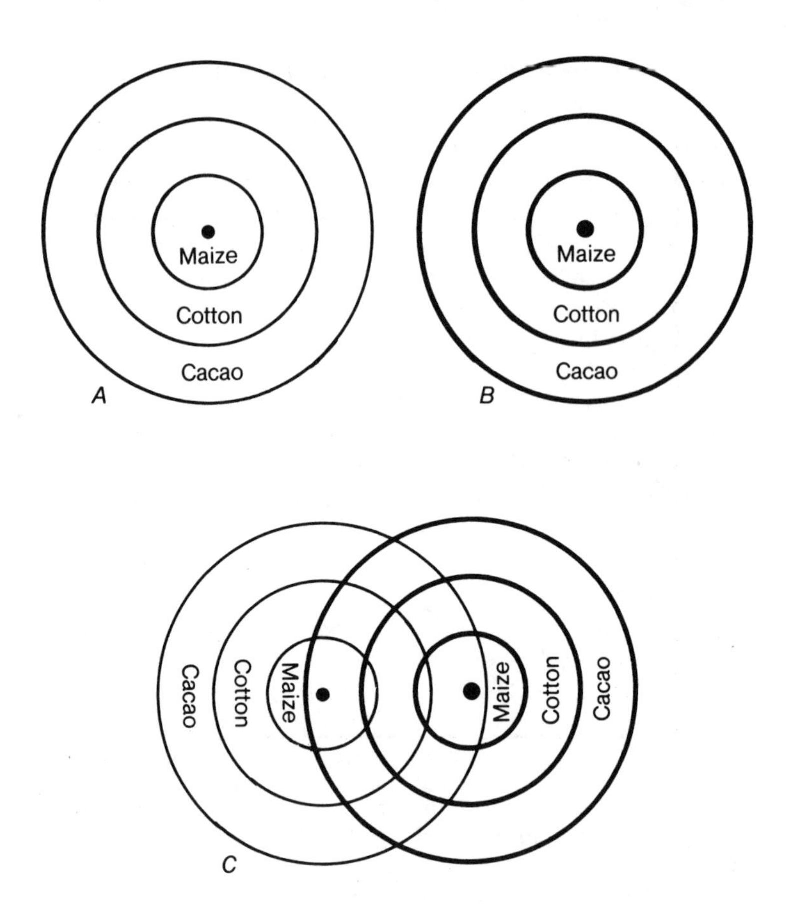

FIG. 2.5. TRANSPORT RANGES. *A:* Distance the producer can transport the commodities he produces and still make a profit. *B:* Distance from which the city can import commodities at a feasible price. *C:* Overlapping ranges of producer and city illustrating market restrictions and potential.

these bulk-value distinctions hold for any transportation system, the disparity in ranges among commodities increases as transport efficiency declines since transport cost becomes a smaller percentage of the total commodity cost. Other factors, such as perishability, nutritional value, market-demand variations by social class, and containerization, affect transport ranges, since these affect value rather than altering the basic equation.

A range can be viewed from two perspectives. From the perspective of the urban center, ranges of various goods appear as concentric zones of commodity procurement illustrating the distance from which various goods can be drawn. From the perspective of the producers, ranges appear as concentric zones within which they profitably sell their goods, illustrating which markets are most advantageous for which goods (see fig. 2.5). Since ranges are ultimately defined by the transportation system, variations in transportation efficiency produce variations in ranges. The result is that the less efficient the transportation system, the smaller the ranges and the smaller the center. This is offset only by differences in productivity per unit of land.

Ranges may be determined empirically (yielding actual range) or logically (indicating potential range). Actual range requires little further comment; an analysis of such ranges, if market value and transport costs are known, would indicate the percentage of price increase the market would bear or the lowest price the producer would be willing to accept before stopping production of that commodity or selling it in another, closer, market. Logically, there is no absolute cutoff in potential range. Any commodity may be transported any distance. The issue is the point at which the cost becomes unbearable. The cutoff point is difficult to assess for such culturally ascribed valuables as gold and quetzal feathers. For foodstuffs, however, a simpler approach may be taken. Regardless of the monetary cost of transport, the nutritional cost may be calculated. Thus a point may be determined at which the consumption of the carrier equals the load carried, yielding a normal maximum feasible range. In fact, foodstuffs can be conveyed even farther if there is some reason to do so, such as religion or status. Supplementary foodstuffs may be purchased en route to sustain the transporter and retain the load intact. But in terms of commodities reaching the center, nothing is gained. The amounts consumed en route are simply removed from the amounts that could have supplied the center from closer areas, thus offsetting the goods which actually do enter, but such tactics do enable a specific load to exceed its normal range.[23] Of course, a maximum feasible load is not the point at which it is exhausted (or half that distance to account for the round trip) but some lesser distance, the cost of the load increasing by a minimum of the amounts consumed. Range is clearly a variable of transportation efficiency.

TRANSPORT

Before the arrival of Europeans, Mexico lacked both wheeled vehicles and draft animals. Although wheels have been found on toys in the Gulf Coast region,[24] they were not used for functioning vehicles, possible owing to the lack of domesticated animals large enough to serve as draft animals.

Tlamemes

Basic transport in Mesoamerica was by human carriers, or *tlamemes* (Nahuatl, sg. *tlamemeh* or *tlamamah* < *tla* "something" + *memeh* or *mamah* "to carry," pl. *tlamemehqueh* or *tlamamahqueh;* the Spaniards called them *tamemes,* and the word is so spelled in colonial documents).[25] They carried goods on their backs in woven cane containers called *petlacalli* (Nahuatl, < *petlatl* "mat" or "matting" + *calli* "house") on carrying frames *(cacaxtli)* supported by tumplines and covered with hides to protect the contents.[26]

There is little information concerning tlamemes before the Conquest, although they are depicted in pre-Columbian codices. Despite the difficulties in interpreta-

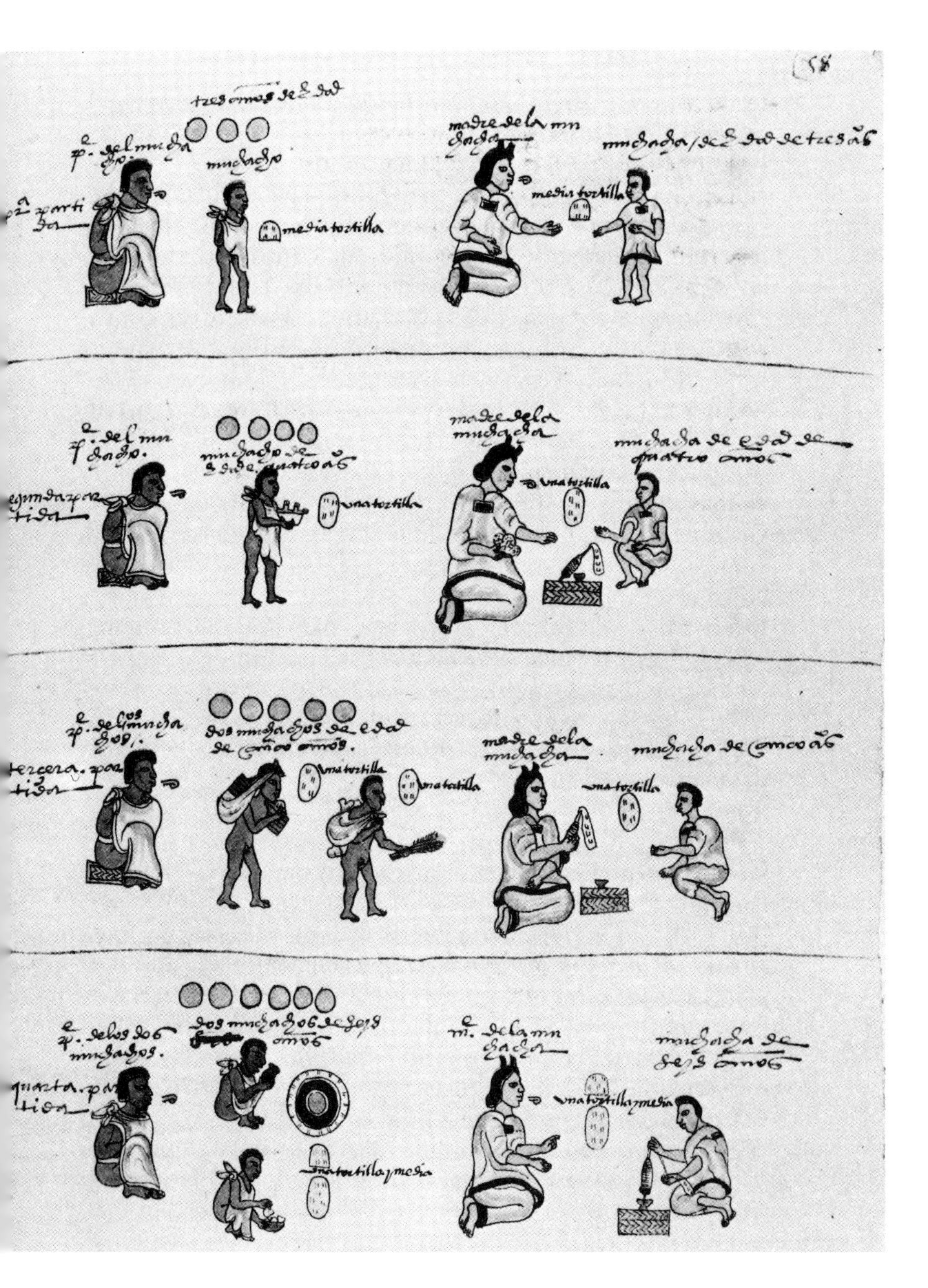

Plate 2. Instructing the children, including training them for tlameme labor (Codex Mendoza *1938, 1, fol. 58).*

tion, the best early evidence comes from the accounts of the conquistadors.

Ultimate origins of tlamemes are unknown. Before the Conquest they formed a separate, probably hereditary occupational group trained from childhood to engage in lifelong portage labor (see plate 2).[27] Codices depict the training of children to carry burdens with tumplines, beginning at the age of five.[28] They have been referred to as a class, but not in a way that distinguishes them from any other low-status workers in an occupation of a predominantly hereditary nature. The image of carrying in the Aztec world is ambiguous. It did have honored and honorable connotations. For example, the metaphor for a ruler was one who shouldered a bundle of people, a carrying frame of people. In discussions of its mythological origin the gods were urged to become the sun, to carry the burden. And marriage was referred to as a large carrying frame, a great burden. Carrying was considered an honest occupation.[29] Yet carrying also had negative connotations. The tumpline was thought to have been given by the deity Cihuacoatl, along with other burdens and undesirable things; and those born in the 13-day series beginning with 1 Ocelotl were doomed to slavery, to the digging stick, and to the tumpline.[30] There is general agreement, however, that tlamemes were on the lower rungs of society.[31]

Hereditary succession was not the sole way one could become a tlameme. Some workers became tlamemes as a form of tribute. This occurred as a result of a political demand originating outside the local political unit, such as the Aztec demands on the city of Tepeaca,[32] rather than as a requirement placed on the local populace by their own rulers. The tlameme occupation may also have been voluntarily adopted in the face of extreme poverty, particularly in cities where there were likely to be large numbers of landless persons, and within the Aztec capital of Tenochtitlan, tlamemes were a different ethnic group.[33] Egress from the tlameme group appears to have been difficult, possibly owing to the lack of alternatives, as the hereditary nature of other occupations, such as the merchants, would tend to exclude aspirants, and the corporate kin and/or residential nature of commoner land would perpetuate their landlessness. Entry into the tlameme ranks, however, appears to have been easy, a reflection of its low status and the increasing demand.

To understand the role of tlamemes, consideration of internal organization alone is insufficient. The road system was a major influence on tlameme portage, channeling the flow of commodities. The terms of portage—loads, distances, and pay—dictated what and how goods were transported. Finally, the relationship of tlamemes to the political organization greatly shaped their role.

Roads

Beyond the confines of major urban centers in central Mexico, roads were not well developed. There were, however, a variety of types: *ohtli,* or road in the general sense; *ochpantli,* or main road, wide, but rough, with holes, muddy spots, and curves; *ohpitzactli,* or trail, which is narrow and straight when other roads curve; *ixtlapalohtli,* or shortcut, which also goes straight when other roads curve; *ichtacaohtli,* or secret road, which few people are aware of; *icxiohtli,* or footpath, which is small and narrow and seldom traveled; and *ohquetzalli,* new road, and *ohcolli,* old road:

> The old people also gave the name coatl to the road, the main road, etc. Thus they said: "Can it be that it is a little danger, a little serpent of our lord?" Or they said: "How hast thou come? Can it be that it is the serpent, the road of stumbling?" Thus they named the road "serpent," because it is long and winding. And they called the road tequatoc, since there is stumbling, there is the running of thorns into the feet.[34]

This did not mean that the roads were undeveloped everywhere. The ochpantli linked nearby cities and are recorded in early accounts as leaving Tlaxcala, Cholula, Huexotzinco, Texmelucan, Chalco Atenco, and Tlalmanalco and going to Tenochtitlan. The ohquetzalli was a royal highway linking the cities of the Valley of Mexico and more distant cities.[35] However, having been built for foot traffic, the indigenous roads were rough and steep, with sharp turns—conditions of little concern to foot traffic.[36]

The principal constraint on foot travel is distance, not turns or grades. Indigenous roads reflected this, stressing directness over gradient in route selection. The lack of stress on formal road building did not, however, indicate a lack of organization. Routes connected towns, local authorities cared for the roads, and inns were built; the organization of labor for public works had a long pre-Columbian tradition.[37] The Aztec system of runners illustrates the organization and serviceability of these roads for foot traffic. Aztec messengers were stationed along the roads at 2-league intervals (1 league = 2.6 miles, or 4.2 kilometers, to 3.6 miles, or 5.6 kilometers).[38] On receiving messages, runners carried them in relays, allegedly at a rate of 4 to 5 leagues per hour or 100 leagues per day. It is claimed that Moteuczomah Xocoyotzin ate fresh fish from the Gulf of Mexico, a distance of 80 leagues by the shortest route.[39]

While there were major routes between regions, such as those going from Tenochtitlan to Soconusco and the Mayan area, the emphasis in road construction was not on the direct connection of terminal points. Rather, routes tended to go through a maximum number of towns, reflecting the preponderance of local over long-distance traffic, the utilization of existing local road networks, and the need for considerable "on line" support services.[40]

Loads and Distances

The actual terms of portage—loads, distance, and pay—for the pre-Columbian period are problematic. Conquistador Bernal Díaz del Castillo[41] stated that each tlameme carried a load of two arrobas (1 arroba 25.36 pounds, or 11.5 kilograms, 2 arrobas thus totaling 50.72 pounds, or 23 kilograms, per load) and went 5 leagues (13 to 18 miles, or 21 to 28 kilometers) to the next district before he was relieved. This statement has been the subject of much repetition and considerable uncritical reliance. Despite some credence given these figures and the possibility that they do reflect pre-Columbian usage, there are reasons for caution in accepting them. The five-league figure is apparently a Hispanic convention for a one-day journey under load. The indigenous measure was most likely on a per-day basis, a method that would take into consideration variations in terrain, loads, weather, and so forth. Furthermore, the 5-league and two-arroba figures reflect later Spanish legal limits on tlameme labor, and since Díaz del Castillo's account was written long after the standards were officially established, even though depicting earlier events, their precision, though not their general accuracy, is questionable.[42]

There is considerable variation in recorded loads and distances, and the data are scattered and incomplete. Portage is clearly a function of terrain, weather, load weights, and distance. Terrain is a factor not only in elevation changes but also in ground cover (e.g., jungles versus plains) and local topography (e.g., broken land, barrancas, and rivers). As for the weather, inclement conditions reduced road serviceability and increased the discomfort of the porters.

Distance and load weight are inversely related. Within a set time span, the heavier the load, the shorter the distance traveled; the longer the distance, the lighter the load. This primary trade-off of distance and load may be reduced further by weather and/or terrain. Thus loads will be lighter or distances shorter when weather or terrain worsen. While extremes are possible, such as carrying very heavy loads or traveling long distances, it is doubtful that they occur in conjunction. Although very heavy loads could have been carried in pre-Columbian times, this would not indicate greater efficiency. Rather, more porters were required to achieve the same distance, each tlameme carrying a very heavy load for a short distance, combining to achieve the total distance traveled, single tlamemes carrying very heavy loads for smaller total distances. The most common example of this is in the portage of people. Litters and hammocks were employed to carry personages of high status, bearers being employed singly, in pairs, and in fours. Individuals were also carried by single tlamemes without litters.[43] The stated practice of pre-Columbian tlamemes carrying two arrobas for five leagues per day appears reasonable as a statement of the general terms of portage, but rather than granting blanket acceptance to these standards, more consideration must be given to loads, distances, terrain, and climate as interrelated variables affecting tlameme portage.

Tlameme Organization

Tlameme organization reflected Mesoamerican political organization. At the local level subimperial or preimperial Indian society was organized by small districts. The native rulers, *tlahtohqueh* (sg, *tlahtohqui*, also *tlahtoani*), or *caciques* (an Arawak word imported from the West Indies by the Spaniards and used to refer to the native rulers),[44] resided in capital towns, called cabeceras by the Spaniards. (In sixteenth-century usage, a cabecera was the capital town of a local Indian ruler who bore the title *tlahtoani*. But since the criterion for cabecera status was based on caciques rather than on tlahtohqueh, it was uncertain. Before the Conquest, tlahtohqueh had been promoted or suppressed for political reasons, leaving a certain ambiguity about who was a legitimate tlahtoani. As the century wore on, the overlap of subimperial or preimperial tlahtohqueh communities and post-Conquest cabeceras was not absolute).[45] The cabecera was the center of the district which included the surrounding politically dependent towns and areas.[46] The districts may or may not have been subject to larger political entities, such as the Aztec or Tarascan empires.

Díaz del Castillo states that the cacique provided tlamemes for portage through his district and that they carried to the next district, where they were relieved. From this statement and later-sixteenth-century practice, it is evident that tlamemes were organized by political districts.[47] However, the precise way they were organized is not clear. The caciques could order them to carry, and, indeed, were obligated to do so,[48] but whether tlamemes could freely carry otherwise is less certain, although such was apparently the case. Tlamemes were paid for their labor,[49] but there were exceptions. Tribute portage to the cabecera was considered part of the tribute and was not paid by the recipient.[50] But since it was the obligation of the payers, professional tlamemes may not have been used for this labor. However, in the post-Conquest period, tlamemes were paid for carrying tribute, although apparently at a lower wage than that for carrying other goods.[51]

Tlamemes also had certain obligations to the nobility. *Principales,* or nobles, exercised limited rights to the labor of tlamemes. These rights are clearly documented for the Hispanic period[52] and presumably arose from pre-Conquest practices. *Principales* could, as a perquisite of nobility, order tlamemes to carry for their personal benefit, but the existence of this right leaves many questions unanswered. For instance, was it a right exercised over all tlamemes or merely over Indians who were dependent on the *principal* in question? Did Indians have this obligation at all times or merely as part of their local tribute obligations, and did they receive any remuneration? In any case, it appears certain that tlamemes were organized by districts, that they resided in or near cabeceras, since they operated from them, and that they were under the direction of the cacique. The nature and extent of the cacique's control over the tlamemes is not clear. The possibilities range from absolute control over work undertaken, loads, distances, pay, and so forth, to nominal authority. But minimally, the cacique's involvement was to guarantee the functioning of portage through his district, as one link in an interlocking transportation network.

Despite their organization by districts, tlameme journeys were apparently from their home cabecera to the cabecera of the adjacent district rather than from border to border within their respective districts. This is suggested on two counts: the logic of such organization and later sixteenth-century practice. Cabecera-to-cabecera portage would allow a simpler, more centralized organization of tlamemes within each district. If border-to-border portage were the practice, tlamemes would necessarily have been stationed at the borders on major routes, or they would have been stationed in or near the cabecera. The former would have entailed an expensive and cumberson organization, and the latter would have required prearrival notification if lengthy delays were to be avoided. The organizational efficiency of cabecera-to-cabecera portage and its use throughout the sixteenth century argue strongly in its favor.[53]

There are at least four exceptions to the practice of local portage. Tlamemes were used for long-distance portage (1) to carry tribute from the provincial centers to Tenochtitlan, (2) to carry some war supplies, (3) to assist in some pochtecah (merchant) trade, and (4) apparently, to engage in public works similar to those levied on other segments of the population. These will be discussed later, as appropriate.

Travelers who hired tlamemes in cabecera-to-cabecera relays may have been rightfully concerned about political relations between the districts they entered and their own, but such was not the case for tlamemes. Despite political enmities between districts, tlameme transport appears to have been routine and largely unaffected, except in the event of actual war. There were politically inspired blockades, such as those maintained by the Aztecs around Tlaxcala and Huexotzingo.[54] Supplies such as salt and cotton were allegedly cut off by the Aztecs, indicating the deliberate disruption of transport. But given the many miles of border involved, the minimal road requirements for foot transport, and the numerous sources and merchants of salt and cotton, a physical blockade of traffic seems unlikely. Rather, Aztec control of supplies and markets was a more probable control mechanism.

There are, however, recorded incidents of attacks on tlamemes during actual war. In 1696, during the entry of

Captain Pedro de Zubiaur into the Maya area, two tlamemes from the village of Tekax were beaten to death by the Itzas during the attack.[55] This example is rather far removed from central Mexico. But during Cortés's siege of Tenochtitlan, tlamemes carrying supplies for the Spaniards were the deliberate targets of the Aztec army.[56] Since the Aztecs were intercepted, it remains uncertain whether the raid was a punitive one directed at the tlamemes or was merely calculated to disrupt supplies. In any event, short of actual combat, tlamemes seem to have enjoyed a neutral status, an eminently reasonable policy that worked to the advantage of all.

Since tlamemes were organized by districts, where these districts formed parts of greater polities, tlamemes would logically be affected. The prime example is the expansion of the Aztec empire. Trade was a major concern of the Aztecs, and when the city of Tepeaca submitted to the Aztec army, part of its tribute consisted in some of its people becoming tlamemes.[57] Tepeaca straddled the main trade route linking central Mexico with all of southern Mexico and the Maya area.[58] Tlamemes would necessarily have already existed there, but given the location of Tepeaca and the Aztec interest in trade, this tribute demand reflected a concern for supporting the expanding interregional trade. As the Aztec empire expanded and interregional traffic increased, the previously adequate district tlameme organization required expansion. This was not a wholesale expansion, but rather a selective one along the major conduits of trade.

There also exist contrary examples of cabeceras with few tlamemes. Epazoyuca (Epazoyucan, Hidalgo)[59] and Mistepeque (San Juan Mixtepeque Juxtlahuaca, Oaxaca)[60] claimed to have lacked tlamemes. Since human portage was an economic necessity, it is unlikely that these claims were strictly true. Tlamemes may have been located in the *sujetos* (dependent towns) of these cabeceras or may have comprised a small portion of the resident population. On the other hand, neither town was on a major trade route,

Plate 3. Tlamemes carrying goods for the Spaniards during the Conquest. (*Muñoz Camargo,* Descripción de la ciudad y provincia de Tlaxcala [*Mexico, 1981*]).

and Mistepeque was not tributary to Tenochtitlan; and thus one would expect their portage industry to have been poorly developed, serving only local rather than interregional trade.

Customs regarding tlamemes varied by province,[61] probably reflecting not only ecological variables but also their respective roles in interregional trade, political assimilation, and so forth. As a corollary to the imperial expansion, tlamemes within the Aztec empire probably enjoyed a greater area of political neutrality reflecting the Aztec interest in establishing and maintaining interregional trade (see plate 3).

Thus the picture that emerges of pre-Columbian tlamemes is of an expanding low-status occupational stratum. Conditions leading to work as a tlameme—landlessness and exclusion from hereditary occupations—tended to perpetuate it in hereditary fashion. With the expansion of the Aztec empire, demand (both market and Aztec) increased, and tlameme ranks swelled, possibly by absorbing persons dispossessed by Aztec and other conquerors. They labored as organized, professional carriers with general standards for portage, probable periodic rest stops, and loads commensurate with distance and road conditions and carried not only elite goods such as cacao and gold but ordinary commodities such as maize and cotton. Since transport was essentially from cabecera to cabecera, this established distance in the load-distance balance. Given a separation of appoximately five leagues between cabeceras,[62] loads were adjusted accordingly, and extreme loads were generally avoided in the interests of reaching the next cabecera within a day.

Cabecera districts were not economically independent entities. Towns were dependent on trading goods to provide what they lacked—salt, maize, cotton, cacao. It was this interdependence that fostered tlameme neutrality, enabling transport to cross political boundaries with relative impunity. Tlamemes were patterned after local political organization and were the vital element linking districts, promoting interregional trade, and uniting the Aztec empire into an integrated economic region.

URBAN DEVELOPMENT

City size depends on the acquisition of a reliable food supply from the surrounding hinterland, but how large an area may be drawn on and the use to which that land is put depend on the efficiency of the prevailing transportation system. The more efficient the system of transportation, the larger the effective hinterland. With an efficient transportation system (e.g., with wagons and draft animals) cities may draw on larger hinterlands and support greater urban populations. As a corollary, the larger the hinterland, the farther apart the cities are. Under conditions of less efficient transportation (e.g., no wagons or draft animals, only human carriers), cities draw on smaller hinterlands, support smaller urban populations, and are closer together.[63]

The few measures available to the Mexicans for expanding their food support areas, such as professionalization of carriers and maintenance of roads, were employed, but in the absence of a technological breakthrough city growth was restricted by the comparatively inefficient tlameme transport system. Limited to a radius of approximately 21 to 28 kilometers (5 leagues) for bulk commodities, city hinterlands were relatively restricted. Thus cities on the central Mexican plateau did not grow very large. Even though hinterlands were small, they suffered the same spatial patterning of production as did larger areas, but the high cost of tlameme transport resulted in a rather sharp decline. What emerges is a general picture of small cities drawing on correspondingly small hinterlands, even in areas of favorable agricultural productivity.

CHAPTER 3

Economic Production in The Valley of Mexico

DESPITE the general constraints on urban growth operating throughout Mesoamerica, the Valley of Mexico was anomalous. It possessed large cities—particularly Tenochtitlan-Tlatelolco—that greatly exceeded both the size of cities elsewhere in Mesoamerica and the theoretical limits predicated on considerations of transportation constraints. This is largely attributable to the unique geographical and ecological circumstances of the Valley of Mexico and to the Aztecs' ability to adapt to and take advantage of them (see map 2).

PHYSICAL DESCRIPTION

Much of economic and political life in the Valley of Mexico was patterned by the topography of the valley. Situated on the southern edge of the Mexican *mesa central* in the *tierra fría*, the Valley of Mexico[1] extends approximately 120 kilometers north-south and 70 kilometers east-west, with an area of 7,853 square kilometers.[2]

There are three distinct horizontal zones in the valley: (1) the low zone, which extends from the bottom of the valley, about 2,236 meters above sea level, to 2,250 meters, with an area of 1,507 square kilometers; (2) the hilly zone, which extends from 2,250 to 2,400 meters, with an area of 2,575 square kilometers; and (3) the mountain zone, which extends from 2,400 meters up and can be subdivided into an intermediate zone, from 2,400 to 2,700 meters, with an area of 2,671 square kilometers, and the mountain zone proper, 2,700 meters and above, with an area of about 1,000 square kilometers.[3]

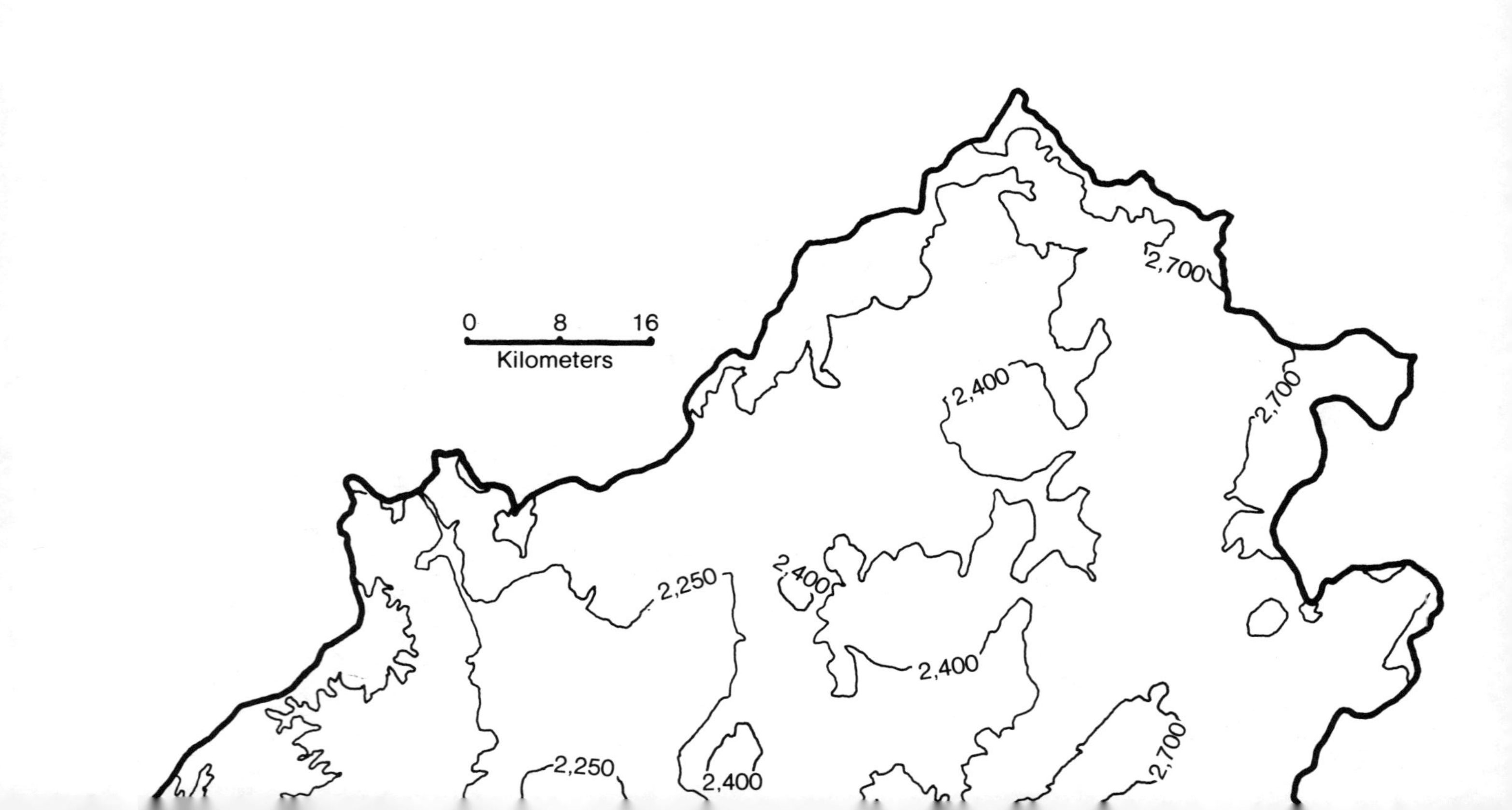
0
8
16
Kilometers
2,700
2,700
2,400
2,250
2,400
2,400
2,250
2,400
2,700

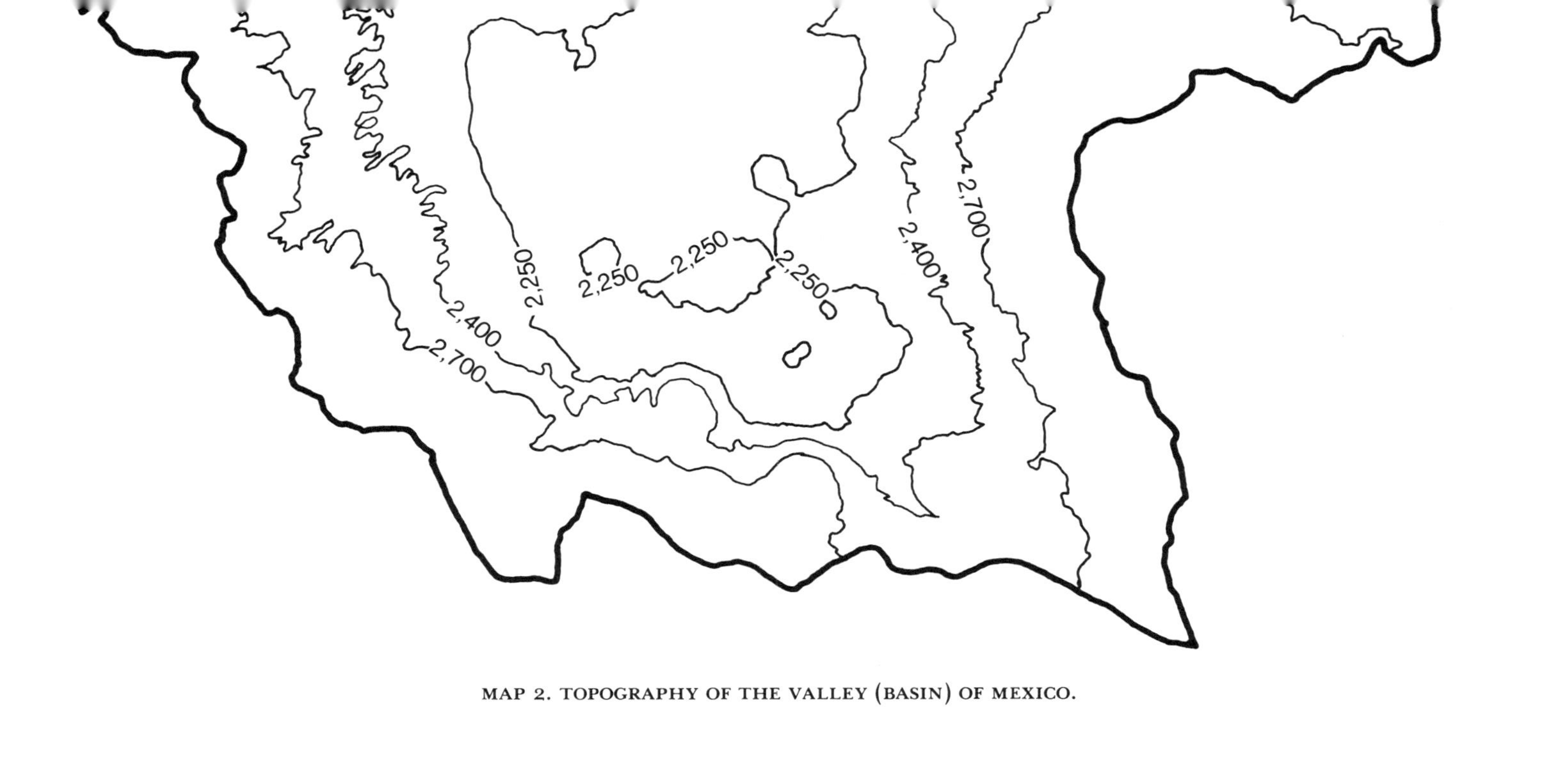

MAP 2. TOPOGRAPHY OF THE VALLEY (BASIN) OF MEXICO.

Table 3.1. Modern Mean Temperatures in the Valley of Mexico

Month	Mean Temperature, °C	Month	Mean Temperature, °C
January	12	July	16
February	16	August	16
March	21	September	15
April	17	October	14
May	19	November	13
June	18	December	12

Source: Mexico, Departmento del Distrito Federal 1975, 1:45–47.

Life in the Valley of Mexico was affected by three climatic factors: temperature, winds, and precipitation. Median annual temperature is 15°C, although it varies throughout the valley, particularly by altitude (see table 3.1). Of major significance is frost. In the lower elevations of the valley frosts normally begin in October and continue until March, although there may be both early and late frosts. The frost season varies throughout the valley, being shortest in the south and increasing as one goes north, and shortest at the lowest elevations and increasing with altitude.[4]

Winds in the valley are predominantly from the northeast and northwest, the windiest months being March through May. Rainfall also varies in the valley, increasing from north to south and from lower to higher elevations. The rains are not constant, however, but concentrate in a rainy season that normally begins in May and extends into October. The remainder of the year is dry (see table 3.2). Thus the valley is not a uniform area but exhibits considerable variation.

In the sixteenth century the Valley of Mexico contained a series of interconnecting lakes, conventionally divided into five. They are, from north to south, Zumpango, Xaltocan, Texcoco, Xochimilco, and Chalco. The lakes were fed by runoff from the surrounding mountains, draining through a series of rivers. In the eighteenth cen-

Table 3.2. Median Precipitation by Hydrological Zone, 1920–70

	Zone	km²	Annual mm	Rain Volume, 1,000 m³*
I	Xochimilco	522	891	465,102
II	Churubusco	234	1,020	230,680
III	Mexico City	725	872	632,200
IV	Cuauhtitlan	972	789	766,908
V	Pachuca (60%)	1,252	312	649,144
VI	Teotihuacan	930	612	569,160
VII	Texcoco	1,146	639	732,294
VIII	Tecomulco	533	651	346,983
IX	Chalco	1,124	855	961,020
Total		7,438	6,641	5,353,491

*Adjusted for 60 percent of Hidalgo.
Source: Mexico, Departmento del Distrito Federal 1975, 1:45, 48, 50, Atlas, tomo 1, plano 11; Kovar 1970:19.

tury Velázquez found only two year-round rivers, Tenango and Tlalmanalco, which ran into Lake Chalco. Palerm makes the same claim today exclusively for the Amecameca River—apparently the same river earlier identified as Tenango. Velázquez lists several additional river systems that fed the lakes during the rainy season: Coyoacan and Mixcoac, Guadalupe, Tlalnepantlan and Azcapotzalco, Cuauhtitlan, Guacalco and Tepotzotlan, Teotihuacan, Papalotla, and Coatepec.[5] The rivers that fed the lakes drained relatively small areas and did so only seasonally, so their numbers and locations changed. Thus an accounting beyond generally noting seasonal watershed drainage is unnecessary and possibly misleading.

Texcoco was the largest and the lowest lake, receiving drainage from the others. In the south, Lake Chalco was fed year-round by the Amecameca River. Chalco flowed into Lake Xochimilco, which was also fed by perennial springs. These freshwater lakes were 3 meters higher than saline Lake Texcoco, into which they drained. In the north, Lake Zumpango was fed seasonally by the Cuauhtitlan River and general runoffs. Lake Zumpango was 6 meters and Lake Xaltocan 3.5 meters higher than Lake Texcoco; thus Zumpango flowed into Lake Xaltocan, and thence into Lake Texcoco. Although Lakes Zumpango and Xaltocan were fed by fresh water, they were brackish owing to the seasonal cutoff of drainage. The entire lake system had a surface of about 1,000 square kilometers.[6] The lakes were shallow, varying between 1 and 4 meters, and were from 2,236 to 2,240 meters above sea level. This situation is now greatly changed, and conventional estimates of the sixteenth-century lake level are based on the placement of pre-Columbian lakeside towns.[7]

Long-term climatic patterns greatly affected the lakes in the valley. It is probable that minor fluctuations in the lake level occurred between the beginning of the formative period (about 1200–1000 B.C.) and A.D. 1519, and that the original lake level was approximately 2,250 meters before its decline. The diminution of the lakes was a result of a change in the prevailing temperatures that reduced rainfall.[8]

AGRICULTURE

The agricultural picture of the Valley of Mexico was somewhat different from that of Mexico generally, not only because of altitude but also because of particular horticultural practices prevalent in or exclusive to the valley. The agricultural picture of the Valley of Mexico is more complete than for Mexico generally (see appendix A), but the complementary difficulties of extent of production and size of population persist without adequate resolution.

General

On the intricate man-land balance, a further consideration is work efficiency. Modern data from Oaxaca indicate that one man using a *coa* (digging stick) can cultivate only two hectares, a figure that agrees with data from present-day highland Tepoztlan.[9]

Another factor in yield levels is fertilization. Fertilizer

boosts yields per hectare and also allows continuous cropping of a field. But before the Conquest there were no large domesticated animals to produce manure. While most studies indicate that little or no fertilizer was used in highland agriculture, it was employed, particularly in chinampa agriculture (see below). The pre-Conquest source was, of course, night soil.[10]

Chinampa Agriculture

One of the most important forms of cultivation in the Valley of Mexico was chinampa agriculture. Chinampa is a form of intensive cultivation on segments of land artificially constructed in lakes. To build a chinampa, posts are driven into the shallow lake bottom; between the posts vines and branches are interwoven to form an enclosure.[11] Soil is placed inside to form the artificial island, and it is eventually anchored more securely by growing trees along its perimeter. The earth used to construct the chinampa comes primarily from the lake bottom, which gives it a twofold virtue. The soil is particularly fertile, and the excavation helps maintain the canals that separate and irrigate the chinampas.

Chinampas were generally rectangular, though of varying sizes: 300 feet by 15 to 30 feet, 100 meters by 5 to 6 meters, 25 to 30 varas by 6 to 8 varas (approximately 21 to 25.5 meters by 5 to 7 meters). Construction of a chinampa 8 by 200 meters required eight days for a group of four to six men, or 32 to 48 man-days (see plate 4).[12]

The surface of the chinampa is, ideally, less than a meter above the water, permitting crop irrigation by the water in the soil. Today, however, the water falls so low during the dry season that manual watering is required.[13]

The exceptional productivity of chinampa agriculture is due, in part, to the year-round cropping it permits. Chinampas are continuously cropped with a great variety of plants—up to four crops a year—with the longest fallow period less than three months once every three or four years. This is possible through a combinaton of mixed

Plate 4. Plano de Maguey, showing chinampa areas in the Valley of Mexico (Díaz del Castillo 1908–16, vol. 3).

cropping, crop rotation, extensive use of seed beds, and extensive use of fertilizer.[14]

Today, as in the past, before each planting, mud is dredged from the lake bottom and spread on the chinampa. This eventually leads to such a large accumulation that the natural chinampa irrigation is impeded; then the excess is excavated and used to repair old chinampas or to construct new ones. This fertile mud is augmented by fertilizer—animal today, but human before the Conquest. At one end of the chinampa a nursery is made by spreading mud over a bed of lake weeds. After several days of hardening, the mud is cut into small rectangular blocks (*chapines* in Spanish) into which a seed is placed and covered with manure. The seedbed is covered with reeds to protect it from the occasional frosts, and the *chapines* are later transplanted. This transplantation was observed with general amazement by the Spaniards. Transplantation was not only within chinampas but also to fields adjacent to the lakes.[15] By using a small portion of the chinampa as a nursery, the chinamperos (chinampa farmers) could not only select the healthiest sprouts for transplanting but shorten the growing season per crop. A variety of crops were grown on chinampas: maize, chili, fruit, tomatoes, amaranth, beans, and flowers.[16]

Chinampas were employed extensively in the Valley of Mexico at Conquest, although lake conditions, such as salinity, hindered their use everywhere. There is no evidence of chinampas in the saline Lake Texcoco. However, in the western portion of Lake Texcoco (Lake Mexico), chinampas did exist, and there are indications that the chinampa zone was advancing in that area. Chinampas were cultivated in and around Tenochtitlan, where chinampa areas attached to residences ranged in size from 0.01 to 0.085 hectares. Most such plots were between 0.01 and 0.04 hectares, but at the extreme southeastern section of the city chinampas were large, up to 0.5 hectares.[17]

The brackishness of the water and seasonality of its drainage hindered chinampas in the northern lakes, although they did exist there to a limited extent, particularly around the towns of Xaltocan and Zumpango. Their greatest cultivation was in Lakes Xochimilco and Chalco, which were virtually filled with chinampas. Towns that were specifically mentioned as having chinampas in the sixteenth century, but where they no longer exist, include Xaltocan, Tenochtitlan, Chalco Atenco, Coyoacan, Ixtapalapa, Culhuacan, Huitzilopochco, Mexicalzingo, Azcapotzalco, Popotla, and Chapultepec.[18]

Attempts at estimating the pre-Columbian chinampa area are fraught with difficulties. Armillas measured the gross chinampa area of the Lake Xochimilco–Chalco region, based on aerial photographs taken in 1930 and estimated its pre-Hispanic expanse at more than 12,000 hectares. He reduced this amount by one-fourth to allow for canals and interspersed pools, leaving over 9,000 hectares of chinampas. J. R. Parsons accepts these figures but increases them by 500 hectares to 9,500 hectares, to compensate for traces of chinampas obliterated before Armilla's survey.[19]

Estimates of the carrying capacity of chinampas presuppose estimates of consumption. Productivity of maize by weight, though difficult, can be calculated.[20] Sanders describes the sowing of maize in rows about 0.8 meters apart, with plants in each row about 0.5 meters apart, four to five seeds per hole. Approximately one *cuartillo* (1.2 to 1.5 kilograms) of seed is used per 0.1 hectare, or 10 *cuartillos* per hectare. He estimates that under conditions of complete drought one man could cultivate 0.5 hectare of chinampa. J. R. Parsons increases this figure to 0.75 by assuming normal rainfall during the summer months.[21] Sanders calculates an average production of about 4,000 kilograms per hectare, a minimum of 3.5 and more probably 4 tons per hectare. For his estimated 10,000 hectares of chinampas in the southern lake region, Sanders calculates a production of 40 million kilograms of maize. He not only estimates 4 tons annually from chinampa agriculture but does so year after year, unlike other forms of production which require fallowing. Thus each chinampero produces between 2,000 and 3,000 kilograms per year.[22] These are, however, estimates from the early 1950s, not pre-Conquest production rates (see appendix A).

Thus estimates of chinampa carrying capacity vary greatly, depending on one's approximation of chinampa area, the estimated level of productivity, and the consumption rate of the populace.

Dates for the construction of chinampas are varied. Earlier estimates place chinampas from 1,000 to 2,000 years old, based on pottery found in canals, and the coincidence of the grid pattern of the Xochimilco chinampas with that of Teotihuacan, 15 to 17 degrees east of true north.[23] But most recent scholarship places them clearly in the Aztec period.[24] This Aztec-period assessment is bolstered by the lack of any pre-Aztec residences in the Ixtapalapa chinampa area and by the almost exclusive presence of Aztec ceramics.

Chinampas were the solution to the twin dilemmas of valley agriculture. If fields are planted early to avoid the autumn frosts, they may be too early to benefit from the summer rains. If they are planted later to ensure adequate rainfall, the crops may suffer from early frost.[25] While chinampa agriculture avoids these problems, it is not without its own difficulties. The construction of chinampa areas is not a simple task. True chinampas are built in shallow lakes that ensure the continuous flow of water to irrigate them and to reduce salinity.

Chinampa agriculture requires two things unavailable naturally in the lakes of the Valley of Mexico: constant fresh water and a stable water level. Fresh water flowed through Lakes Chalco and Xochimilco. But because of seasonal fluctuations in lake levels, drought, and storms and winds in Lake Texcoco, saline water was washed back around the Ixtapalapa peninsula that separated the freshwater lakes from the saline ones. Consequently, Lake Xochimilco, if not Lake Chalco, was subject to periodic increases in salinity that were detrimental to chinampa agriculture. Chinampas also require a fairly constant water level: too low, and the crops require watering; too high, and they are drowned. Thus conversion of the southern lakes to chinampas required a considerable investment in hydraulic works.

During the reign of King Itzcoatl (ca. A.D. 1426–40), a system of dikes, canals, and aqueducts was begun which served to separate fresh and salt waters and to regulate the levels of the lakes (see table 3.3).[26]

Records of the labor ordered by Cortés on the canal at Texcoco indicate that the Ixtapalapa-to-Tenochtitlan causeway (9,000 meters long and 7 meters wide, with an estimated height of 5 meters, since the lake depth was 3.6 meters), which had a volume of 300,000 cubic meters, would have required 4 million man-days to construct. If similar widths and heights are assumed, the causeways listed above would have required 25 million man-days to build, a considerable investment. That extensive hydraulic works were important is also readily apparent from the complex and elaborate terminology used by the Aztecs to describe them.[27]

The process of creating a freshwater chinampa zone[28] required the following steps. First, an area of the lake was

Table 3.3. Estimated Dimensions of the Causeways in the Valley of Mexico

Causeway	Dimension, Meters
Tlahuac (Cuitlahuac)	4,000
Santa Catarina to Cerro de la Estrella	2,500
Coyoacan-Ixtapalapa to Tenochtitlan	6,000
Culhuacan to Coyoacan	2,500
Nezahualcoyotl's dike	16,000
Ixtapalapa to Tenochtitlan	9,000
Tenochtitlan to Tacuba (Tlacopan)	8,000
Tenochtitlan to Tepeyac	6,000
Chapultepec to Tenochtitlan	2,500

Source: Palerm 1973:73–74.

closed off with dikes to isolate it from the salt water. Second, by taking advantage of the rainy and dry cycles, the area was drained by means of sluice gates in the dikes. Third, fresh water was reintroduced. Fourth, the chinampas were built.

The development of these large chinampa areas must have been the action of a highly centralized political entity, as witnessed by the massive effort involved in constructing the dikes and also by the grid pattern of the chinampas themselves, indicating centralized planning.[29]

Overview

The original pattern of agricultural production in the Valley of Mexico was one in which each polity had its own agricultural producing area. After the rise of the Aztecs this was superseded by a valley-wide pattern of land use illustrated by the von Thünen model. Extremely productive labor-intensive chinampa agriculture was instituted as close at hand as possible. Lakeshores were irrigated, and banks were terraced. Transplantation from chinampa seedbeds further enhanced the productivity of the areas adjacent to the lakeshore. Production intensified throughout the valley, but this occurred to the greatest extent in the southern areas.

URBAN FOOD SUPPLY

The ideal support area describes a circle around the urban center. Although it is actually a series of concentric commodity ranges, bulk foodstuffs—maize, beans, squash—are the items of real concern, for they determine the size of the urban population. In dealing with a specific location, such as the Valley of Mexico, the ideal model of urban economic hinterlands is considerably modified. This ideal, or potential, hinterland is circular, but the actual support area is subject to irregularities both in production and in transportation. Production irregularities are evident when areas within the potential hinterland cannot be used for production. These include (1) unusable lands, such as swamps, rock outcrops, and ponds, (2) areas used for activities other than primary production, such as housing and roads, (3) areas used indirectly for production, such as forests needed for foraging and land not currently in production owing to fallowing, and (4) areas of marginal lands that may or may not be brought under cultivation, depending on demand and location. Thus the actual maximum productive area is much smaller than the potential area.

Transportation irregularities stem from such obstacles as cliffs, rivers, and mountains. What constitutes an irregularity varies, of course, with the type of transportation used. Furthermore, the smaller the range of the commodity being transported, the greater the relative hindrance posed by any transportation obstacle, since it dominates a larger percentage of the trek and is thus more difficult to avoid.

A model of these irregularities yields four logical possibilities, with two subtypes: (1) regular-production–regular-transportation area, (2) regular-production–irregular-transportation area, (3) irregular-production–regular-transportation area, and (4) irregular-production–irregular-transportation area, which is further divisible depending on (*a*) congruence or (*b*) lack of congruence. Deserts or dry salt lakes are obstacles to production but not to transportation. Rugged but terraceable mountains and cultivable swamps are obstacles to transportation but not to production. The occurrence of either of these irregularities removes that area from the actual support area. Transportation distance is the crucial limiting factor. Further expansion in the production zones to offset areas lost by transport obstacles merely stretches the transport beyond the commodity range, and hauling from a productive area of difficult transport has the same net effect. The increased difficulty of transporting the goods has the same effect on time and expense as does greater distance over favorable terrain. Thus areas within the center's potential support area fall outside in terms of commodity range owing to the increased effort necessary to utilize it (see fig. 3.1).

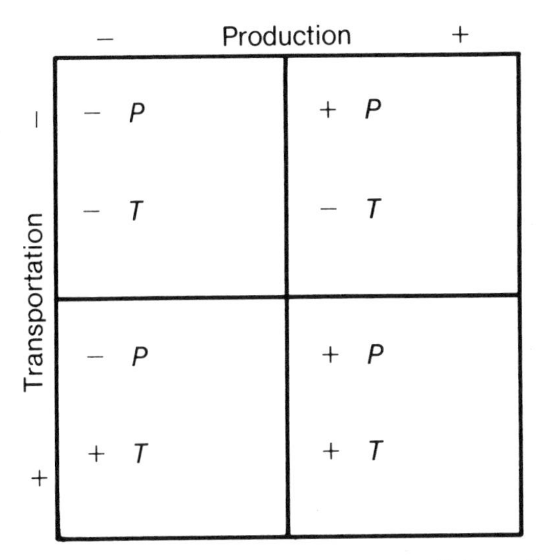

FIG. 3.1. PRODUCTION–TRANSPORTATION MODEL. Schematic representation of the four possibilities in a hinterland. One (−*P*/−*T*) precludes any use of the land for production for the market; a second (+*P*/−*T*) permits production but not transportation; a third (−*P*/+*T*) permits transportation but not production; and the fourth (+*P*/+*T*) permits both production and transportation.

While differences in transportation efficiency affect the size of potential and actual hinterlands, they do not alter the basic pattern. The patterns of shifts in production with distance remain the same: it is the dimensions that change. Aside from major technological improvements, the efficiency of a transportation network may be increased by organizational means, such as professionalization of the carriers, or by technological means within the capacity of the society, such as improving the roads. A more efficient transportation system permits a larger support area and, consequently, a larger center. Differences in transportation systems may be manifested in differences in city size and placement. Cities with more efficient systems may either draw on a larger area and thus grow larger and be more widely spaced or remain small but require smaller hinterlands than those of comparable cities elsewhere. If a region has two types of transportation systems of unequal efficiency, the more efficiently served area should have larger centers and exercise greater influence than that of the less efficiently served areas. Differences in transportation systems may occur in three ways: (1) simultaneously, as above, (2) sequentially, in which case the more efficient system should displace the less efficient one with consequent effects on city growth and location, or (3) through a combination of the first two, resulting in differential acceptance of the new system, depending on relative efficiency. However, not all systems of transportation are equally efficient in every context, so mixed systems may occur, with concomitant consequences for urban growth and patterning.

Examination of a lakeshore city shows that the support area is, in effect, halved, since its hypothetical expanse includes the lake itself, an area containing neither arable lands nor consuming or producing populations. There are, of course, compensatory products, such as fish and waterfowl. But in terms of land support area these cities should be smaller than their contemporaries on plains, reflecting their reduced hinterlands. For Tenochtitlan, however, such was not the case.

TRANSPORT

Tlamemes were employed in the Valley of Mexico, as they were throughout Mesoamerica, and politically mandated road maintenance and intercabecera linkage increased the efficiency of the system. However, the Valley of Mexico also enjoyed a second system of transportation, canoes (Nahuatl, *acalli*; the Spanish form of the Nahuatl word was rendered *acale*).[30]

The canoes used in the Valley of Mexico were dugouts—shallow-draft, square-bow craft hewn from single trees—and were of many varieties. They were rowed or poled, but lacked sails.[31] Although sails were used in pre-

Columbian South America, and early pre-Columbian voyages between Mexico and South America seem probable, as does later extensive sea trade in the Gulf of Mexico–Caribbean area, and sails may have been in use among coastal groups such as the Huastecs, these navigational arts did not extend into the highlands, and the use of sails was unknown in the Valley of Mexico.[32] Tenochtitlan was highly dependent on canoe transport. The city was built on an island (as was Tlatelolco) artificially expanded by the creation of chinampas, and laced with canals,[33] which facilitated the movement of goods.

Even during the early phase of Tenochtitlan's development, when it was little more than a simple village, subsistence was a problem, since the town lacked substantial agricultural areas. Tenochtitlan was dependent upon supplies from lakeshore sites, notably Azcapotzalco.[34] This difficulty increased as the town expanded to a metropolis of more than 200,000 inhabitants[35] because the areas from which it could draw subsistence goods did not expand proportionately. Indeed, in terms of agricultural self-sufficiency, Tenochtitlan was unfortunately situated, standing on an island in brackish western Lake Texcoco.[36] Although the Aztecs expanded their productive areas by constructing chinampas in the lake adjacent to the city, these local resources accounted for only 5 percent of the city's subsistence needs.[37] Throughout its history Tenochtitlan was dependent on the surrounding lakeshore cities and their agricultural hinterlands for its food supply.[38]

Tenochtitlan was connected to the adjacent shore by three major causeways: north to Tepeyacac, west to Tlacopan, and south to Ixtapalapa and Coyoacan. These highways were major constructions—6,000 by 7 by 5 meters, 8,000 by 7 by 5 meters, and 6,000 by 7 by 5 meters, respectively (see map 3).[39] The basic pattern of Tenochtitlan was cruciform, but it lacked the precision of earlier Mesoamerican cities such as Teotihuacan, for the pattern was superimposed on an original, spontaneous one. Causeway construction dated from the reign of Itzcoatl (ca. A.D.

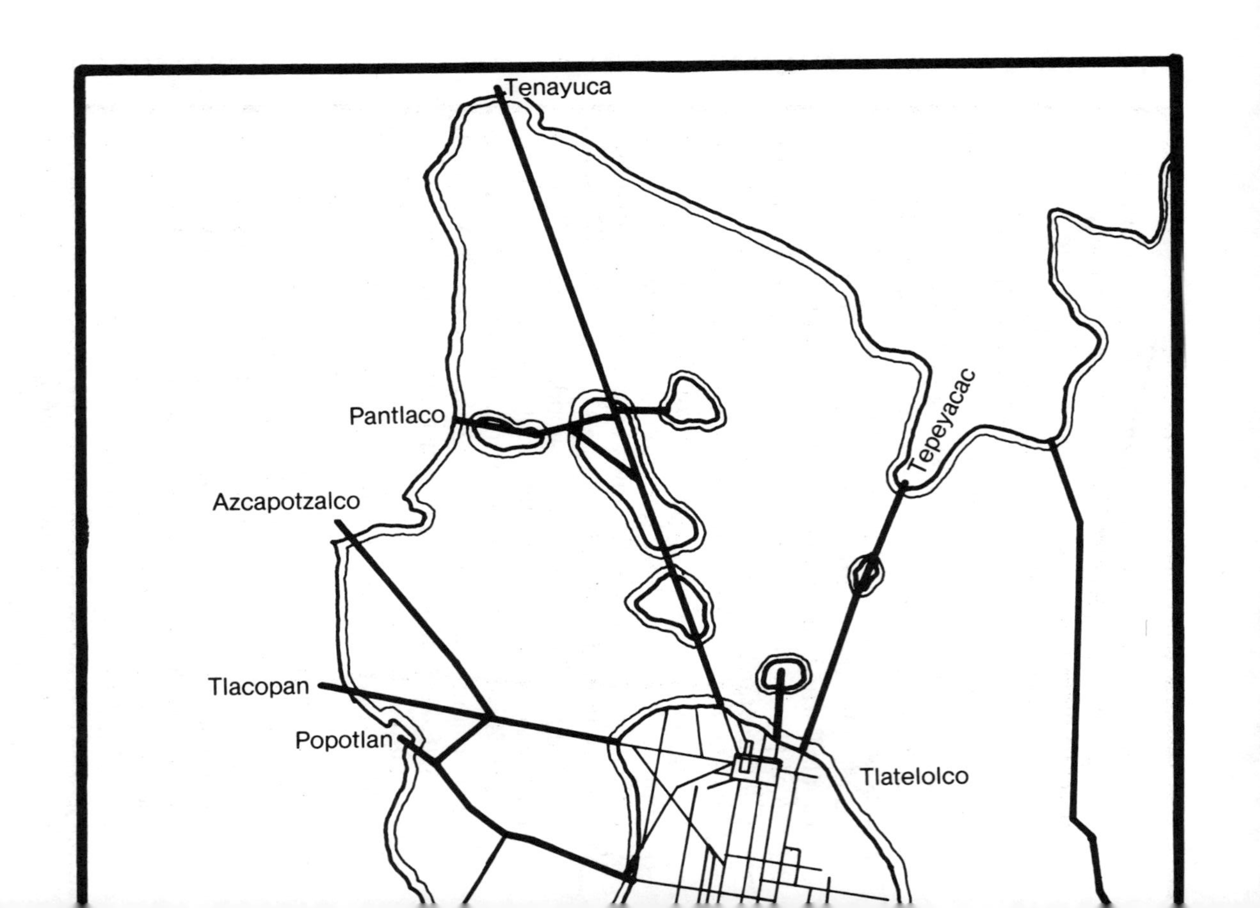
Tenayuca
Pantlaco
Tepeyacac
Azcapotzalco
Tlacopan
Popotlan
Tlatelolco

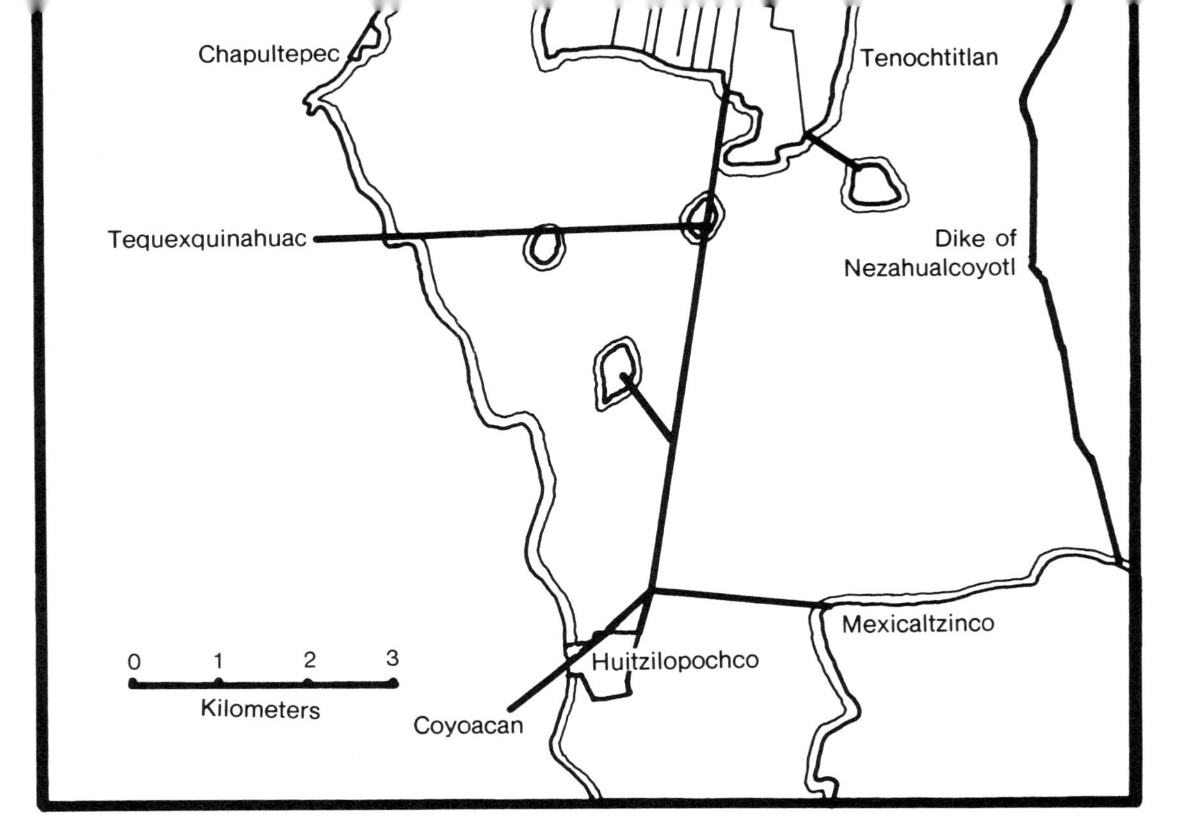

MAP 3. TENOCHTITLAN AND CONNECTING CAUSEWAYS (from Sanders, Parsons, and Santley 1979, map 19).

1427–40), and so, possibly, did the cruciform plan. The two axes crossed in the center of the city, dividing it into four great districts. In the center was a plaza containing the great temple, markets, and religious and political structures. Four great highways radiated from this plaza, those to the north, west, and south continuing out of the city by means of the causeways, while the eastern highway led to the city's edge and the canoe dock.[40] Texcoco was 24 kilometers due east of Tenochtitlan, so the canoe port was established to accommodate its trade, as well as that with Chimalhuacan and other cities around the lake periphery. Canoe transport was preferred for most commodities, even from sites connected to Tenochtitlan by causeways.

The systematic pattern of Tenochtitlan, which gave it a grid-style layout, is the result of two factors.[41] First, rectangular grids are more practical for chinampa construction, for this is an expensive process and constructing sharp angles is unproductive. Second, since thousands of canoes entered the city daily, straight, orderly canals were built to ensure a smooth flow of traffic. City markets were adjacent to canals to permit easy supply.[42] The implication is that, from the time of Itzcoatl, or at least by midcentury,[43] Aztec urban planning took into consideration not only population growth but—critical to Tenochtitlan—traffic flow, upon which the city depended for its subsistence.[44]

Canoe traffic economically linked the entire lake system of the Valley of Mexico.[45] The flow was predominantly into Tenochtitlan and consisted largely of foodstuffs and other provisions, but Tenochtitlan-Tlatelolco also served as a market for the hinterlands, so the canoe trade went in both directions.[46] While areas sending goods into Tenochtitlan from the west employed tlamemes, those able to use canoes did so, and this channeled the flow through several prominent *embarcaderos* (docks) in communities specializing in transport. Not only was canoe transport more efficient and cheaper, but in many instances the water route was shorter than the land routes, as between Texcoco and Tenochtitlan, where the canoe journey was 3 leagues and the two land routes were 7 and 8 leagues, respectively.[47]

Traffic on the lake system of the Valley of Mexico was influenced by several factors: the configuration of the lakes, differences in production around the lakes, and the location of interregional trade routes. Despite the distances involved, traffic from the northern lakes to Tenochtitlan clearly occurred.[48] That it did not extend from the northern extremes to the southern has less to do with efficiency than with marketing behavior. Tenochtitlan reaped the complementary benefits and burdens of its island location. Unlike lakeshore sites, it had no adjacent agricultural hinterland, and it necessarily relied on lake-borne commerce to a greater extent and also benefited by its greater centrality. Furthermore, Tenochtitlan's bulk-import–manufactured-goods export also benefited by the hydrology of the lakes.

Lakeshore production of agricultural surplus was greatest in the southern two lakes, where the chinampa system was most extensively developed. However, other goods also flowed in from beyond the valley. Trade routes from Morelos fed into the Chalco region,[49] the Azcapotzalco-Tlacopan area received trade from the Valley of Toluca, and Texcoco received trade from the Puebla area. In the center of this trade flow was the great consuming city of Tenochtitlan.

The current that flowed from the higher peripheral lakes to the lower central lakes coincided with the economic flow of bulk goods from the peripheries to the center. Thus heavily laden canoes bound for Tenochtitlan were assisted by the current, while the lightly laden returning canoes met little resistance. The lake system served as a large and efficient conduit of goods, the flow being rural to urban, and predominantly into food-deficient Tenochtitlan.[50]

The ease of canoe transport allowed an unprecedented degree of regional economic integration; early chroniclers often commented on the extent of the trade.[51] The docks of several prominent transit points around the lake are frequently mentioned: Chalco Atenco, Ayotzingo, Tetelco, Xochimilco, Mexicalzingo, and Huitzilopochco.[52] However, these reflect southern-lake usage that was more important during the colonial period. Specific documentation is less forthcoming for the other lakes, but canoe transport clearly did occur, as, for example, from Xaltocan and Ataltepeque.[53]

Canoers were specialized and highly organized, their responsibilities extending only to the conveyance of goods from dock to dock and not to extraneous matters concerning their sale or storage.[54] Canoe work was sufficiently specialized that some workers—presumably dock workers—did nothing but launch canoes.[55] They also controlled the size of the canoe cargoes.[56]

How extensive canoe traffic was is uncertain, although it was large. Early-sixteenth-century accounts vary, but all indicate great numbers of dugout canoes: 200,000 canoes, 60,000 to 70,000 large canoes, and 50,000 canoes. As late as 1580, 3,000 to 4,000 canoes passed Mexicalzinco daily on their way to Mexico City.[57] Modern estimates place the number of canoes in the valley in colonial times at 100,000 to 200,000 (see plate 5).[58]

The size of the canoes is as important as their numbers, however. Estimates of size were recorded not only as dimensions but also in terms of cargo capacity and numbers of passengers. One modern estimate puts the size of canoes during the colonial period at between 14 and 50 feet.[59] There were clearly great variations in sizes; one colonial writer described large canoes bigger than the Capilla de la Congregación (or 110 *pies* long and 35 *pies* wide; 1 *pie* ≐ 28 centimeters, thus 30.8 by 9.8 meters, or about 100 by 32 feet).[60] Another writer recorded various lengths: 15 *pies* (4.2 meters), 20 *pies* (5.6 meters), 40 *pies* (11.2 meters), and 50 *pies* (14 meters).[61] Modern data describe 7-meter and 10- to 15-meter canoes in the lakes of the Valley of Mexico, similar to those mentioned by Díaz del Castillo, in which a single man could pole over a ton of maize.[62]

Plate 5. Canoe with Moteuczomah Xocoyotzin going to Tlachtonco (Durán, Historia 1. *52, Biblioteca Nacional, Madrid).*

The cargoes conveyed by canoe probably included everything produced in central Mexico, but most were bulk commodities, stones, sand, wood, maize, grain, salt, meat, fish, fruit, flowers, and vegetables.[63] Canoe loads in the colonial period were as large as 15,000 pounds and at least 20 cargas, or, if maize, 35 cargas, and, if flour, 52 cargas, varying by weight and volume. At 23 kilograms per carga, this is a hauling capacity of 460, 805, and 1,196 kilograms, respectively.[64]

Numbers of passengers also give an indication of canoe sizes. Colonial sources record various canoe sizes, from one- and two- to sixty-man canoes.[65] One modern estimate, based on 130 to 140 pounds per man, yields a capacity of about 4 tons for a 60-man canoe.[66] Estimates of size and capacity will probably never be adequate for precise freight calculations, but recorded sizes, haulage, and passengers clearly indicate the presence of multiton haulage by single canoes. Speed, however, does not seem to increase with the size of the canoe; it merely requires additional paddlers to push more dead weight at an average speed.[67]

To preserve the produce, canoe journeys were made at night. The trip from Ayotzingo to Mexico City was six to eight hours, but various factors affected the time required. For instance, canoe journeys between Xochimilco and Mexico City quadrupled or quintupled from a normal one-day trip to a four- to five-day journey when the canals became clogged with tule weeds.[68] One sixteenth-century source records the distance by canoe from Chalco Atenco to Mexico City as five *leguas pequeñas* (small leagues),[69] a rate of travel of between 2.6 and 3.5 kilometers per hour; the rate dropped to about 2.1 kilometers per hour in the 1950s, as the canal system deteriorated.

In the plateau area of central Mexico, the size of urban hinterlands (and consequent city size) was determined by the efficiency of *tlamemes* (23 kilograms carried 21 to 28 kilometers per day), but the Valley of Mexico also contained a five-lake system that provided the opportunity to use two systems of transportation, *tlamemes* and canoes,

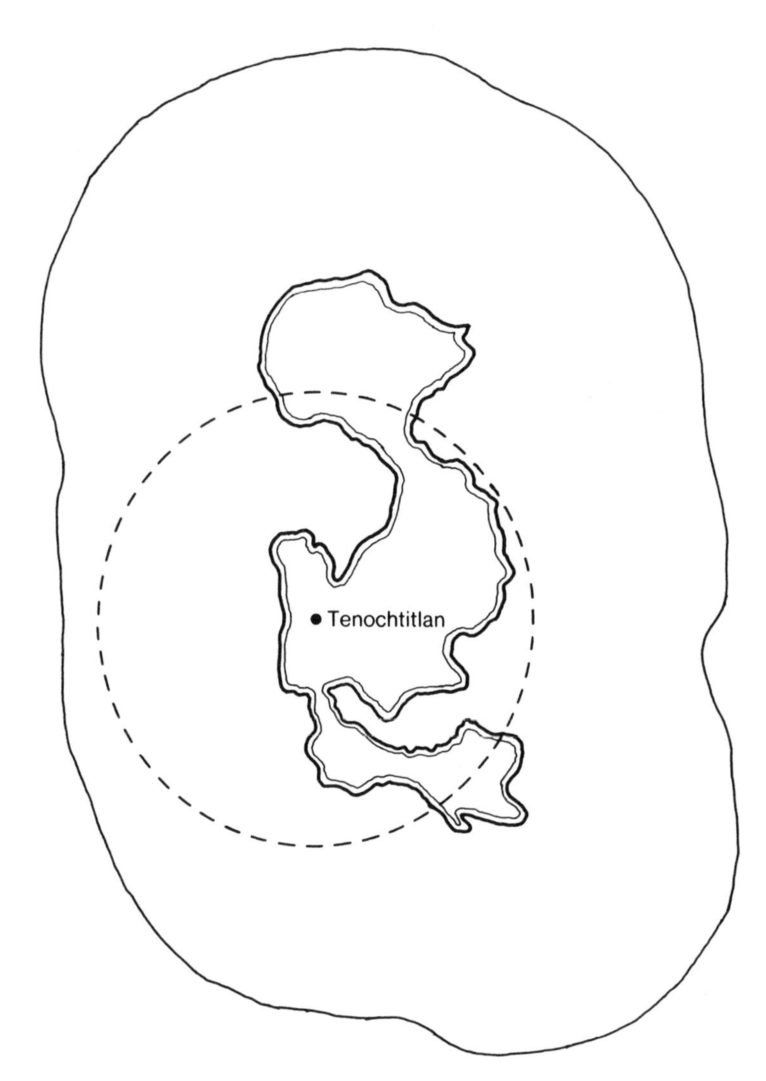

MAP 4. TENOCHTITLAN'S ECONOMIC HINTERLAND. Defined as one tlameme-day distance (18 miles), the area from which Tenochtitlan could ideally attract foodstuffs on a remunerative basis is represented by a dotted line if the city were landlocked. The solid line indicates the same one tlameme-day radius, considering the vastly more efficient canoe transportation.

the latter being forty times more efficient than the former in terms of bulk transported. Consequently, Tenochtitlan's effective hinterland was not a 5-league radius around the city but a 5-league radius along the entire lakeshore (see map 4). This hinterland was determined by the high cost of transporting goods from the point of production to the lakeshore and the low cost of further transport to Tenochtitlan.[70] The net effect was to allow the city immediate access to an economic hinterland much larger than that available to other Mesoamerican cities and to increase its population potential. This larger hinterland was a potential, not necessarily an actuality; how it was taken advantage of is at issue.

CHAPTER 4

Economic Distribution

WHILE local food production and procurement play a major role in the supply of all cities, for Tenochtitlan the lack of immediate arable lands forced the creation of chinampas and the political co-option of productive areas elsewhere in the Valley of Mexico. But of greater significance to Tenochtitlan than to more conventionally sited cities was the way markets interacted to facilitate the flow of goods into and out of major centers. To a large extent Tenochtitlan's economic life was structured by formalized exchange, both marketing and long-distance trade.

TRADE AND MARKET

The markets (*tianquiztli*) of central Mexico were a significant factor in the economy of the region. The markets—at least the largest of them—were held in marketplaces built for that purpose. Often they were adjacent to the residences of the rulers, possibly indicating a conjunction of the economic and the political, if not a dominating role of the latter over the former.[1] The markets were laid out in a planned manner, like commodities being sold in separate sections (see plate 6) and, in Tenochtitlan, began and ended with the sounding of the drum from the temple of Quetzalcoatl in the morning and evening. Officials patrolled the market to ensure fairness in transactions, quality, and price, and a merchants' court, composed of twelve senior merchants, stood ready to hear business disputes and decide cases of alleged fraud.[2] Of all that was brought into the market, part was paid to the ruler. Goods were sold by count and measure, not by weight, and although the Aztecs lacked a unitary system of money, cacao beans,

Plate 6. Aztec marketplace (Durán, Libro de los Ritos, 1. *28, Biblioteca Nacional, Madrid)*

mantas (blankets), quills filled with gold dust, and small copper axes had standardized values and augmented the prevalent barter system.[3] Regulations not only required periodic attendance at the markets but prohibited the sale of goods outside the markets.[4]

While markets admirably serve the purpose of concentrating both goods and services produced within their areas of interaction and the consumers of those goods, to address the needs of a larger area, market interaction and integration are necessary. Market economies possess central places that are hierarchically organized and interrelate in patterned ways.[5] Various centers have markets at times and locations that permit the movement of people and goods between them, providing for greater seller and buyer flexibility, as exemplified by central-place theory. This theory assumes that the location of market centers is determined by competition, market size (reflecting goods and services offered and area), and population served. Given an inhabited landscape, central-place theory predicts where cities must be situated, reversing von Thünen's assumption that a city determines how the land will be utilized. Central-place patterns are based on the distance consumers will travel for various goods and services, such centers arising in proportion to the demand. Proportional demand is as follows: many centers provide the basic goods, and fewer centers provide more esoteric goods, each center drawing on a sustaining population. The range of a good or service (the area beyond which consumers will not travel for the commodity) and threshold (the amount of business needed to sustain a supplier) are interdependent variables, the range equaling or exceeding the threshold of a successful firm. Whereas von Thünen's center yields a circular hinterland, the central-place landscape, occupied by equidistant centers, yields a hexagonal pattern—the most nearly circular form which can exclusively occupy a plain.

Central-place theory is further elaborated by the nested hierarchy of centers and hexagons, reflecting increasingly comprehensive hinterlands of the increasingly scarce and/or costly goods and services. Consequently, less expensive, more common goods would be available in many centers, since their sale would be frequent and the population necessary to support their sellers would be small. More expensive, less common goods would be available in fewer (larger) centers, since their sale would be infrequent and the population necessary to support their sellers would be large. Commodity types and consumer demand would result in a marketing pattern in which small centers are common and evenly distributed over the landscape (to maximize the population on which each would draw) while large centers would be less common (to draw on larger areas of population). Thus a given consumer may occupy the hinterland of several centers for different purposes. Among the assumptions of central-place theory are market rationality, an isotropic landscape, even dispersal of population, and homogeneity of taste and income (see fig. 4.1). Despite the unreality of these assumptions, central-place theory provides a useful model from which

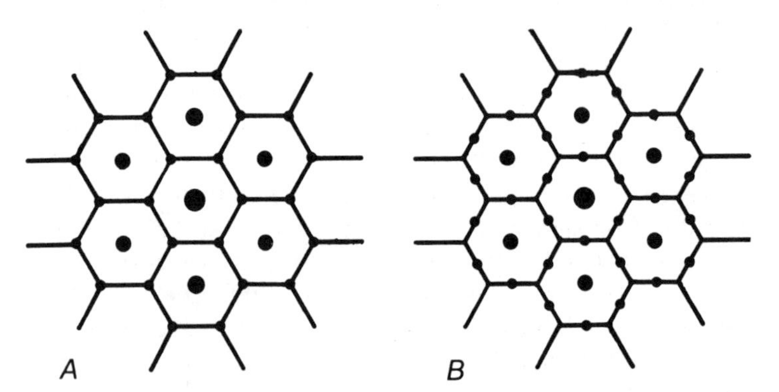

FIG. 4.1. CENTRAL-PLACE MARKETING MODELS. *A: K*-3 retailing pattern in which each small center has three higher-level markets with which to trade, but roads do not link major centers directly. *B: K*-4 transport pattern in which each small center has only two higher level markets with which to trade, but roads link major centers directly.

to consider regional economies and to illustrate the effects of actual variations of the assumed conditions. The very unreality of the model's conditions, as well as its elaborateness, requires good data concerning actual market behavior. City size is a function of all central functions, not just retailing, and settlement patterns alone do not provide a reliable indication of marketing systems.

There are several variations of the central-place pattern. The K-3 pattern emphasizes marketing since it maximizes the number of markets available to any given seller-buyer. The K-4 pattern emphasizes transport, since it minimizes travel distance between major centers. The K-7 pattern emphasizes administrative functions (see fig. 4.2). In contrast to central-place systems in which all markets have access to at least two higher-level markets, marketing centers in dendritic patterns do not. In dendritic systems each marketing center has access to one and only one higher-level center, thus skewing the economic system.[6]

Market integration is largely a function of the frequency and periodicity of markets. Demand density affects the frequency of markets; the larger the population, the greater the demand for market goods, and the more frequently a viable market can be held to satisfy those demands.[7] Where the population is large, as in Tenochtitlan, the demand is sufficient to allow daily markets. Where there are smaller population centers, markets are held periodically. Ideally (but by no means invariably) the periodic markets of a given area are staggered so that their markets do not conflict. This permits traders to travel between markets, furnishing goods and services otherwise not available to such small population centers, and to transport goods between smaller and larger marketplaces.

Before Tenochtitlan rose to a position of dominance, patterns of exchange within the Valley of Mexico were affected by ethnic and political divisions. The main ethnic groups in the Valley of Mexico during late pre-Columbian times were the Acolhuas, on the eastern shore of Lake Tex-

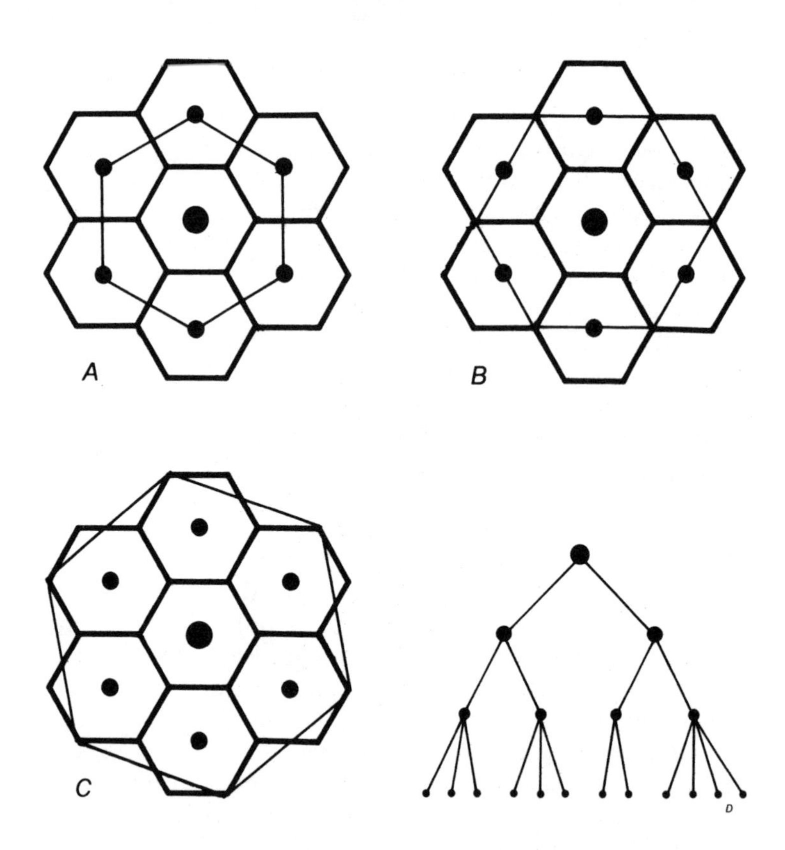

FIG. 4.2. ECONOMIC EXCHANGE MODELS. *A: K*-3 central-place retailing model. *B: K*-4 central-place transport model. *C: K*-7 central-place administrative model. Thick lines indicate marketing areas of respective towns; thin lines indicate the respective areas (and forms) of dominance of the central town. *D:* Dendritic model in which each center is dependent on one and only one higher-level market.

coco; the Tepanecas, on the western shore of Lake Texcoco; the Xochimilcas, on the southern shore of Lake Xochimilco; the Chalcas, on the eastern shore of Lake Chalco; the Cuitlahuacas, at Cuitlahuac, between lakes Xochimilco and Chalco; the Mixquicas, at Mixquic, on the southern shore of Lake Chalco; and the Mexicas, or Aztecs, centered in Tenochtitlan, in western Lake Texcoco. It is apparent that many goods not produced locally were fed into the valley and exchanged within it—notably cotton, obsidian, and cacao. Other goods were produced or processed for regional consumption within the valley. Specialization was the result of unequal availability of certain goods, such as salt extracted from the lakes and lime from the northern area.[8] There was also politically maintained market specialization, as witnessed by the markets for slaves at Azcapotzalco, dogs at Acolman, and cloth and pottery vessels at Texcoco.[9] The basic pattern of commodity production and distribution, however, appears to have been fairly localized, as evident from the excavations at Huexotla.[10] This is consistent with a marketing pattern in which the lowest-level, or primary, markets were periodic within a five-day cycle and focused on the secondary markets of their respective cabeceras (see fig. 4.3; the term "primary market" is used here to designate the lowest-level market, "secondary market," the next higher market, and so on).

Although some regional exchange existed, it was not pervasive in the economy and seems to have resulted primarily from resource specialization. In short, the pre-Aztec marketing patterns appear to have been solar systems in which markets were oriented around single centers, creating simple two-level hierarchies.[11] Marketing systems tended to remain bounded by political borders, and little interpolity trade existed in commodities other than elite goods.

MARKET PERIODICITY

Market periodicity permits an easy and simple economic integration of an area. However, economic rationality does

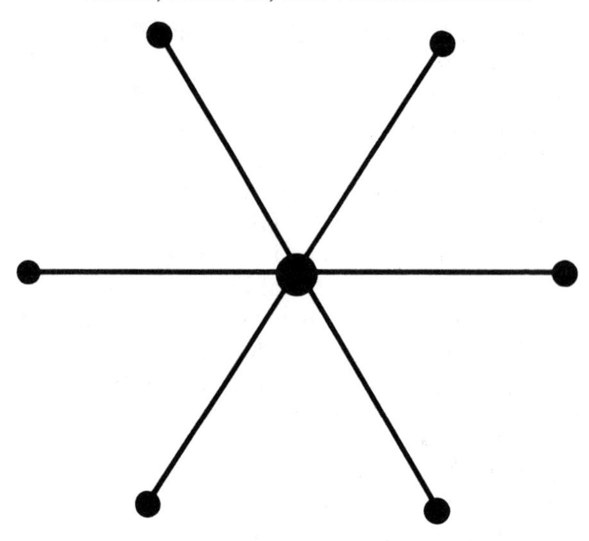

FIG. 4.3. SOLAR SYSTEM. The center town, or *cabecera,* exchanges goods with each dependency, or *sujeto,* but there is no direct trade between *sujetos* or with other marketing systems.

not necessarily dictate periodicity. Periodic markets, which generally meet in smaller population centers, have three interlocking advantages: they allow exploitation of low-consumer-demand areas by mobile traders, they offer consumers a greater variety of goods by periodically concentrating supply, and, by meeting on different days, they facilitate the redistribution of commodities in the marketing system to and from higher-level centers.[12] However, cultural factors are as much a determinant of market frequency as is the logic of market efficiency.

While an understanding of periodic markets does not necessarily explain a marketing system in its entirety, knowing how they function is a vital component in comprehending the whole. Although the data on indigenous market periodicity are thin (the lack of indigenous dates is apparently due to the complementary factors of rapid conversion to the European calendar and literacy in New

Spain being a Christian skill), they can be profitably examined in light of our knowledge of the Aztec calendar.[13]

Calendrical systems have a great influence on the temporal patterning of markets. One of the basic concerns of market scheduling is simplicity. It is crucial that buyers and sellers alike know when markets are held. Consequently, those schedules that fit the fundamental units of time of a given calendrical system are best and most easily remembered.[14] Regularity alone is insufficient.

Markets of many different frequencies are recorded for the Aztecs, from daily markets in large cities, such as Tenochtitlan, to 5-, 8-, 9-, 13-, and 20-day markets.[15] There is an assumption that the largest centers held markets most frequently (daily) and the smallest centers held markets least frequently (every 20 days).[16] Despite its consistency with marketing theory, this correlation of town size and market frequency finds only limited support in the Aztec data. To assess the significance of the recorded 1-, 5-, 8-, 9-, 13-, and 20-day sequences, as well as to understand why these particular sequences were used, a brief consideration of Aztec calendrical system is in order.[17]

The central Mexican calendar is based on two major cycles, one of 260 days and one of 365 days, and within each there are other shorter cycles. In the 260-day cycle (the tonalpohualli, "the counting of the days"), each day is represented by a day-number accompanied by a day-sign, the combination producing a day-name. There are thirteen day-numbers and twenty day-names, the two enmeshing to create a 260-day sequence (see table 4.1). This sequence is an indigenous convention used throughout Mesoamerica and does not indicate the fundamental starting point in a 365-day year anymore than our Sunday-through-Saturday sequence indicates on which day of the week a new year will begin.

The 13-day sequence is not linguistically recognized in Nahuatl (i.e., there is no word equivalent to "week" or "fortnight"), but its viability as a unit is suggested by the existence of the thirteen day-patron gods, known as the

Table 4.1. The Twenty Tonalpohualli Day-Signs in Conventional Aztec Sequence

Day-Sign	Day-Sign
1. Cipactli (caiman)	11. Ozomahtli (monkey)
2. Ehehcatl (wind)	12. Malinalli (grass)
3. Calli (house)	13. Acatl (reed)
4. Cuetzpalin (lizard)	14. Ocelotl (jaguar)
5. Coatl (snake)	15. Cuauhtli (eagle)
6. Miquiztli (death)	16. Cozcacuauhtli (vulture)
7. Mazatl (deer)	17. Olin ([earth]quake)
8. Tochtli (rabbit)	18. Tecpatl (flint)
9. Atl (water)	19. Quiahuitl (rain)
10. Itzcuintli (dog)	20. Xochitl (flower)

Lords of the Day (see table 4.2). Since the lowest common multiple of 13 and 20 is 260, a given day-name (i.e., a given combination of day-number plus day-sign) will recur only after 260 days. This 260-day period was therefore the longest period within which the cycles of 13 and 20 would uniquely identify a day.

In the 365-day cycle, there are eighteen named "months" of twenty days each, totaling 360 days, plus five additional days, called nemontemi or nentemi. The

Table 4.2. The Thirteen Lords of the Day

Day-Name	Day-Name
1. Xiuhteuctli (Turquoise-lord)	9. Quetzalcoatl (Plumed-serpent)
2. Tlalteuctli (Earth-lord)	10. Tezcatl Ihpoca (Mirror That Smokes)
3. Chalchihuitl Icue (Her-skirt Is Jade)	11. Chalmecateuctli (Lord who dwells in Chalman)
4. Tonatiuh (Sun)	12. TlahuizcalpanTeuctli (Lord of Dawn)
5. Tlahzalteotl (Filth-goddess)	13. Citlalli Icue (Her-skirt Is Stars)
6. MictlanTeuctli (Lord of Mictlan)	
7. Centeotl (Dried-ear-of-maize God)	
8. Tlaloc (Landlier)	

nemontemi days are intercalated at the end of the eighteenth month.

Although the question which month began the year is unresolved,[18] there is a generally accepted *sequence* of the eighteen months (see table 4.3).

Both the 260-day cycle and the 365-day cycle operate simultaneously, running in independent cycles. The multiples of the 20 day-signs, 13 day-numbers, and 18 months (plus 5 days) generate unique combinations through 52 solar years and constitute the Binding of the Years, after which the entire cycle begins anew.

The solar years are named for the day-name (i.e., the day-number and day-sign combination) on which they begin. The formal solar year is 360 days of 18 complete 20-day cycles. The cycle does not include the nemontemi (lit. nen ontemi, "it becomes full in vain") days, omitting

Table 4.3. The Eighteen "Months" of the Solar Year

Month	Month
1. Atl Cahualo (Water Is Abandoned)	10. Huei Miccailhuitl (It Is the Great Festival of the Dead)
2. Tlacaxipehualiztli (It Is the Flaying of Men)	11. Ochpaniztli (It Is the Road-sweeping Action)
3. Tozoztontli (It Is the Short Vigil)	12. Pachtontli (It Is the Little Spanish Moss)
4. Huei Tozoztli (It Is the Long Vigil)	13. Huei Pachtli (It Is the Great Spanish Moss)
5. Toxcatl (It Is a Drought)	14. Quecholli (Macaw [*lit.* It Is Rubber at the Neck])
6. Etzalcualiztli (It Is the Eating of Bean Porridge)	15. Panquetzaliztli (It Is the Flat Raising)
7. Tecuilhuitontli (It Is the Little Festival of the Lords)	16. Atemoztli (It Is the Descent in the Form of Water)
8. Huei Tecuilhuitl (It Is the Great Festival of the Lords)	17. Tititl (It Is a Shrunken [or Wrinkled] Thing)
9. Miccailhuitontli (It Is the Little Festival of the Dead)	18. Izcalli (It Is a Sprout)

5 days each 365-day year, but the tonalpohualli is oblivious to the nemontemi days. Each 365-day year runs 18 complete 20-day cycles plus 5 additional days each solar year. Consequently, the years always begin on one of 4 days, known as the yearbearers, which are 5 days apart in the day-sign sequence. Each of these days—calli, tochtli, acatl, and tecpatl—designates a year thirteen times during the Binding of the Years.[19]

An additional cycle of days, although by no means the only other one, is that of the nine Lords of the Night, the Yohualteuctin (see table 4.4). This series of nine is generally attributed to the tonalpohualli but does not fit into it evenly (unless there was a doubling of the gods on the last day of the cycle), running in continuous cycles apparently independent of both the tonalpohualli and the solar-year cycles.[20] The central Mexican calendar can be viewed as a series of different-sized cogs, each turning at its own rate but combining as the various cycles coincide, to create larger temporal units.

The issue is how the 1-, 5-, 8-, 9-, 13-, and 20-day sequences fit the calendar. The 20-day sequence is based on the 20-day month, the 13-day sequence is based on the 13-day Lords of the Day cycle, and the 9-day sequence is based on the 9-day Lords of the Night cycle. The 8-day sequence, however, does not fit the calendar in any obvious

Table 4.4. The Nine Lords of the Night

Day-Name	Day-Name
1. Xiuhteuctli (Turquoise-lord)	Mictlan)
2. Itztli or Tecpatl (Obsidian or Flint)	6. Chalchihuitl Icue (Her-skirt Is Jade)
3. Piltzinteuctli (Child-lord)	7. Tlahzolteotl (Filth-goddess)
4. Centeotl (Dried-ear-of-maize God)	8. Tepeyollohtli (Mountain-heart)
5. MictlanTeuctli (Lord of	9. Tlaloc (Landlier)

fashion. The probable explanation of its occurence lies in the misinterpretation of early Spanish chronicles. Seven-day markets, based on the European calendar (initially Julian, then Gregorian), appeared after the Conquest. Although English practice is to say "every seven days" to describe a weekly event, Spanish practice includes the day the count is begun as well as the day it ends. Thus, "every seven days" is rendered in Spanish "de ocho en ocho días," literally "every eight days," but meaning weekly.[21] This, in conjunction with the absence of any mention of an 8-day market in Molina's classic Nahuatl dictionary—which does refer to 5-, 9-, and 20-day markets—and the lack of supporting evidence from sixteenth-century chronicles and colonial documents, indicates that the 8-day market was probably a post-Conquest chimera.

The 5-day sequence is not obvious in the Aztec calendar either, but it does constitute a basic unit of time. In the 20-day month, the 4 yearbearer days have a greater significance than the remaining 16 days, each yearbearer beginning and dominating a 5-day segment of the month.[22] Thus, although it is not a formally recognized cycle, as were the 9-, 13-, and 20-day cycles, the 5-day cycle emerges from the way the calendar functioned.

That there were articulating periodic markets is repeatedly supported by sixteenth-century chronicles and later colonial practices, but the 5-, 9-, 13-, and 20-day cycles represent two distinct types of marketing sequences. If the 5-, 9-, 13-, and 20-day cycles were actual marketing cycles, their use, even at different levels in the marketing hierarchy, would result in adjacent markets meeting on the same day with relative frequency, thus undermining the primary advantage of periodic markets. Furthermore, these conflicts would appear to occur irregularly, so that dropping one of the conflicting markets would introduce an undesirable element of randomness into the system. Although the sequencing of the resultant conflict between adjacent markets could be calculated, it is a complicated matter. In practice, the market deletions necessary to avoid conflicts would appear to be irregular. This is similar to the situation with respect to Easter. Easter is celebrated on the first Sunday after the full moon following the vernal equinox. In other words, it is loosely tied to Passover and is set according to the Jewish lunar calendar. Thus, despite its regularity, Easter appears irregular from the perspective of the Gregorian calendar.

The 5-day sequence was the basic Mesoamerican marketing unit. A market might be held on any day within the 5-day unit. For example, a town may have its market on the third day of the 5-day sequence or twice within the sequence, as was the case in Zapotitlan.[23] Daily markets were a subset of the 5-day market, merely meeting every day to ensure the provisioning of the largest centers, an example of periodic markets filling up the calendar until there was a continuous market, although Tenochtitlan's daily market had a "bulge" in attendance on a 5-day schedule, as expected.[24] However, the remaining market sequences—9-, 13-, and 20-day—differed fundamentally from the 5-day sequence. The 9-, 13-, and 20-day markets were not cycles indicating the temporal spacing of markets. Rather, they were ritual temporal units with markets held the first day of their respective cycles, and only on the first day.

Among the Toltecs the 20-day market was held on the first day of each month.[25] Given the striking calendrical and ritual similarity, if not unity, throughout Mesoamerica,[26] this practice appears likely to have persisted for that reason as well as for others to be discussed later. A festival is associated with each 20-day month, but there is a certain amount of debate over which day the 20-day festival was celebrated, the first or the last day of the cycle. Some modern opinion holds that festivals began on the last day of the 20-day month,[27] but Ixtlilxochitl clearly states that the market was held on the first day of the month. The discrepancy is whether it was on day 1 or day 20 of the month. I support the former interpretation because the market would then correspond not only with the yearbearer days but specifically with the yearbearer days that named the current year, making the event all the more important.[28] Unfortunately, sixteenth-century sources differ on the subject, some favoring the last day of the month and some the first.[29]

In addition to the support of most sixteenth-century sources of the first-day interpretation and the increased stature of the market falling on a yearbearer day, two additional considerations argue in favor of a first-day interpretation. First, there is a question about when the Aztec day began. The four logical possibilities are midnight, sunrise, sunset, and noon, with any but the first making the selection of a specific Gregorian day not quite accurate. Second, in the Maya area, festivals "seat" by beginning on the day before the formal festival day.[30] Thus the conflicting positions may have arisen by confusing the festival, variously given as the first and last day of the 20-day cycle, with the market, unambiguously stated as being held on the first day.

Data concerning the 9- and 13-day markets are more scarce than those for the 20-day markets, but they also marked fundamental cyclical units and similarly appear to have been ritual in nature, since they were based on ritually related calendrical units—the nine Lords of the Night cycle and the thirteen Lords of the Day cycle, as is the 20-day cycle, in marked contrast to the 5-day cycle. In all probability the 9- and 13-day markets also met only on the first day of their respective cycles.

Although the 5-day market indicates a temporal unit within which markets were regularly held on any day(s), the same was not true for the 9-, 13-, and 20-day markets. Being held on the first day of their respective cycles, the latter markets were held relatively infrequently and were uniform throughout the area, since they were dictated by the calendar. Thus their significance for articulating markets was minimal.

The frequency of a market generally indicates the population it serves; the larger the population, the more frequent the market. Thus daily markets in central Mexico were held in the largest centers, such as Tenochtitlan, Texcoco, and Tlaxcala. Five-day markets were the norm for most towns. However, in towns holding daily markets, the 5-day sequence was cumulative, the 5-day market being larger and more important than the daily one.[31]

Which day of the 5-day sequence was the market day in specific towns is unknown. Basic market principles would indicate, however, that lower-level markets did not conflict with adjacent markets of the next higher level but, rather, dovetailed with their schedules, a pattern supported by the extant data. Within the 5-day sequence the most important day was the yearbearer day. Thus it is plausible that the cabecera of a region held its market day then, just as, in 1547, the city of Tlaxcala claimed exclusive use of Saturday for its market in the state of Tlaxcala.[32] There is support for such a pattern beyond the logic of the system. The market days for Tenochtitlan-Tlatelolco (since it had several major markets, this presumably referred to the most important of them, probably Tlatelolco) were recorded as the third, eighth, thirteenth, and eighteenth days of the month, not the first, sixth, eleventh, and sixteenth, as one would assume if they were yearbearer days.[33] However, the same source continues and lists the market days as calli, tochtli, acatl, and tecpatl. Since these are the yearbearers, it is clear that the statement about the third, eighth, thirteenth, and eighteenth days refers not to the yearbearers as they function in the system but to their order in the indigenous conventional sequence. Mexico City's market days did, in fact, meet on the first, sixth, eleventh, and sixteenth days of the month—the yearbearer days—supporting the theory that major centers held markets on the yearbearer days. Unfortunately, the paucity of marketing data recorded in the indigenous calendrical system prevents a fuller examination of this issue.

The 9-, 13-, and 20-day markets were most likely not independent but were superimposed on the 5-day sequence much as the 5-day market was superimposed on the daily markets, cumulative celebrations being common in the Aztec system.[34] Furthermore, extant documents record the occurrence of 20-day markets in larger cities rather than in small towns, as one would expect if they were truly periodic markets, their infrequency indicating small populations and small consumer demand. The neatest fit with the 5-day markets was the 20-day market. The 20-day market, being held on the first day of the month, would have been held on the first yearbearer of the month. Although the name of the solar year rotated among the four yearbearers, the first yearbearer of each month was also the yearbearer for which that 365-day year was named. Presumably this market was larger and of more importance than the other markets, including the other yearbearer markets, just as the 5-day market was more important than the daily markets.

The 9- and 13-day markets do not fit as neatly into the annual cycle. They were apparently celebrated on the first day of their respective cycles,[35] rather than randomly throughout. But even only initial-day markets based on such eccentric cycles would introduce excessive randomness to an otherwise regular, predictable marketing system. The 9- and 13-day markets were probably celebrated only in those towns whose regular 5-day markets coincided with the 9- and 13-day markets. This practice of selective celebration would have been compatible with existing patterns, for it is clear that festivals varied in importance throughout central Mexico.[36] Only one town in a marketing system would celebrate that 9- or 13-day market, making its regular market slightly more important than it would ordinarily be and avoiding the economic chaos that would result if every town held a market on the ninth and thirteenth days—similar to the way in which the 20-day markets operate.

Thus the system as reflected in the documents, the calendar system, and the logic of marketing appears to have been one of daily markets in major cities and articulating 5-day markets elsewhere, with the yearbearer 5-day markets being held in the dominant center of each area. The 9-, 13-, and 20-day markets, held on the initial day of their respective cycles, were not celebrated in every town but were held only in those towns with whose market days they coincided. The 20-day markets were likely held only in large centers, as evidence of their occurrence in Tulanzingo and Huitzilopochco (and also in Toltec Tula, Teotihuacan, Tulanzingo, Cuauhnahuac, Cholula, and Tultitlan) suggests,[37] whereas the 9- and 13-day markets probably rotated among the various markets of the region. This cumulative market celebration permitted special markets to be held without generating chaos in the system. What this does indicate, however, is a marketing region of basically two levels—important centers all holding their markets on the same days, the yearbearers, and their subordinate towns holding markets on the nonyearbearer days. The use of the 5-, 9-, 13-, and 20-day cycles as periodic marketing cycles would logically result in apparently irregular conflicts between adjacent markets. But the use of a 5-day cycle alone, with the ritual 9-, 13-, and 20-day cycles being cumulative rather than independent, permits a marketing pattern that would not conflict with adjacent markets, even if the yearbearer day was reserved for the cabecera. Market articulation above the cabecera level was not a matter of periodicity.

This marketing situation, then, fought against the economic integration of areas larger than those encompassed by the small city-states of the Valley of Mexico. The challenge faced by the Aztecs was to channel more goods into Tenochtitlan than were available through the original marketing system, to make Tenochtitlan the dominant market in the valley. But this was primarily a political problem, not an economic one.

CHAPTER 5

The Political Structure and the Economic Reorganization of Central Mexico

MUCH OF Tenochtitlan-Tlatelolco's food requirement was met through market mechanisms. Virtually the entire Valley of Mexico was within Tenochtitlan-Tlatelolco's economic hinterland and supplied foodstuffs to the city. Remuneration alone did not account for the entire flow of commodities entering the city, however. The Aztecs exercised their political power in a deliberate effort to augment the economic means of supplying their capital.

Patterns of compliance may be divided into coercive and remunerative power, although in their actual functioning they are almost always mixed, with the proportions shifting.[1] A third type of compliance, normative, is omitted for present purposes, in part because it is not a major focus of this study, although it assuredly exercises influence, and in part because of the relative difficulty of assessing normative power, particularly for the period in question. With respect to procurement in particular, it is unlikely that normative power played a significant role in securing the goods required for urban consumption.

Remunerative compliance operates within the area from which commodities flow into the center on an economic basis. The existence of good markets coupled with high demand and high prices is sufficient to stimulate the flow of goods without requiring the exercise of other compliance strategies. Coercive compliance operates within the area from which commodities flow into the center on a political basis. Policies supported by military force (or the threat thereof) account for goods being brought to the center in such forms as taxation, corvée labor, and forced attendance at markets.

Remunerative-coercive strategies operate when both forms of power are mutually supportive. On the ground, compliance systems usually involve a power mix, and in this model we may conceive of a continuum varying between the two "pure" types with goods being drawn into the center through a variable mix of the two strategies. Thus such factors as high demand and high prices are augmented by pressures of taxation and required market attendance, the situation more closely approximating the actual mix of reasons for supplying the center.

POLITICAL HINTERLANDS

In addition to their analytical distinctions, these compliance strategies can also be distinguished spatially. Compliance zones—the areas within which each of the compliance strategies operate—may describe actual hinterlands (the area drawn on in practice) or potential hinterlands (the area maximally feasible to draw on with a given compliance strategy). Economic hinterlands are determined by commodity range (the value of the commodity plus the cost of transportation), and political hinterlands are determined by the exercise of power and may extend to a greater or smaller area than the economic hinterland. An urban support area is the area from which the center draws commodities by whatever compliance strategy.

A center extracts goods from its political hinterland through coercive means, such as taxation or tribute. Where political and economic hinterlands overlap, political measures may not be needed; where they are necessary, one typically finds mixed strategies, such as required attendance at markets (with all the economic benefits that entails), coupled with penal sanctions for failure to attend. Where the economic hinterland extends beyond the political hinterland, the market alone is operative. Where the political hinterland extends beyond the economic hinterland, however, goods will not flow in response to the market. It should be remembered, though, that an area not within range for one commodity may be within range for another, so economic zones decline by gradients, leaving hinterlands where remunerative factors operate for decreasing types of increasingly valuable commodities. Thus even when political extractive measures are employed, they do not exclude the possibility of attenuated economic intercourse as well. Nevertheless, much of Tenochtitlan's economic needs was supplied as a result of political dominance.

AZTEC EXPANSION

The Aztec empire expanded into areas producing or having access to desired goods and stabilized the flow of specific types and quantities of goods by means of the tribute system.[2] Despite attempts to categorize periods of Aztec expansion, the fortunes of Aztec expansion do not lend themselves to easy divisions beyond those of reign periods (see fig. 5.1).[3]

Conquests before the reign of Itzcoatl took place while the Aztecs were under the domination of the Tepanec empire and are thus best interpreted as Tepanec conquests in which the Aztecs played a role. During Acamapichtli's rule (ca. 1376–96), campaigns within the Valley of Mexico were aimed south at Xochimilco, Cuitlahuac, and Mixquic and north at Xaltocan, and further campaigns were waged against Cuauhtinchan, in Puebla, and Cuauhnahuac (Cuernavaca), in Morelos. Huitzilihuitl's reign (ca. 1396–1417) saw attacks to the north on Tula, and east on Texcoco, Acolman, Otumba, and Tulanzingo. The reign of Chimalpopoca (ca. 1417–27) was largely uneventful.

During Itzcoatl's reign (ca. 1427–40) the Aztecs overthrew the Tepanec empire, and Tenochtitlan, Texcoco, and Tlacopan formed the Triple Alliance. Conquests were carried out in an area bounded by Tula on the north, Huitzilapan on the west, Xiuhtepec (southeast of Cuernavaca) on the south, and the Texcoco area on the east, as

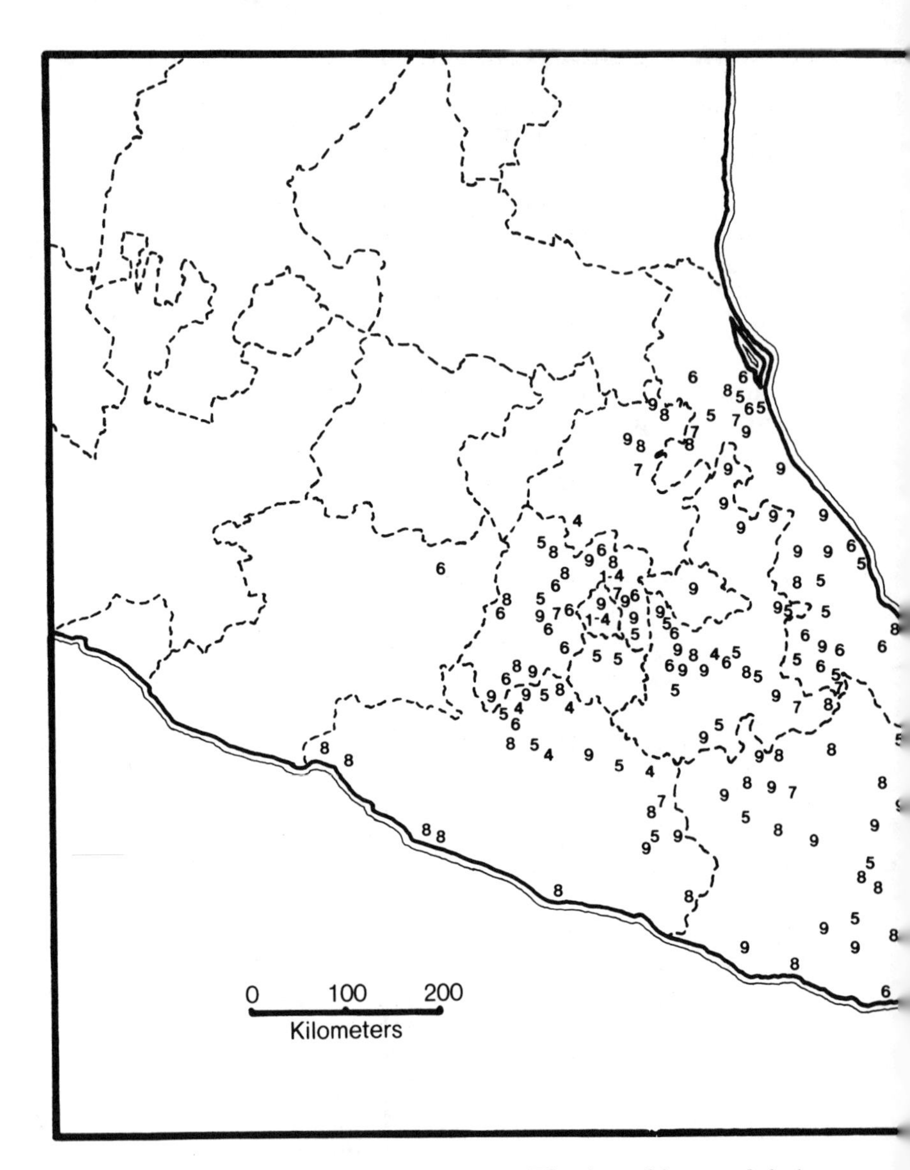

FIG. 5.1. AZTEC RULERS AND CONQUESTS. The Aztec kings and their reigns are listed, with their conquests enumerated on the map by their numbers. For purposes of clarity, the numbers indicate areas of conquests, not necessarily individual towns. Conquest sequence is based on Kelly and Palerm 1952 (but cf. Gibson 1971). Dotted lines indicate modern state and national boundaries.

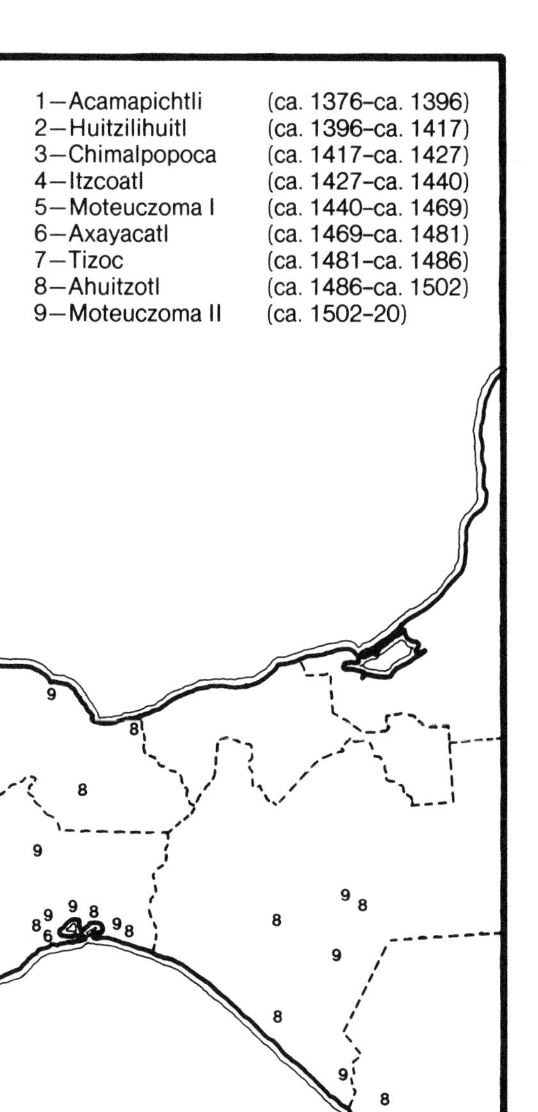

1—Acamapichtli (ca. 1376–ca. 1396)
2—Huitzilihuitl (ca. 1396–ca. 1417)
3—Chimalpopoca (ca. 1417–ca. 1427)
4—Itzcoatl (ca. 1427–ca. 1440)
5—Moteuczoma I (ca. 1440–ca. 1469)
6—Axayacatl (ca. 1469–ca. 1481)
7—Tizoc (ca. 1481–ca. 1486)
8—Ahuitzotl (ca. 1486–ca. 1502)
9—Moteuczoma II (ca. 1502–20)

well as in northern Guerrero. Under Moteuczomah Ilhuicamina (ca. 1440–69) the immediate vicinity was consolidated, including Chalco, the northern Tepanec towns of Xilotepec, Tula, Atotonilco, Hueypuchtla, and Itzcuincuitlapilco, and their armies marched successfully to the Gulf Coast, Veracruz, Puebla, and northern Oaxaca. Axayacatl's reign (ca. 1469–81) was one mainly of consolidation, but with substantial expansion westward and in the Tuxpan area. Tizoc's reign (ca. 1481–86) was a military failure, which may have led to his early (and involuntary) demise.[4] Ahuitzotl's reign (ca. 1486–1502) was another period of great expansion, north, east, and south. The Aztecs conquered large stretches of both coasts and marched into areas of Oaxaca, Tehuantepec, and Chiapas. Moteuczomah Xocoyotzin (ca. 1502–20) expanded further into central and southern Oaxaca, northern Puebla, and adjacent areas of Veracruz, consolidating sections between the areas conquered by Ahuitzotl.

THE TRADITIONAL VIEW

Despite these impressive military gains, the Aztec empire has often been criticized as an inadequate political organization, lacking internal cohesion and displaying an apparent inadequacy in its military organization. The theoretical underpinnings for this perspective derive from Clausewitz, whose basic premise is that war is inherently political, that its purpose is not random violence but the furthering of some goal of the polity. While Clausewitz's works permit many arguments to be made, the basic principle extracted and applied to the Aztecs is that the enemy must be controlled after conquest, a task best accomplished by disarming the vanquished and occupying their territory.[5] The main concern of empires is territorial expansion, internal control, and the maintenance of secure borders, which entails the existence of a standing army, control of the enemy's will (most easily accomplished by control of the territory and leadership), and fortifications to guarantee territorial defense.[6] The Aztecs are generally regarded as not having effectively controlled vanquished territories. The cause, from a Clausewitzian perspective, is the absence of a standing army, on which garrisons and fortifications are, in turn, dependent.

However, the nature of the Aztec empire and its military organization has been misconstrued owing to overreliance (implicit and explicit) on the Clausewitz view of empire. To assess the accuracy of traditional views of the Aztec empire, three related factors must be considered: the professionalism of the Aztec military, the existence of fortifications, and the presence of garrisons throughout the empire.

Aztec warriors have not been considered professional soldiers—despite the existence of military orders—because membership in the army was neither a means of support nor a full-time occupation.[7] Each time the need arose, the military was reconstituted from the populace. There was no permanent standing force, without which the political directives of the capital could not be effectively imposed on the conquered territories. Thus political centralization was impossible.

Fortifications likewise require the presence of a sophisticated military organization.[8] Despite the many reports of fortified sites throughout Mesoamerica (implying military professionalism),[9] the actual nature of these sites is unclear. The existence of walls does not imply the kind of military professionalism required for actual fortifications. Such strongholds as existed were simply matters of expediency and not permanent military installations. This is necessarily so if there was no standing army. However, Aztec garrisons were reported throughout the empire by the conquistadors and in native accounts as well.[10]

A recent refinement of these general requisites adds further to our knowledge of the dynamics of empire by focusing on internal spatial variations of polities. In traditional empires there is a systematic relationship between space and defense.[11] In the center of the polity there is little governmental concern with defense, while at the frontier the opposite is the case. This results from spatial variations of threats to security—low in the center where homogeneity is high and the likelihood of external support for revolt is slight, and high at the periphery, where heterogeneity is high, likelihood of external support for revolt is great, and a breakaway alliance with bordering polities is possible. This spatial refinement of empire lends cogency to the emphasis on standing armies, border fortifications, territorial control, and suppression of potentially subversive local governments.

However, these logical requisites are based not on the way the Aztec empire functioned but on a European conception (and type) of empire entailing the territorial expansion of influence into previously sovereign areas (frequently ethnically and linguistically diverse) and the exercise of political domination, achieved and maintained militarily, not only to guarantee territorial integrity but to replace or control conquered governments. In other words, "empire" seems to demand a standing army, territorial control, border and internal fortifications, and the removal or subordination of indigenous governments. This basic concept of empire pervades the European literature on Mesoamerica.[12] However, the way the Aztec empire was organized was tied to the ecological and technological constraints it faced and to the economic needs of Tenochtitlan.

THE HEGEMONIC EMPIRE

Rather than viewing the Aztec empire as a deficient political entity, as the traditional approach requires, an alternative perspective displays the data in a better light. In reanalyzing the Roman Empire, Edward Luttwak[13] has presented several alternative imperial models, the earliest of which, the Julio-Claudian system, is applicable to the Aztecs. Under this system the empire was one of hegemonic expansionism. The Roman Empire did not fortify and man the frontier. Rather, beyond their nuclear zone of direct control (the territorial empire) lay two zones of diplomatic control, an inner one composed of client states and an outer one composed of client tribes. Unlike the passive true buffer states, the client states actively supplied auxiliary troops and provided peripheral security against "low-intensity" threats. Roman troops were deployed as a field army, available to meet threats rather than being tied to territorial defense. The army was defensive, aimed at internal unrest. The empire was one of political rather than territorial control, buttressed by the threat rather than the presence of Roman military might, thus achieving great economy of force:

> By virtually eliminating the burden of maintaining continuous frontier defenses, the net "disposable" military power generated by the imperial forces was maximized. Hence, the total military power that others could perceive as being available to Rome for offensive use—and that could therefore be put to political advantage by diplomatic means—was also maximized. Thus the empire's political military power could be converted into actual political control at a high rate of exchange.[14]

While the similarities between the Romans and the Aztecs can be overstated, they did share certain characteristics: (1) expansion of political dominance without direct territorial control, (2) a focus on the internal security of the empire by exercising influence on a limited range of activities within the client states, and (3) the achievement of such influence by generally retaining rather than replacing local officials. Because their imperial concerns were limited, maintenance of the empire was achieved with great economy of force, local resources being relied on for local security and order. The Aztec army did not have to maintain a presence. It was mobilized only for further conquests, rebellions, and other major disruptions. In lesser matters the threat of its inexorable presence was sufficient to achieve the compliance of the clients. In such a system a standing army, garrisons, and fortifications take on a different significance from that in a territorial empire. By adopting this alternative model, the heretofore "inadequate" pivotal characteristics of the Aztec empire can be profitably reanalyzed.

Aztec expansion was neither continuous nor smooth but punctuated by revolts and reconquest (see table 5.1), usually following the succession of a new ruler. However, the Aztecs did engage in successful imperial expansion,[15] and there was at least some internal cohesion.

Army

The Aztec army was drawn from both noble (pipiltin) and commoner (macehualtin) ranks, most of it coming from the macehaultin, not the middle, or artisan, class.[16] In short, the calpolli (originally probably a kin group, but by the time of the Spanish conquest a social organi-

Table 5.1. The Provinces That Revolted

Province No.*	Province Name	Number of Revolts
2	Tepecuacuilco	2
3	Tlachco (Taxco)	1
7	Cuahuacan	1
10	Cuauhtitlan	2
11	Xilotepec	1
18	Tlapacoyan	1
19	Atotonilco el Grande	2
21	Chalco	4
22	Cuauhnahuac	3
23	Huaxtepec	1
26	Tlatlauhquitepec	1
27	Cuauhtochco	1
28	Cuetlaxtlan	2
32	Yoaltepec	1
35	Coayxtlahuacan	1
37	Citlaltepec and Tlatelolco	2
38	Petlacalco	2

*Based on Barlow 1949b.
Source: Holt 1976:61.

zational grouping centered around a barrio, or ward, temple) formed the basis of the commoner units. The nobles lacked an analogous organizational unit and fought as members of military orders. Men were trained in schools, nobles in the calmecac and commoners in the telpochcalli, and underwent brief retraining before a war. Weapons were stored at the entrances to the temples, apparently in each barrio.[17] The Aztec military organization was complex, distinguishing between higher, noble, and lower, commoner, ranks, each graded by valor and military success and permitting limited penetration of the noble ranks by meritorious commoners.[18]

Although technically a standing army may have been absent, the existence of military ranks, grades, and offices clearly indicates a military infrastructure running through Aztec society, providing the organizational basis for mobilization. Males were instructed in the art of war, public armories existed, and a quiescent chain of command lay ready. Atop this massive force stood highly trained, and largely noble, military orders that formed the vanguard and elite of the army. But only in time of war was it mobilized.

Fortifications

While fortifications may bear directly on the nature of the military, the issue in Mesoamerica is a thorny one, varying with one's basic assumptions. Central Mexico is dotted with sites that were arguably fortified.[19] However, the designation of specific sites as fortified meets with less agreement.[20] Numerous arguably fortified sites exist, but their significance is subject to different interpretations, especially insofar as their existence and dispersions reflect directly on imperial territorial extent.

For the period of Aztec dominance, historic and protohistoric sources clearly indicate some type of political empire in which the capital and constituent parts are detailed, so its expanse is known. But that it fits the territorial empire model is more assumed than demonstrated.

Furthermore, from the hegemonic-empire perspective, a correlation between polity size and fortification distribution is less compelling. The extent to which these sites were permanent fortifications is pertinent only when territorial control is a goal. Where it is not, the role of fortifications is different, and criticisms based on their inadequacy—judged as permanent fortifications—are hollow.

Garrisons

The issue of garrisons also bears directly on the nature of the military and is, to a large extent, definitional. In normal parlance, garrison *(guarnición)* may refer either to a place or to the troops manning it, but it is the conjunction of the two that makes the term's application to troops meaningful. This is what Covarrubias intends, not only from the context of the full entry but from the sentence in question, "Guarnicion de soldados, porque guardan y asseguran la fuerza o plaza donde estan" ("Garrison of soldiers, because they guard and protect the fortress or fortified place where they are"). More light may be shed by examining *guarniciones* as revealed in sixteenth-century documents.

Despite an armed Aztec presence in many parts of central Mexico and the existence of regular troop-transit areas,[21] *guarniciones* were apparently limited to frontier areas, Tarascan, Gulf Coast, and Chichimec.[22] They were adjacent to hostile polities and areas of imperial expansion.[23] Rather than being an accidental collection of transitory troop locations, the geopolitical distribution of the *guarniciones* indicates an orderly pattern. From site surveys and sixteenth-century accounts, *guarniciones* appear to have been strongly fortified sites and to have had resident Aztec troops.[24] However, some, if not all, of the forts were unoccupied during peacetime,[25] and it frequently fell to local towns to man and arm them on a rotating, periodic basis in lieu of other tribute.[26] While *guarniciones* may have been less than armies from Tenochtitlan permanently stationed in farflung areas of the empire, they were considerably more than merely temporary camps for transient troops.[27]

Logistics

The Aztec military organization was not simple, nor was its task. There was an effective army, but the hegemonic empire, which yielded benefits in lower cost and wide-ranging control, had complementary burdens. Enforcing Aztec desires and defending tributary areas placed enormous stress on the military system since it lacked permanent occupying forces and suffered under the severe transportation constraint of having only human porters to supply large numbers of men not only in battle but on marches of considerable duration. These problems were largely overcome by relying on the resources of the local tributaries to maintain Aztec forces at minimal cost.

In the field the Aztec army required, and received, considerable auxiliary support in the form of Aztec colonists relocated in potentially troublesome areas, supplies provided as tribute en route, allied troops from various places in the empire, and local troops manning the frontiers in lieu of tribute.[28] The difficulty of Aztec military logistics leads to the conclusion that their military efforts were greatly handicapped.[29] However, these constraints were largely overcome by royal granaries spread throughout the empire to store tribute grain[30] and by local support in areas of transit.

With imperial expansion lands (milchimalli or cacalomilli) were set aside for the support of the army and as part of their tribute towns en route supplied both food and weapons to the army when it passed.[31] Food was also supplied to the *guarniciones*, as were arms, and lands were set aside for the provisioning of *guarniciones*.[32] Thus military supplies provided under the tribute system allowed the army to move through the empire relatively quickly and unencumbered.

The supply problem was further reduced by the use of local troops. Although most of the soldiers were drawn from the Triple Alliance (Tenochtitlan, Texcoco, and Tlacopan) and other cities of the Valley of Mexico (Mexicalzingo, Chimalhuacan, Acolman, Tenochtitlan, Texcoco, Tlacopan, Xochimilco, Chalco, Culhuacan, Ixtapalapa, and Huitzilopochco),[33] others could be drawn from a larger area, and providing troops for the army when it passed through was common in such subject towns as Tepexpa, Totolapa, Alahuiztlan, Tetela, Atitalaquia, Tuchtepeque, Teticpac, Chichicapa, Petlaltzingo, Texaluca, Chilapa, and Zultepec.[34] Thus supplies for the whole armed body for the entire march from Tenochtitlan to the site of the battle were unnecessary, for many troops were added en route, which increased Aztec strength at a relatively low cost in supplies.

Added to the troops collected en route were frontier armies. Peoples occupying regions bordering such hostile groups as the Yopes, Tlaxcalans, and Tarascans—towns like Acapetlaguaya, Teloloapa, and Tamazola—were exempt from the payment of tribute goods in return for military service.[35]

During the reign of Ahuitzotl married men were recruited from various cities of the empire—most from Tenochtitlan, Texcoco, and Tlacopan, but also from subject towns—and sent to distant regions to settle.[36] This occurred in Oztuma, Alahuiztlan, and Teloloapan, Tuchtepeque, and also in Oaxaca.[37] These colonies have been interpreted as the *guarniciones* discussed above,[38] but the few colonies, in contrast to the oft-mentioned and scattered *guarniciones* (and in view of the functional characteristics of *guarniciones*), argues forcefully against their being the same in all instances, although an argument can be made for specific sites. At a minimum, the presence of Aztec colonists in distant settlements would have provided security for transient soldiers, local levies in time of war, and a loyal force to suppress possible revolts. Thus the Aztec war complex consisted of a core army drawn from the cities of the Valley of Mexico augmented by proportionally cheaper troops gained en route and supplemented at the frontiers by loyal colonists and local armies providing border defense in lieu of tribute.

Internal Control

Despite the ingenuity exhibited by the Aztecs in overcoming some of the difficulties inherent in their imperial organization, such an organization necessarily permitted the existence of largely autonomous local governments. This limited imperial control led to the perception of the Aztec empire as an inferior political system, an inadequate, possibly embryonic, empire.[39]

The inadequacy of the Aztec empire was indicated by endemic internal revolts. Unlike territorial empires where the threat to centralized control is greatest at the periphery of the systems, hegemonic empires are not primarily concerned with territorial integrity. Force and the threat of force supply the cohesion. The imperial structure does not offer substantial differences in feasibility of revolt, depending on proximity to the center. In contrast to revolts in territorial empires, virtually all of the provinces that revolted were near the center of the empire, not at the periphery, contrary to Davies's assertion.[40] That the revolts were close to the center of the empire might have reflected the length of time over which provinces were incorporated into the Aztec empire; the greater the time, the more the revolts. However, that does not appear to have been the case. A long time period may present more occasions for revolt, but this is only one factor and does not directly correlate with incidence of revolts.

The Aztec empire cannot fairly be faulted for lack of proper local control or for the recurrent revolts. These were logical consequences of a hegemonic empire. Although hegemonic empires enjoy certain advantages over territorial empires, such as economy of force, greater expanse, smaller army, and greater economic return where that is a goal, their structure entails certain disadvantages as well. External threats of low intensity may be resolved locally without the intervention of imperial forces, but high-intensity threats can be dealt with by imperial forces only after the fact, in response.

Impact

Hegemonic empires are well suited to endemic threats, because forces can be deployed to specific areas for some duration, but sporadic threats, such as rebellions, are kept in check by the "armed suasion" of absent imperial forces or are put down after the fact. Hegemonic empires do not rely on immediate force to deter revolt. They are oriented toward maintaining tranquillity, not toward maintaining fortified imperial boundaries, thus freeing forces for the former use. Backed by eventual imperial force, client states are largely responsible for their own security.

Despite intimations of fortified positions and border sieges,[41] the number of imperial soldiers, their placement, their permanency, the use of local auxiliaries in perimeter defense, and the intermittent nature of border fortifications argue strongly against a determined defense of the perimeter of the Aztec empire. Rather, these factors slowed intruders and acted as a trip wire for response. Seizure and exclusive control of territory was not an Aztec goal; tapping into local economic productivity was. Cities and the control of populations were the objects of war, and defense was structured accordingly.

Imperial exploitation varies in degree rather than in kind. As the degree of exploitation varies, so too do the political-administrative costs involved in overseeing the dominated regions. While there are always costs involved in managing the dominated areas, if exploitation is low, so too are the administrative costs. Where exploitation is high, economic extraction in the form of taxes, tribute, escheated lands, corvée labor, and so forth, requires greater coercive control, raising political-administrative costs (see fig. 5.2). Although other factors, such as nationalism and ethnic and religious divisions, may alter the relationship between conquered and conquering groups, there is, in general, considerable congruence in compliance strate-

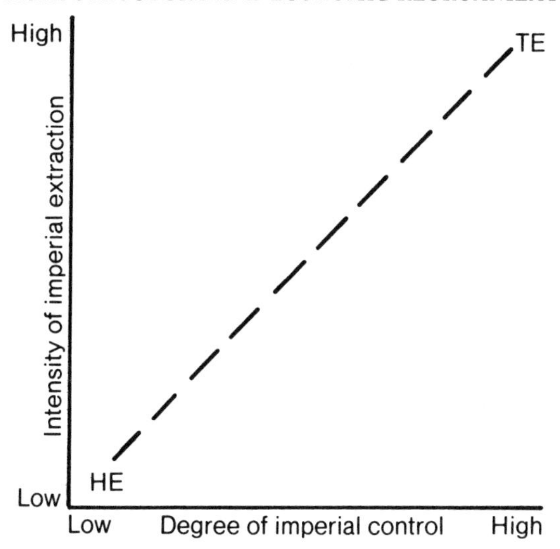

FIG. 5.2. TYPES OF IMPERIAL SYSTEMS. Imperial systems are distinguished by degree of extraction and control of conquered areas. Hegemonic empire is low control–low extraction while territorial empire is high control–high extraction.

gies, goals, and response.[42] While both imperial types exploit dominated areas, the territorial system emphasizes the incorporation of regions, while the hegemonic system emphasizes their exploitation.

The Aztec system sacrificed depth of control and extraction for breadth. Although the high-extraction territorial empire yields a larger return per area, the political-administrative costs are higher, and use of the army to maintain the situation keeps the imperial expansion to a relatively limited area. This permits the empire to expand no farther than the area it can immediately occupy. By adopting an imperial system based on low-extraction hegemony, the Aztecs achieved a moderate gain in tribute from all areas, and they did so without maintaining a standing army. By exercising a controlling influence over the main cities of provinces rather than over their territorial expanse, the Aztecs tapped into the local commodity flow at the highest level, exercising very little administrative control. Since tribute demands were moderate, they could be backed by the threat of Aztec reprisal, rather than by a military presence. This allowed the perpetuation of the empire in the absence of a standing army and also allowed the army, when in action, to sweep successively more distant areas since it was not fragmented by the need to station detachments in conquered areas to ensure compliance.

Tribute was not, however, uniform throughout the empire. One reason for this (and strong evidence of Tenochtitlan's greater concern for expansion of the empire rather than the largest possible tribute exaction) was the sliding scale on which the Aztecs assessed tribute. If a city became a subject of the Aztecs on being asked by imperial ambassadors sent for that purpose, its tribute was relatively low. If the city refused, the demand was restated after the arrival of the Aztec army, and the tribute was raised. If the city once again refused, battle was joined, and the tribute demands escalated accordingly. However, the battle need not continue to its logical end but could be ended through a negotiated settlement, varying with the battle success of the combatants.

In general, tribute may be viewed as analogous to agricultural production in which cultivation goes from more intensive at the center to more extensive at the periphery owing to transportation costs. Transportation costs are reflected in generally decreasing bulk, if not value, with distance. More important, however, extraction per se varies with distance. Even if the imperial strategy is a trade-off of depth for breadth of control, this varies with proximity to the center. The closer a tributary province is to the center, the less effort is required to dominate it, for the center can mobilize more forces more quickly and more cheaply and can afford to exert more coercion. As a consequence, within a general breadth-over-depth strategy there is also a systematic variation of coercion in space—more at the center and declining toward the periphery.[43]

Virtually all of the provinces of the Aztec empire that revolted were near the center of the empire or located throughout, but they were certainly not clustered at the periphery.[44] Clearly the greatest threat of revolt in the Aztec empire was near the core region, with little danger on the periphery. Of course, part of this pattern may be related to the time each province was under domination, those near the core generally having been dominated for the longest period of time. There is apparently no consistent relationship between the value required and the distance from the center (there was, of course, a regular variation in bulk). In a hegemonic empire there is no more territorial integration or comprehensive political structure to maintain cohesion at the core than there is at the periphery. All subordinated areas have equal opportunities to revolt. It is only coercive force that keeps subjects. Thus, as the exercise of that force becomes more difficult and expensive with distance, its effectiveness declines. Because of the overwhelming reliance on force and the threat of force in a hegemonic empire, it has the characteristic of declining military might with distance.

Although Tenochtitlan was organized on preexisting Mesoamerican patterns, it was qualitatively different as a result of its historical peculiarities. Unlike the other cities in the Valley of Mexico, Tenochtitlan was founded on an island without access to agriculturally productive areas of its own; it was always dependent on other city-states for its sustenance. One of the main purposes behind Aztec imperial expansion was the acquisition of productive lands and tribute.

TRIBUTE

Tribute, the revenue collected by the militarily dominant state from conquered regions,[45] was not an Aztec innovation in Mesoamerica (they themselves had been tributaries of Azcapotzalco), but they did make effective use of the system. A truly comprehensive analysis of the pre-Hispanic tribute system has yet to be satisfactorily accomplished, although there are some excellent studies of selected aspects.[46] There is no consensus on the nature of the system, nor is there likely to be, given the divergent perspectives from which various scholars have approached the subject (see appendix B). The two major points of agreement are virtually definitional truths: that it was a politico-military stratagem and that economic extraction was a primary goal.[47] But the role that tribute played in the economy, as well as its part in imperial expansion, has met with less agreement. One perspective sees the tribute system as fueling expansion of the empire, Valley of Mexico cities, and the upper strata of Aztec society.[48]

Because of the nature of Mesoamerican warfare and the limitations on political consolidation, conquest did not mean complete territorial domination and control. Rather, conquest was of political centers. Control of territory per se was not a major consideration. Once a political center was dominated, so too were its dependencies, and tribute, flowing from dependency to cabecera to provincial capital, could be drained from an entire region simply by dominating the center.

In the ordinary course of maintaining the tribute empire, the local political structure and personnel were retained, although there are some instances of local tlahtohqueh being replaced by Aztec governors, for example, in Coatepec, Tepexpa, Tlacotepeque, Tetela, Cuetzala, Apastla, Taxco, Miaguatlan, Coatlan, Tlacotlalpa, Piastla, Texaluca, and Temazcaltepec.[49] Why these particular towns had governors appointed by the king of Tenochtitlan while others did not is uncertain. There are several possible explanations concerning replacement of local rulers by Aztec governors. Some centers whose rulers were replaced, such as Taxco and Piastla, occupied sites on strategic routes. But all such strategic sites did not suffer leader replacement. Some centers (e.g., Temazcaltepeque, Tetela, Apastla, Tlacotepeque, and Cuetzala) whose rulers were replaced shared borders with hostile neighbors. But many border towns retained local rulers. Some centers (e.g., Tepexpa) were coopted through marital alliances with the Aztecs, and others, such as Coatepec, were ostensibly (but unconvincingly) placed under Aztec governance until youthful local rulers became old enough to govern. Some coopted centers (e.g., Miaguatlan, Piastla) apparently acted to ensure peace with traditionally enemy towns, now within the empire.

The Aztecs' policy may have been strategically consistent—pacifying small or weak areas while destabilizing large or powerful areas—but tactically their approach varied enormously. A satisfactory resolution requires both more theoretical research and additional data. Local rulers were replaced under several circumstances, most notably when they were hostile.[50] But even while they were replacing local tlahtohqueh, the Aztec nobles married into the local ruling families, so their offspring were de jure as well as de facto rulers.

The actual functioning of the tribute system may be analyzed at the imperial level and at the provincial level. At the imperial level the Aztecs (or, more properly, the Triple Alliance) drew tribute from thirty-eight provinces[51] that had only their tributary status in common. At the provincial level, goods were channeled from *sujetos* to dependent cabeceras to provincial centers. The officials who controlled the tribute system were the calpixqueh, either imperial or local.[52] Imperial calpixqueh were sent from Tenochtitlan to conquered regions to collect tribute from the rulers and forward it. Dealing as they were with kings, the imperial calpixqueh were drawn from the ranks of the nobility. Local calpixqueh, on the other hand, were commoners. Their lower status not only mirrored their lesser role as intermediaries between tributary commoners and the local rulers, but permitted delegation of authority by the ruler which would not have been feasible had they been nobles. Only nobles could own land and have subjects, yet these holdings frequently exceeded their individual capacities to administer them. By appointing local calpixqueh, administration was safely achieved, since their commoner status removed the threat of usurpation.

The system thus relied on a local official (tequitlahtoh) to collect tribute goods at the local, or calpolli, level and take them to the regional center. There the calpixqueh transferred them to the provincial center, where imperial calpixqueh supervised their delivery to Tenochtitlan.[53] One also finds exceptional arrangements, such as that whereby Otlatlan sent its tribute directly to Tenochtitlan rather than to the provincial center of Tepecuacuilco.

One unresolved issue is the division of tribute. While it is frequently stated that the shares within the Triple Alliance were 2 to 2 to 1, (Tenochtitlan, Texcoco, Tlacopan),[54] the picture is more complicated, with some towns paying to all three, some to one, and so forth. Although the tribute system operated in a pyramiding fashion—*sujeto* to cabecera to provincial capital to Triple Alliance—the burden was not spread evenly throughout the system (see fig. 5.3). Inevitably, commoners paid the tribute, but not all commoners. Nobles were exempt,[55] as were administrators and governmental officials, priests and teachers of various temples, commoners who had distinguished

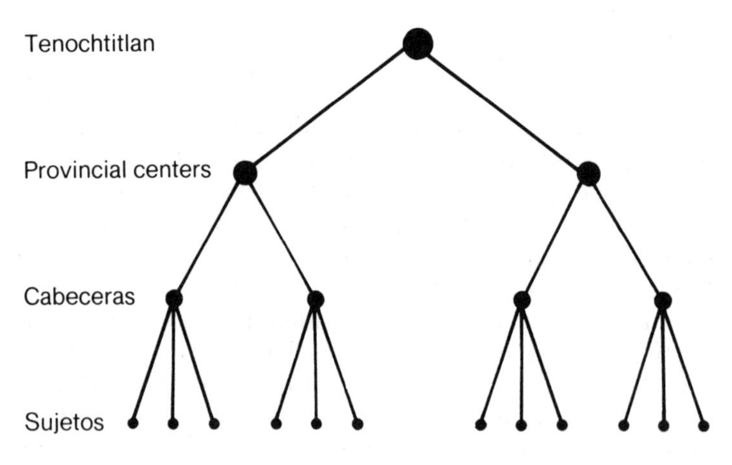

FIG. 5.3. UPWARD FLOW OF TRIBUTE.

themselves in war, slaves, and mayehqueh ([lit., "hand-owners,"], they were the Mesoamerican equivalent of serfs, peasants tied to the lands of nobles. However, Hicks[56] maintains that there was no such group in central Mexico, the misconception springing from the work of Zorita). Artisans and merchants did pay tribute, but in kind, not in service.

Tribute was paid at several levels: imperial, provincial, town, and lower groupings such as calpolli. Nobles and cults also had lands from which they received tribute, and *guarniciones* were also supplied by tribute.[57] Aztec imperial control was exercised at the level of provincial capitals, with the installation of imperial calpixqueh. The thirty-eight capitals listed in the *Codex Mendoza* appear to be the locations of calpixqueh.[58] While this implies a funneling of goods from the bottom of the system to the top,[59] the amounts reaching the Triple Alliance were actually comparatively small, the heaviest burden being local and provincial tributes. Not all imperial tribute reached the Valley of Mexico: as mentioned, some was used in the provinces to maintain *guarniciones.*

Warehouses for tribute existed in each town or at least province,[60] although their capacity and distribution are as yet undetermined. The wooden cribs, or *trojes,* in which grain was stored, held 4,000 to 5,000 fanegas of maize (tribute corn was shelled).[61] Based on their careful construction (as depicted in the *Matricula de tributos;* see plate 6), it is probable that they were imperial granaries.[62] The royal granary, or petlacalco, of Tenochtitlan is recorded as holding 2,000 measures of dried grain.[63] Five factors affected the tribute demands of the Triple Alliance:[64]

1. Time of conquest and distance from the capital. The closer provinces provided foodstuffs, clothing, and warriors' costumes, while the more distant provinces (conquered later) provided some of the same goods, though generally in smaller quantities, as well as luxury goods. Other than foodstuffs, the goods paid in tribute were over-

whelmingly manufactured rather than raw materials.[65]

2. Availability of goods. Tribute was ostensibly paid in goods locally produced or available, although this was clearly not the case in all instances.[66]

3. Initial resistance and subsequent rebellion. If towns resisted conquest, their tribute assessments were greater, as they were if they rebelled.[67] The penalty for rebellion was reputedly a doubling of their assessment, although the records of increases do not support this, so it was, perhaps, a doubling of value rather than a simple increase in quantity.[68]

4. General increase in tribute demands. In addition to rebellions, there was a general increase in assessments over time, possibly reflecting population increases rather than per capita increases.

5. The growing requirements of the Aztec state. Requirements expanded in Valley of Mexico towns, not only because of population increase but also as a result of the proliferation of political and religious offices, expanding nobility, and growth in number of artisans.

Town assessments varied widely.[69] Although the pre-Hispanic tribute system was not uniform even within a single tributary province, there were regularities in the system.[70] Warriors' suits came from all but eight provinces (the most distant) and Tepeaca, which was unique in giving war captives. Similarly, major feather-paying provinces gave fewer suits. In addition to tribute commodities, assessments were also made for service, food, and public works, as well as for war service, particularly in border areas where such service exempted the towns from other tribute assessments.[71] In tribute systems elsewhere in the world, goods also flow back down the system, ensuring allegiance of the local rulers or cementing economic and political relations.[72] However, such does not appear to have been the case with the Aztecs. The few occasions on which rulers in Mesoamerica gave gifts to other rulers appear to have been associated with royal succession, and these events were not just lord-vassal reaffirmations but included gifts between formal enemy kings and were reciprocal.[73] Since there were some benefits to being a tributary, however, the lack of information concerning gift giving to tribute payers may be due to the lack of focus on this subject by the colonial chroniclers and the disinterest of the Spaniards in this aspect of the system.

Tribute demands were not entirely based on goods available within the individual provinces.[74] All but one of the adjacent tributary provinces plus distant Coyolapan gave grain. The province of Citlaltepec and Tlatelolco gave only nominal amounts of foodstuffs. Unlike the *troje* quantities given by other provinces, Citlaltepec and Tlatelolco gave baskets of chianpinolli and baskets of cacao ground with maize in nominal quantities. However, the province of Citlaltepec and Tlatelolco was unique in being the only area giving cacao that did not also produce it, yet the amounts given were not greatly different from cacao-producing provinces. The explanation of this anomaly lies in the special relationship of Tlatelolco to Tenochtitlan. As the incorporated sister city of the Aztec capital, Tlatelolco shared Tenochtitlan's urban-supply problems. Thus requiring grain in tribute would merely shift the flow of foodstuffs from Citlaltepec and Tlatelolco and result in no additional supplies for the overall urban population. Consequently, the higher-value cacao offered a more reasonable demand, from the perspectives of both income to Tenochtitlan and maintenance of food supplies for Tlatelolco.

Clearly the relationships among the various tribute demands were complex. Nevertheless, even with such exceptions as grain from Coyolapan and lime from Tepeaca, it was generally true that low-value–high-bulk items came from nearer provinces, while more distant provinces supplied high-value–low-bulk elite goods.

The consequences of a tribute system can be further analyzed, in terms not only of its impact on the tribute recipient but also of the impact on the tribute payers.

While the worth of the tribute goods to the recipient was substantial, the gross cost to the payers included transporting them to Tenochtitlan as well as producing them. This entailed a large outlay, the net effect of which was to depress the population of the paying areas below the levels they could have supported otherwise (although this is not to say that there was necessarily an absolute decline in population in the tribute-paying areas),[75] while artificially raising the population level of the Tenochtitlan area above its already high carrying capacity.[76] Consequently, studies of population in Mesoamerica that strive to achieve population totals ignore spatial population variations, just as studies based on the carrying capacity of given regions fail to see their socially induced distortion.

POLITICAL IMPACT ON TRADE

Regional Markets

Another consequence (if not purpose) of Aztec conquest was the reorganization of the relatively autonomous market centers into a more systematic and integrated marketing system. Regional markets were not unique to the Valley of Mexico. The pattern was pre-Aztec, but the Aztecs manipulated markets within their empire. Local rights and marketing patterns were altered to focus specific items of commerce (those not general everywhere) in certain locales (usually on major trade routes) at advantageous prices, and the pochtecah then funneled these goods through other regional markets and into the Valley of Mexico. This reorganization resulted in an efficient marketing structure, coupled with the pochtecah trade, and tolerating competition at only the intraregional level. Regional markets were a third level in the Aztec marketing hierarchy, above the *sujeto* and cabecera levels. Although the typical local-level marketing pattern was characterized by a dominant yearbearer market and subject nonyearbearer markets, forming basic solar systems, there was another type of market (or tianquiztli) that played a major role in Mesoamerican exchange, the regional market. Regional markets dealt in exotic goods, as well as in ordinary wares. They occupied a more elevated position in the marketing hierarchy than that of ordinary cabecera markets, some achieving such prominence that they became famed for particular products. For central Mexico the most noted were Tepeaca, Acapetlayocan, Otumba, and Tepepulco (birds); Azcapotzalco and Itzocan (slaves); Acolman (dogs); Cholula (jewels, precious stones, "rich" feathers); and Texcoco (clothes, "rich" pottery vessels).[77]

Data are not readily available concerning these markets, although a few facts may be gleaned. Regional markets were not wholly distinct entities. Rather, they operated in conjunction with the ordinary markets. At Azcapotzalco and Itzocan, the site where the slaves were sold was at one side of the tianquiztli (slaves to be sacrificed to the god Quetzalcoatl).[78] Furthermore, to judge by the bird markets of Tepeaca and Acapetlayocan, regional markets adhered to the regular marketing schedule of their respective towns —every five days in these two instances.[79]

The location of markets was based on political considerations. Rulers established new markets[80] and shifted existing ones. For instance, Azcapotzalco's slave market was originally at Cuauhtitlan. In the early fifteenth century, King Maxtla of Azcapotzalco, conquered Cuauhtitlan, sowed its marketplace with cactus, and removed the slave trade to his own city.[81] In addition, the rulers established regulations that markets were to specialize in certain goods.[82] Although regional markets resulted from political power, it is clear that this exercise was a necessary but not a sufficient condition of their existence and location. Azcapotzalco took its slave market by force, yet it retained the slave trade for almost one hundred years after its own subjugation by the Triple Alliance, reflecting either a more subtle subimperial power or other, as yet undiscerned, variables.

Political power was only one factor in the continuation of regional markets. Markets shifted as a result of war as well. For example, the regional market was moved from Chalco Atenco to Tlalmanalco after the latter aided the Aztecs in their war with Chalco.[83]

What did such a shift of regional markets mean? When the market was changed from Chalco Atenco to Tlalmanalco, what was affected? Chalco Atenco continued to have a market, and, to judge from the populations of both Chalco Atenco and Tlalmanalco and the numbers of their respective *sujetos,* they did so on a yearbearer day. What changed was the right—overseen by the Aztecs—to traffic in certain types of commodities. These commodities were not the more mundane goods of the ordinary markets but the elite goods produced within that region and those brought in from elsewhere for consumption within the region. The ordinance concerning specialization applied to markets generally. Specialization operated with respect to higher-value goods, not those available everywhere. The regulation applied to certain goods only—above the ordinary 5-day market level and probably above the level of most of the yearbearer markets as well.

This, then, was the sine qua non of the regional market—the right to traffic in certain goods, which involved reorienting the flow of goods into and out of a new center, with all the attendant benefits such commerce entailed. Basic principles governing regional markets were recognized throughout central Mexico, and there were regional markets, such as Cholula, which were not politically subservient to the Aztec empire. Regional markets and their relocation were not an Aztec innovation, but they expanded the practice.

Despite the appearance of a regional market trade monopoly in certain goods, it is clear that such markets were not the sole purveyors of these goods. Implicit in the prohibition against buying sacrificial slaves outside the Azcapotzalco and Itzocan markets was the admission of their availability elsewhere.[84] Dogs were obviously sold in many other markets, despite Acolman's specialization in them.[85] Specialization in certain commodities did not lead to the elimination of wholesale trade. Birds from the markets of Otumba and Tepepulco were taken to Mexico City for resale.[86] Quite simply, regional markets were social devices to concentrate both the supply of and demand for particular goods at selected points. Trade went from regional to other markets, relying on the lower prices in the regional markets and the higher prices for the same goods elsewhere. Professional merchants traded in these regional goods (e.g., the oztomecah slave traders). Thus the regulation of regional market commodities did not promise exclusivity of certain wares to those sites but instead provided focal markets concentrating certain goods and lowering prices. They drew elite goods from the producers and supplied them to local consumers in what appears to have been an otherwise free market. But while these regulations channeled the local flow of elite goods, they apparently left unhindered, and perhaps even encouraged, professional trade. Regional markets were sites that had the social and political right to trade exclusively, or semi-exclusively, in certain types of goods. They accordingly served not only as suppliers and consumers of the products at the regional level but also as bulking points for the area and facilitated their monopolistic pochtecah dissemination at the interregional level.

Pochtecah Trade

A second consequence of the Aztec conquest was the way it facilitated long-distance trade. The pochtecah were hereditary merchants, organized in guild fashion, and occupying separate barrios, or wards, of the city, at least in Tenochtitlan-Tlatelolco. Fray Bernardino de Sahagún[87] chronicled the rise of the pochtecah of Tenochtitlan-Tlatelolco, as well as their expansion in trading areas and commodities. However, the existence of organized, long-distance merchants predates the rise of the Aztecs.[88] It has been suggested that the pochtecah originated during the time of Teotihuacan,[89] although their qualitative continuity has been challenged.[90] In his seminal work on the pochtecah, Acosta Saignes[91] suggests a Toltec origin, basing his theory on the widespread existence of merchant guilds in places known to the Toltecs. Merchant guilds existed not only in Valley of Mexico cities, such as Tenochtitlan, Tlatelolco, Chalco Atenco, and Cuauhtitlan, but also in Tepeaca, in Tochtepec, in the Mixteca, in Acalan, and in Yucatan, all places of known Toltec presence, some of which—Tultitlan, Cuauhtitlan, Tulanzingo—were the locations of important Toltec fairs. From a comparison of the merchant festivals to the god Yahcateuctli in Tenochtitlan with those to Quetzalcoatl in Cholula, itself an Olmec import from the Gulf Coast, Acosta Saignes concludes that the pochtecah, or some similarly structured trading group, were founded before the Toltec migrations and were possibly of Gulf Coast origins (see plate 7).

When the merchants of Tlatelolco first began trading, during the reign of the Tlatelolcan king Cuacuauhpitzauac (ca. 1350–1409), they dealt only in red arara and blue and scarlet parrot feathers. During the reign of Tlacateotl (ca. 1409–27), their wares grew to include small quetzal feathers, troupial feathers, turquoise, green stones, and capes and breechcloths of fine cotton. During the reign of Cuauhtlahtoatzin (ca. 1427–67), the merchandise also included gold lip and earplugs, necklaces with radiating pendants, fine turquoise, enormous green stones, long quetzal feathers, wild-animal skins, long troupial feathers, and blue cotinga and red spoonbill feathers. During the reign of the last independent sovereign of Tlatelolco, Moquihuitzin (ca. 1467–73), costly red capes with the wind-jewel design, white duck-feather capes, capes with cupped-shaped designs in feathers, embroidered breechcloths, embroidered shirts and shifts, long capes and chocolate were added to their inventory.[92] Assessing these goods in relation to the conquests of the Aztecs, it is apparent that the merchants' trading areas were expanding with the empire. As the borders of the empire were pushed back, Aztec merchants traded within these areas. While trading beyond the confines of the empire during this time may have been possible, the regularly acquired goods need not have

Plate 7. Yahcateuctli, patron god of the pochtecah (Sahagún 1979, 1:12r).

derived from areas beyond those controlled by the Aztecs.

Pochtecah trade was far-flung, extending as far south as Guatemala and, it is claimed, as far north as the Chaco Canyon area of New Mexico.[93] However, detailed records of their trade routes are lacking, except for the one serving the rich regions of Anahuac (the lands beyond the empire). From Tlatelolco, the pochtecah crossed the lake and proceeded to Teotihuacan. Skirting the territory of Tlaxcala, they continued to Tehuacan and thence to Tochtepec. There the road divided, the merchants from Tlatelolco, Tenochtitlan, Huitzilopochco, Azcapotzalco, and Cuauhtitlan going either to Anahuac Ayotlan, the Pacific Coast lands around Tehuantepec, or to Anahuac Xicalanco, the Gulf Coast lands.[94] This description may be overstylized and fail to take into account the undoubted variations of many pochtecah practices. For instance, one colonial source states that they began their journeys on the day 1 Coatl,[95] but in all probability this was a statement of ideal rather than actual behavior. Roads were maintained and lodging houses were kept along the routes, and at Tochtepec the pochtecah of each city maintained separate storehouses and resthouses.[96]

Traditionally the pochtecah have been viewed as somewhat anomalous:

> . . . long-distance trade was an institution apart: geographically, it was trade beyond the borders; its personnel formed a distinct social group; its members only exceptionally made their appearance in markets; both the organizing of caravans and the negotiating of exchange in foreign countries formed part of this specialized occupation.[97]

Much of what is written about the pochtecah is based on Sahagún.[98] Although it is a laudable account, it stresses the more spectacular aspects of pochtecah trade (such as the journey to Anahuac bearing goods from King Ahuitzotl), leading to the conclusion that these were the norm. Consequently, the pochtecah have been classed as long-distance traders of elite goods to and from foreign markets, an overnarrow and misleading characterization. Typically, Aztec economy is described in such a way as to leave a considerable gap between local market exchange and long-distance elite trade.[99] Much debate has arisen over the proper characterization of the Aztec economy, largely over the extent to which the economy was or was not free of political control. One side of the debate maintains that the polity was paramount in instigating and maintaining economic organization,[100] while the other side maintains that market principles and free economic exchange were paramount.[101] These differences arise from the emphasis each writer places on the same data. While there are indications of state intervention in trade, both long-distance[102] and marketplace,[103] there is also considerable indication of free exchange.[104]

Part of the problem of pochtecah activities is semantic: Who are pochtecah? Pochtecah was a generic term for merchants, the subdivisions of which have been variously stated (see table 5.2).[105]

The pochtecah were a hereditary occupational group, although a limited number of outsiders appear to have been admitted by royal permission.[106] As described, the pochtecah of Tenochtitlan-Tlatelolco occupied separate barrios; Pochtlan, Ahuachtlan, Acxotlan, Atlauhco, Tzon-

Table 5.2. Types of Aztec Merchants

Type	Description
Pochtecatlahtohqueh	Principal merchants
Pochtecah	Merchants
Oztomecah	Vanguard merchants
Nahualoztomecah	Disguised merchants
Teyahualoanimeh	Spying merchants
Tecohanimeh	Slave dealers
Tealtianimeh	Slave bathers
Tlacohcohualnamacaqueh	Peddlars
Tlanamacanimeh	Peddlars
Tiamicqueh	Traders, dealers

molco, Tepetitlan, and Itzcalco. They were internally governed by two principal merchants and formed a political enclave in Aztec society with their own courts and laws.[107] Their relation to the polity was a close one, although its exact nature is unclear. They were not nobles, yet they affected attire that included sumptuary goods that were normally prohibited to commoners (see plate 8). Although they gave the king tribute in kind, they supplied neither personal service nor war service. There are indications that pochtecah organization spanned at least the cities of the Valley of Mexico.[108]

Despite the picture presented by Sahagún of a highly organized and rigidly controlled body of elite merchants, several factors argue for a full complement of merchants, bridging the gap between the elite pochtecah and the producer-seller; the availability of more plebeian goods in the markets, and the simultaneous existence of regional markets concerned with elite goods. While it is clear that not all of these traders were pochtecah, it is equally clear that pochtecah did perform some of these functions. There were, in fact, various alternatives open to the pochtecah. Rather than engaging in long-distance foreign trade, pochtecah could, and did, begin their careers by entering the system at a low level that did not require a major capital investment. Many of them traded within the empire, circulating among the markets, benefiting by price differences between them. The poorest pochtecah traded in salt, chili, and other inexpensive articles door to door and in the smaller markets.[109] Indeed, merchanting seems to have been relatively open at the lower end of the trading spectrum and was a major way to rise in social status.[110] That these mundane aspects of merchant life did not receive the treatment accorded more exotic activity is not surprising.

One theory of pochtecah activities that has gained widespread acceptance is Chapman's[111] dictum that tribute follows trade. Her theory, briefly restated, is that the pochtecah engaged in simultaneous foreign trade and covert military reconnaissance. From this intelligence, the Aztec

Plate 8. Aztec merchants before the king, on the road, and with their wares (Sahagún 1979, 2:316r).

army conquered cities and incorporated them into the tribute-paying empire, whereupon the pochtecah ceased trading there and went farther afield to repeat the process. The theory is based on several facts:

1. The pochtecah did engage in foreign trade.
2. They did have political connections with the Aztec state.
3. They did engage in espionage and undertake conquests.
4. Only the pochtecah of the Valley of Mexico entered foreign territory.

The pochtecah traded manufactured goods and Valley of Mexico products (mentioned are worked cotton capes, golden crowns, rosettes and necklaces, and rings, as well as crystal and obsidian earplugs, tin, obsidian razors, and needles and lake products) for raw materials (e.g., feathers, turquoise, green stones, amber, and animal skins) which were used primarily by artisans.[112] This part of pochtecah trade formed a partly closed cycle: raw goods were imported into Tenochtitlan, crafted by artisans, and exported to the rest of Mexico as manufactured wares.[113] The closed nature of this trade is evidenced by the close association between the pochtecah and the artisans, particularly the featherworkers.[114] Since this most famous trade was basically of an elite nature, a recurrent theme has arisen dividing Aztec trade into local exchange and long-distance (foreign) trade.[115] In view of the value-bulk divisions of commodity ranges, as well as historical practice, such a dichotomization is easily seen to be distortive. Certainly the long-distance trade served different consumers from those served by local trade, but it was one end of a trading continuum, not a qualitatively distinct enterprise.

The pochtecah did have definite, although imprecisely understood, political connections with the Aztec state. Closing roads to commerce was a frequently cited cause of war, as was killing merchants.[116] This does not appear to have been a blind exercise of martial force by the Aztecs, but was a recognized casus belli extending throughout central Mexico. For example, when Triple Alliance merchants were killed, Moteuczomah Ilhuicamina raised men for a punitive expedition, appealing to allies and enemies alike in the common interest.[117]

There was a more active element in the pochtecah political connection, however. Some merchants entered foreign lands in disguise for the purpose of reconnoitering the land, and they did so (in at least one instance), by order of the king (Ahuitzotl). Furthermore, some of them were also warriors who did conquer cities.[118]

The passage of Sahagún upon which the emphasis on foreign trade by the pochtecah rests states: "And where they entered Anauac was not the place of entry for everyone, because it was the trading area of (the merchants of) Auitzotzin. There went, there entered only those of Tlatilulco, Tenochtitlan, Uitzilopochco, Azcapotzalco, (and) Quauhtitlan. They always were accompanying one another."[119]

To return to the "tribute follows trade" thesis, the pochtecah were, to some extent, a political arm of the Aztec state, and they did undertake some conquests. Furthermore, the Aztec empire was expanding. However, this does not mean that there was a systemic relation between political expansion and foreign trade, aside from the axiomatic truth that once areas were politically incorporated, trade with them was no longer "foreign." Nor is it likely that the existence of the pochtecah was the sine qua non of Aztec expansion, although they did perform a complementary function. A better understanding of the situation requires a consideration of the nature of pochtecah foreign trade.

Sahagún's great work on the pochtecah is based primarily on Tlatelolco, but merchants were similarly organized in many different towns. Only twelve cities in the Valley of Mexico had professional merchants. Azcapotzalco, Chalco Atenco, Coatlichan, Cuauhtitlan, Huexotla, Huitzilopochco, Mixcoac, Otumba, Tenochtitlan, Texcoco,

Tlatelolco, and Xochimilco.[120] For Mexico as a whole, however, Acosta Saignes locates their presence in many other towns.[121]

Since many of these cities with merchants were not within the Aztec empire, and in fact, many were enemies of the Aztecs, the restrictions recorded by Sahagún clearly do not apply uniformly. Merchants from towns other than the five named Aztec cities also visited coastal areas, merchants from Tehuantepec were in contact with Soconusco, Teotitlan del Camino traded with Soconusco and Xochitepec, and Cholula traded with Soconusco and Guatemala.[122]

The issue, then, is whether these restrictions indicate a managed economy. That the pochtecah trade is an example of administered economy (trading operated through government-controlled channels by administrative methods)[123] is widely accepted.[124] However, the main evidence of this is an example of semiritual exchange between the ruler of Tenochtitlan and the rulers of commercial centers in Tabasco and Soconusco, with the pochtecah acting as agents.[125] But even in this example, the pochtecah took along their own private goods, apparently free of state control.[126] In addition to the state manipulation of foreign trade, prices were regulated somewhat and foreign merchants were excluded from trading in markets within the Aztec empire.[127] While it would be hasty to deny totally any political molding in the trading process, simpler processes were also involved which acted to restrict foreign trade.

A major factor in structuring long-distance (and other) trade was the transportation system. As previously described, the tlamemes, upon whom portage depended, were organized by cabeceras. Thus merchants trading in or passing through a district did so with the assistance of hired porters who carried from their cabecera to the next. This system was elaborated by the Aztecs within the area of their empire. Beyond the borders of the empire, however, tlameme transport may or may not have been organized at a supra-cabecera level, depending on the dominant polity.

The areas beyond Tochtepec were actively hostile for the pochtecah. The exception to this was in the actual market town itself. Unlike markets, these "ports of trade" were neutral grounds where long-distance merchants could meet directly and where the security of entering merchants was guaranteed.[128] The danger to Aztec merchants in these areas is evidenced by the fact that if the disguised merchants were discovered they were slain and that the pochtecah passed through the lands of their enemies at night.[129] The combination of secrecy and nocturnal passage argues against the use of local tlamemes. Yet tlamemes were necessary and were used. This conclusion is based on two aspects of Sahagún's description of a journey to Anahuac. First, the pochtecah took 1600 mantas for King Ahuitzotl, as well as their own trade goods, amounting to an additional 80 tlameme loads, clearly not a minor burden easily carried by the pochtecah themselves. Second, the use of tlamemes is specifically mentioned. They carried only small, measured loads and were organized into caravans, and small boys were taken along to learn the occupation. Thus it is apparent that the Aztec pochtecah were not employing tlamemes from towns along their route. Rather, they employed their own tlamemes from the Valley of Mexico for the entire trip. In a trade involving export of manufactured goods and import of raw materials, the total burden capacity of the tlamemes is dictated by the largest loads, the raw materials. Therefore, on the outward leg of the journey, the tlamemes would have been underutilized, each carrying a small load, as indeed appears to have been the case.

An alternative explanation of the long-distance tlamemes is their location in Tochtepec, whence they carried to and from Anahuac, the pochtecah relying on the local tlamemes for the remainder of the trip. However, four factors argue against this explanation. First, although Tochtepec was on the frontier of the Aztec empire, the boundary was changing so even if that city had been a major tlameme supplier, its position was, as a border city, a fleeting one. Second, Tochtepec was too small to supply the numbers of tlamemes necessary in addition to the normal portage traffic. Third, since Tenochtitlan-Tlatelolco was both the beginning and the ending point of the treks, its centrality made it a logical place to station the long-distance tlamemes and it had a sufficiently large population to support such an industry. Fourth, the cited use of tlamemes from Tenochtitlan-Tlatelolco indicates that they were long-distance porters. Had they been local tlamemes carrying in relays to Tochtepec, their numbers would have been fewer and their loads heavier than indicated. The number of long-distance tlamemes was dictated by the return trip, so on the outward leg the size of the load, rather than the number of porters, was reduced.

The effectiveness of a strictly political ban on trade appears questionable, given the numerous merchants and many markets in central Mexico, the fluidity of borders, and the virtual impossibility of rigorously controlling traffic over a wide area when neither roads nor vehicles were required. The necessary reliance on long-distance rather than on local tlamemes was an effective deterrent to foreign trade and provided the real incentive to observe the restriction.

The remaining major issue is why the pochtecah would have abetted the political expansion of the state if it meant loss of nearer markets. Despite Chapman's contention that "Once a territory was conquered and thereby subjected to tribute payments, the pochtecah ceased to trade there,"[130] as stated above, pochtecah trade did not cease. Four reasons can be cited. First, nontribute goods continued to enter Tenochtitlan-Tlatelolco from areas after their subjugation. Second, since the pochtecah from only five Valley of Mexico cities were permitted to trade beyond Tochtepec, the others were clearly trading internally. Third, the existence and continuation of regional markets required merchants at a higher level than merely local producer-sellers. Fourth, the types of goods entering Tenochtitlan-Tlatelolco in tribute were not usually the same as those entering by means of pochtecah trade. Hence the expansion of the Aztec empire did not mean the loss of marketing areas. Possibly, spying by the merchants was largely a way to gain honor and by no means their primary concern. Yet it did facilitate imperial expansion.[131] This, under the Chapman thesis, was extremely detrimental to trade, given the increase in trade distances and the high costs of transport. True, the pochtecah did benefit by Aztec honors, apparent trade monopolies, and a certain amount of military protection, although self-help appears to have been the major component. But there must have been further, more tangible benefits to induce the pochtecah to assist in the ebbing of their foreign markets. Here again, transport provides at least part of the answer.

When new areas were incorporated into the Aztec empire, not only was the safety of merchants enhanced, but in addition transport became more efficient. While long-distance tlamemes were reliable, as well as essential, beyond the confines of the empire, they were costly for three reasons. First, since they carried day after day, the continual burden would have been felt in reduced loads, reduced distances, periodic rest days, or some combination thereof. Second, since the number of carriers was dictated by the maximum load (on the return journey), more tlamemes were employed than were necessary during at least part of the trip. Third, since the tlamemes were engaged for the entire trip, they were a constant expense, whether or not they carried. The corollary of the above is that local tlamemes were more efficient for the inverse of the same three reasons. First, since they carried only one day, local tlamemes were less fatigued and could carry larger loads longer distances. Second, since tlamemes were hired by the day, only the number necessary to carry the loads at that particular point in the trip were employed. Third, they were employed only when carrying, causing no additional expense to the merchants on the days they stopped in markets or towns. Thus one of the benefits to the pochtecah of expanding the imperial domain was to increase the size of the domestic trading area. Within this area the local tlamemes were more highly organized and augmented where needed, so merchants within the imperial borders benefited by this cheaper, more efficient transportation system, in addition to prospering under peace.

There is relatively little evidence for state intervention in pochtecah trade, and the formidable natural and organizational obstacles to long-distance and foreign trade would have made control difficult. The Aztec state did not engage in controlling commerce in a heavy-handed, directed way. Rather, the state molded trade by more subtle strictures. Political control was exercised over the economy in two fundamental ways. First, the time, place, and nature of markets was determined by the polity, and regulations requiring attendance while banning extramarket sales reinforced their significance. Second, access to transportation was controlled by the polity. Unless the pochtecah procured tlamemes through the local rulers they were virtually unavailable. Considering both the limits and the potential of the extant transport system, the indeterminacy of political borders, and the difficulty in controlling traffic that was independent of roads or vehicles, it is evident that martial enforcement of trade restrictions was both unwieldy and unnecessary. This perspective clarifies the situation in which independent states such as Tlaxcala and Huexotzinco claimed to suffer from embargoes of salt and cotton by the hostile Aztecs, and yet there is little or no evidence of any military blockade. Since it is virtually impossible to curtail all traffic into a region when the dominant form of transport is by foot, only the sorts of controls outlined here (market and transport control) could be effective.

The picture presented in many sixteenth-century chronicles of a free economy—including laissez-faire entrepreneurs, supply-and-demand markets, bargaining, and freely hired professional porters—is accurate. All this took place. The control exercised by the state operated on a more subtle level, controlling the nature and locale of exchanges and overseeing the transportation needed to benefit by the transactions.

CHAPTER 6

The Valley of Mexico as a Regional Economy

THE economic and political pattern encountered by the conquistadors in the Valley of Mexico in 1519 was neither a long-standing condition nor a natural result of market forces. Rather, it was brought about by the increasing political and economic power of Tenochtitlan in response to that city's needs. It was a city always dependent on the agricultural lands of others, yet as its population expanded, the areas from which it could draw subsistence goods did not grow apace. To meet the increasing food demand, two initial strategies were adopted: the acquisition of lands by political means and the creation of new lands from within the lakes.

While the reasons for and purposes of political expansion were many and varied, one of the persistent practices of Mesoamerican conquest was the confiscation of part of the subjugated groups' land. The Aztecs benefited by this system even while they were tributaries of Azcapotzalco, and they made substantial gains after they allied with Texcoco and Tlacopan to overthrow the previously dominant Tepanecas.[1] The lands taken from the Tepanecas were divided (unequally) among the Aztec nobility and calpolli[2] and worked for the benefit of the victors. The direct benefits drawn from conquered lands were augmented by tribute that the vanquished paid from their own labor.[3] The strategy of conquering areas and confiscating land and/or exacting tribute was continued by the Aztecs until their defeat by the Spaniards. As the success of the Aztec political expansion increased, however, the effectiveness of the tribute system in supplementing Tenochtitlan's food supplies decreased.

As discussed earlier, the primary means of transportation in Mesoamerica was the tlameme, and although data on their costs are lacking and the post-Columbian political situation considerably distorted the actual costs of such a system during the earlier period, the system had marked limitations.

Each 13 to 18 miles of a journey from the city entailed two days of travel, one going and one returning. Because tlamemes were professional carriers, not merely casual porters, their minimal costs can be estimated as the subsistence rate of the tlameme and his dependents. An estimated family size of five would require an average of 8 pounds of maize per day.[4] This is not to say that the husband was the sole provider in the Mesoamerican family. Undoubtedly wives, children, and elderly dependents were economically significant, but considering that tlamemes likely came from the landless portions of the populace, it is unclear what role their dependents played in providing subsistence. Consequently, I have chosen to use the five-member family to illustrate the probable cost of tlamemes, but this figure is not an absolute for family dependency or consumption, nor does it consider profit, and it may easily be revised. Based on these conservative estimates, the minimum cost of transport for bulk goods, such as maize, was around 30 percent of the value of the load per day's distance from the market (calculating the cost for a round trip). Given the problems with the pre-Columbian data and the approximation of subsistence needs, neither an exact cost nor an economically feasible transport range can be established with any certainty. Nevertheless, it is readily apparent that this form of transportation did pose rather serious problems.

One would not expect tlameme-borne bulk goods to be conveyed any great distance, save for those goods received in tribute where the tribute costs necessarily included transportation—an expense borne by the givers, not by the recipients.[5] This expense was implicitly recognized since, even as tribute, bulk goods generally declined with distance.

The second measure designed to ease pressure on resources was the conversion of thousands of square meters of freshwater Lakes Chalco and Xochimilco into chinampas. The exceptional productivity of the converted lands, along with such spinoff benefits as providing seedlings for lakeshore gardens, eased the demand for food in the capital but did not completely satisfy it.

Faced with additional and increasing demands for food, the Aztecs had few alternatives available: intensify the areas already under production, further expand the area of production, or both. An increased reliance on aquatic resources was another possible response. However, as with hunting and gathering, these resources were culled from natural abundance rather than subject to increased production. There were highly nutritious and abundant lake foods, such as *ahuauhtli* (insect larvae) and *tecuitlatl* (blue-green algae, *Spirulina geitleri*).[6] But there is little evidence that such food sources played more than an ancillary role in the support of the valley population. Chinampa cultivation was already highly intensive, and creation of additional chinampas was greatly hindered, if not halted completely, by the salinity of the remaining lakes.[7]

The second option, expansion into areas beyond the Valley of Mexico, did not constitute an efficient strategy for augmenting Tenochtitlan's food supplies because food costs rose as transportation distance increased. Rather, effective areal expansion and agricultural intensification would have required the further appropriation of areas already within reasonable distances of the capital. Although this strategy was technically feasible, it was not adopted, possibly because it entailed at least two difficulties. First, many of the available lands were already allied with, dependencies of, or tributary to other Triple Alliance cities.[8] Second, even if these areas had been made direct tributaries of Tenochtitlan, additional exactions would most likely have met resistance. While such resistance would probably have been unsuccessful, the increased costs to Tenochtitlan of military and administrative control to achieve the additional extraction would have largely offset the benefits of such an approach. Thus the Aztecs were hemmed in by political constraints and areal limitations, and their existing acquisition strategies were substantially exhausted. The solution lay not in extending them but in adopting a radical alternative.

To overcome these difficulties, Tenochtitlan devised a strategy that resulted in the creation of a more efficient economic symbiosis encompassing a larger region—an economy of scale. The extant pattern of producing manufactured wares (secondary goods) within each major city and foodstuffs (primary goods) in their respective surrounding areas was efficient for localized production and consumption. Each cabecera produced secondary goods for both its own consumption and that of its rural hinterland; its hinterland produced primary goods for urban consumption. This pattern fostered the centrality of each town within its dependent area by maximizing the range of its goods and minimizing the travel distance within its hinterland. While this arrangement was advantageous when focusing on each such city-hinterland unit as a separate entity, it was not necessarily efficient when production was destined for a larger market.

Tenochtitlan altered this pattern by encouraging primary production throughout the Valley of Mexico while simultaneously discouraging secondary production.[9] It did so by controlling the flow of tribute[10] and by exercising monopolistic control over much pochtecah trade, rendering the valley cities incapable of effectively competing with the secondary production of Tenochtitlan for several reasons. First, overall craft specialization in these cities was weakened by the influx of competing tribute goods from the outside. Nominally Tenochtitlan received only two-fifths of the Triple Alliance tribute (Texcoco receiving two-fifths and Tlacopan receiving one-fifth).[11]

But this was more ideology than reality. Tenochtitlan's share of the tribute increased with time, both absolutely as more areas were conquered, and relatively as it appropriated increasing percentages of its partners' shares. These goods consisted primarily of finished goods[12] that could then be rechanneled into the valley economy through the markets. The cost of tribute goods to the recipients was nil. There were, of course, both military and administrative costs involved in tribute, but the costs weighed more heavily on the commoners than on the nobility while benefiting the latter disproportionately. These tribute goods could be sold at or below the cost of production of similar wares produced within the Valley of Mexico.

Vast quantities of tribute foodstuffs entered Tenochtitlan annually, estimates differing according to interpretation of the historical sources. Carrasco[13] maintains that the tribute stimulated provincial production without increasing provincial consumption and that this reinforced the concentration of power in the Valley of Mexico. Although many of the tribute goods entered the market system, many were sumptuary goods and did not. How goods passed from tribute to merchandise is not clear. Berdan maintains that tribute goods were redistributed through administrative channels to support royal households, to supplement commoner production, and to be placed in storage against famine or disaster. This was accomplished by merchants selling goods received from the king. Berdan[14] suggests that tribute supplied support for the secondary producers of the Valley of Mexico, military expansion, and the growth of the nobility and specialized groups. Whatever the mechanism, tribute goods apparently did enter the market system. Litvak King[15] argues that this lowered Valley of Mexico prices since the cost of production to the seller was zero. Because tribute was a revenue-generating device, it seems unlikely that lower prices would have been a deliberate policy. Rather, the general price decline was a result of the massive influx of goods which met or exceeded demand. Thus, secondary production throughout the valley was undermined by the influx of goods with which they could not compete economically.[16]

Second, monopolization of trade in certain goods and concentration of craft production in Tenochtitlan led to more and better wares being produced there than elsewhere in the Valley of Mexico, further undermining local competition. Although twelve cities within the Valley of Mexico had pochtecah merchants, not all these groups possessed the same functions. The pochtecah of only five cities in the valley were permitted to trade beyond the borders of the empire:[17] Tenochtitlan and Tlatelolco, accompanied by merchants from Azcapotzalco, Huitzilopochco, and Cuauhtitlan, the latter as auxiliaries rather than as independent merchant groups.[18] The pochtecah of the remaining cities—Chalco Atenco, Coatlichan, Huexotla, Mixcoac, Otumba, Texcoco, and Xochimilco—could not trade outside the empire. This restriction illustrates the Aztecs' control of long-distance trade and monopolization of exotic goods from areas beyond the imperial borders.

Goods imported by the pochtecah consisted largely of raw materials—hides, feathers, precious stones, and so forth—that fueled craft production within the Valley of Mexico. Merely controlling the influx of these goods would not have resulted in any advantage in secondary production for Tenochtitlan. Craft specialization was increasingly centralized, however, by the movement of the better craftsmen from other cities into Tenochtitlan.[19] This was due, in part, to the negative impact of competing tribute goods and to the positive impact of closer ties with the pochtecah which afforded the craftsmen direct access to imported raw materials. This was particularly true of the pochtecah from Tenochtitlan and Tlatelolco, who had access to extraimperial exotic goods that were either denied to artisans of other cities or made available to them through the market at greater cost.[20] In short, manufacturing was more effective in Tenochtitlan than in outlying towns because its artisans were better craftsmen, they had access to material largely unavailable to craftsmen located elsewhere in the valley, and they produced on a larger scale, not only for local consumption but for export as well. Thus secondary production became increasingly difficult and certainly less profitable in other cities.

While the concentration of secondary production was taking place, overall population growth increased the demand for foodstuffs, primarily in Tenochtitlan. As the profitability of secondary production decreased in other cities, the demand for foodstuffs grew, and the profitability of primary production increased. Since high-bulk–low-value goods such as foodstuffs could not travel great distances, the demand for them had to be satisfied locally. Thus the profits of local primary producers could increase to include the extra amounts that consumers would have paid for food transported from more distant areas. As a result, the predominant economic pattern of the Valley of Mexico shifted from a mosaic of small producing and consuming areas to a primary-producing periphery and a secondary-producing core. As a consequence of this new symbiosis, markets now drew on goods from the entire valley.[21] Gradually the economic balkanization of the valley diminished, owing partly to increasing political integration, but crucial factors in integrating the markets were the changing pattern of production and the use of a different system of transportation.

Whereas land transport in Mesoamerica was by tlamemes, within the Valley of Mexico transportation was also provided by canoes that traveled at approximately the same speed as tlamemes yet propelled one ton per person —an efficiency ratio of 40 to 1 over tlamemes.[22]

Canoes permitted the flow of commodities over much greater distances than was possible in most other places in Mesoamerica. The lower cost of transport (or flow from a much greater distance at the same cost) enabled Tenochtitlan to trade throughout much of the valley, and it therefore enjoyed a much larger hinterland than that available to landlocked cities. Yet the greater efficiency of canoe transport did not simply draw towns closer in terms of commercial interaction.

The use of canoes distorted the transport space, so that actual linear distance did not accord with social interactional distance. Consequently, the unmodified application of spatial marketing models to topographical space is, in this instance, unrealistic. Since marketing models are indicators of human interaction, differentials in the flow of commerce must necessarily be taken into consideration.[23] Lacustrine areas must be reduced by a factor of 40 for the transport of goods by water to be represented as comparable to the transport of goods by land. It follows that the relationships among cities are not indicated by relative distance unless the very real differences between water and land transportation are taken into account. Transport distance, not linear distance, is the crucial variable.

Canoe transport economically integrated the valley in terms of commodities but did not greatly affect consumer movement. Travel time to market remained substantially the same since canoes increased haulage, not speed. Canoe efficiency can be calculated in two different ways: in cost per ton per mile and in speed. Canoes enjoyed a great advantage over tlamemes in terms of cost per ton per mile but no advantage in terms of speed (except where the water routes were more direct than land routes, as between Tenochtitlan and Texcoco, the canoe route being 3 leagues while the two land routes were 7 and 8 leagues, respectively.[24]

The effect of this lower cost was to increase greatly the flow of goods within the valley, but not the flow of consumers. The primary constraint on consumers was not the monetary cost of transport but the time cost, which was not substantially reduced by the use of canoes. Consumers remained tied to local markets for the most part, while middlemen moved goods to and from Tenochtitlan-Tlatelolco. This differential strengthened the economic position of the other valley cities vis-à-vis their subject towns because it gave the city markets greater access to goods from Tenochtitlan without a complementary loss of consumers to that still temporally distant market. The increased economic significance of Tenochtitlan, however, affected the location of the cities in relation to their respective subject towns.

Until the greatly increased reliance on canoe transport and valley-wide economic integration, the pattern of urban-rural interchange was based on the central location of the secondary-producing–primary-consuming city within the primary-producing–secondary-consuming hinterland. This changed with the shift in productive patterns. The cities were no longer major producers of secondary goods but rather producers of primary goods for Tenochtitlan, whose secondary goods they now consumed. This shift in production and consumption entailed a major economic reorganization, not merely the addition of Tenochtitlan as the dominant market. The importance of valley cities was no longer determined by centrality within their respective economic systems but was determined by their role as conduits, standing midway in the larger exchange system between Tenochtitlan and their respective subject towns. Thus the previous locational advantage declined. The increased trade with Tenochtitlan had the effect of shifting the secondary-market centers toward the lakeshore.[25] Lakeshore locations enabled the cities to control the flow of primary goods from their respective hinterlands into Tenochtitlan, as well as the reverse flow of Tenochtitlan's secondary goods into the hinterlands. The predominance of lakeshore locations resulted from the intermediate position of the cities in the flow of goods and also because the lakeshore was a transition area of transportation types (land-water) and a break-of-bulk point, both factors encouraging the exercise of economic control.

The shift of cities to the lakeshore during Aztec times was closely associated with the emerging trade network. At first glance the market pattern appears to have been dendritic, in which lower-level centers were tributary to only one higher-level center, with centers becoming progressively smaller with distance from the major center that controlled the economic flow.[26] A more graphic model, however, is that of the gateway city. Gateway cities,[27] unlike central-place cities, are situated eccentrically toward one end of their hinterlands and control entrance into the extended hinterland. They tend to be located at transportationally important sites. The Valley of Mexico cities were such, the shift between canoes and tlamemes being both a major transport break and a bulk-break point. Before the rise of the Aztec commercial network, the important cities were situated back from the lakes, in the centers of their hinterlands, but as the intralacustrine trade grew, Tenochtitlan-Tlatelolco became increasingly important, and so too did the cities located between it and the hinterlands. Whereas pre-Aztec hinterlands were supplied by their central cities, the Aztec-era hinterlands were supplied from Tenochtitlan-Tlatelolco. Centers situated at points that controlled that flow enjoyed a substantial advantage over the earlier hinterland-centered cities.

Gateway cities permit market interaction but do not exclusively control it. Rather than controlling trade in a region through a rigidly tiered and exclusive marketing structure, gateway cities owe much of their importance to their fortuitous position vis-à-vis their hinterlands and the major supplier, with strict market structuring incidental. In the Valley of Mexico the gateway cities owed their positions to the lakes.

While this alteration of production and marketing patterns in the Valley of Mexico changed the vertical integration of markets by placing them within a larger marketing hierarchy, it did little for their horizontal integration. Trade between yearbearer systems could be expected, political boundaries aside, when one produced a commodity the other lacked or when one served as intermediary between the source and the consumer. But aside from larger specialized marketing or artisan centers, most of the towns in the Valley of Mexico produced similar goods. Furthermore, since all lakeside cities or areas had substantially equal access to the dominant market by means of efficient canoe transport, trade with adjacent markets for items originating in Tenochtitlan-Tlatelolco merely interjected an additional intermediary in the marketing process and raised the prices. There was little advantage in establishing sustained trading relations between yearbearer systems since access to each other was not substantially easier than entry into the Tenochtitlan-Tlatelolco market and certainly lacked many of the benefits. Produce from the hinterlands was bulked at subordinate five-day market centers and then flowed into the nodal yearbearer markets and thence by canoe to Tenochtitlan-Tlatelolco. Both elite items and costlier mundane articles, such as cotton mantles, reversed the sequence, flowing back down the system, supplying the hinterland. Little incentive remained for lateral trade, since it would not increase the diversity of commodities and merely added another wholesaling layer; it increased costs without increasing benefits.

Tenochtitlan-Tlatelolco was clearly the dominant market of the valley, but there was competition. Although it nominally possessed great political and economic significance, Azcapotzalco, capital of the earlier Tepanec empire, was not a serious competitor; neither was the Triple Alliance city of Tlacopan, or the great agricultural centers of Xochimilco or Chalco Atenco. Despite its reduced role in pochtecah trade, Texcoco was the valley's second most important market, but it did not owe this position simply to its size or political prominence. The valley's economy was not nurtured by a constant and unchanging flow of goods. Climatic factors affected both the flow of goods and the relative significance of the participating centers.

While 2,240 meters is generally accepted as the level of the valley lakes at Conquest, this was their normal crest and did not reflect year-round lake conditions. In fact, lake levels fluctuated considerably. An understanding of short-term lake fluctuation requires some consideration of basin hydrology. Basically, the operation of a basin hydrological cycle is simply approximated as

Precipitation = basin channel runoff + evapotranspiration + changes in storage.[28]

Basin-channel runoff is not a factor, since the Valley of Mexico is an internal drainage basin. The hydrological cycle of the basin was simple. Rain in the mountains drained into the central plains and evaporated in the lakes:

Rain = evaporation + storage.

The probable ratio was 6 = 5 + 1. Overall, the lakes were shrinking, and evaporation was greater than precipitation.[29] Cloud cover kept temperatures lower during the rainy season, thus reducing evaporation, but prodigious amounts of moisture were lost throughout the year. In the mountains, south, southeast, and southwest evaporation was much lower than in the north and northeast. It currently varies between 900 and 2,100 millimeters a year and surpasses the annual rainfall.[30] Annually, 5.4 billion cubic meters of water fall into the drainage area of the lake system. Of this, 0.89 billion cubic meter goes into ground storage, the remaining 4.5 billion cubic meters evaporating.

Calculating evaporation rates for extinct lakes is a precarious undertaking. Vital information is lacking, such as water volume actually entering the lakes, changes in evaporation rates throughout the year, and losses from the higher lakes into Lake Texcoco. However, a prodigious average of 12 million cubic meters of water is currently lost through evaporation per day. Only 2 million cubic meters of water separate the high-water estimate of 2,240 meters and the scattered pools at 2,238 meters, and in the face of a valley-wide evaporation 2,000 times this amount, together with the fact that the lakes comprised

10 percent of the total surface, the periodic reduction to scattered pools is a foregone conclusion (see map 5).

The actual situation in the Valley of Mexico was, of course, complicated. Evaporation played a smaller part in lake water loss than did drainage, except for Lake Texcoco and the northern two lakes during the dry season, when drainage ceased. Lakes Zumpango and Xaltocan drained into Lake Texcoco seasonally, permitting transit only part of the year. Lakes Chalco and Xochimilco, having permanent water sources, allowed year-round passage into Lake Texcoco. Depending on the amount of runoff and the discharge ratio into Texcoco, periodic flooding could temporarily reverse the flow, sending saline water back into Lake Xochimilco. In short, owing to evaporation the lakes were subject to considerable annual fluctuation in size. The water loss was made particularly acute by the shallow lake beds, and interlake transit was periodically interrupted. Durán relates that even in the fifteenth century canoes were not able to make the journey from Tenochtitlan to Acuecuexco, southwest of the city, during the dry season because of the low water level.[31]

Interruption of interlake transit was the most obvious consequence of shallow lakes, rainy and dry seasons, and a high evaporation rate. Reduced water levels that may not have interrupted transit on a single lake would nevertheless cause major inconveniences. Lake depth decreased, and water receded from cities normally served by lake transit, reaching its nadir just before the annual rains.

Despite the general picture of placid lake transport, this flow of commodities fluctuated throughout the year. In the early 1950s, June to October was the period of heaviest traffic, the average farmer making two trips a week from the chinampa area to Mexico City.[32] Not only the agricultural cycle but also the climate affected the amount of commerce. During the spring, when water transport was difficult because of large waves blown up on the lakes by the winds, canoe trips decreased. Furthermore, some areas were seasonally cut off from the main areas of

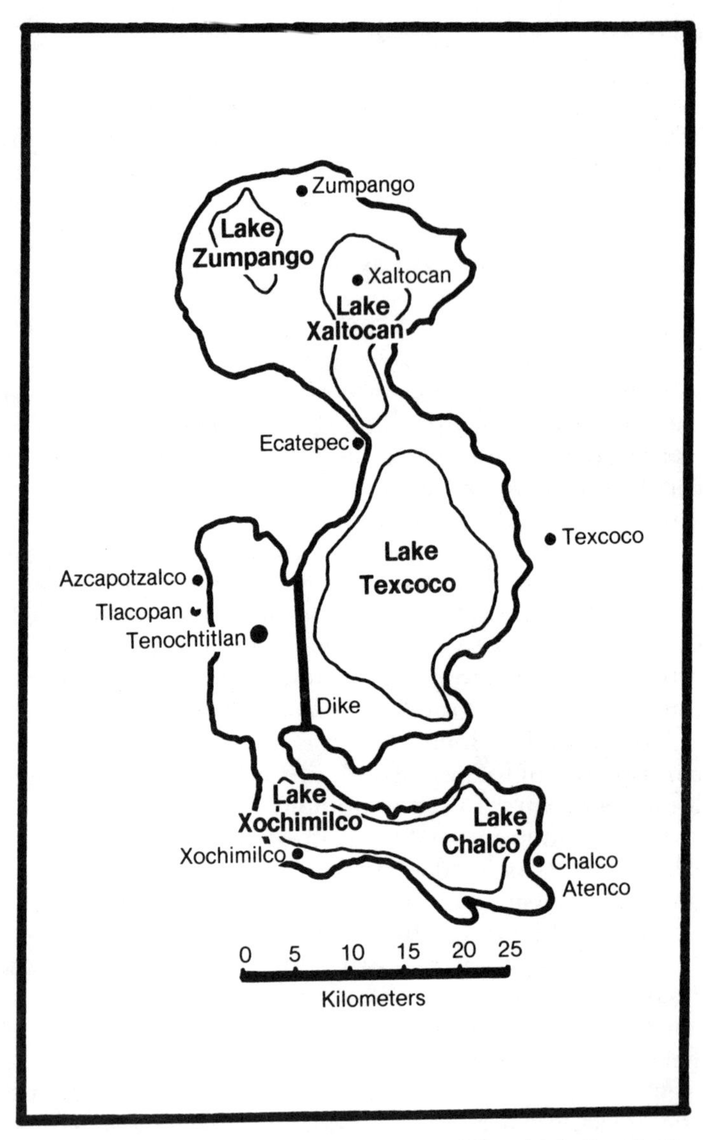

MAP 5. LAKES IN THE VALLEY OF MEXICO. The thick line indicates the lakes' maximum expanse in 1520: the thin line indicates their late-colonial expanse. The pre-Columbian annual division occurred at similar points in the lakes. Lakes Zumpango and Xaltocan were separated from Lake Texcoco at Ecatepec, and Tenochtitlan was severed by lowered water surrounding that city. Lakes Xochimilco and Chalco remained connected to Tenochtitlan year round by canal.

lake traffic because of the wet-dry cycle of the valley, the elevations of the various lakes, and the shallow lake bed. The decline in lake level did not greatly affect the southern two lakes, but the northern two experienced an annual blockage that completely cut off canoe traffic. Moreover, the shallowness of the lakes often resulted in an annual retreat of the lake, inconveniencing lakeshore sites; in very dry years the inconvenience could become totally incapacitating.

During late winter and spring lake levels declined to the point that the northern lakes, Zumpango and Xaltocan, were cut off, and the water receded in Lake Texcoco (Lakes Xochimilco and Chalco also experienced fluctuation in water levels but their perennial water sources guaranteed year-round traffic to Tenochtitlan-Tlatelolco). The spring winds blew so violently that the little canoeing that was still going on in the lowered lakes was extremely hazardous, a condition made worse by the shallow draft of the keelless vessels.[33] Consequently, the northern area was completely cut off from Tenochtitlan-Tlatelolco, and the eastern shore of Lake Texcoco experienced markedly reduced traffic. These periods coincided with the lowest level of food transport, since the harvests generally occurred throughout the summer and autumn, so presumably these factors were taken into consideration in the annual scheduling of canoe traffic.

Tenochtitlan-Tlatelolco was connected to land by three causeways leading to four cities on the western shore and the Ixtapalapa peninsula and was fed by the canal from Chalco Atenco. It thus remained the primary market of the southern and eastern regions during the annual segmentation of the valley. Cut off from Tenochtitlan-Tlatelolco, the northern-lakes marketing region experienced a marked decline in the quantity of incoming goods.

The eastern shore of Lake Texcoco also experienced annual changes in trade owing to lake fluctuations. Although trade was seldom completely severed, the flow of goods into the eastern-shore area from Tenochtitlan-Tlatelolco was hindered, as it was from western Mexico. However, wares from southern and eastern Mexico entered the Texcoco area, as well as Tenochtitlan-Tlatelolco, by way of the canal from Chalco Atenco. The impact of this annual trade quietus on the eastern shore was lessened by the suitability of the city of Texcoco to fill the role of regional market, since it too received tribute and trade goods, although on a lesser scale than those entering Tenochtitlan-Tlatelolco.

Thus what was essentially an integrated valley-wide macromarket drawn together by efficient canoe transport during most of the year, was segmented during the late winter and spring into an autonomous northern marketing region, a semiautonomous eastern marketing region, and the remaining southern and western marketing region. However, the economic effects of this were muted by the coincidence of heavy traffic and harvest seasons and the relative self-sufficiency of the yearbearer systems. The affected commodities were basically elite goods and relatively costly mundane articles, such as mantas, that could more easily bear the increased cost of foot transport if essential, were easily stored, and did not suffer the inelastic demand of foodstuffs. More important than the diminished flow of goods was the establishment of trade networks at a level below that of the overall valley-level system. This permitted the annual opening and closing of the lacustrine marketing system to proceed without undue disruption as well as patterning relations within the three areas in ways that are unintelligible when the lake marketing system is viewed as an unchanging whole.

The annual opening and closing of the valley macromarket system had profound effects on cities in the valley. As the primary terminus for tribute and elite trade goods, and as the largest agricultural market in the Valley of Mexico, Tenochtitlan-Tlatelolco exercised major economic influence that was virtually irresistible when coupled with their politico-military power. Cities of importance before the rise of the Aztecs—Azcapotzalco, Culhuacan, and Coyoacan, as well as Tlacopan (one of the members of the Triple Alliance that overthrew the Tepanec empire)—were never of great economic significance after the establishment of the Aztec hegemony. They were utterly dominated by the economic power of Tenochtitlan-Tlatelolco into whose marketing network they were tied year round. The eastern shore was spared this complete domination. Towns of earlier importance there, Acolman and Coatlichan, were eclipsed by Texcoco, but the eastern-shore cities were not reduced to the status of mere economic appendages of Tenochtitlan-Tlatelolco as were the western-shore cities. Although Texcoco had a large population, received tribute, and possessed its own pochtecah, it owed its relative autonomy from Tenochtitlan-Tlatelolco to its geographical position rather than to its economic or political might. Texcoco's status as a recipient of tribute and elite trade goods, at least from southern and eastern Mexico, was insufficient to account for its relative independence from Tenochtitlan-Tlatelolco since Tlacopan was also a tribute terminus. Furthermore, the pochtecah of Texcoco were subordinated to those of Tenochtitlan-Tlatelolco and were not free to trade beyond the empire.

In sum, Texcoco presents a picture of economic subordination belied by its population and cultural significance. Its autonomy was a consequence of the annual segmentation of the valley marketing system. Since trade between the eastern shore and Tenochtitlan-Tlatelolco greatly diminished each spring, the yearbearer-market systems of the eastern side of the lake were not totally dependent on Tenochtitlan-Tlatelolco. The Aztec capital easily dominated the entire valley marketing area during the high-water months, for it was the source of most secondary goods available to the smaller marketing towns. For all but the landlocked towns of the eastern valley Texcoco offered no advantages as a market, merely adding another marketing (and cost) layer for goods available directly from Tenochtitlan. During the low-water months, however, eastern valley towns were deprived of direct access to these goods, and of the eastern-shore towns only Texcoco possessed both direct access to Tenochtitlan and a marketing area of sufficient size to offer specialized goods and services. The eastern-valley towns were part of a marketing subsystem that swelled and subsided in counterpulsation with that of Tenochtitlan-Tlatelolco. Thus the lake fluctuations, agricultural cycle, and winds fortuitously combined to stave off the economic domination experienced by those cities more permanently tied to Tenochtitlan-Tlatelolco. The northern-lakes area retained a certain amount of autonomy not only because of its annual separation but also because of its smaller population and lower agricultural productivity.

Between early (ca. 1150–1350) and late (ca. 1350–1520) Aztec times,[34] the urban pattern of the Valley of Mexico changed to reflect the increased importance of lake transport and the dominance of Tenochtitlan-Tlatelolco as supplier of manufactured goods and consumer of the valley's agricultural produce. By its political control of trade and tribute, Tenochtitlan converted the Valley of Mexico to a core-periphery structure: the core supplied secondary goods unrivaled in the rest of the valley, and the periphery produced primary goods that the growing demand and distance factor made increasingly profitable. As a consequence of this altered economic pattern valley cities moved toward the lakeshore and adopted eccentric locations within their hinterlands that perpetuated economic control over their respective hinterlands. These positions were strengthened by canoe transport that facilitated the flow of goods but not of consumers. Canoe transport also increased hierarchical market integration by giving secondary centers direct access to Tenochtitlan but discouraged horizontal integration by minimizing the impetus for trade among secondary centers. Thus the valley was converted from loosely linked disparate economic areas into a largely unified core-periphery system. Primary markets fed into their respective secondary markets, and each of these fed into Tenochtitlan to form a dendritic central-place system.

CHAPTER 7

Summary of the Pre-Columbian System

MESOAMERICA was unique in having highly urbanized states that lacked both wheeled vehicles and draft animals. Primary transport was by means of tlamemes, a low-status, hereditary occupational group whose members engaged in lifelong portage. Based in the main town, or cabecera, of a political district, they carried burdens from their cabecera to the next, where other tlamemes picked up the load, thus transporting it for great distances in relay fashion. Generally, tlamemes carried loads of about 23 kilograms a distance of 5 leagues (21 to 28 kilometers) per day.

The few measures available to the Aztecs for expanding their food-support area, such as professionalization of carriers and maintenance of roads, were employed, but in the absence of a technological breakthrough the economic hinterlands of cities remained quite small. The net effect of this was that Mesoamerican cities, having smaller economic hinterlands, had smaller populations and were closer together than cities in the Old World. However, the same was not true of the Valley of Mexico.

In the examination of a lakeshore city, the support area is, in effect, halved since its hypothetical expanse includes the lake itself, an area containing neither arable lands nor consuming or producing populations. There are, of course, compensatory products, such as fish and waterfowl. But in terms of land support area, these cities should be smaller than their contemporaries on the plains, reflecting their reduced hinterlands. Such did not prove to be the case, however. The Valley of Mexico contained a five-lake system that provided the opportunity to use two systems of transportation, tlamemes and canoes, the latter being forty times more efficient than the former in terms of bulk transported. Consequently, Tenochtitlan's effective hinterland was not a 5-league radius around the city but a 5-league radius along the entire lakeshore. The net effect was to allow the city immediate access to an economic hinterland much larger than that available to other Mesoamerican cities.

Although Tenochtitlan was organized on preexisting Mesoamerican patterns, it was qualitatively different as a result of its historical peculiarities. Unlike the other cities in the Valley of Mexico, Tenochtitlan was founded on an island without access to agriculturally productive areas of its own; it was always dependent on other city-states for its sustenance. Consequently, when it embarked on political expansion, it adapted a preexisting tribute pattern but laid heavier emphasis on access to productive areas and spurred valley-wide lake-system economic integration. Cities had existed in the valley for over a thousand years, but the Aztec period differed in that, unlike earlier eras, cities were now situated along the lakeshore. This important shift owed much to the Aztec political organization.

While an economic hinterland is defined by transportation efficiency, a political hinterland is determined by power. In this the Aztecs were aided by their disproportionately large population resulting from its location in a favorable transportation network. The Aztec empire has been depicted as politically unstable and unsophisticated because of its lack of areal integration and the frequency of internal revolts, but such criticisms rest on a fundamental misconception of the nature of the Aztec expansion. Political expansion to benefit the urban center can be schematically analyzed by the presence or absence of exploitation and territorial incorporation. The alternatives vary by yield and military-administrative costs, and the Aztecs adopted a nonincorporated low-exploitation approach. On conquering a new territory, they generally left the indigenous political structure intact and relied on local means of extracting tribute for the empire. The cost was very low: the system required only two tribute administrators in each province. Thus the benefits were relatively high, and the system had the advantage of not tying down the army in occupation but permitting it to sweep ever-increasing areas that it could incorporate as tributaries. Rather than viewing the Aztec imperial system as an inadequate territorial empire, it can more profitably be viewed as a hegemonic empire. It did not maintain a standing army but relied on the threat of force and its reputation to enforce compliance. The effect of such a system was to operate with a considerable economy of force. Rather than being indicators of the decay of a territorial empire, revolts are expected in hegemonic empires.

The net effect of this system was to enable Tenochtitlan to extend its economic hinterland artificially by political means, placing the cost of transport (as well as the cost of production) outside its own system and on the shoulders of the tribute-paying groups. It was, in essence, a social adaptation to severe ecological and technological constraints.

One benefit of expanding the empire was that it permitted the economic integration of areas within it. By welding together the local tlameme organizations, it made trade more efficient, particularly long-distance trade. Although the long-distance pochtecah trade appears to have been an old institution in Mesoamerica, the Aztecs expanded it, tying its fortunes to imperial conquest. Despite the existence of pochtecah guilds in twelve Valley of Mexico cities, the extraimperial trade was overwhelmingly dominated by Tenochtitlan-Tlatelolco. The pochtecah trade of the other cities was subordinated to the economic interests of the Aztec capital.

The distribution throughout the Valley of Mexico of local agricultural production, tribute goods, and elite goods was not an automatic occurrence but required an organized distribution system. Much of the distribution occurred through markets and were a function not only of consumer demand but of time as well, and time is a culturally determined phenomenon.

Aztec markets were based primarily on a five-day week, with smaller satellite markets permitted around those of cabeceras on complementary days so that each market could attract the largest feasible consumer population. The important markets in the Valley of Mexico were held on the same days, the first day of every five-day week (yearbearer days). Lower markets were oriented toward and met in sequence with these cabecera markets, but cabecera markets did not articulate with each other.

The efficiency that canoes offered was in hauling capacity: the effect of the canoe system on the valley economic system was to integrate more closely not the flow of consumers but the flow of commodities. Customers did not generally come from the farthest cities to market in Tenochtitlan. Rather, the transporters shipped their products efficiently into Tenochtitlan and returned to their home markets laden with products from Tenochtitlan to be sold. This capacity had profound consequences for the economic patterns of the valley. Before the Aztec era most cities in the valley had engaged in considerable craft production. With the rise of the Aztec economic center there was an increase in Aztec craft products, exotic trade goods, and tribute goods, all centering on Tenochtitlan. Goods produced in Tenochtitlan took advantage of economies of scale, and tribute goods were recirculated from the city through the marketing system, probably at or below production costs. The effect was to reduce the number of craftsmen in other cities in the valley and to shift the economies of those cities toward more intensive primary production to supply the large and growing demand in Tenochtitlan. This flow of goods fostered the shift of Valley of Mexico cities away from the centers of their respective hinterlands to the lakeshores, since in the latter locations they were gateway cities, controlling the flow of goods from Tenochtitlan to their subordinate centers. Thus for the first time the Valley of Mexico was converted from an area of distinct and frequently warring city-states into a truly symbiotic macroregion, based on economic interdependence.

The three basic economic flows into the Valley of Mexico—local trade, long-distance trade, and tribute—represented three distinct patterns. Local tlameme traffic and local marketing presented a solarlike yearbearer marketing pattern, flowing into and out of the cabeceras. Pochtecah trade over longer distances presented a modified dendritic pattern. The pochtecah linked the Valley of Mexico with the rest of Mesoamerica. As presented by sixteenth-century sources, the picture is one of trade to and from Tenochtitlan-Tlatelolco, but the clear evidence of more elaborated pochtecah trade, both internal and external to the empire, leads to the conclusion that they linked most major markets. Whether this linkage was incidental to serving Tenochtitlan-Tlatelolco is not known, but is unlikely. Whatever the case, the pochtecah served the larger communities, leaving local distribution to local means. The tribute system was, however, a unidirectional dendritic pattern. Unlike the normal dendritic flow, goods did not flow both up and down the tribute system. Goods went from *sujetos* to cabeceras to provincial centers and thence to Tenochtitlan. Any return was incidental to the system.

Tenochtitlan was fortuitously situated to take advantage of a more efficient transportation network, allowing it a larger economic hinterland. It intensified production to the highest level in the New World, and it expanded politically to augment those resources. To feed its burgeoning population, Tenochtitlan used both its physical and its economic location in the valley to restructure economically most of the outlying regions into areas of primary production while reducing them to dependence on itself for goods they could not otherwise obtain or produce competitively.

An understanding of the political and economic structure of the Aztecs clarifies why the Spanish conquest happened the way it did. The Conquest changed much, but from the perspective of urbanism it was not the cataclysm it is depicted to have been. The fact of conquest was a logical consequence of the Aztec political structure. The Aztec empire was never a territorially integrated system that could stand in opposition to an outside threat. In the absence of any competing power, the Aztec empire functioned admirably in augmenting Tenochtitlan's supplies. The endemic revolts show a certain amount of continual hostility, so the appearance of Cortés, rather than being simply a new and opposing force of equal organization, was instead a small wedge driven into a nonintegrated empire, splitting it along the cleavages inherent in its structure.

PART TWO

The Post-Columbian Era

CHAPTER 8

Colonial New Spain

THAT the Spanish conquest had an enormous impact on the New World is unquestionable, but that the impact of this conquest was fully foreseen or intentional is unfounded. What took place in New Spain throughout the sixteenth century (and beyond) was not simply the transplantation of Iberian culture to a new locale. Rather, the Spaniards had to contend with (and often relied on) preexisting cultural practices and patterns, as well as a large native population. What the Spaniards introduced was superimposed on the indigenous schema.

The preexisting relationships between dependent native cities and their sustaining hinterlands underwent massive assault. The balance between urban demand and areas of economic and political sway was upset—new needs, newly emergent regional competition, and political factors dominated the creation of new urban-rural relationships. The same four factors of significance in Aztec times—population, productive potential, consumption, and transportation—also structured Hispanic-era relations, but their values were greatly altered by the Conquest.

The Spaniards, particularly after their experiences in the West Indies, were prepared with many policies and directives for the conquered areas and peoples, such as the idea of conquest as vassals on behalf of the king, exploitation of native tribute and labor, and Christianization of the Indians. Thus some of the impending changes in New Spain were intentional, the result of conscious decision, as were many later policies, such as the establishment of the *alhóndiga* (public granary), the creation of roads, and so forth. However, these reasoned (albeit often unreasonable) policies also had consequences that were unintended, such as the chaotic reshuffling of indigenous markets, the new competition among cities for foodstuffs, and the shift in tribute. There were wholly unanticipated consequences of the Conquest, such as the devastating depopulation of the natives. As a result of the foregoing, many of the changes that New Spain underwent in population, agricultural production, and transportation were unintentional ones, far different from those envisioned by the Spaniards, if they were predictable at all.

Many changes occurred, but in analyzing the pre-Columbian situation, I have addressed chronological developments in only the most general manner. This approach was dictated not only by the scale of the approach but also by the paucity of detailed and reliable sequential information. The post-Columbian situation presents the opposite problem, however. Although highly variable, Spanish data from the sixteenth century offer a flood of detail that threatens to drown the general patterns of accommodation by both Indians and Spaniards. Consequently, time periods of relative homogeneity (based on both demographic factors and social events) are used to display general patterns and changes throughout the sixteenth century.

CHAPTER 9

Demographic Changes

THE size of the native population at Conquest is crucial to an understanding of many of the subsequent events in New Spain. The issue of population size in the New World is a thorny one and has been much debated without the emergence of a general consensus concerning its size. That there was a large population before the Conquest and that it was drastically reduced by the end of the sixteenth century is generally conceded, but the specifics remain in question.

Direct Spanish activity in the form of war, maltreatment, and neglect was not the main cause of Indian mortality in the sixteenth century. Famines such as those in 1558, 1579, and 1587 were responsible for some deaths, but the vast majority resulted from disease (see table 9.1). Although of great significance for the history of Spanish-Indian interaction, disease did not play the pivotal role in the Conquest that is often claimed for it.[1]

The demographic changes that took place provide both a background for events in the sixteenth century and a possible basis for dividing that century for analysis. While there is no general agreement on the size of the population at the time of the Conquest in central Mexico (roughly Mexico from the Isthmus of Tehuantepec to the desert north of Mexico City), Cook and Borah estimate the immediate pre-Conquest population at better than 25 million with a decline of 95 percent by the end of the sixteenth century (see table 9.2).[2]

Although the trend was continually downward, the sixteenth-century Mexican population experienced three

Table 9.1. Causes of Indian Mortality, 1520–1602

Year	Disease*
1520–21	*Viruelas, huey zahuatl*
1531	*Zahuatl, sarampión, viruelas, zahuatl tepiton*
1532	*Viruelas, zahuatl*
1538	*Viruelas*
1545–48	Great pestilence, *cocoliztli*
1550	*Paperas*
1558	Death and famine
1559	Pestilence with symptoms like those of 1545 and 1576
1563–64	*Zahuatl, sarampión, matlaltotonqui*
1566	*Cocoliztli*
1576–81	Great *cocoliztli*
1587–88	*Cocoliztli*
1590	*Tlatlaciztli*
1592–93	*Tlatlaciztli, sarampión, cocoliztli*
1595–97	*Sarampión, paperas, tabardillo*
1601–1602	*Cocoliztli*

*Gibson (1964:448–49) gives the following probable definitions of disease terms: *matlazahuatl* is typhus or yellow fever; *huey zahuatl* and *zahuatl tepiton* may refer to different intensities of the same disease or to different diseases, possibly smallpox *(viruelas)* and measles *(sarampión)*, respectively; *matlaltotonqui* may be pleurisy; *tlatlaciztli* is a disease like influenza with a cough; *paperas* is a form of mumps; *tabardillo* is an unidentified fever; and *cocoztli* refers to general sickness or plague.

Source: Gibson 1964a:448–49.

precipitous declines following major epidemics: in 1520–21, 1545–48, and 1576–81.[3]

The demographic effects were marked, but they were not uniform throughout the region. The lowland coastal areas experienced a much more precipitous drop in population than did the highland plateau area, although the decline in both areas was major. Sixty percent of the pre-Conquest population lived in the highlands,[4] but as the century progressed, the lowland percentage dropped from

Table 9.2. Population Estimates for Central Mexico, 1519–1608

Year	Plateau	Coast	Total, Central Mexico
1519	–	–	25,200,000
1532	11,226,336	5,645,072	16,871,408
1548	4,765,000	1,535,000	6,300,000
1568	2,231,176	418,397	2,649,573
1580	1,631,129	260,138	1,891,267
1595	1,125,172	247,056	1,372,228
1608	852,244	217,011	1,069,255

Source: Cook and Borah 1971:80–82.

40 percent in 1519 to 34 percent in 1532, 24 percent in 1548, and 14 percent in 1580, at which point the decline eased and was overtaken by the rate of decline in the highlands. The lowland-population percentage (not total numbers) then rose to 18 percent in 1595 and 20 percent in 1608. However, the coastal areas experienced massive depopulation even within the context of the loss in central Mexico as a whole (see fig. 9.1). The primary reason for the disparity in mortality between the lowlands and the highlands was not the difference in virulence of the epidemics but the difference in diseases between the two regions.

How any disease affects individuals depends on the characteristics of the disease and the hosts' susceptibility. In terms of populations, however, disease symptoms are of less consequence than the manner in which the disease is communicated. "Civilized" diseases—those depending on person-to-person contact for transmission—are relative newcomers to the human scene, having evolved only after there were sufficiently large host populations capable of sustaining a chain of infection. These conditions did not exist before the development of urbanism with its large population concentrations and continual human interactions.[5] Consequently, most of the major contact diseases, such as measles, mumps, chicken pox, and smallpox, are concomitants of urbanization, dating from about 3000 B.C. in the Old World. In Mexico urbanization began at the outset of the first millennium A.D., a scant fifteen hundred years before the Conquest. Contact diseases had had little time to evolve.[6] This did not mean that the New World was disease-free before 1492;[7] it was, however, free of major epidemics and generalized chronic endemic ailments. Newman (1976:669–71) lists the likely aboriginal New World diseases as follows:

1. Bacillary and amoebic dysentery
2. Viral influenza and pneumonia
3. Various arthritides
4. Various rickettsial fevers, such as verruca or Carrion's disease
5. Various viral fevers
6. American leishmaniasis, such as uta or espundia
7. American trypanosomiasis, such as Chagas' disease
8. Roundworms, especially ascarids
9. Nonvenereal syphilis and pinta
10. Nutritional deficiency diseases
11. Bacterial pathogens, such as streptococcus and staphylococcus
12. Salmonella and other food-poisoning agents and possibly typhus *(matlazahuatl)*.

The scourges of the Old World—smallpox, mumps, measles, scarlet fever, yellow fever, chicken pox—were absent.[8] However, Mexico had achieved population densities sufficiently large to sustain contagious disease organisms in a human-to-human chain.[9] Thus the pre-Columbian environment was a tinderbox into which Old World diseases dropped. Lacking prior contact with the diseases, the population also lacked immunity to them and was devastated by their introduction.[10]

Most of the Mesoamerican epidemics were contact diseases. Survivors of such diseases acquire immunity to further attacks. Thus an outbreak cannot remain at epidemic proportions for long, since exhaustion of the susceptible population eliminates further hosts for the disease. If it persists, the disease is reduced to endemic status.

Regardless of the seriousness of the outbreaks, the greater urban densities of the *tierra fría* should have produced a higher mortality rate.[11] And insofar as contact diseases are concerned, this was apparently the case. However, in addition to European contact diseases the Spaniards also introduced African diseases as an inadvertent consequence of the early slave trade.[12] The most significant of these diseases was malaria.

Malaria is a protozoan disease transmitted by mosquitoes. Although the host mosquito, the anopheles, is indigenous to Mexico, the protozoa are not.[13] Once introduced, however, the disease flourished and, unlike contact diseases, could do so in areas of low population density. But the range of the anopheles generally limited the disease to the tropical lower altitudes. Thus, in addition to the situation in the *tierra fría,* where urban disease was periodically epidemic, the *tierra caliente* also became an area of endemic malaria, slowly but steadily depleting the populace, both Indian and Spanish.

Because of the prevalence of malaria in the lowlands (to which the Spaniards had no more immunity than did the Indians) and the Spaniards' predilection for urban living, the conquerors settled in the highlands, virtually shunning the lowlands. While all of central Mexico experienced a decline in Indian population, it was most marked in the lowlands. As the native population shrank, the Spanish population grew, largely in the highlands, and the slaves the Spaniards imported from Africa, being less susceptible to malaria, were employed and increased largely in the lowlands.[14]

CHAPTER 10

Changing Economic Patterns

BASIC changes in Mexico City's economic pattern were due to (1) new flows of goods, (2) new systems of transportation, and (3) changing labor patterns, inter alia. One factor that greatly shaped Mexico City's post-Conquest role was its relative economic position.

MEXICO AND THE EXTERNAL ECONOMY

Pre-Columbian Tenochtitlan was the apex of a four-tiered marketing structure: *sujeto*-cabecera-regional market-imperial capital. Much of what transpired economically in central Mexico did so at the behest of Tenochtitlan. After the Conquest, however, Mexico became part of a wider economic network.[1] A fifth economic level was added—Spain—and Mexico City no longer independently dominated its market system. Not only were the colonials a ready market for Spanish wares, but the Mexican silver with which they purchased these wares fueled the worldwide flow of goods into Spain. Mexican silver went to Spain as payment for consumer wares and as the royal fifth of all precious metal production: there it was used to support the spice trade with Asia.[2] Much of the flow from and economic development of Mexico was spurred not by internal needs but by those of Spain. The primary flow of goods was no longer to Mexico City (at least not as a final destination) but to Spain. The Mexican economy as a whole was subordinated to the expansive economy of the Spanish empire. While much of New Spain's early economic life was based on indigenous patterns of trade and production, new colonial developments were focused primarily on the needs of the external economy. Thus, while post-Conquest Mexico saw the linkage of major cities and economically productive areas, the newest and most significant development of roads was from these areas to the major ports, reflecting the colonial emphasis on production for export over that for local consumption.

SHIPPING

Spanish shipping had a large and immediate impact on the economic life of Mexico, the internal flow of goods, and existing transportation systems. Although there had been some pre-Columbian coastal shipping, the volume was low, and the transport vessels were rafts and canoes that could be landed and launched from virtually any point along the coast.[3] Spanish shipping altered this. Not only were European goods foreign to Mexico, but quantities were greater, and the requirements of oceangoing ships focused the commerce on fewer suitable ports. Although they were substantially larger than native vessels and also had keels which required greater water depths, the generally small size of Spanish vessels made service feasible to virtually all coastal sites.[4] Other factors, however, further concentrated this commerce in a few sites. Spain's trade with the New World quantitatively expanded preexisting patterns[5] and had a major impact on indigenous economic and transportation patterns.

The economy of New Spain operated along two axes; east–west, connecting Mexico City to the Atlantic port of Veracruz–San Juan de Ulua and the Pacific port of Acapulco, and north–south, connecting Mexico City both to the expanding northern regions of mines and haciendas and to the southern productive areas of Oaxaca and Guatemala as well as to the Pacific ports of Huatulco and Tehuantepec (see map 6).[6] By the early seventeenth century, Thomas Gage was able to say:

> For contraction Mexico is one of the richest cities in the world. By the North Sea cometh every year from Spain a fleet of near twenty ships laden with the best commodities not only of Spain

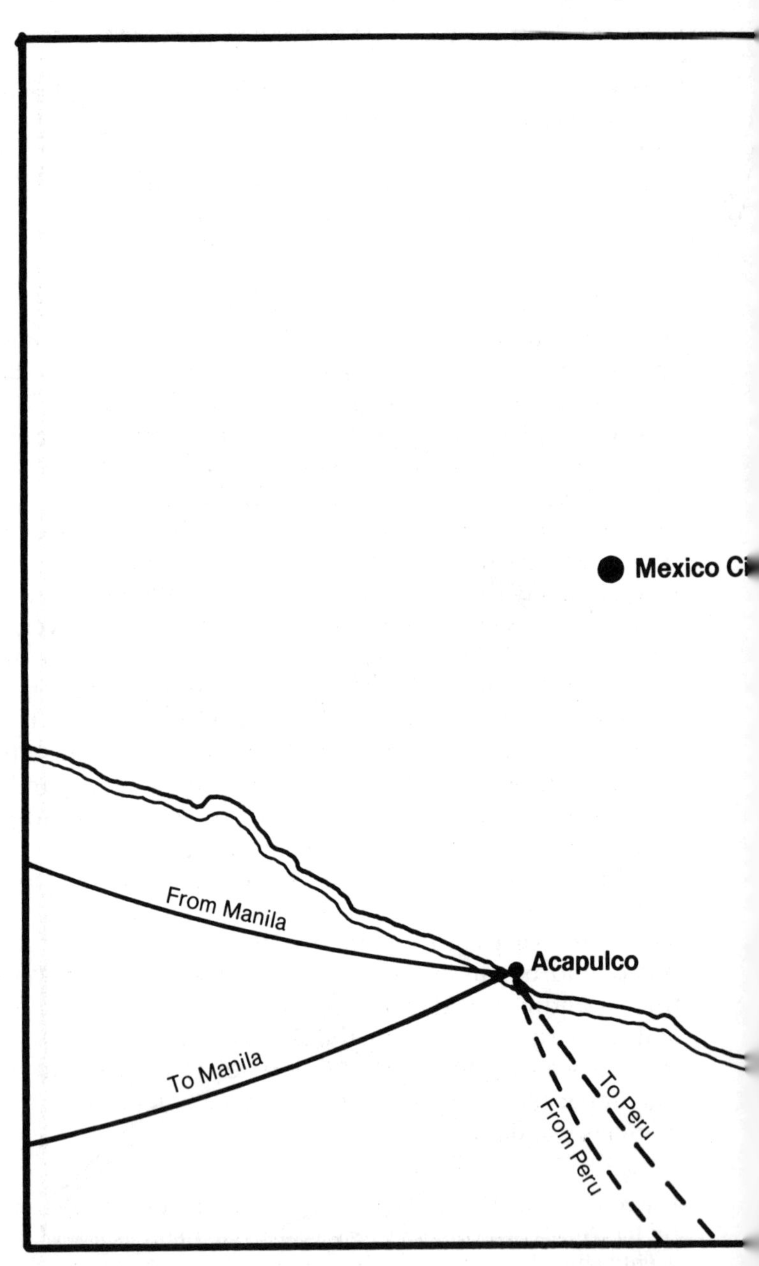

MAP 6. NEW SPAIN'S SHIPPING. Solid lines indicate shipping to and from Spain, Peru, and Manila. Dotted lines indicate the Peruvian shipping routes as of the mid-1570s.

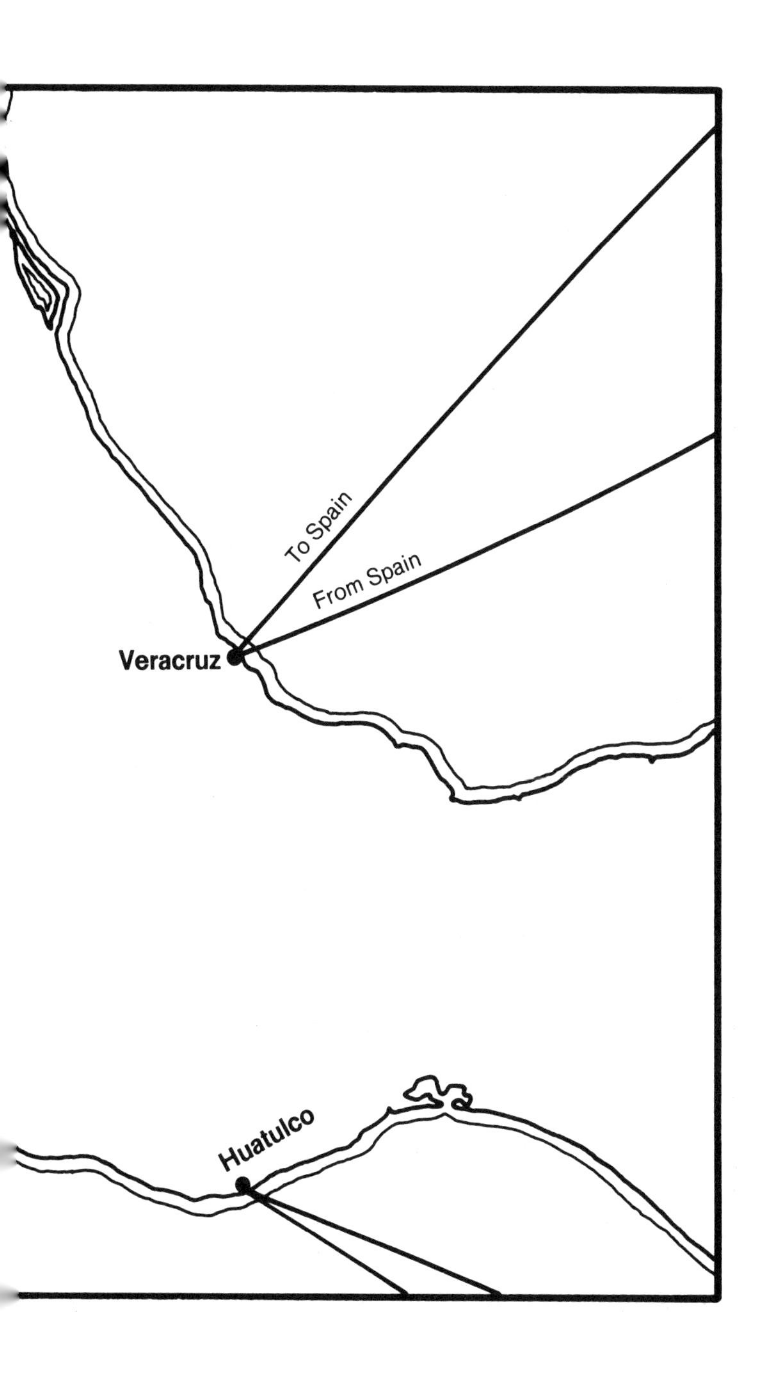
To Spain
From Spain
Veracruz
Huatulco

but of the most parts of Christendom; by the South Sea it enjoyeth traffic from all parts of Peru. Above all, it trades with the East Indies, and from thence receiveth the commodities as well from those parts which are inhabited by Portuguese, as from the countries of Japan and China, sending every year two great *caracas* with two smaller vessels to the Philippine Islands, and having every year a return of such-like ships.[7]

European trade was a new factor in the Mexican economy, and it caused several new problems. The effects of these different goods entering New Spain (some of which could not be sold to or by Indians) was significant, but also important was their impact on the existing transportation systems. Not only were unprecedented quantities arriving in ports, but the timing of their arrival created transportation bottlenecks.

Spain

The Spanish trade originated in Seville and its subsidiary, Cadíz, where it was controlled by comparatively few commercial houses.[8] During the early colonization of the New World, Santo Domingo was the undisputed major port. Its dominance lasted until the early 1520s, when the islands' share of Spanish trade fell off, dropping from three-fourths to one-third by the 1530s. Operating from Veracruz–San Juan de Ulua, Mexico overtook the islands as the major port, but the Peruvian market (and the transshipment of goods across the Isthmus of Panama) rapidly outstripped the Mexican. By the end of the 1540s the islands accounted for 29 percent of the Spanish trade with the New World, Mexico 32 percent, and Panama 39 percent.

For thirty years after 1559, the number of ships engaged in the New World trade remained fairly constant, but the size of the ships increased, rising from an average of 200 tons between 1506 and 1515 to 360 tons between 1600 and 1604. However, Benzoni states that vessels as large as 360 tons were reaching Nombre de Dios between 1541 and 1556.[9] The flow of Spanish wares into Mexico, largely in the form of manufactured goods and some Spanish consumables, such as wine and oil, was met by a counterflow of Mexican silver.[10]

Initially, shipping to the New World was relatively unorganized, but climatic conditions and political events altered this. As trade increased, a standard route came into use. Leaving from Cadíz or San Lucar, Spain, ships sailed south to the Canary Islands, then west, catching the trade winds and westward currents to the Antilles. There they diverged, the ships engaged in the Peruvian trade going to Panama, while the ships bound for Mexico and the West Indies sailed north to Santo Domingo and Veracruz.[11] The journey from Cadíz to Veracruz took two to three months.[12] The return voyage was by way of Havanna, through the Bahama Channel, then northeast between the Virginia capes and the Bermudas to about 38 degrees latitude to catch the southward winds, and east to the Azores and Spain.[13] The return journey was somewhat longer than the voyage to Veracruz, requiring about four and a half months.[14] Sailings to the New World usually took place in the spring to avoid the hurricane season and the "northers" in the Gulf of Mexico,[15] but the flow of traffic was otherwise little organized.

In 1543 war broke out between France and Spain, and French predations on Spanish shipping forced some changes. Convoys had been instituted as early as 1537, but in 1543 the Indies trade was limited to ships of at least 100 tons and convoys of ten or more ships. The organization of these convoys varied during the early years, but by the mid-1560s it had become standardized. There were two sailings per year from Spain, one in April (advanced to May as of 1582) for New Spain, known as the *flota,* or fleet, and one in August for Panama, known as the *galeones,* or galleons.[16] Both fleets wintered in the New World and returned to Spain together to protect the rich return cargoes from pirates. They sailed from their respective ports to Havana, where they formed the armada, sailing for Spain in June.[17] Without exception all ships in port lading for Spain were required to sail with the fleet.

Thus imports entered New Spain through the port of Veracruz–San Juan de Ulua in June or July, and exports exited in May. Although adherence to this schedule was loose, the net effect of the *flota* system was to concentrate arriving traffic and imports in a few peak weeks. The concentration of shipping had two important consequences; land conditions, such as the seasonal rains, determined the schedules and quantity of tlameme journeys in pre-Columbian times. But now, the demands of the *flota* schedule were of primary consideration. Moreover, the relatively low but steady demand for land transport generated by the pre-*flota* pattern of casual shippage was now concentrated into a few peak months (see fig. 10.1).

Peru

Although both New Spain and Peru were linked to Spain by ships supplying basically similar goods, a profitable trade sprang up between the two countries as early as 1536. In addition to maintaining considerable traffic in passengers, Mexico exported manufactured goods, horses, and European foodstuffs, in exchange for silver. Peru traded with Mexico because it was cheaper to import Mexican goods—goods of Mexican manufacture or surplus Spanish goods—than to import goods directly from Spain. The Peruvian civil wars of the 1530s, 1540s, and 1550s increased the demand for Mexican horses and arms, while the specie shortage in New Spain was partly alleviated by the quantities obtained from silver-rich Peru. The mercury-amalgam mining process, introduced in New Spain in 1555, further spurred the Peruvian trade. Following the discovery of a mercury source at Huancavelica, Peru, in 1567, mercury was exported to Mexico, although the Spanish policy of protecting its own mercury exports periodically disrupted this trade.[18]

Climatic factors concentrated this trade temporally, causing some difficulties, but ships plying the Peruvian trade were smaller than the Atlantic ships (private vessels ranged from 35 to 180 tons, whereas royal treasure ships

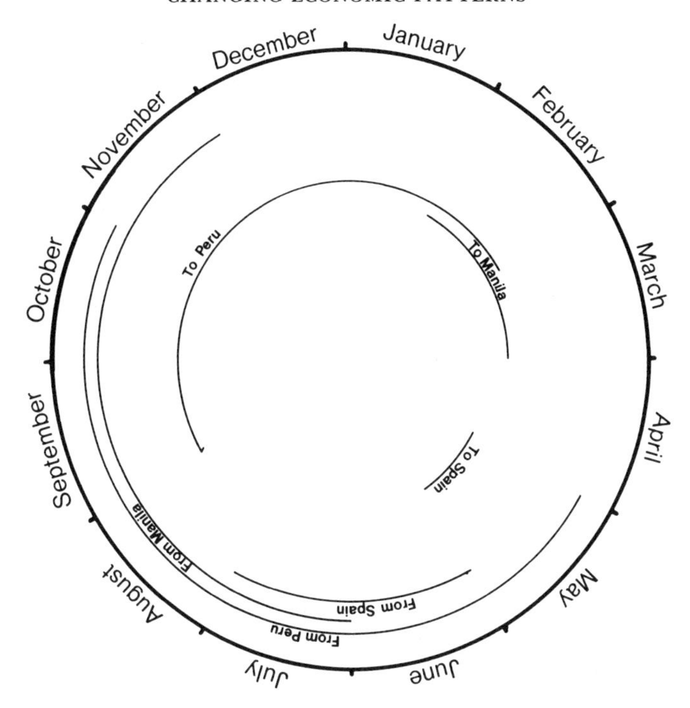

FIG. 10.1. PORT TRAFFIC. Arrivals and departures for the three major overseas commodity flows.

ranged from 200 to 365 tons), so this transport bottleneck was less severe than the one in Veracruz. Most of the year, especially from April to September, the prevailing winds along the South American coast are from the southeast, while uncertain winds and frequent prolonged calms typify conditions along the Central American coast. Consequently, travel southward was slow and difficult, requiring seven or eight months. Travel northward, however, was favorable, requiring only four to six weeks. From October to April there is a partial shift in winds and currents, resulting in northern winds. Movements southward normally began between late September and the end of

February and required two to three months or more.[19] Thus goods for export flowed into the port of Huatulco from September to February, while imported wares arrived from May to October. Initially the Peruvian trade was concentrated in the port of Tehuantepec, but greater storm protection and a better harbor led to an early shift to the port of Huatulco, 80 miles west of Tehuantepec by sea.[20] Huatulco was the principal harbor from 1537 to 1575 because it could be easily reached by land. Although not as good a harbor as Acapulco, Huatulco remained the focal point of Pacific shipping because upgrading the existing Indian trail to Huatulco was much easier than building a road to Acapulco.[21] After 1585, with the increased importance of the Manila trade, Acapulco became the principal Pacific port and Huatulco declined.[22]

Manila

Although Magellan visited the Philippines in 1521, the Spanish presence there did not begin until 1565.[23] Trade between Mexico and the Philippines began in 1573 and consisted of Chinese and Japanese goods—silks, satins, and porcelain—flowing into Mexico in exchange for silver and smaller quantities of cacao, cochineal, oil, and wine.[24] Acapulco was probably settled as early as 1530, but the port was little used, for the trip from Mexico City took a month by tlameme. A road between the capital and Acapulco was built in the 1560s, but Huatulco remained easier to reach until a better road was constructed in 1573 or 1574, reducing the travel time to six to ten days.[25] The Pacific port of La Navidad on the north had handled some of the early Manila trade, but that traffic too shifted to the superior natural harbor of Acapulco.[26]

Climatic conditions in the Pacific patterned the flow of trade to an even greater degree than they did in the Atlantic. The journey from Acapulco to Manila was relatively safe and easy. Although pirates were active, they did not prove to be a serious threat to the Manila galleons during the sixteenth century. However, one galleon was captured off Baja California by English pirates in the early seventeenth century.[27] Ships usually sailed from Mexico in late February or early March, taking advantage of the westward trade winds between the equator and the 30 degrees north parallel,[28] and arrived in Manila eight to twelve weeks later. The return journey, however, was long and hazardous. Leaving Manila in March, between the two regular monsoon seasons, the ships sailed northeast for two months to get above the westward flows. In the 30s and 40s north latitudes an eastward wind propelled the ships to the coast of California, whence they sailed southeast to Acapulco. The entire journey from Manila to Acapulco required four to eight months, averaging six.[29]

Thus goods for export to Manila entered Acapulco during January and February while imported wares from Manila arrived in Acapulco between July and November. The volume of the Manila trade was relatively low, the Pacific ships being limited to 300 tons or less.[30] But Manila was not Acapulco's sole trading partner: coastal and Peruvian trade made up a large portion of the port traffic. The Peruvian trade pattern of September-to-February sailings and May-to-October arrivals largely complemented the Manila trade pattern of February-to-March sailings and July-to-November arrivals.

The impact on the indigenous transportation systems of local changes, such as great quantities of goods, heavy loads, long distances, and general depopulation, was dramatic. But New Spain's incorporation into a larger economic system also undermined the tlameme system and promoted the development of competing Spanish systems. Climatological factors (winds and currents) and political events (wars and pirates) combined to foster a tighter scheduling of sailings. These sailings, for both imports and exports, were responsible for the commercial pulsations of Mexican foreign trade.

Spanish goods entered the Atlantic port of Veracruz during June and July, and Mexican goods left during May. Huatulco experienced its greatest exodus from September to February and its greatest influx from May to October, and Acapulco subsequently picked up this pattern in Peruvian trade plus adding the Manila trade leaving Mexico in late February or early March and returning between July and November. The Veracruz goods arrived at the beginning of the rainy season, as did much of the Peruvian and Manila trade. Furthermore, these arrivals occurred during the summer months, the most unhealthy period in the *tierra caliente.* Mexican exports, however, did benefit by this scheduling, commodities going to the ports during the cooler dry months. The schedules of arrivals and departures did not affect imports and exports equally, however, since goods for export could flow more casually into the ports, whereas the imports had to be removed from the unhealthy lowlands to more suitable locales with all haste.

The foregoing merely highlights the inconveniences generated by the scheduling of shipping. A more significant consequence was its impact on the tlamemes. The steadily increasing, and now intensely concentrated, shipping from Spain and elsewhere strained the tlameme system beyond its limits. Previously the numbers of tlamemes available had been adequate given the gradual flow of goods year round. But now the concentration of demand far exceeded the numbers of bearers available at one time. Overland haulage had to be increased but the men necessary to expand the labor-intensive tlameme system were unavailable. The growing Spanish transport systems—*arrieros* (mule drivers) and *carreteros* (wagoneers)—now proved indispensable. Although expanding these systems required a greater capital investment, they required a much smaller increase in manpower per ton-mile, and only by expanding these Spanish transportation systems could the volume of shippage be maintained. Tlamemes continued to play a part in New Spain's transport system and to supply ancillary services, both separately and in conjunction with *arrieros* and *carreteros,* but the concentration of demand had revealed the inelasticity of the indigenous system in contrast to that of the Spaniards.

ROUTE DEVELOPMENT

Internal colonial economic development and Mexico's external trade were tied to the development of roads. The indigenous roads were woefully inadequate for Spanish transport needs. Pre-Columbian roads were not well developed beyond the confines of major urban centers, particularly beyond the central highlands.[31] Not intended for wagons or draft animals, the indigenous roads were rough, hilly, and twisting, factors of little concern for foot traffic.[32] In the course of the sixteenth century new ones were constructed. The pattern of these roads followed the Mexican economic growth along east–west and north-south axes. East–west was the Veracruz–Mexico City–Acapulco axis, and north–south followed the continued northern expansion of the Camino Real as mining and cattle areas opened up and proceeded southward through Oaxaca. The axes crossed in the commercial hub, Mexico City (see map 7).[33]

The first and most important of the major routes was that between Veracruz and Mexico City. In 1524 or 1525, Cortés ordered the establishment of inns *(ventas)* to serve traffic from Veracruz to Mexico City, but during the first half century there was no fixed route between the two cities.[34] The routes gradually stabilized as establishments such as inns, monasteries, and hospitals developed.

Traditional Indian labor drafts were used for road maintenance, but Spaniards were placed in authority at an early date.[35] It was charged that needed repairs were not made owing to the absence of anyone paid to oversee the work.[36] The first evidence of government road construction dates from 1530, when the cabildo (city council) of Mexico City referred to a new road running to Veracruz that would allow passage of wagons, although the first wagons were not introduced until 1531.[37] This road de-

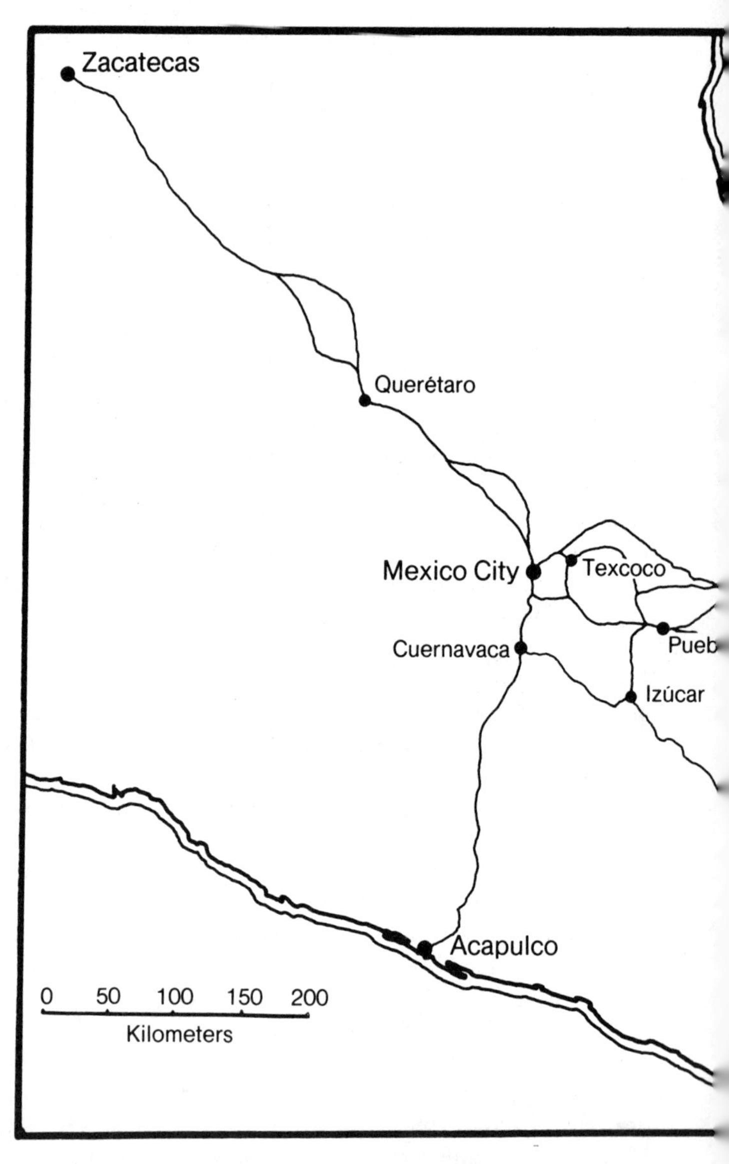

MAP 7. THE MAIN ROADS IN NEW SPAIN IN THE SIXTEENTH CENTURY (derived from Borah 1954:27; Chance 1978:54; Powell 1952:20; Rees 1971:112; and Schurz 1939:385).

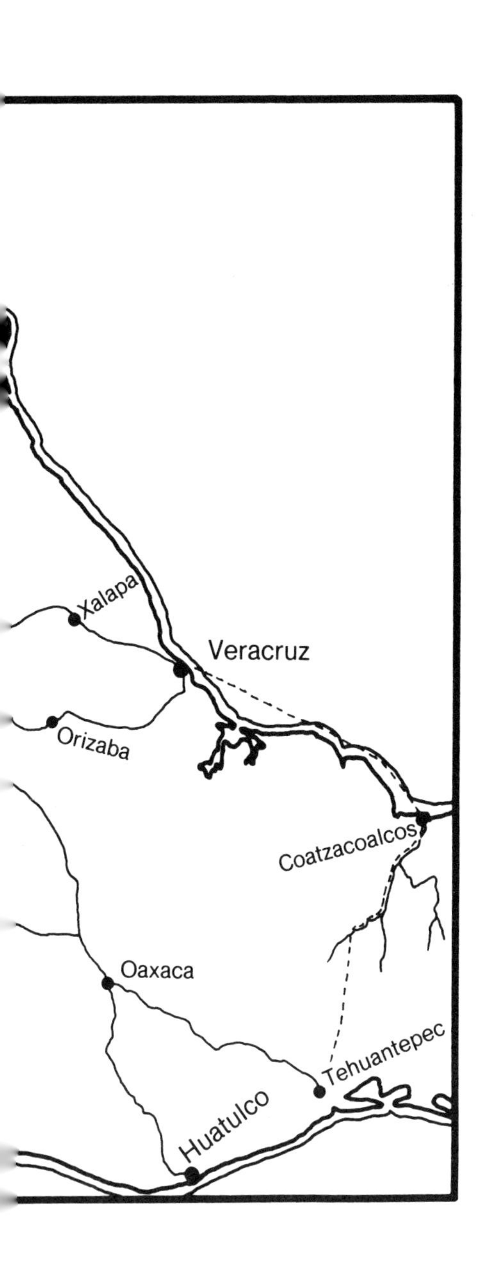

Xalapa
Veracruz
Orizaba
Coatzacoalcos
Oaxaca
Tehuantepec
Huatulco

parted from the route previously used to avoid difficult terrain and because of the need for adequate water and pasturage for the animals.[38]

The Spanish practice of staying in private Indian homes and eating the Indians' food without adequate compensation led to a regulation prohibiting the practice where there were inns on the road. Where there were none, Spaniards could continue to stay and eat in Indian homes, but these services had to be paid for at the common value.[39] Although Spanish officials attempted to shift the wagon route away from Indian villages[40] to avoid the damage caused by travelers, this did not lead to the establishment of an exclusive route. Rather, two main routes developed between Mexico City and Veracruz. One passed through Indian villages, and the other traversed an unpopulated area, but there were inns where all the necessary goods could be bought. Despite this, the removal from Indian towns was not always popular. Speaking of La Rinconada in the early seventeenth century, Thomas Gage stated: "This place stands so far from any other town that travellers can scarce make their journeys without either baiting there at noon, or lying there at night, or declining three or four miles out of the road to some Indian town."[41] It was by this latter route that wagons and mule trains traveled, few Spaniards going by the populated route except for those on horses.[42]

Puebla was founded in 1531 between Mexico City and Veracruz, but it did not lead to an immediate shift in route. Some wagon traffic was passing through Puebla by 1550, but most continued to use the older, more direct route to Mexico City.[43] By 1570 the two major routes to Mexico City ran to the Venta de Caceras (present-day Oriental), where the route divided into the Puebla road and the Camino de las Ventas. They were of roughly equal distance, but the wagon route passed through less populated and flatter land. By this time the previously important commercial city of Texcoco was no longer on the route, the two roads skirting the city and going either south through Chalco (the Puebla route) or north through Ecatepec (the wagon road). By 1590 an alternate route from Mexico City to Veracruz ran through Orizaba, leaving two major routes, one by way of Orizaba and the other by way of Xalapa.[44]

The route from Mexico City south to Oaxaca passed through existing towns. Spanish road building began in 1529, and by midcentury Antequera (Oaxaca City) was a major stopping point,[45] connected to Mexico City by several major routes. One ran south through Cuernavaca, then southeast to Izúcar, where it joined the other road from Mexico City that ran through Puebla. From Izúcar the road ran southeast through Acatlan and a series of valleys—Tamazulapan, Teposcolula, and Nochixtlan—and into the Valley of Oaxaca. Another major road from Mexico City went to Puebla and proceeded through Tepeaca, Tecamachalco, Tehuacan, and Cuicatlan, both major roads passing through Seda. The sequence in which these roads were developed is uncertain.[46] Apparently the Mexico City-Puebla-Tehuacan-Antequera route was one of the first, construction having begun in 1531, the Antequera-Tehuacan portion being completed by 1544. The impetus for building the road was to allow the passage of mule trains and wagons from Mexico City, and from Veracruz by way of Puebla, to Oaxaca. The Mexico City-Izúcar-Antequera road was less used. By midcentury two other important routes were in use[47] to Huatulco by way of Miahuatlan and to Tehuantepec (and thence to Guatemala) by way of Tlacochahuaya, Tlacolula, Totolapa, Nejapa, and Jalapa del Marqués.

In a report of 1547 the viceroy recorded having opened roads from Mexico City to Acapulco, Oaxaca, Huatulco, Tehuantepec, Michoacán, Colima, Jalisco, Pánuco, the mines of Taxco, Zultepec, and Zumpango, while repairing those to Veracruz.[48] A lesser though still important route connected Tehuantepec to Veracruz.[49] Traveling by sea from Veracruz to Coatzacoalcos, canoes were employed to go up the Coatzacoalcos River to Antigua Malpaso, where land transport was employed for the remaining 12 leagues to Tehuantepec. This route was also employed in traveling between Mexico City and Tehuantepec or Huatulco, for the Mexico City–Veracruz road was the best in New Spain, and water transportation was easier than overland travel. The route was also used to transport bulky objects, such as ships' gear, brought into Veracruz and bound for the Pacific ports.

The route from Mexico City northward developed as the economic potential of that region was exploited. The decade between 1545 and 1555 saw the real opening of roads into the mining areas of the north, spurred by the silver strike at Zacatecas. No effective Spanish entry into the north had been made beyond the area inhabited by sedentary Indian groups until 1543,[50] when Viceroy Antonio de Mendoza began making land grants in the area, largely for livestock pasturage. The discovery of silver at Zacatecas in late 1546, however, proved to be the real stimulus for road construction. The Camino Real was extended from Mexico City to Querétaro and Zacatecas between 1550 and 1555, allowing the passage of mule trains and large wagons,[51] and supply routes were opened between Zacatecas, Michoacán, and Guadalajara.

The western route ran from Mexico City to Acapulco. Although Viceroy Mendoza mentioned having built the road by 1547, whatever work was done was of minor consequence, and the route was not important until the beginning of the Manila trade in the 1570s. The road began in Acapulco and ran through Chilpancingo, crossed the Río de las Balsas, and continued through Tuspa and Cuernavaca to Mexico City. Although adequate for *recuas* (packtrains), the road could not accommodate wagons during the sixteenth century.[52]

In addition to these major long-distance routes, construction began on roads directly concerned with the provisioning of Mexico City. Thus roads were opened to the Valley of Matlatcingo and the villa of Toluca,[53] and repairs continued on roads to closer towns.

Much of what dictated route patterns was not simply the productive areas of Mexico, although these were important, but also ports. What determined ports was primarily the existence of good harbors. In keeping with this concern, the original settlement of Veracruz was moved 6 leagues to a harbor offering ships greater protection from northern winds.[54] Other significant factors in selecting a port were the distance of their routes to Mexico City and proximity to areas above the unhealthy *tierra caliente.*[55] Veracruz was a wealthy town, being the focal point of trade from all the New World and the Orient bound for Spain. But because of endemic disease the town had few inhabitants.[56] The merchants lived above the *tierra caliente* in Xalapa, the nearest town so situated and to which the imported goods could be quickly removed. There the merchandise was sold to other merchants at the annual *feria* (fair).

The ports held a *feria* following the arrival of the ships. Patterned after the fairs of Spain, and distinguished from *mercados,* or markets, by their annual rather than monthly or more frequent occurrence, they were primarily wholesale markets for merchants. The fair for the port of Veracruz was held in Xalapa owing to the climate. The first formal fair in Xalapa was held in 1561, and the practice persisted until 1778. Since Acapulco lacked a convenient *tierra fría* location, it was the site of its own fair, lasting twenty to thirty days, beginning as early as January 20 and lasting as late as February 25. This fair, with the attendant swelling of Acapulco's population, lasted into the nineteenth century.[57] Neither the Atlantic port of Veracruz nor the Pacific port of Acapulco was occupied during much of the year.[58]

LABOR

One of the most crucial factors in New Spain's economy was, of course, labor and its availability. While there was always some free Indian labor that, other than through taxation, remained uncommitted to the Spanish colonial economy, much Indian labor was organized for effective exploitation by the Spaniards. These labor systems, encomienda, repartimiento, and "free" labor, changed during the century, each yielding to its successor grudgingly and varying by locale and political influence. Under the encomienda system Indians were assigned to specified Spaniards, often as a reward for service to the crown. The Indians held in encomienda were not chattel, but the encomendero was allowed to exact tribute from them in goods and labor. In return the encomendero was obliged, among other things, to provide military service and to Christianize his charges. Thus wealth in early New Spain was the recognized right to Indian labor. This system was abused, however, and the crown sought to curtail it in the Indies as early as 1513 and to end it in 1520. Faced with the demands of the conquistadors, the effort failed, but repeated attempts to curtail the institution led to its replacement (though hardly its extinction) by the repartimiento after 1550. Repartimiento, or corvée, was the allotment of Indian labor to Spanish employers by Spanish political authorities. The laborers assigned in repartimiento were drawn from each Indian community and were allocated for specific durations and tasks. This practice too was abused, and in the late sixteenth century the crown sought to replace it with "free" Indian labor.[59]

Encomienda was established in an era of plentiful labor. But with a declining population, it was doomed as a form of labor extraction. Attempts to alter the prevailing labor systems antedate the epidemics of 1545–48 and 1576–81, and ethical and religious motivations for their change cannot be discounted. But the effective shift in labor systems closely followed the major population declines in New Spain, and the explanation of the changes has been closely allied with these. That is, traditionally, both the shift in labor systems and the health of the economy have been viewed as altering in direct response to these precipitous declines.[60]

Certainly a population loss of the magnitude suggested for New Spain would have had a major impact on the economy, but these epidemics were not the proximate cause of the change in labor systems. As appealing as is the apparent causal tie between total population and labor, the emphasis on gross population has been misplaced. The demographic characteristics of the population in question, and not merely its size, are of primary importance in understanding the shift in labor systems. Unfortunately, the available sixteenth-century data are not sufficiently detailed to reconstruct the actual characteristics of the Mexican population, particularly for the years before the 1560s, and population reconstructions by modern scholars have not met with general agreement. And, in any case, these modern estimates have concentrated on total population and not on such demographic characteristics as age and sex. Actual population data are inadequate, unavailable, or unreliable, but reconstructions based on a detailed demographic model are also unrewarding.[61] In light of what is known of sixteenth-century conditions and events, a general consideration of population dynamics is more persuasive in outlining central Mexican demographic history.

As mentioned above, there were many epidemics in sixteenth-century central Mexico (although the diseases responsible were not always clear) and several famines. The demographic consequences of both these types of events, pestilence and famine, are marked. In both pestilence and famine mortality increases, while fertility remains constant in the former and declines sharply in the latter.[62] Following these catastrophes there is a population rebound as the famine-induced fertility decline reverses itself, and also because the mortality rate is abnormally low, the more vulnerable segments of the population already having died under the stress of famine and plague. Thus the progression of the population, even in sixteenth-century central Mexico, was not unrelievedly downward. Of more significance, however, was the age-sex structure of the surviving population. Both disease and famine strike hardest at the most vulnerable segments of the population, the young, the old, and the infirm. While this is generally true of famine,[63] the mortality rate differs by disease. Various segments of society were affected in varying degrees by the main epidemic diseases of the sixteenth-century, smallpox (variola major) and typhus.

Smallpox is a self-immunizing disease. Survivors acquire immunity to further attacks. Thus although the entire Mexican population was susceptible to the initial smallpox outbreak in 1520, subsequent outbreaks affected only those not immune, that is, the young born since the last epidemic. The much lower incidence of smallpox among those over twenty-five is usually explained as the result of previous contact with the disease, but this lower incidence among older persons cannot be explained solely on that basis.[64] Consequently, the age pattern of those stricken may be skewed further than mere epidemiological factors would indicate.

Data for unvaccinated populations are scarce and those that are available are not reflective of the immunologically virgin populations present in sixteenth-century Mexico. Nevertheless, it is clear that the mortality rate among the young (birth to ten years of age, but especially for those birth to five) was the highest,[65] because that age group had both a higher death rate and a greater incidence of infection. Thus, the mortality rate would be further skewed against the young.

Typhus, also a self-immunizing disease, has a 10 to 40 percent fatality rate. However, this mortality rate is also skewed by age, ranging from 10 percent for those under thirty years of age to 50+ percent for those over sixty. Again, however, the incidence of disease (not the mortality rate) appears to be much higher among the young.[66] Consequently, typhus also would skew the mortality rate against the young.

Although there are general estimates of disease-induced mortality, such as 30 to 50 percent for the epidemic of 1520,[67] a simple reduction of the total population by such an amount is misleading. Neither disease nor famine is age-blind (nor is it sex-blind, although this factor is of less significance for the issue at hand).[68] Consequently, the aftermath of these catastrophes would not see the pre-event population uniformly diminished. The disease would have thinned the population of its old and young to a much greater extent than its middle ages, leaving a smaller but age-skewed population.

While the pestilence deaths were individually tragic, at the population level there were beneficial consequences. The population reduction permitted the abandonment of less fertile lands in favor of more fertile ones, thus increasing individual agricultural productivity. But, more important, the dependency ratio—the number of dependents per productive adult—changed. Since dependents, the old, the young, and the infirm, died in disproportionate numbers, their numbers dropped relative to productive adults. Consequently, regardless of any increase in individual productivity, economic surplus increased as goods were freed that previously had gone to support the more numerous dependents. The surviving population thus not only was more vigorous but produced a greater surplus: the postpestilence economic situation was actually favorable, particularly to the Spaniards, whose incomes came from Indian surplus. Although the numbers of Indians were reduced, the per capita surplus they generated was increased.

This favorable circumstance was, however, temporary. The portion of the population that survived in greatest numbers (those between the ages of about fifteen and forty-five) was the most productive, both economically and sexually. And since this age group now made up a disproportionately high percentage of the total population, per capita fertility was higher than it was in the prepestilence population. Consequently, ten to fifteen years later, the population profile had greatly altered, and so too had its economic profile. Many of the people who had been in the productive ages were now older, having become dependents themselves, and the baby boom had produced a larger population. But since this segment of the population was still under fifteen years of age, the boom produced only additional dependents and not yet any productive adults. Thus the dependency ratio had swung disadvantageously. The population deficit created by the pestilence was no longer concentrated among the dependents; rather, as that cohort aged, the deficit had as well, until the productive ages now suffered from a dearth of workers. Moreover, per capita production of surplus was down, most economic production going to support the increased percentage of dependents in the population. Consequently, while the total population may have been as large as or larger than the immediate postpestilence population, economically it was inervated (see fig. 10.2).

This trend was further accelerated by recurrent pestilences. Not only were the young more susceptible anyway, but the older segments of the population had acquired immunity by virtue of their prior exposure. So the population continued to age, with a dwindling percentage of productive workers to support it. By focusing on the timing of the major epidemics (those of 1520–21, 1545–48, and 1576–81), the mortality characteristics of the diseases (and famines) involved and the ripple effects they had through time, it is apparent that the economic and labor problems experienced by New Spain during the sixteenth century were not simply the result of the epidemic-caused population declines. Rather, these pestilences cut away at the existing population in such a way that initially invigorated it yet contained the seeds of its destruction. And the problems this caused can be seen before the major declines. The first major labor shortage arose in the latter part of the 1530s, not because there were fewer Indians but because there were fewer Indians of the appropriate age category. Thus a law restricting the use of Indians under eighteen years of age as tlamemes reflected the increasing practice among Spaniards of seizing younger men as laborers.[69] This was the period in which the encomienda began to crumble.

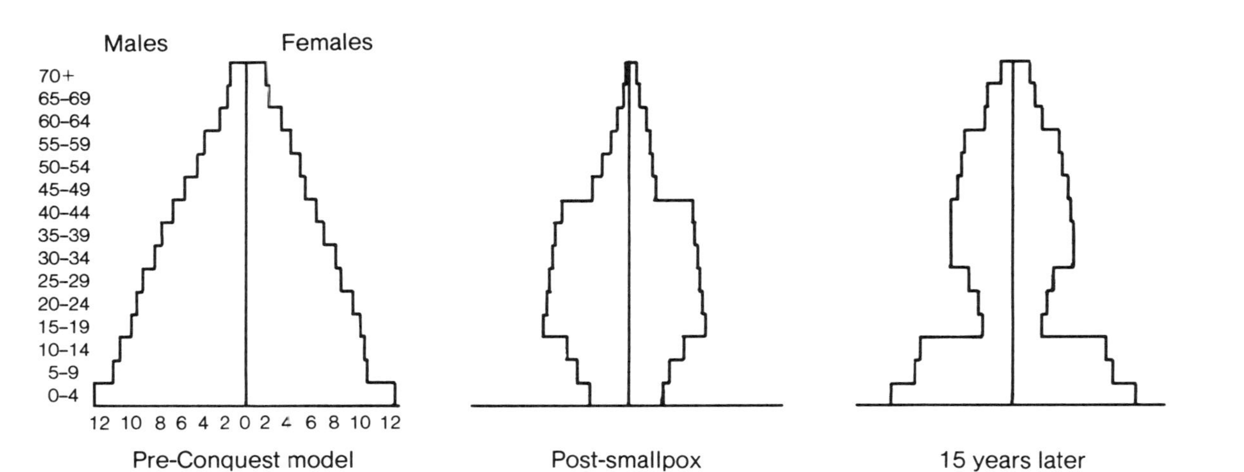

FIG. 10.2. POPULATION STRUCTURE. Indigenous population of central Mexico displayed according to age and sex. The first population pyramid presents the pre-Conquest population, the second the immediate post-smallpox population, and the third the resultant populational skewing fifteen years after the epidemic. (These are models only; actual calculations based on West model and unvaccinated European populations produced unreliable estimates.)

The depopulation of 1545–48 probably had another beneficial effect by temporarily reducing the dependency ratio and economically reinvigorating the population. But the economic cycle that followed necessarily began on a lower scale because the overall population was seriously reduced. A similar though necessarily smaller-scale pattern probably occurred in the mid- to late 1560s as the productive-population bulge aged and the deficit moved into the productive age range, again reversing the dependency ratio, changing it from favorable to unfavorable. No doubt a similar pattern followed the population declines of 1576–81, but the effects were of even less significance, for by then the total population had been so seriously eroded that the dependency differential would have had an insignificant impact on New Spain's economy. While the pestilence-induced population declines were the most salient demographic features of the sixteenth century, particularly when seen from a distance of four hundred years, they were not the cause of the shifting labor systems. The precipitating factor in altering these labor systems was the 10- to 15-year delayed demographic consequences of the diseases and famines that led to an age-skewed population.

Both the shifting labor pool and the massive native population decline during the sixteenth century had profound effects on the Spanish colonists. By virtue of their status as conquerors, as colonists, and simply as Spaniards, the Europeans entered New Spain's economy at the higher levels, as the de facto upper class. Any upper class is necessarily small in relation to the number in the middle and lower classes that support it. Immediately after the Conquest the large Indian population easily supported the few Spaniards as well as the indigenous elite. The initial depopulation (following the plague of 1520–21) had little impact on the Spaniards, for their entry into the economy postdated it. In fact, the resulting lower dependency ratio was beneficial to the Spaniards' intrusion into the native economy in providing a greater per capita surplus that could then be appropriated. During the century, however, this Spaniard-native population ratio shifted. While the Indians were massively and disadvantageously affected by disease, the Spaniards were not. Centuries of acclimation had left the Spaniards less vulnerable to Old World diseases than were the Indians. Accordingly the Spaniards died in smaller numbers. The result was that the Spaniards then constituted a larger percentage of the total population.

In a society in which the upper class is directly supported by the middle and lower classes, any erosion of the latter undermines the position of the former, since a diminished lower class cannot support the resulting larger per capita upper class. Time and native depopulation increased the burden on the lower classes, which were unable to continue supporting the Spaniards as they had. Consequently, Spaniards increasingly occupied lower relative positions in society as previously upper-class Spaniards shifted downward to occupy the middle classes.[70] Thus in population the Spaniards suffered less than the Indians, but their relative social standing declined more precipitously.

The overburden of Spaniards was further accelerated by their continual immigration from Spain. The flow of immigrants was affected not only by the eroding Spanish social position in New Spain but also by their arrival in relation to the shifting native labor pool. The state of that labor pool largely determined the economic prospects of the immigrants. One's economic fortunes were considerably enhanced if immigration occurred at a time when the Indian dependency ratio was low. Entry into the upper ranks of society was considerably easier when Indian labor was plentiful and the natives' per capita production of surplus was high. Conversely, when the Indians' dependency ratio was high and little per capita surplus was produced, entrenched Spanish interests and the lack of available Indian labor combined to exclude the immigrants from the upper classes. Accordingly, migrants in these years were middle class and came to the New World with professional or artisan skills,[71] entering professions analogous to those of the Indians; that is, a Spaniard would not become a tlameme or a mano-and-metate corn grinder, but he might become an *arriero* or a miller.

Since voluntary migration is motivated by opportunities in the land of immigration,[72] the shifting native labor situation in New Spain (and consequent economic prospects) should have had an impact on Spanish immigration. Thus immigration should have been greater when the Indian dependency ratio was low and less when the ratio was high, although the impact of such shifts should have lessened through the course of the sixteenth century as the total Indian population declined. And such appears to have been the case, for Spanish immigration experienced severe drops in the 1540s and 1550s and again in the 1580s and 1590s.

The dip in migration to New Spain is not unambiguous, however.[73] Immigration to Peru accelerated at this time and could account for the decline in those bound for New Spain. But this would still indicate that there was no decline in potential immigrants in Spain and would reflect a perception of greater promise in Peru and a lesser promise in New Spain. Also, when the New Laws of 1542–43 threatened to curtail Spanish rights to Indian labor (at a time when the Indian dependency ratio was unfavorable), more than six hundred families left New Spain, and arguments were made that legal reforms should encourage migration there.[74]

Thus the changing demographic situation in New Spain resulted in a continuous degrading of the social status of Spaniards. And the fluctuating native dependency ratio affected both the rate of Spanish immigration and the economic and social fate of those who did migrate. Such prospects may also have altered the social composition of migrants, since the varying social prospects in New Spain would undoubtedly have attracted different groups with different aspirations and expectations.

TRANSPORTATION

Patterns of production shifted substantially throughout the sixteenth century, partly owing to changes in demand but in large part owing to changes in the transport systems that hauled the produce to the major markets. Indigenous forms of transportation were augmented by Spanish forms, wagons and draft animals.

Pack animals are an improvement over foot travel, and animal-drawn wagons are an improvement over pack animals, but each method of transportation has its own topographical limitations.[75] To the extent that improved transportation affects regional economies, the introduction of Spanish systems of transportation into New Spain may be justifiably seen as a major revolution.[76] But while the impact of these systems in New Spain was significant, it was neither as immediate nor as devastating as would be expected a fortiori. Rather, existing social institutions and cultural practices mediated and moderated their adoption.

Overland

Tlamemes, the basic means of transport before the Conquest, did not vanish with the introduction of mules despite the apparent advantages of the latter.[77] One reason for the continued reliance on tlamemes was the lack of viable alternatives. Until midcentury both livestock numbers and production were low in New Spain.[78] Faced with the great expense of shipping animals from Spain, crown policy was to encourage livestock production in the New World. Having begun in the Indies, livestock production remained centered there, and the 1520s saw a struggle between island and mainland producers for the right to breed livestock. Initially mainland producers were not allowed to engage in stock raising, but the ban was finally lifted in 1525.[79] The initial hindrance to the Spanish transport systems caused by the dearth of draft animals did not trouble tlamemes. The patterns of tlameme use, as well as the conditions of their labor, did, however, change substantially.

The Spaniards did little about most of the factors affecting tlameme use—depopulation, increasing transport demand, rudimentary support systems, and inadequate numbers of draft animals. Indeed, many of these difficulties were not fully recognized by the Spaniards. Even had they been aware of the problems, they would have been able to do little about them. Instead, the Spanish response was to mandate legal restrictions on Indian labor, and it is the records of these efforts that largely trace the patterns of tlameme use.

Royal and viceregal laws and policies repeatedly tried to curtail the exploitation of native labor, including tlamemes. Spanish regulation of Indian bearers began in the West Indies before the Conquest of Mexico. In 1511 the king prohibited the use of Indians of Hispaniola to carry burdens since their numbers were greatly diminished, and the Indians of San Juan were prohibited from carrying loads greater than 25 pounds and from carrying them over rough terrain.[80] From the outset royal policy was concerned with the effects of portage on the natives and sought to place limits on its use. In New Spain tlamemes were employed from the earliest contact, but in 1528 the Ordinances of Toledo forbade forcing Indians to become tlamemes.[81] Rather than imposing an absolute ban on their use, the Council of the Indies (which was subordinate only to the king) recognized the necessity of tlamemes and outlawed only their use by force. As long as their labor was voluntary and compensated, it remained permissible.[82] The king did, however, ban the use of tlamemes to supply the mines.[83] Massive labor drafts occurred during those early years, however, such as Nuño de Guzmán's use of 1,500 tlamemes to carry maize from Huexotzinco to Mexico City.[84]

Tlamemes were regarded as necessary and were recognized as a legitimate occupational class whose livelihood depended on this form of labor.[85] Thus by 1531 the governing Audiencia (the ruling body of New Spain, subordinate to the Council of the Indies and to the viceroy) established regulations for their use: carrying was to be voluntary; tlamemes were to be paid 100 cacaos a day (worth about 1 real—one-eighth peso—at that time); their loads were to be limited to 2 arrobas (although official pronouncements occasionally varied, allowing 3 arrobas, 1.5 arrobas, and 2 arrobas, 5 pounds),[86] and they were to go no more than one day's journey from their pueblos. Intended as a temporary expedient, the use of tlamemes was to be discontinued once pack animals became available.[87] However well intended these reforms were, they did not alleviate the situation. For example, in 1532, Cortés violated the one-day journey limit by sending tlamemes on a round trip from Cuernavaca to Acapulco,[88] although he did pay them the required 100 cacaos a day. The dilemma faced by the crown was the excessive hardship that portage caused the Indians—heavy loads, long journeys, and harsh treatment—versus the need of the Spaniards for such transport, particularly merchants, who could not travel as swiftly or gain access to many places without tlamemes. This impasse was resolved in favor of the Spaniards and tlameme use and abuse continued.[89] But when it was in the crown's interest to overlook "illegal" use of tlamemes, it was done.[90] This decision was not an unalloyed evil. While it supported Spanish interests, it also allowed the continuation of an established indigenous occupation.

Although tlamemes were often used with callous disregard for their well-being, official concern that using natives as porters was seriously diminishing the indigenous population began in the Indies as early as 1511. It quickly became apparent that tlamemes were dying in New Spain as well, but the reasons are not clear. Sometimes weather was a factor. In 1531 witnesses in litigation between Hernán Cortés and Nuño de Guzmán testified to the deaths of many tlamemes en route from Huexotzinco. Two to three thousand maize-laden tlamemes were sent to Mexico City despite the winter season. Caught by snow in the Chalco pass, many died—the accounts vary, ranging from 30 to 113—and more succumbed from fatigue after returning to Huexotzinco.[91] The pass was recognized as dangerous: according to legend, the vassals of Quetzalcoatl had died there, between Iztac Tepetl and Popoca Tepetl, when they were caught in the snow.[92] Excessive loads were also a common complaint, as was the length of many journeys.[93]

The most crucial variable, however, was change in climatic zones. Portage from the *tierra caliente* to the *tierra fría* was devastating.[94] The Indians of the *tierra fría* were popularly thought to be stronger and to work better than those of the *tierra caliente,* and the lowlands were regarded as unhealthy.[95] However, a simple lowland-to-highland movement was not the sole cause. Deaths occurred as a result of journeys in either direction. Royal officials modified the existing regulations prohibiting tlameme travel beyond the confines of their home provinces and extended the prohibition to journeys between climatic zones within single provinces as well.[96] Viceregal regulations on the use of tlamemes restricted them primarily to the central plateau area of New Spain.

The organization of tlamemes by districts persisted throughout the sixteenth century,[97] partly because of restrictions on tlameme journeys between climatic zones, but also because of the ease with which the existing organization could be used to recruit and direct tlamemes, and to ensure efficient portage by being able to employ a series of fresh carriers.

Although official Spanish concern for the tlamemes began early and was persistent, it was often ineffective. When Antonio de Mendoza became the first viceroy of New Spain, he was ordered to see whether the existing regulations provided adequate safeguards, and, if not, to determine what additional measures could be taken.[98] In 1537 the legal limit of one day's journey (5 leagues) was reiterated, and the use of tlamemes was prohibited in the tropical areas of Veracruz, Soconusco, Tehuantepec, Oaxaca, Huatulco, Colima, Zacatula, and Pánuco, as well as between climatic zones,[99] pointing up the high mortality rates among those so employed. During New Spain's early years Spanish merchants relied on tlamemes, arguing to the king that only by so doing could they effectively compete with the Indian merchants.[100] Spanish regulations concerning the use of tlameme labor (effective and otherwise) did not apply to the native population. Consequently, a dual system existed in which Spaniards were legally bound to guarantee certain working conditions but Indians were free to use tlamemes without restrictions (presumably in the traditional manner). Indian merchants were thus unfettered by Spanish restrictions on tlamemes, which allowed them entrée to areas inaccessible to wagons or mules.

Viceroy Mendoza complained to the king about this inequity, stressing the injury to poor Spaniards who could not afford pack animals and were therefore forced to sell their goods to Indian merchants employing tlamemes. Also, business trips would be prohibitively expensive if one were forced to hire an *arriero* rather than tlamemes.[101] These complaints were apparently effective, for the next year merchants were granted the right to use tlamemes to carry cacao to Mexico City,[102] although the age at which Indians could carry as tlamemes was regulated,[103] reflecting a lack of sufficient laborers at this time. The earliest licensed use of tlamemes occurred along the major arteries running from Mexico City to Veracruz, Oaxaca, and Acapulco. Tlamemes were employed to carry a wide variety of goods, from bulk commodities, such as maize, to cacao (in which there was considerable official interest), imported plants, and bellows and tools for the mines at Culiacán.[104] The official attitude was that using tlamemes was acceptable as long as pack animals were unavailable, because of either scarcity or prohibitively high cost. However, attitudes among the Spaniards differed. While the king tried to curtail reliance on tlamemes, Spanish colonists favored their extensive use, and the royal officials were placed in the uncomfortable position of mediating conflicting demands, commands, and flagrant violations.

The New Laws of 1542–43 restated the previous general restrictions: that tlamemes were limited to areas where pack animals were unavailable, that their burdens were to be moderate, that they were to be paid, and that the work was to be voluntary.[105] The ban on forced tlameme labor was reiterated, including work for clerics.[106] Repeatedly, the lack of roads and animals was held to be sufficient reason to employ voluntary tlamemes, but it did not excuse forcing them to carry. It was common, however, for Spanish merchants simply to use tlamemes and then to claim that the conditions under which they did so were legal.[107] It was the responsibility of the governors and other justices of each jurisdiction and district to oversee the regulations and grant licenses for tlameme use where justified and to establish the number of tlamemes needed, the distance they were to go in one day, and their pay.[108] Indians continued to be exempt from these regulations on tlameme use, but the newly emerging group of mestizos was not. When the New Laws were announced, there was general opposition among the Spaniards amid dire predictions that the merchants would abandon their trade.[109] Widely disregarded, the New Laws were suspended in 1544.[110]

Whether the threat of the New Laws stimulated greater compliance or whether greater care was taken to enforce existing regulations to show that new laws were unnecessary, there was an increase in the number of complaints by Indians, denunciations of Spanish abuses, and the issuance of licenses for legitimate Spanish use of tlamemes. The licenses granted during the 1540s were generally for small parties of tlamemes, ranging from fifteen to thirty-five (although one cacao merchant was permitted to bring 1,000 cargas (tlameme loads—50 pounds each) by tlameme to Mexico City).[111] There was considerable small-scale and local use of tlamemes, for which pay schedules were enacted. But the main routes continued to see most of the tlameme flow, despite the prohibition on taking them to the ports of Veracruz or Huatulco.[112] Wages were uncertain, although ostensibly based on load and distance or time, and the enforcement of the regulations was uneven and subject to considerable official abuse. It was generally considered that the Spanish officials were concerned only with their own profits, not with enforcing the regulations.[113]

During these early years some of the demand for tlamemes was removed by competing Spanish *arrieros* (and the few Indians who also became *arrieros*),[114] but they were too few to satisfy the demand,[115] and their fees were so exorbitant that the Mexico City cabildo was forced to set standard rates.[116] Wagons too were introduced, although not until 1531,[117] but, being dependent upon roads, they were primarily used locally and to service the mines.[118] Rather than being displaced, tlamemes were used in conjunction with both *arrieros* and *carreteros,*[119] although often illegally.[120]

Mules were the most prominent means of bulk transportation in New Spain after the Conquest. Operating with strings of pack animals (*recuas*), predominantly mules but also horses, the *arrieros* traveled all the major routes in Mexico. To judge from sixteenth-century contracts as well as modern practice, there was one *arriero* or helper for every four or five animals (see appendix C).[121] These constraints indicate relatively small *recuas,* 12 to 30 animals[122] in the sixteenth-century and an average of 50 mules in the early seventeenth century.[123] The standard load (carga) for a mule was 10 arrobas (approximately 250 pounds, or 113 kilograms), as indicated by convention,[124] by law (at least for cargas of iron)[125] and a mule rental contract,[126] despite von Humboldt's early-nineteenth-century estimate of 300 pounds.[127] Such a load also accords well with modern practice.

Although mule raising is a relatively complex matter, the efforts are well rewarded. Mules are sterile hybrids, bred by mating a male donkey and a female horse.[128] (The offspring of a male horse and a female donkey, called a hinny, lacks the desired characteristics of a mule, notably size.)[129] Thus mule raising requires three separate breed-populations. Jacks and jennets (male and female donkeys, or asses) must be bred to produce jacks. Stallions and mares must be bred to produce mares. And jacks and mares must be bred to produce mules.

An act of 1526 of the Mexico City cabildo required that anyone owning a mule must also own a horse.[130] This regulation was apparently aimed at maintenance of the necessary parent stock for mule production, as it is horses generally and mares in particular, rather than jacks, that are the limiting factor.[131] The organization of mule production is thus not a simple or haphazard affair. Mules are the premier pack animals: they are capable of subsisting on poorer feed than that required by horses, they are more surefooted, and they are less susceptible to disease and more resistant to heat. Although colonial documents are replete with accounts of a local reed (zacate) being cut for fodder in the Valley of Mexico,[132] apparently an Indian monopoly, nearly all the cultivated grasses important for grazing in the Americas are of Mediterranean and northern Eurasian origin and were introduced into the New World, [133] a factor that likely made the durable mule of even more importance in the early years of colonization. Though capable of hauling great loads, mule transport was slow (see table 10.1).

During the early period (1521–50), most *arrieros* were Spanish although some Indians were similarly employed. Complaints during those years indicate that the number of *arrieros* was insufficient to meet the demand,[134] and the exorbitant amounts charged by the *arrieros* led to price regulation by the Mexico City cabildo.[135]

Spanish wagons also played a significant part in augmenting transportation in New Spain. Wagons can haul larger and bulkier items than can mules, and where terrain does not require repeated unloading for portage over obstacles, such as rivers or ravines, wagons save time required in dismounting and unloading pack animals.[136]

Table 10.1. Time and Distance of an *Arriero* Journey from Mexico City to Veracruz, 1803*

Location	Day No.	Distance† Leagues	Kilometers
Mexico City–			
Carpio	1	6.4	27
Otumba	2	8.3	35
Apam	3	9.8	41
(Rest)	4	0	0
Atlangatepeque	5	8.8	37
Piedras Negras	6	4.8	20
San Diego	7	6.0	25
Tonquita	8	7.1	30
(Rest)	9	0	0
Tepeyagualco	10	6.7	28
Perote	11	4.8	20
Vigas	12	6.0	25
Xalapa	13	6.7	28
(Rest)	14	0	0
Ensero	15	4.8	20
Plan del Río	16	5.5	23
Rinconada	17	3.6	15
Paso de Varas	18	2.9	12
Antigua	19	2.4	10
Veracruz	20	7.1	30
Total	20	101.0	426

*The *arrieros* arrived in Veracruz on August 19, 1803.

†Distance estimates from Rees 1971:219. The average distance traveled per day on this trek was 6 leagues if the rest days are excluded or 5 leagues if the rest days are included. While this trip required only 20 days, Rees (1971:214–15) estimates the usual time during the dry season at 20 to 22 days (an average of 4.6 to 5.1 leagues, or 19 to 21 km, per day) and during the rainy season up to 35 days (an average of 2.9 leagues, or 12 km, per day). Since the trip from Mexico City to Veracruz is predominantly downhill, the return journey presumably took somewhat longer. In 1841 the trip from Veracruz to Mexico City took 18 to 25 days by mule and wagon (Mayer 1844:283).

Source: AGN-Con 179, n.p.

However, carting had a late start in Mexico; wagons were not introduced until 1531,[137] the early demand for transport being met by mules and tlamemes. Part of the reason for the late introduction of wagons was their greater dependence on roads. Three basic types of wagons were used in Mexico: two types of *carretas* and the *carro.*[138] One *carreta* was a wagon with relatively small wheels of heavy timber, nearly solid, and rimmed with wooden strips. The other type of *carreta* had larger, spoked wheels, often with metal rims. The first type was the basic freight wagon of Spain, pulled by two oxen with a third in reserve and capable of hauling up to 40 arrobas (454 kilograms) 10 to 12 miles (16 to 19 kilometers) a day. The third type of wagon commonly used in Mexico was the *carro,* an outgrowth of the freight *carreta.* The *carro* had four times the *carreta's* capacity and required up to sixteen mules when fully loaded.[139] During the early period (1521–50), only the two types of *carretas* were employed.

The initial use of wagons was on the Veracruz–Mexico City route. Rather than following the road used by the *arrieros,* the Spaniards had a wagon road constructed in 1530–31.[140] The new route was the result of different needs of this new technology.[141] Not only were wagons more sensitive to topographic obstacles than were tlamemes, but the increased numbers of mules for both wagons and mule trains required more water and pasturage. The availability of pasturage on the plateau varied greatly owing to microenvironmental differences, particularly during the dry season, and the route change reflected this. Furthermore, the wagons and wagoneers (*carreteros*) damaged Indian towns by draining local resources and by forcing tlamemes to work for them, which led to official attempts to locate the early roads away from these towns.

Since they were limited to roads, the use of *carretas* in interregional trade grew slowly, devoted for the most part to early transport to the mines.[142]Lead, an essential ingredient of the smelting process then in use, made up many of the loads.[143] Despite the viceroy's statement of

1547 that he had opened roads for horses, mules and *carretas* to Acapulco, Oaxaco, Huatulco, Tehuantepec, Michoacán, Colima, Jalisco, Pánuco, Taxco, Zultepec, Zumpango, and Veracruz,[144] not all of these were accessible to *carreta* traffic (e.g., Acapulco).[145] In addition to the Veracruz–Mexico City road, the greatest use of *carretas* was for local transport in areas around urban centers. In 1543 the Indians of Azcapotzalco and Tacuba (Tlacopan) were ordered to repair the road from Mexico City to the quarries so that wagons could use them, and Mexico City itself was so crowded with *carretas* that a tax was imposed in an effort to discourage them.[146] Apparently the attempt was a failure, for the following year the citizens were forbidden to have *carretas* in the city altogether.[147]

Thus in the early years of colonization tlamemes bore the greatest transport burden. But the shipping situation greatly accelerated the demand along Mexico City–port routes, and Spanish demands grew while the native population declined. *Arrieros* first picked up the deficit, followed by *carreteros,* particularly on major routes, but adequate numbers of draft animals were unavailable, and tlamemes continued to be a flexible and much-sought-after means of transport.

Between 1550 and 1580 depopulation severely reduced the number of tlamemes, although their decline was partly offset by the greater number of mules and horses available.[148] At the same time, however, the opening of the northern mines increased the overall demand for transportation. Pursuant to royal order, the second viceroy, Luis de Velasco, implemented the previously suspended New Laws,[149] but with limited success. In 1568 and 1580 the king again ordered the viceroy to stop tlameme portage.[150] Spanish merchants continued to employ tlamemes,[151] and the established patterns of use continued, with the commodities carried changing very little.[152] Throughout this period, as in the previous one, complaints came to the viceroy of Spanish travelers forcing the Indians in the villages en route to become tlamemes, often for little or no pay, and for long and arduous journeys.[153] Even persons legally entitled to limited use of tlamemes such as clergymen and the Spanish officials entrusted with enforcing tlameme regulations, were guilty of extorting free labor. Thomas Gage states:

> For our comfort in our further travelling, we were informed in Oaxaca that in most towns of the road through that country, the Indians had an order from the High Justice to give unto friars travelling that way either horse to ride on or to carry their carriages, and provision of food freely without money, if they had none, so that at their departure they should write it down in the town book what they had spent, not abiding above four and twenty hours in the town. The Indians afterwards at the year's end of their ordinary justice and officers were to give an account of these expenses of travellers carrying their town book unto the Spanish justice to whom they belonged. By so doing, these expenses were allowed of to be discharged by the common town purse or treasure, for the which a common plot of ground was allotted to be yearly sown with wheat or maize.[154]

Though widespread, the mistreatment of tlamemes was not universal and some priests decried it on moral as well as pragmatic grounds. As a practical matter, however, maltreatment was commonplace,[155] and the consequences of violating the laws protecting the Indians were minimal. For instance, in 1580 the Indians of Teutitlan complained to the viceroy that Diego Pizarro, a mestizo who resided in the village, forced them to carry as tlamemes. Pizarro had previously been banished from the village of Teutila by viceregal order for the same offense, yet further banishment was the only penalty assessed against him.[156]

In 1579 the earlier requirements of voluntary paid portage with moderate loads where roads and animals did not exist were restated, reflecting a continuation of the banned practices.[157] Spanish officials entrusted with enforcing the regulations concerning tlameme use were also the objects of Indian complaints. They abused their authority in compelling the Indians to carry for them.[158] These impositions were visited on the Indians by others besides Spaniards and mestizos, however. Complaints reached the viceroy that Indian officials not only forced tlamemes to work for them but also gave tlamemes to others.[159] The use of tlameme labor by Indian nobles, a right presumably balanced by reciprocal obligations in pre-Conquest times, was also abused.[160] Complaints were made that *principales* forced tlamemes to work, although sometimes the nobles joined in the commoners' complaints to the viceroy about Spanish abuses.[161] On leaving office in 1550, Viceroy Mendoza admonished his successor, Viceroy Velasco, not to allow the *principales* to abuse the macehuales (commoners) by demanding too much tribute or service.[162] The problem, recognized by the viceroy, was one of balancing the nobles' rights and those of the commoners. If the nobles were allowed to demand too much service, the commoners would suffer, but if the Spaniards unduly restricted the nobles, they would lose their authority over the commoners.[163]

The system under which native nobility had freely exercised its rights to tlameme labor was breaking down, owing to the rise of "nobles" of questionable title, a decline in the commoners' sense of obligation as the nobles provided fewer traditional services, or an attempt by the nobility to increase commoner services, either absolutely or per capita as they attempted to maintain traditional rights in the face of demographic decline.[164] In any case, the Spaniards felt that the caciques and nobles were exploiting their own people.[165] While Indian officials remained responsible for tlamemes, the extent of their control was diminished. For instance, in 1580 the priest of Pachuca sought two tlamemes from the Indian governor of Tolcayuca to take some clothes to Texcoco. The two tlamemes, Juan Yautl and Miguel Huicitl, fled with the goods. Although the governor was manifestly neither implicated in the actions of the tlamemes nor able to control their actions, the priest seized him and forced him to pay for the missing goods.[166]

Indian merchants continued to use tlamemes.[167] Reflecting both earlier and later conditions and practices, tlamemes ritually consumed tobacco and invoked the gods to protect them from robbers and other dangers during their journeys and to aid them with their burdens.[168] The physical conditions of portage are unrecorded for pre-Columbian times, but during the colonial period allegations were made (or implied in their denial)[169] that heavy loads bore down on the tumplines of the tlamemes, causing bleeding of the foreheads and occupationally induced baldness. Thomas Gage claimed that "by the end of the journey this [*the tumpline*] makes the blood stick in the foreheads of some, galling and pulling off the skin, and marking them in the fore-top of their heads. So these carriers, who are called *tamemes,* are easily known in a town by their baldness, that leather girt having worn off all their hair."[170]

During these decades, however, there was a great rise in the number of *arrieros.* With the increase in livestock and demand for *arrieros,* many Indians entered the profession. Licenses were required but appear to have been easy to obtain.[171] The prohibition against Indians' use of horses was relaxed, probably because of the increase in available livestock and because of the increased competition for tlamemes. Allowing Indians to use horses thus freed many tlamemes. Mules were used for local transport of bulk commodities, and it became common for Indians to engage in long-distance commerce,[172] some entire Indian towns, such as Tepoztlan, specializing in transporting goods.[173] There were considerable efforts at regulating *arrieros,* focusing mainly on the effects they had on grain supply in various regions. *Arrieros* were to bring in grain from within a certain, variable number of leagues of Mexico City and they were forbidden to remove grain from the region of Mexico City to the mines of Zacatecas.[174]

These years also saw the true florescence of wagons in Mexico. Spurred by the opening of the great silver-mining areas of the north, carting expanded greatly, further facilitated by the expanded supplies of draft animals and the abundant grazing lands in the north. The Royal Highway (Camino Real) from Mexico City to Zacatecas was opened between 1550 and 1555.[175]

The mines required large quantities of supplies, not only labor and foodstuffs from the area of Mexico City but also goods shipped from Spain by way of Veracruz and Mexico City, such as mining equipment and lead for the smelting process, and later salt and mercury with the introduction of the mercury amalgam process during the 1560s and 1570s.[176] Wagoneering was helped by the demand for goods at the mines and the high value of the silver that offset the high transport costs, but the terrain also played an important role. The trip from Mexico City to the mines was entirely on the central plateau, which afforded relatively level and easily crossed terrain over long distances, cut only by the occasional barranca, or ravine. These favorable conditions fostered the development of the large freight *carro*. Rather than using oxen, as was customary in Spain, these wagons employed mules (six to sixteen on *carros*), as did most of the wagons in Mexico.[177] By 1555 the Camino Real to Zacatecas was opened to the heaviest wagons.[178] *Carros* traveled through the hostile northern territories in convoys, some as large as 80 wagons, but even large convoys were not immune to Indian attack.[179]

Although draft animals and freight wagons accounted for much of the traffic, tlamemes were still employed.[180] The major problem was the extension of the route into unsettled areas. The mining area stretched into lands inhabited by roving Chichimecs where there were few or no settled communities. Using tlamemes thus meant long-distance treks requiring food, shelter, and protection in a manner similar to that required for Spanish systems of transport. Consequently, much of the advantage of employing tlamemes was lost, and they were not used as extensively on these routes as they were elsewhere in New Spain. There was also an increase in wagon traffic between Veracruz and Mexico City,[181] but the use of Indians on this route, even as *carreteros,* was legally restricted to the autumn and winter months.[182] By this time black slaves were also employed in *recuas,* each having one to three.[183]

Wagon traffic from Veracruz to Mexico City also increased, the wagons pulled by mules, horses, and the slower oxen, and grain was shipped into Veracruz by wagons for the supply of that city and of the fleet.[184] By 1570 the wagon industry was sufficiently developed that Mexico City had a section, the parish of Santa Catalina, with 200 Spanish citizens who were *carreteros.*[185] Indians had entered the profession as well,[186] but their use on the Veracruz–Mexico City route was limited to September through March (later May). This restriction was ostensibly for health reasons, although in 1568 the trip was regarded as impossible after February owing to the poor pasturage for oxen.[187] The conditions under which Indians could be employed were subject to official scrutiny: they were, however, frequently abused.[188] The trek from Mexico City to the mines was also well established, difficulties arising only over the siphoning off of foodstuffs for the mines from the area in and around Mexico City.[189] Despite the growth of wagon transport, however, most of the supplies for the mines continued to go by pack animals and tlamemes.[190]

The third major area of wagon use, and perhaps its greatest, was in and around urban areas, particularly around Mexico City. Local transport of bulk goods, such as firewood, charcoal, and fodder, was largely by wagon.[191] Outlying areas that produced foodstuffs for consumption in Mexico City were increasingly linked to the urban market by wagons and the expanding road network: Atitalaquia, Atotonilco, and Tlemaco, in the province of Tula, on the north; Toluca; and the Valley of Matlatcingo.[192] Although the route south to Oaxaca, Tehuantepec, and Huatulco could accommodate packtrains, it was too rugged for wagons, and their use remained restricted to intravalley transport.[193]

Draft animals having become plentiful, *arrieros* and *carreteros* grew in significance, particularly along the major routes and on the relatively flat central plateau. Tlamemes continued to be employed, but their numbers had been further reduced through depopulation. The growth of Spanish roads into the silver-mining areas stretched *arriero* and *carretero* lines into the unsettled north, and although tlamemes were used as auxiliaries, their usefulness declined.

Tlamemes continued carrying the same types of goods after the pestilence of 1576–81, but they were used to a much greater extent in carrying local commodities; wood, fodder, charcoal, stone, and clothing.[194] Royal orders to halt the practice were again issued[195] but without significant impact. Spanish travelers continued to force the Indians to carry as tlamemes,[196] a situation exacerbated by their reduced numbers. There was a further surge of complaints to the viceroy of tlameme abuse, but these were more localized and less general than earlier ones. Pueblos on major routes were constantly forced to supply tlameme labor for travelers, a fact readily apparent to the Indians. When they moved away from the road, the problem lessened,[197] but was not eliminated. Towns at some distance from main routes did not supply tlamemes frequently and when they did, they were usually used for local trips. Towns on main routes, however, were often compelled to supply tlamemes, frequently for long distances.

The impact of Spanish expansion on tlamemes can be seen at Epazoyuca (Epazoyucan, Hidalgo).[198] Situated on the road to the mines of Pachuca, Epazoyuca claimed to have lacked tlamemes before the Conquest, but it was a tlameme town by 1579. During the waning decades of the sixteenth century the most noticeable pattern in native portage was an increase in the number of non-tlamemes who were forced to carry. Previously the large numbers of tlamemes had been adequate for Spanish needs, but as the population dwindled, increasing complaints to the viceroy indicate a shift to coerced portage by commoners who were not professional tlamemes. The practice of indiscriminately forcing Indian laborers to serve as porters had occurred earlier, but the practice now became widespread. The previous reliance on professional tlamemes often gave way to simple coercion of available Indians by Spanish travelers. The treatment received by these porters was often abusive and led to personal losses of animals, fields and homes.[199]

Many Indians entered or continued in transportation, but often by adopting Spanish roles. As mule trains increased, so too did Indian *arrieros,* although the number of draft animals they could own was restricted.[200] This period also witnessed the crest of the *carretero* development, their numbers waning after 1600.[201] Tlamemes under license were used in conjunction with *arrieros* (to whom they were often in debt), and tlamemes, their horses and mules, were forced to carry to the mines.[202]

These years saw a continuation of earlier trends. The number of Indians working as *arrieros* increased greatly. However, Indian *arrieros* were subject to regulations limiting the number of mules they could own. Those owning horses or mules were limited to two animals, increasing to six in 1588,[203] and were required to grow 20 *brazas* (1 *braza*=2 *varas*=1.68 meters) of grain for each horse, a reflection not only of the increase in horses but also of the decrease in Indian cultivators and the drain of many of them into trade.

The period from 1580 through 1600 saw the peak of the wagoneering industry as well as its greatest expansion. The patterns of the early years were continued. The Veracruz–Mexico City traffic continued, as did road construction.[204] Around Mexico City wagon traffic increased. Goods continued to be brought into the city by wagon,[205] but the quantity of wagon traffic and the damage it did to the streets led to the banishment of all iron-wheeled vehicles in the city.[206] Other cities also experienced rapid *carretero* growth, particularly those situated on or near major routes, such as Puebla and Cholula, which could readily supply wagoneers.[207] By 1585, Mexico City was connected to Veracruz by two major roads and by others to Amecameca, Tochimilco, Texcoco, and Tlalmanalco.[208] The mines continued to absorb much of the wagon traffic, although it declined after 1600 as Indian depopulation and Spain's counterproductive tax policies slowed the flow of silver.[209] The large *carros* designed to supply the mines never reappeared after their seventeenth-century demise, and wagons in general fell into disuse except on the plateau.[210]

Both *arrieros* and *carreteros* expanded, but the decline of the native populations greatly undermined the tlameme system. Some Indians entered the burgeoning *arriero* and *carretero* trades, but human portage had suffered irreparable damage and was finally effectively banned.

Because the exception under which tlameme use had previously been allowed had been abused and had led to great excesses,[211] tlameme use was virtually banned by 1609. Only limited portage of *corregidor* and ecclesiastical goods was still permitted, although in practice, tlamemes use continued,[212] possibly because enforcement of the restrictions was put in the hands of the priests, the efficacy of which the viceroy doubted. In addition, the use of tlamemes by Indians remained unregulated,[213] and their use by Spaniards remained legal within the confines of cities, provided it was voluntary and paid and conformed to city laws.

Despite these prohibitions and others reiterating the ban,[214] tlameme use persisted. It was, of course, illegal but widely recognized as occurring,[215] even to the extent that while decrying the use of force, the viceroy continued to demand that the tlamemes receive their "usual" pay. That the avoidance of regulations designed to safeguard the tlamemes was widespread can be seen from the century-long pattern of excessive loads and distances. Complaints about burdens generally state just "excessive loads," but distances are more explicitly given (see table 10.2). The number of complaints, however, greatly decreased from the high of the sixteenth century. Rather than indicating a discontinuance of the illicit practices, the dearth of complaints reflected the nadir of the indigenous population and the rise of competing forms of transportation, many employing Indians.

Royal and colonial officials struggled with the problems of tlameme use, seeking to find a satisfactory course amid the conflicting needs, demands, abuses, and continuing common practices. From 1521 to 1550 tlameme use was variously curtailed and/or outlawed, the system settling into a pattern of regulated loads, distances, and pay under established conditions—the absence of horses, mules, and roads. Tlameme use was regarded as a necessary evil until Spanish transportation systems could take over. From 1550 to 1580 regulated use of tlamemes continued about the same as before. Spanish policy was based on the assumption that tlameme use would decline as roads and mules opened larger regions. But the voluntary relinquishment of tlamemes by the Spaniards never materialized. After 1580 further restrictions were implemented until the only legal use of tlamemes by Spaniards in the

Table 10.2. Distances Tlamemes Were Forced to Carry, Taken from Complaints to the Viceroy

Distance, Leagues	Source
25 (5 *jornadas*—5 leagues per day for 5 days)	Libro 1952:71, 1548
12–15	*CI* 4:296, 1552
12–15	Cuevas 1975:197, 1554
20–30	Cuevas 1975:243, 1555
35 (7 *jornadas*—4 leagues per day for 7 days)	*FHT* 2:224, 1579
10–12	*FHT* 2:89–90, 1580
8–10	*FHT* 2:411–12, 1581
12–15	AGN-I 6-1a-656-175v, 1593

early seventeenth century was within cities. Tlameme use continued, however, for Indians were never subject to any restrictions on their use, and the Spaniards kept violating the regulations. General use of tlamemes by poorer Spaniards to take produce to markets can also be inferred, although such uses are not directly reflected in documentary sources.

The history of *arriero* use throughout the sixteenth century reflects demand. Basic constraints, such as mule loads, *arriero*-to-mule ratios, and speed, changed little, but the numbers of *arrieros* increased. Mule driving was initially a Spanish occupation, but by midcentury, increased demand born of mining coincided with increased livestock, and the occupation opened up to Indians and mestizos. Throughout the remainder of the century restrictions on Indians becoming *arrieros* lessened, and mules came to be used for local haulage and for everyday goods.

As with the use of *recuas*, wagoneering changed in response to demand throughout the sixteenth century. The basic constraints of loads per mule and speed changed little, but freight wagons grew to enormous proportions in response to the demands of the mining industry and the security afforded by larger wagons when traveling through the largely unsettled and dangerous Chichimec territory. With the midcentury increase in livestock the number of wagoneers increased, and their use expanded to more mundane wares and local needs.

Lake-borne

Lake transport continued to be important throughout the sixteenth century, but it underwent changes. The most important factors influencing lake transport after the Conquest were changes in the lake system itself. By 1543 the two northern lakes (Zumpango and Xaltocan), that had previously supplied foodstuffs to Tenochtitlan were permanently cut off from the other lakes.[216] Cutting of trees to rebuild Mexico City and to supply firewood led to massive deforestation. This and overgrazing by Spanish livestock caused erosion and silting in the lakes,[217] and a general pattern of desiccation followed. Traffic continued by canal to Mexico City from the towns bordering Lakes Chalco and Xochimilco, but traffic on Lake Texcoco faced growing obstacles. The dike separating the saline and fresh waters was a partial barrier to traffic between Mexico City and Texcoco, but more important was the water level.

The level of the lake dropped during the dry season with the result that canoe traffic slowed or stopped during those months.[218] Even more devastating for this commerce, Lake Mexico (the portion of Lake Texcoco surrounding Mexico City, diked off from the main body of the lake) began drying up as early as 1524.[219] Despite this trend, there were also years of periodic flooding.[220] The decline in the importance of east-west lake traffic, even where feasible, is indicated by numerous reports concerning the provisioning of Mexico City. The towns of the southern lakes supplied Mexico City by land and water, and the roads running north to Guadalupe and Veracruz, to Pánuco, to Xochimilco, and to Tacuba were all major conduits to Mexico City. Supplies entered the capital from Guatemala, Cuernavaca, Acapulco, Michoacán, Jalisco, and elsewhere, but Texcoco was conspicuous by its absence as a source.[221] In 1582, Pomar noted that there was lake traffic between Mexico City and Texcoco across the 3-league expanse but that two roads used by wagons ran north (seven leagues) and south (eight leagues),[222] indicating the greater significance of land transportation by that time. The situation with regard to east-west traffic is in marked contrast to the continuously navigable Mexico City-southern lake route where land routes are scarcely mentioned.[223] Even in the seventeenth century more than a thousand canoes supplied foodstuffs to Mexico City daily.[224] Some of Texcoco's canoe commerce continued, but by 1625 the city was reduced to one hundred Spaniards and three hundred Indians.[225] Thus the early sixteenth century saw the bulk of the lake traffic flowing into Mexico City from Lakes Chalco and Xochimilco and the towns of Chalco, Ayotzingo, Tetelco,

Xochimilco, Cuitlahuac, Mixquic, Amecameca, and Mexicalzingo (see map 8).[226]

In an effort to prevent flooding—largely the result of Spanish-caused ecological changes in the Valley of Mexico—the Spaniards undertook the drainage of the lakes.[227] In 1609 construction was begun on a canal running north to the Tula River and draining into the Gulf of Mexico.[228] While this drainage system was not fully completed for centuries, it immediately reduced the lake levels, further adversely affecting not only canoe transport but also the supply of aquatic products such as fish, insect larvae (ahuauhtli), algae (tecuitlatl), and waterfowl.

The organization of the canoe system remained largely intact following the Conquest. Indians retained control of the boat traffic, but Spaniards controlled the docks where the canoes loaded. Unloading the canoes was regarded as part of the canoer's responsibility.[229] So, despite their continued control of the actual means of transport, the canoer's responsibilities extended only to actual haulage, while the Spaniards controlled the overall flow of goods.

Although Cortés built ships to blockade Tenochtitlan during the Conquest, the Spaniards did not engage in lake shipping in the Valley of Mexico. There are several reasons for this. First, the Spanish ships were too large. Cortés's thirteen brigantines measured 42 feet (the flagship was 48 feet long). From this length Gardiner estimates that the ships were 8 to 9 feet abeam, drawing 2 to 2.5 feet of water and having a freeboard of 4 feet at the waist and 6 to 7 feet at the forecastle and the poop.[230] Each ship carried twenty-five men (twelve of whom manned the oars) and had one or two masts. They were probably flat-bottomed, and it is likely that they had keels. While some Indian canoes were of similar length and breadth, such dimensions allowed their use only in deeper water, and, as has been noted, the water level declined seasonally and throughout the century. The sails in use during the sixteenth century were of two types, square-rigged and lanteen,[231] The former being better before the wind but not very maneu-

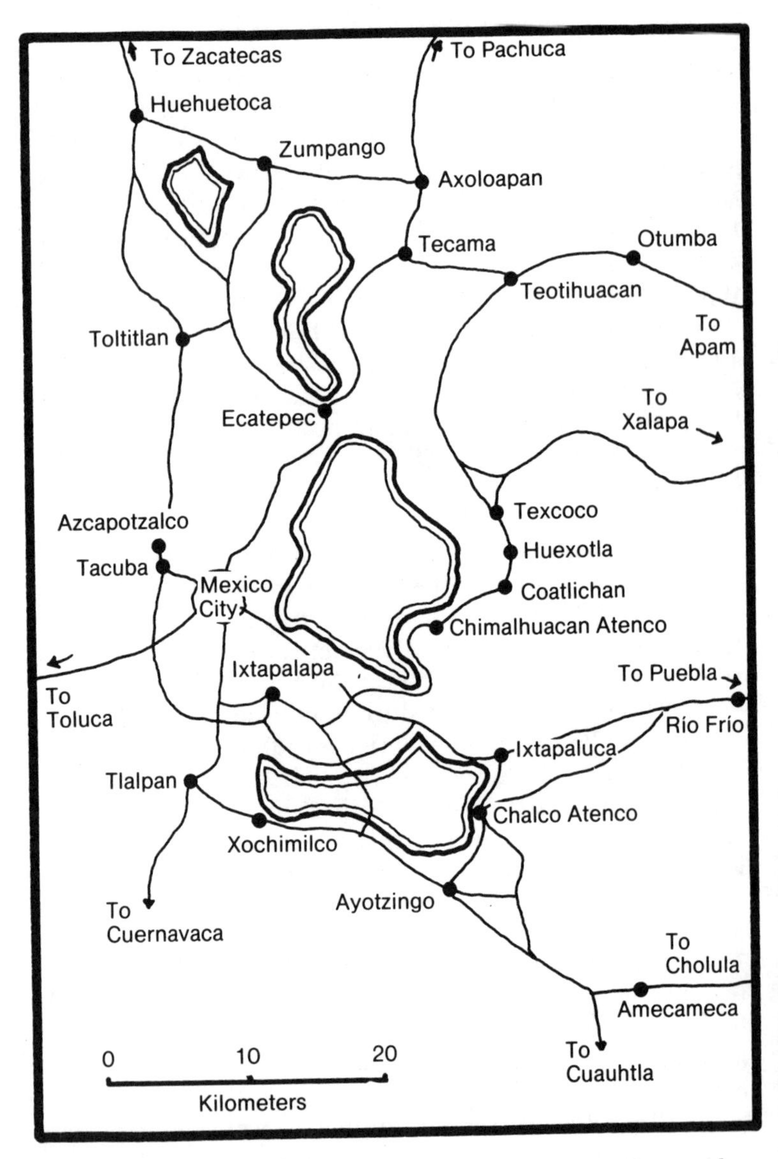

MAP 8. THE MAIN COLONIAL ROADS IN THE VALLEY OF MEXICO (derived from Gibson 1964a:363).

verable, the latter having the opposite characteristics. Thus to use sails in the Valley of Mexico lakes would have required either a loss of speed or maneuverability or two sets of sails requiring constant adjustment. Keels would have added draft and seriously reduced the lake area usable by the boats. Use of large vessels for transport also involves increased loading and unloading time. To fill the ships to capacity, large quantities of goods must be immediately available, or smaller loads must wait further stores before shipping. In short, large Spanish vessels were not economically feasible in the restricted valley lake system. The indigenous canoes were poled, not sailed, and were the most efficient means of water transport under the existing conditions. It is unlikely that Spaniards would have effectively competed with them or would have wanted to in view of the canoers' generally lower wages.

Indians were responsible for the upkeep of the canals, which gradually declined through neglect.[232] The Spanish colonial government took over the canoe-regulation functions of the Aztec government, notably taxation. Regulations paralleling those for other forms of transportation stipulated that canoes could not unload or sell goods anywhere but the designated market.[233] And, as with other Indian enterprises, Indian canoers were often forced to take Spaniards' and Indian nobles' wares to Mexico City without pay.[234]

Although canoe practices remained relatively unchanged throughout the sixteenth century, the area in which canoes trafficked changed radically. From the extensive commerce of pre-Conquest days canoe traffic dwindled in Lake Texcoco and ceased between Lakes Xaltocan and Zumpango and Mexico City. However, the year-round canal to Chalco permitted a considerable flow of goods from Lakes Chalco and Xochimilco into the capital.

TRANSPORTATION COMPARISONS

The issue of tlameme costs is a complicated one, and payment varied in amounts received and distances carried (see table 10.3). Maize, however, not coinage is the important consideration here, providing a more meaningful basis of wage comparison than the constantly depreciating real (see figure 10.3). A cursory glance at the actual worth of the wages calculated in maize reveals a gap in some of the later cases between the amounts paid and the quantities necessary to support the tlamemes and their families. This shortfall was avoided in two ways. Although pre-Conquest tlamemes most likely owned no lands, many of the tlamemes recruited after the Conquest undoubtedly had land, and the lands vacated owing to deaths from disease were redistributed by the viceroy, so tlameme labor wages were not the sole income in many cases. As the numbers of livestock increased throughout the sixteenth century, they gradually became available to Indians of lesser means, and it became increasingly common to find complaints to the viceroy concerning not only the coerced labor of the Indians, particularly tlamemes, but of seizures, for varying periods, of their animals for hauling loads. Most of the complaints dealt with the hardships this caused in delaying planting, so the situation was not one of commercial animals being seized. Nevertheless, some tlamemes owned horses, and they were employed in conjunction with them,[235] for which they were to be paid an additional sum, double that for the tlameme.

Arriero costs are difficult to assess. The most specific evidence consists of contracts. From these, two basic patterns of hiring can be seen: by set periods (usually a year) and by trips between specified points. Contracts made during the early years of colonization show a wide variation in *arriero* salaries, from a high of 210 pesos a year to a low of 90 pesos a year. The contracts are not sufficiently complete to indicate the reason for such a great disparity; perhaps it rested on experience or numbers and ownership of the animals employed. On a per-trip basis the cost ranged from 23 pesos per round trip (Mexico City to Medellín) with five beasts of burden, which was stated as the customary price, to 15 pesos per trip. One contract specified

TABLE 10.3. TLAMEME PAYMENTS, 1523–96

Rate or Trip	Payment in Cacaos*	Payment in Reales
Per day	100	0.5
Toluca to Ucareo	500	2.5 per 40 leagues
Cholula to Tepeaca	100	0.5
Cholula to Mexico City	200	1.0
Villa Alta to Oaxaca	600	3.0
Tehuacan to Tultitlan (2 days)	160	1.6
Tehuacan to Tecamachalco (2 days)	160	1.6
Tehuacan to Cozcatlan (1 day)	60	0.6
Amecameca to Los Ranchos, Puebla	80	0.8
Amecameca to Chimalhuacan, Mexico	40	0.4
Amecameca to Ecatzingo, Mexico	50	0.5
Amecameca to Tepopula	40	0.4
Amecameca to Tlalmanalco	40	0.4
8 leagues	–	1.0
1 league	–	0.5
1 day	–	1.0
Ocumatlan, Guerrero, to Tecuisiapa (2 leagues)	–	0.5
Ocumatlan, Guerrero, to Apongo (6 leagues)	–	1.5
1 *tomín* per day	–	1.0
4 leagues	–	1.0

*Between 1544 and 1550 cacao was worth 1 real per 200 beans (*AC* 5:61–63, 1544; 5:289, 1550), so pay rates given in cacao beans are calculated at that rate.

Source: *ENE* 2:116, 1532; AGN-M 1-138-67, 1542; AGN-M 2-109-43v; AGN-M 2-452-182, 1543; AGN-M 2-558-227, 1543; Simpson 1938:70, 1543; AGN-GP 1-141-28, 1575; AGN-I 4-649-185, 1590; AGN-I 4-840-228v, 1590; AGN-I 5-52bis-85, 1590; AGN-GP 4-289-81v, 1591; AGN-I 6-1a-1130-310, 1596.

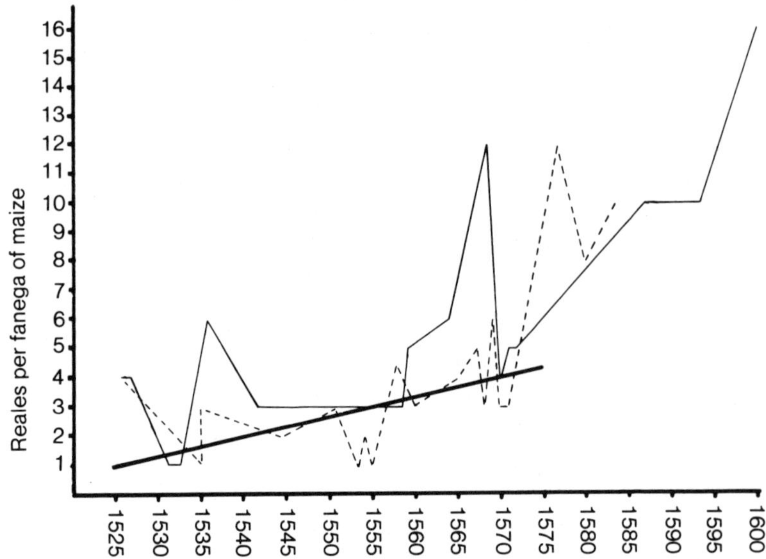

FIG. 10.3. MAIZE PRICES. Maize prices in Mexico City (thin solid line), in the region (dotted line), and the general price trend as calculated by Borah and Cook (thick solid line) (adapted from Florescano 1965:601, based on Borah and Cook 1958 and Gibson 1964a).

three pesos per carga (mule load, i.e., 10 arrobas), while a breakdown of other contracts yields 4.6 and 1.6 pesos per carga (3.2 pesos if construed as round trip).

The later contracts (1590–1601) indicate a great disparity in salaries. Although *arriero* salaries on the Cortés estate in Cuernavaca averaged 113 pesos a year, the contracts divide into high pay (240 pesos a year) and low pay (25 to 48 pesos a year), with one moderate wage of 60 pesos a year.[236] This range appears to reflect ethnicity, Spaniards receiving high salaries, mestizos receiving medium salaries, and Indians receiving low salaries, compounded by the hiring of Indians, and possibly mestizos, as helpers, not primarily as *arrieros.*

Given the variations in stated *arriero* wages, perhaps a

better estimate of *arriero* costs can be obtained from more generalized statements. In 1525, Cortés established official rates for various commodities sold in the inns on the Veracruz–Mexico City road. Locally obtained goods, such as chickens, turkeys, and maize, had a constant price, but imported goods, such as wine, increased with distance from the port of Veracruz.[237] One *azumbre* (2 liters) of wine sold in inns cost 4 reales within 10 leagues (42 kilometers) of Veracruz, 6 reales within 20 leagues (84 kilometers), 8 reales within 30 leagues (126 kilometers), and an additional 4 reales per each 10 leagues thereafter. This price increase cannot be used to calculate actual transport costs, since it leads to impossibly high totals. In 1525 clothing transported from Veracruz to Mexico City cost three reales per arroba, or 30 reales per mule load.[238] In 1528 part of a debt was repaid by transporting 24 arrobas of wine from Veracruz to Mexico City for 48 pesos.[239] In 1531 the Mexico City cabildo acted to restrict *arriero* charges to 10 pesos (of 8 reales each) per ten-arroba carga, rather than the 15, 18, and 20 pesos commonly charged.[240] Thus, an increase in *arriero* rates can be seen between 1525 and 1531, from three reales per arroba in 1525, to 16 in 1528, to 12, 14, and 16 in 1531, before regulations lowered the rates to 8 reales per arroba. Before 1550, when animals were scarce, the price per carga rose from 5 pesos to 10 (4 to 8 reales per arroba).[241] Despite the regulations, prices were probably not uniform. As a minimum, in 1587, the pay for transporting maize to the public granary was 12 maravedis (34 maravedis per real) per fanega per league,[242] or 60 maravedis per mule-carga league, the equivalent of 22 pesos, 2 reales, per mule carga from Veracruz.

Data on carting costs are scarce. Wagoneers with oxcarts were paid 3 reales per fanega for hauling 330 fanegas of maize from Tecamachalco to Cholula (15.5 leagues, or 65 kilometers by air).[243] At midcentury the cost of a *carreta* with iron-rimmed wheels was more than 100 pesos; a *carreta* with wood wheels was worth only 20 pesos.[244] Generally, the slower carts were cheaper than *recuas.*

Canoe costs are unknown for the pre-Conquest period, but in the 1560s the cost rose from 6 reales to 2 pesos (16 reales) for the trip from Ayotzingo to Mexico.[245] For Ayotzingo, at any rate, the pre-1560 cost was 6 reales for a six- to eight-hour trip to Mexico City (and back, presumably) carrying amounts ranging from 1 to 4 tons. The attempted price increase was apparently unsuccessful, as was a later one in 1633, from 6 to 20 reales between Mexicalzingo and Mexico City.[246] Thus the cost was between 0.83 an 0.21 reales per ton-league.

Ideally, a comparison of transportation systems would include a cost analysis and comparison on a uniformly applicable basis, such as cost per ton-mile. Unfortunately, the data do not permit such precision. Only rarely are comparative prices mentioned, and in the few instances that they are given, other crucial data, such as distance or load, are omitted, or the conditions of haulage or the years are too widely separated to make comparison meaningful. Given the disparate prices recorded within each of the transportation systems surveyed and the difficulty in ascertaining the circumstances that affected these variations, a direct comparison of these costs would not be very reliable (see table 10.4).

While there is a dearth of recorded costs, some comparative estimates of transport costs are available: one tlameme cost 1 real per 4 leagues, while his horse cost 2 reales per 4 leagues.[247] In the early nineteenth century, von Humboldt[248] put the cost of mules at 2 shillings, 8.75 pence per 300 pounds between Huehuetoca and Mexico

Table 10.4. Early Comparative Estimates of Transportation Costs

Means of Transport	Estimated Costs
Tlameme	23 kg/21 km/day
Mule	105 kg/21 km/day
Wagon	Up to 1,800 kg/16–19 km/day
Canoe	Up to 6,800 kg/29 km/day

City, while an Indian canoe with 15,000 pounds cost 17 shillings, 6 pence, or 0.109 pence per pound by mule versus 0.014 pence per pound by canoe—8.4 percent of the cost of transport by mules. Similarly, a 1785 analysis[249] estimated that 60 or 70 canoes could replace 1,500 beasts of burden since the former could carry 35 mule cargas of maize or 52 mule cargas of flour. Obviously a canoe load is dictated more by space than by weight, so canoe efficiency would fluctuate with the type of cargo.

In fact, the disparity between canoe and mule transport appears to have been twelve to one, based on von Humboldt, rather than the two to one indicated above. The disparity between tlamemes and mules is not two to one based on rentals of Indian horses but five to one based on loads carried by single mules and tlamemes. From the pre-1560s canoe price of six reales (and twenty reales thereafter) from Ayotzingo to Mexico City, the disparity between canoes and tlamemes would have been about thirteen to one, pre-1560s, and two to one thereafter. Unfortunately, all these calculations are based on considerable guesswork and comparison of nonequivalent data. It is enough to state that canoes were substantially more efficent than any other available form of transport.[250] Where wagons could effectively compete, they were even cheaper than *recuas* (e.g., the fanega-league cost of wagons was up to half the cost of the general fanega-league rate paid for *alhóndiga* grain.)[251] *Recuas, carros,* and *carretas* were more efficient than tlamemes for long hauls and over favorable terrain, but during the first half of the sixteenth century tlamemes were profitably used under those conditions because of lack of transport animals and under conditions of coercion.

In analyzing transport efficiency, however, linear efficiency is inappropriate for the analysis of canoe transport, for the size of the lake limited its impact. Thus canoe transport within the Valley of Mexico was highly competitive, but beyond the valley only wagons, animals, and tlamemes were used. Consequently, the effects of these transportation systems on urban hinterlands is dependent upon geographical factors that encouraged or discouraged their use.

Use of land transport systems was hierarchically ranked, depending on roads. The pre- and post-Conquest transportation systems fit together in complementary fashion. Indigenous patterns were not summarily replaced. Where there were poor roads or none, tlamemes continued to operate almost exclusively. This was a consequence not only of road conditions but of terrain and weather as well. Where there were roads, *arrieros* could effectively operate, but not exclusively; tlamemes also used these routes. On the better routes, particularly on the central plateau, within valleys, and around urban centers, *carreteros* operated, also in competition with tlamemes and *arrieros*. Each system had particular strengths and weaknesses that allowed the others to compete. They occupied spatially and temporally separate but overlapping transportation niches.

Mules were, in general, less expensive than tlamemes, so larger loads favored their use. Tlamemes could be employed under several circumstances: where there were not enough *arrieros*, where the loads to be carried were not large enough to warrant hiring an *arriero*, where treks were difficult or impossible for mules, or when the cost of tlamemes was artifically lowered, as by coercion or as part of encomiendo labor. Wagons competed where terrain permitted, not only for safety in the hostile northern territories but as an economical form of transport and the only one capable of hauling large single-unit items. In time Indians moved into these occupational niches, becoming *arrieros* at an accelerating rate throughout the century.[252] Thus although these systems operated best under differing conditions, they were not mutually exclusive. Tlamemes were used in conjunction with both *arrieros* and *carreteros*.[253]

In the Valley of Mexico both land and lake transportation were used. As the lakes dried up, the northern areas became tied to Mexico City by land rather than water transport. The northeastern section of the valley was also connected by land transport, for the lake separation allowed a major road to cross the lake bed between Ecatepec and Chiconauhtla, serving the Veracruz trade. On the southern lakes, however, canoes proved a durable and efficient system of transport, and towns such as Xochimilco, Tetelco, Chalco, and Ayotzingo not only shipped their own products but were important ports to which *recuas* brought goods from Veracruz, southern Mexico, and Guatemala for transshipment by canoe to Mexico City.[254]

CHAPTER 11

The Functioning of the Political Economy

CHANGE IN Mexico City's economy was partly due to alterations in economic flow, systems of transportation, and labor patterns. But in its extraction of goods from throughout the country, New Spain's economic system cannot be disentangled from the political. Tribute, marketing, and grain legislation were shaped by the political might of Mexico City, which was deployed to meet its economic needs. During the early stages of Mexico City's political control of the economy (1521–50), the indigenous economy and tribute system were continued, with a gradual shift from grain to monetary tribute. From 1550 to 1580, however, the general Indian depopulation and a growing Spanish population in Mexico City led to a reorganization of the tribute system that emphasized grain over money, expansion of Spanish agricultural production, and organization and restructuring of markets to ensure maximum influx of goods to Mexico City. After 1580 depopulation led to a decline in the importance of tribute; grain supplies were more rigorously controlled, primarily through the *alhóndiga;* and Spanish commercial cultivation and ranching increased.

Several factors combined to alter the political hinterland of Mexico City from its pre-Conquest pattern. Technological innovations altered economic hinterlands, and the Spanish political structure differed markedly from its Aztec predecessor, but within the context of these changes the massive Indian loss of population and the Spanish increase altered drastically both the needs of Mexico City and the strategies by which they could be met.

CHANGES IN PRODUCTION

Population shifts had a major impact on New Spain, but the way the cities' economic hinterlands were structured also underwent major changes. New systems of production and goods affected the economy of central Mexico, and new transportation systems altered relations among the various regions. None of these changes in production were immediate; many developed slowly (e.g., changing crop complexes), others depended on discoveries and on technological innovations (e.g., silver mining), and others came about as adjustments to changing social conditions in New Spain (e.g., haciendas).

The Spaniards played little direct role in agriculture until the 1550s, when the decline of the Indian population began to be felt.[1] During the early colonial period (1520–50), Spaniards were granted rights to Indian labor and essentially replaced the indigenous elites at the apex of the economic hierarchy, being supported by Indian tribute and labor. During the second period (1550–80), Spaniards actively engaged in agriculture (primarily cultivating wheat) and other commercial activities, such as mining, manufacturing, cattle ranching, and cash cropping, producing such items as sugar and indigo. The Indians were left to raise maize, vegetables, and farmyard animals, as well as labor-intensive commercial crops, such as cotton, silk, cochineal, and cacao. The third period (1580–1600) saw the rise of large landed estates (haciendas)[2] and an emphasis on "free" labor.

Although the Conquest did not cause an immediate revolution in agricultural practices and production, central Mexico underwent marked changes during the course of the sixteenth century.[3] Some of the new technologies and domesticates introduced by the Spaniards spurred productivity. Iron tools, such as the hoe, the ax, and the plow, altered cultivation practices, making farm labor more productive.[4] Some Old World domesticated animals, such as chickens and pigs, provided important additions to the indigenous crop complexes, while others, such as horses and mules, supplied both animal power and increasing quantities of fertilizer.[5] New plants, such as wheat and barley, were also brought into production, although the additional labor required for their cultivation held little appeal for the Indians.[6]

The impact of introduced crops and domesticated animals on indigenous groups was not uniform but varied by plant or animal and by area. Although the haba bean was readily accepted by the Indians, most other Spanish crops had little impact on Indian producers. Much of the difference in production among areas in Mexico was due to altitude and climate. While maize could be grown profitably from sea level to above 3,000 meters,[7] as could many other traditional foodstuffs, the same wide growing range did not characterize European plants and animals. The pattern of production varied temporally as well as spatially. In the lowlands of the *tierra caliente,* Old World plants made few inroads until the development of sugarcane plantations late in the century.[8] Wheat, however, was grown in both the *tierra templada* and the *tierra fría.* Spanish attempts to induce or force the Indians to grow wheat were largely futile.[9] Spaniards grew the limited quantities of wheat that were produced, but the vast bulk of agricultural production in New Spain rested in the hands of the Indians, who continued to raise indigenous crops primarily. Much of the difference between Spanish and Indian agriculture can be attributed to the Spanish emphasis on cash crops rather than on the subsistence crops that characterized Indian production.

Altitude and climatic zones were also important in livestock raising. Although the climate was not ideal for the animals, livestock grazing was developed in the *tierra caliente.* The *tierra templada* permitted better livestock raising, both cattle and sheep,[10] but it was in the *tierra fría* that the practice flourished.

The chicken (the *gallina de castilla,* as opposed to the *gallina de la tierra,* or turkey) proved to be the most popular introduction, plant or animal, and was quickly and widely adopted by the Indians.[11] Small livestock *(ganado menor)*, such as pigs and sheep, was raised by the Spaniards and multiplied rapidly during the early years with a resultant drop in price for both pork and mutton in the late 1520s. Large livestock *(ganado mayor)*, such as cattle, horses, and mules, lagged behind the *ganado menor* and did not become plentiful until after 1550.[12] Very early in colonial times possession of a horse was the distinguishing mark of a gentleman, and Indians had to petition the crown individually for the right to own one. In the latter half of the century, however, their use became common among Indians, particularly traders, and farm use increased as well. In general, livestock flourished, particularly smaller animals. Ranching, however, was primarily a Spanish enterprise and often proved detrimental to native farming because the animals ate and trampled crops, a development noted as early as 1526.[13] Although livestock quickly became part of the Mexican scene, apart from chickens, none of the introduced animals were raised in large numbers by Indians.

Two major events dictated the next period of production: the depopulation of 1545–48 and the discovery of silver. The decades from 1550 to 1580 saw an increase in the consuming European population, a decline in the producing Indian population, and a major shift in the price of foodstuffs, with high-labor grains growing more expensive and low-labor meat becoming cheaper. This affected both quantities of food available and areas of production. Increasingly agricultural production took place under repartimiento, a forced but paid Indian labor-draft system adopted in the later years of the century. Commercial production was largely in the hands of Spaniards, and many Indian producers withdrew into subsistence agriculture.[14] At the same time the northern territories were opening up following the discovery of silver, and cattle ranching and horse raising expanded northward.[15] This expansion occurred for several reasons. The indigenous population was sparse,[16] and the northern area lacked the developed agriculture with which cattle raising conflicted elsewhere. The mines and their settlements required meat for food, as well as tallow, hides, and draft animals.[17] The natural fecundity of the livestock led to greatly expanded herds, but as cattle increased, their market value declined, forcing cattlemen to shift from small-scale production to the more profitable large-scale, extensive ranching.[18] While ranching increased in the north, stock raising also continued in the central plateau, primarily more labor-intensive sheep raising in the areas north of Mexico City, around Puebla, Tlaxcala, Toluca, Ixtlahuaca, Huichapa, San Juan del Río, and Querétaro, and in Oaxaca.[19]

The third period (from 1580), the era of the large hacienda, also followed massive Indian depopulation. Production in the greater Puebla region (Atlixco-Tlaxcala-Tecamachalco) expanded further, and it became the most important area of European production in Mexico, largely of wheat.[20] Because wheat farming requires special techniques and treatment, such as plows and irrigation, it did not become an important part of Indian production.[21] Wheat was twice as costly to produce as maize, its yield was much smaller, and its nutritional value less.[22] However, it could produce two and sometimes three crops a year, with *riego* (irrigated) harvest in June, *temporal* (rainy-season) harvest in October, and sometimes *aventura* (hazardous) harvest in early spring.[23] To produce wheat on a large-scale basis, a well-integrated system of canals was constructed in the Valley of San Pablo in the Puebla region. This intensification resulted in the production of 70,000 to 80,000 fanegas of wheat a year with only sixty Spaniards, and the Valley of Atlixco yielded 100,000 fanegas,[24] although it displaced indigenous maize cultivation. Other major agricultural centers included the province of Xaltocan, the Valley of Cuauhtitlan, the area of Azcapotzalco, Tacuba (Tlacopan), Tacubaya, Los Remedios, and Santa Fé, as well as Chalco, Tepotzotlan, Texcoco, and Toluca.[25]

Thus the initial reliance on Indian cultivation and small-scale livestock production gave way to greater Spanish control of agricultural production and large-scale ranching in the face of population decline, livestock expansion, and a per capita increasing demand. Further depopulation and labor decline led to additional expansion of Spanish agricultural activities and increasingly extensive cattle ranching. This development took place primarily in the north but also in the south to a lesser extent,[26] leaving the central plateau to agriculture and *ganado menor.*

TRIBUTE

One major factor in changing the political hinterland of Mexico City was the restructuring of the tribute system to correspond with the new Spanish reality. In the wake of the Conquest, Mexico ceased to be an area of scattered kingdoms, city-states, and hegemonic empires. It was politically unified on the Spanish pattern.

The Spanish Empire was hierarchically organized. The king exercised overall authority in the empire. Below the king was the royal Council of the Indies, exercising delegated authority over the New World and the Philippines, and below the Council was the Audiencia of New Spain. The viceroy system, which remained in force throughout the colonial period in Mexico, was instituted in New Spain in 1535, when Antonio de Mendoza was appointed to remedy the abuses of the first Audiencia. New Spain was subdivided into *gobiernos* (provinces), each presided over by a governor responsible to the viceroy. The governor could delegate authority to a subordinate official, the *teniente de gobernador,* but often he governed through subordinate officials known as *alcaldes mayores* and *corregidores,* who were in charge of jurisdictional areas known as *alcaldías mayores* and *corregimientos,* subordinate units that often overlapped and whose status was in a constant state of flux throughout the sixteenth century. These officials also exercised judicial powers and were known collectively as *justicias.* Between 1550 and 1570, New Spain was divided into forty *alcaldías mayores,* increasing to seventy by 1580, and over more than two hundred *corregimientos.* The smallest administrative unit of consequence was the *municipio,* or township, governed by a cabildo or *ayuntamiento.* In contrast to the separate or tenuously connected polities of the Aztec empire, New Spain was a unified political entity.[27]

One consequence of this political change was the alteration of the tribute system. There was a basic divergence between the Aztecs' and the Spaniards' approaches to tribute. The Aztecs used the tribute to support their urban population (at least the nobility), so that the transportation cost was not their primary concern, although they were cognizant of it. In the Spanish system tribute belonged to the king, and the concern was primarily for revenue. The supply of foodstuffs for Mexico City from tribute sources was a secondary consideration. During the first half of the sixteenth century the Spaniards basically perpetuated the Aztec system, with tribute assessments recorded by pueblo, although the assessments were never uniform.[28] Once New Spain was politically unified, however, the Aztec tribute system was not economical. Since under the Aztecs the cost of transporting tribute had been borne by the payers, that expense was extraneous to the recipient. But once the paying areas were politically incorporated, the cost of transport was no longer displaced outside the polity. Now transportation expenses were essentially lost revenue, increasing the payers' cost out of proportion to the recipients' benefit. Even in view of monetary devaluation and maize inflation, it was cheaper for the crown to permit on-site payment of tribute in money, which was easily transported, or to collect foodstuffs and sell them locally, than to require maize payments and then, in effect, subsidize its conveyance to Mexico City.

Since the Spaniards possessed more efficient transportation systems than those of the Aztecs under whom the tribute system had been organized, it was more economical to receive monetary tribute than maize, particularly from distant areas, and then pay for the transport of foodstuffs from nearer and more productive regions, as well as from areas that catered to Spanish demands for wheat. For example, at the authorized rate of 12 maravedis per fanega per league for tribute maize conveyed to Mexico City, tribute from Coyolapan, Oaxaca, would cost over 28 pesos per fanega, or over 14 pesos per tlameme load for transportation alone, while one tlameme load purchased in Mexico City at the highest black-market prices (32 reales per fanega) cost only 16 reales. Still, the Spaniards perpetuated the Aztec system because it was already operating and could be taken over intact. Initially, any costs to the Indians caused by transportation were not of concern to the Spaniards, for they saw themselves as part of a different society. It was only the income that was of concern to the Spaniards, not the total cost to the society. Indians were still plentiful, their labor was cheap, and Mexico City had to be provisioned.

In 1536, in a royal *cédula* (a pronouncement to a subordinate official) to Viceroy Mendoza, the king sought to convert the tribute goods, such as mantas and maize, into gold or silver.[29] The shift to specie was generally well received by the Indians and was often requested by them. Although both specie and maize assessments remained fixed, the value of the maize rose throughout the century, so a monetary assessment meant a de facto lowering of the tribute.[30] The towns paying tribute in maize or other foodstuffs were obligated to take it to Mexico City or to the Spanish town closest to them.[31] With the decline in cheap available labor, concern arose for the continued supply of Mexico City, and there were attempts to rationalize the tribute system. After 1550 grain tribute (wheat and maize) was restored,[32] but the way it was collected changed. Rather than being required to take their tribute grain to Mexico City or another major Spanish city, the Indians were now permitted to pay tribute in their own towns or to take it to a Spanish town no more than one day's journey distant.[33] However, some Spanish officials continued to require tlameme portage of tribute under the pretext that the land was hilly and horses could not carry it, resulting in tlameme journeys of up to 30 leagues.[34] Although maize continued to be required of each tributary, specie made up the bulk of their assessments throughout the latter half of the century.[35] The net effect of these changes was that money from tribute continued to flow into the royal treasury in Mexico City from throughout New Spain, but maize did so from a much smaller area. Maize within one day's journey (approximately 21 to 28 kilometers) was carried in as part of the assessment, but for more distant areas other means were required, most often the intermediary services of the *regatones* (merchants who purchased goods for resale, usually at exorbitant prices).

A major consequence of the reduced area of "free" transportation of tribute was to redefine what had been under the Aztecs, Mexico City's politically expanded economic hinterland. Since New Spain now constituted a unitary political system, the consequences of the tribute system changed radically. While the benefit to Mexico City of tribute goods was substantially the same under both the Aztecs and the Spaniards, the consequences for the respective political systems were quite different. In both systems tribute transport consumed substantial sums, but the difference lay in who bore the cost. The tribute payer, of course, paid for both goods and transport, but since these people were previously not part of the Aztec city-state, this expense was "free" to the Aztecs. With the Spanish conquest these tribute payers became part of the same polity to which they paid tribute, and the cost of transport was either recognized as a larger tribute or was a cost borne by the state in lost potential tribute.

MARKETS

Goods and Measures

Although they were ostensibly economic mechanisms, markets in Mexico were subject to considerable political control. With the Conquest markets underwent several changes, in the kinds of goods available in them, in the distances from which these goods came, in the periodicity of markets, and in the political control exercised over the markets. Some of the changes in the kinds of goods available in the marketplace arose from differences between Spanish and Indian values. Thus, such food as ahuauhtli (insect larvae) and tecuitlatl (algae) declined, and elite goods such as quetzal feathers and *chalchihuitl* (jade) became less important, while gold and silver became more so. Other items were simply replaced. Although dogs continued to be eaten throughout the century, Spanish livestock provided a better source of meat. Some crops, such as chia *(Salvia chia)*, were not well received as staples by the Spaniards and declined. Others, such as *huauhtli* (amaranth), had religious connotations and were suppressed by the Spaniards as diabolical. Precious metals, such as gold, were increasingly extracted directly by the Spaniards and dropped out of the marketplace.[36] Cacao, used as a beverage, had been an elite good before the Conquest but declined in value and became accessible to the commoners during the sixteenth century. Aside from these shifts in goods, the markets continued to supply basically the same types of wares as before.[37]

Indian markets continued much as they had before the Conquest. The Indian market judge in Mexico City was not replaced until after 1533,[38] when control of the markets passed into Spanish hands. Some Spanish control had been exercised earlier, however, as when a Spanish *alguacil* of the *tianguiz* (native market) was appointed in 1526,[39] and the Indian governor of Mexico City had to petition the cabildo as early as 1533 to make changes in the *tianguiz*.[40] The Indians were allowed to manage the day-to-day affairs of the markets, but overall control had been co-opted by the Spaniards. However, the replacement of native market officials proceeded more rapidly in urban than in rural areas.

Not only were market officials changed, but so too were accepted practices. The measures in use in the markets were changed. Pre-Columbian trade was based on measure and count[41] and on the vigesimal (base-20) system. The Spaniards not only introduced their own decimal (base-10) system and specific units of measure but added weight as a new category. Weight was quickly adopted, as witnessed by an ordinance of 1524 assessing penalties for using false weights, and an early ordinance required that both Spanish and indigenous goods must be sold by weight.[42] Weight was used successfully for many goods, such as grains, salt, fish, oil, butter, and honey,[43] but for other goods it was less successful. Furthermore, the possibilities for fraud were great, and false weights were used by Indians and others.[44] Cacao was ordered sold by weight rather than by count,[45] but the pre-Columbian unit of 8,000 beans, the *xiquipilli,* was retained and adapted to a 24,000-bean load (3 *xiquipiles*). Thus, despite the introduction of Spanish units of measure and official pressures to adopt them, many Indian units survived, largely where to do so was beneficial to both Spaniards and Indians (see table 11.1).

Spanish units were adopted most readily in conjunction with grain, since tribute assessments were stated in terms of fanegas.[46] Spanish money was also quickly adopted,

Table 11.1. Conventionalized Loads

Tlameme load:
1 carga = 0.5 fanega
1 carga of mantas = 20 mantas
Indian-derived units of measure:
1 carga = 20 units
1 *zontle* = 400 units
1 *xiquipil* = 8,000 units
For cacao:
1 *zontle* = 400 cacao beans
1 *xiquipil* = 20 *zontles,* or 8,000 beans
1 carga = 3 *xiquipiles,* or 24,000 beans

Source: Borah and Cook 1958:10–12.

again owing to tribute. Market taxes, assessed in coin,[47] were imposed on both Spanish and Indian goods.

Before the Conquest markets were held in the great public plazas of each city,[48] but data about market location in pueblos is scant. After the Conquest, there were many instances when *tianguiz* were changed from their original locations or abolished altogether. These changes were recorded because the viceroy exercised control over the existence and location of Indian markets. Viceroy Velasco went so far as to abolish all markets within 10 leagues of Mexico City before complaints led to the repeal of the order. Attempts were made by native officials—*calpixqueh* and *alguaciles*—to abolish some *tianguiz,* usually those held in smaller centers, to the benefit of larger towns.[49] For example, a *tianguiz* held in an estancia was moved to the cabecera of Tetepango, Hidalgo, by the *alcalde mayor,* although the action was rescinded by the viceroy.[50] In Ocotlan, Jalisco, the customary *tianguiz* was held at some distance from the houses and was not felt to be convenient, so the Indians petitioned the viceroy to be allowed to change it to a better location near the Church of San Pedro.[51] Since these cases represent the contested changes, they reflect only a small percentage of actual changes that took place. Many of these market changes reflect alterations in market schedules that were an unanticipated consequence of the Conquest.

Scheduling

As discussed earlier, the pre-Columbian marketing schedule was based on a 5-day cycle, with larger centers holding daily markets, and the entire system participating in the cumulative 9-, 13-, and 20-day cycles. These sequences derived from the Mesoamerican calendar, which quickly succumbed to the Spanish priests' efforts to eliminate "heathen" practices. With the introduction of the Christian calendar, the basic functional cycle of days shifted from a 5-day week to a 7-day week.[52] In the Valley of Mexico this change had occurred by midcentury, with minor exceptions, and by the end of the century in most other locations.[53]

The imposition of the 7-day week began early, but not in a direct effort to eradicate the native calendar. Although the Indians were generally free to continue following their own calendar system, Cortés prohibited markets from being held on Sundays and fiesta days.[54] While this order did not directly force a shift to a 7-day week, it did require Indian awareness of the Christian calendar. Furthermore, the result of retaining a 5-day marketing schedule while simultaneously observing the Sunday and fiesta day bans was chaotic, for it made it necessary to cancel whichever market happened to fall on Sunday. In a 5-day marketing system the result was the omission of the first, third, fifth, second, and fourth market days which fell on Sunday during each five repetitions of the 7-day week, or, at the level of a specific market, its 5-day market would be omitted every seventh scheduled meeting (see table 11.2). The result was a very disruptive and not easily calculated sequence, aside from the 9-, 13-, and 20-day cycles. To retain any of the indigenous market cycles, both calendrical systems had to be grasped, and, as the dominant system, only the Christian calendar could be relied on to accurately establish market days.

In all instances in which market-days changed, there was an acute awareness of market conflicts. While most areas converted quickly,[55] the 5-day cycle lingered. Cuestlahuaca, in the Mixteca Alta, originally had a 5-day market and then changed to a Saturday schedule,[56] but a conflict existed with another market, and the Indians petitioned the viceroy for a change back to the 5-day system or, in lieu of that, to a Tuesday market.[57] In the Valley of Mexico, Santiago Mamalhuazuca, a *sujeto* of Chalco, successfully petitioned the viceroy for permission to hold a 5-day market on the basis that many Indians used it.[58] While the viceroy controlled marketing schedules, since he did not demand absolute conversion to the Christian calendar but merely required that market schedules did

Table 11.2. The Meshing of Indian and Spanish Calendars in the Marketing Cycle

Indian Perspective	Spanish Perspective						
	Sun.	Mon.	Tues.	Wed.	Thurs.	Fri.	Sat.
	1	2	3	4	5	1	2
	3	4	5	1	2	3	4
	5	1	2	3	4	5	1
	2	3	4	5	1	2	3
	4	5	1	2	3	4	5

not conflict, 5-day markets coexisted with 7-day markets in some circumstances. But the requirement to avoid conflicts meant that the 5-day markets were ultimately doomed.

The shift from a 5- to a 7-day sequence presented several difficulties for the indigenous marketing systems. Markets meeting on a 5-day schedule articulated smoothly, but the switch of any one of them to a 7-day system caused major conflicts—an occurrence likely to happen first in the larger centers or missionized towns. Even when an entire region adopted the Christian calendar, there were problems. When the markets shifted from a 5-day week to a 7-day week, difficulties were introduced that could be solved in one of two ways: each location could keep a single market per cycle, or they could adopt multiple markets, or possibly two, per cycle. However, assuming the populace had access to multiple markets, a 5-day *tianguiz* had a potential market share of 20 percent, whereas a

7-day *tianguiz* had a potential market share of only 14.3 percent. Thus, having only one market in a 7-day cycle would result in a significant economic loss, while two markets a week would be a major gain (28.6 percent of the market share). The issue of which *tianguiz* received two market days, rather than only one, was apparently resolved on the basis of the town's political importance.

Even after the adoption of the Christian calendar markets were not stable, for the day of the week on which they met was frequently changed. In Mexico City, there were three major markets—San Juan, San Hipólito, and Santiago Tlatelolco—and markets were held every day in the city, but the days on which the markets had their main market days changed. San Juan, the most important market, met daily, but its main market day was on Saturday,[59] the most important day of the market cycle, analogous to the earlier yearbearer market day. It was to this market that the Indians were required to go in 1552.[60] San Hipólito was a Spanish creation, ordered established for the greater convenience of the Spaniards. It met on Wednesday and Friday, until 1545, when it was changed to Wednesday and Thursday. And in 1579 it was reported that San Hipólito held its market on Monday, while San Juan was held on Saturday and Saint James (Tlatelolco?) was held on Thursday. In 1592 San Hipólito was apparently on Wednesday and San Juan was on Thursday.[61]

While some of these conflicts can be ascribed to incomplete lists of the multiple market days, there were many changes in marketing days, even within the same city, and of important markets. Whatever day a major market met had an effect on the other markets in the area, since they had to shift to nonconflicting days in a ripple pattern. Famous markets that were close together were scheduled on different days to avoid prejudicing each other.[62] However, this complementary scheduling was not always voluntary. In 1547, the cabildo of the city of Tlaxcala ordered that no Saturday markets were to be held anywhere in the province of Tlaxcala except in the city of Tlaxcala.[63] The markets cited as conflicting were Topoyanco, Hueyotlipan, Atlangatepec, and Tecoac, 2, 5, 5.5, and 8.5 leagues distant measured by air, respectively. Since most of these distances were too great to compete seriously with Tlaxcala for customers, the matter was not one merely of local scheduling but an attempt to establish the dominant market of the region on an exclusive day, at least for merchants. Similarly, important towns of smaller regions also tried to dominate their local marketing systems by taking more and better market days. For example, Tula had held its market on Friday and Saturday but tried to add another market on Wednesday. This conflicted with the Wednesday *tianguiz* one air league distant in Xicapacoya.[64] That town was in the province of Tula but had been independent before the Conquest and had its own *tlahtoani*.[65] The viceroy required the customary market days to be observed. But in 1597, Michinaloya, an estancia of Tula 1.5 air leagues away, was ordered to move its *tianguiz* from Monday to Tuesday. Since this would conflict with a market in Tula, however, the viceroy rescinded the change. Similarly, in 1595, the pueblo of Tetepango, Hidalgo, sought relief from the viceroy when Axacuba, one air league distant, tried to change its *tianguiz* from Tuesday to Saturday, the day of the Tetepango *tianguiz*.[66] The viceroy ordered Axacuba to have only one *tianguiz* a week, on Tuesday.

Tula was trying to exercise its political dominance over the smaller pueblos to gain more and better markets, probably a common occurrence by cabeceras over their *sujetos*. But both Tetepango and Axacuba were cabeceras (although Axacuba was in private encomienda by this time)[67] and were not subservient to each other, though they were in the same *partido* (parish) of Pustla. Thus shifting market days occurred not only within political hierarchies but between them, although the viceroy tried to ensure nonconflicting schedules. Requests were sent to the viceroy by towns wanting to move to less favorable market days when there were conflicts, probably as a matter of self-preservation by the less important markets. These are examples of relatively close markets in conflict (except for the instance of Tlaxcala), and the pattern seems to have been one of towns expanding their markets to include more and better days if the town had the political power to do so, while moving away from conflict when one was likely to lose to a dominant market.

The calendrical change alone would be expected to cause a reorganization of marketing schedules within cabecera-*sujeto* units, but two other factors also led to market conflicts. First, Hispanic political unity promoted conflicts between towns. Social and political barriers between previously independent towns (and markets) were lessened so that there was now competition from consumers, whereas before the Conquest each politically autonomous unit had had a virtual monopoly on its citizens. Second, wagon and animal transportation introduced by the Spaniards made the movement of goods less costly, expanding their range and hence the size of each town's economic hinterland and promoting more distant economic interaction. As a consequence, markets that previously had been situated beyond a town's economic hinterland now found themselves within it, creating new conflicts, particularly along the main routes that were experiencing greater traffic.

It was these changes in hinterland sizes and in the calendar, along with depopulation in many places, that were responsible for the changes in marketing. These changes included not only overt scheduling changes but the absorption of smaller markets by larger ones.

Thus the marketing system of New Spain underwent considerable change throughout the sixteenth century, despite apparent Spanish attempts to retain the indigenous *tianguiz.* Not only did the types of goods sold change, but the units in which they were measured also changed, weight being added, and various indigenous units were amalgamated with similar Spanish measures. There was some explicit market control by Spanish authorities, but more important than the politically inspired changes were the incidental ones. Not only did depopulation affect markets, but the change in calendrical systems threw the articulating markets into chaos, as did the expansion of their economic hinterlands. Thus the sixteenth century saw numerous shifts in marketing schedules as various towns sought to accommodate or intimidate adjacent markets.

Political Regulation of Markets

Although tribute and the way it was reorganized was one way the viceregal government exercised political control over the economy, it was not the only way. A less blatant but more pervasive exercise of coercion was the colonial government's persistent attempts to restructure the economy of central Mexico by regulating the distribution of agricultural products. Spanish attempts to regulate Mexican economic life were early and frequent. Ostensibly the aim of these regulations was to perpetuate the smooth operation of markets and to restrict Spanish interference in Indian marketing activity, while guaranteeing adequate supplies to sustain Mexico City. The regulations were extensive. The types of goods sold by both Indians and Spaniards were controlled. To reduce speculation in commodities, Spanish merchants importing goods into Mexico City were required to disclose their merchandise to city officials:[68] they could not sell to strangers in the city who had come from farther away than 20 leagues, and they were required to announce their wares publicly on entering the city so that the citizens could buy them.[69] There was also a concern for ensuring that Indian merchants were not molested by Spanish merchants. Accordingly, Spanish merchants were prohibited from buying wax, honey, feathers, clothing, eggs, or anything else from the Indians for resale.[70]

The cabildo of Mexico City controlled its markets in more general ways, as by setting market days and location through regulations aimed at Spaniards and Indians alike.[71] Indians perpetuated the markets and the trade in native products, while the Spaniards controlled the trade in Spanish wares. Indians could trade freely with Spaniards, but they were prohibited from trading in Spanish goods.[72] Since Spaniards could not trade in native goods (nor could blacks), the regulations were aimed at maintaining not just a dual economy in which Spaniards dealt in Spanish goods while Indians dealt in Indian goods but one that permitted a flow of goods between economies in only one direction, from Indian to Spaniard. Thus the burden of Spanish regulations fell most heavily on the producers of basic commodities, the Indians.

One area of major regulation was the control of grain. The history of grain legislation in sixteenth-century New Spain has been divided into three major phases.[73] During the first phase (1525–50), legislative attempts at regulating grain prices were early and repeated. The aim of these regulations was to ensure a supply of foodstuffs for the cities and to regulate the *regatones.* Many goods were regulated, including clothing, cacao, and firewood.[74] The prohibition, aimed at Spaniards,[75] sought to restrict price increases resulting from supposedly unnecessary resale, although a certain amount of retailing was allowed in such goods as clothes, maize, sandals, honey, birds, and other items if not purchased within 5 leagues of Mexico City.[76] Despite some attempts at price control (e.g., maize, 4 reales per fanega; cacao, 1 real per 200 beans; mantas, 4 reales each; salt, 4 reales per fanega; salt, 6 reales per fanega),[77] most efforts at price moderation appear to have focused on regulating the markets.

During this period indigenous markets and goods were left in Indian hands, while the sale of Spanish goods was left to Spaniards. Spaniards were not allowed to purchase basic commodities in Mexico City for resale within 5 leagues. This kept Mexico City prices low by eliminating competing markets and ensured a larger supply from more distant areas of production when prices in Mexico City rose enough to justify transportation costs. The net effect was that only Indians supplied basic goods and were subject to these regulations. Consequently, the early-sixteenth-century economy operated on two tiers: foodstuffs and indigenous products were traded by Indians and could be purchased by Spaniards for consumption only; Spanish wares were traded by Spaniards and could be bought by Indians for consumption only (with some restrictions, such as wine).[78] Although the aim of these regulations was to retard unnecessary price increases, their consequences were quite different. City supplies were not adequate; repeated scarcities are indicated by Spanish seizures of goods from Indians, although this occurred largely in famine years.[79] In general, cabildo control of prices discouraged production.

Despite the regulation of local markets and the stifling effect of Mexico City's control over foodstuffs produced in surrounding hinterlands, long-distance trade flourished.[80] Spanish merchants were in competition with the still-wealthy pochtecah and lodged complaints that they could not effectively compete without using tlamemes.[81] Although the pochtecah continued to compete effectively with the Spanish merchants, they were increasingly hindered in conducting their trade by local Spanish officials and often turned to the viceroy for licenses.

The period from 1550 to 1580 began with two major problems, a reduction in the flow of supplies into Mexico City, caused primarily by the decline in Indian population, and a drain of foodstuffs from the Mexico City region to other areas, such as Zacatecas. In 1551 in an effort to overcome lower production (the result of depopulation and the disincentive of price regulation) and funnel more supplies into the city, Viceroy Velasco abolished all markets within 10 leagues of Mexico City except those of Texcoco and the capital itself.[82] The Indians within that area were to be required to bring goods into Mexico City rather than to their local markets. But complaints of hardships and suffering caused by the order led to its rescission,[83] at least to the extent that necessities could be sold in local *tianguiz.* This was not construed to mean, however, that the king intended the Indians to cease bringing food into the city.[84] The requirement that Indians within

20 leagues of the city must bring food to sell in the market each Saturday continued, being modified only to the extent that it was to be made more convenient for the Indians and less vexatious,[85] largely through the increased use of beasts of burden and wagons.

Another threat to Mexico City's food supply appeared with the discovery of silver in the north. Foodstuffs from the Mexico City region began moving to the northern mines, further depleting local supplies. To safeguard the city's food, buying goods to be sent to the mines was forbidden within 6 leagues of Mexico City.[86]

While local production languished, long-distance trade flourished, though not in its pre-Columbian form. Under colonial conditions the special social standing of the pochtecah eroded, their position undercut by competition from Spanish goods and merchants and new forms of transportation in conveying traditional wares. But after the plague of 1545–48, many Indians took up occupations as traders, frequently claiming to be descendents of pochtecah.[87] Throughout the rest of the century Indian merchants persisted, although they were increasingly hampered by bureaucratic requirements. For example, in 1570 many of the Indians of Temascaltepec were merchants.[88] After midcentury these merchants began increasingly to rely on horses and mules in their trade.

The expansion of Indian traders was not without opposition, however. Indian merchants were frequently hindered by officials, notably the *alcaldes mayores,* who felt that they had exclusive rights to buy and sell in their respective jurisdictions (a fact noted as late as the nineteenth century), despite explicit regulations to the contrary.[89] These officials customarily engaged in the business of raising and selling foodstuffs—meat, fruit, bread, and other items—in the cities, villas, and pueblos, a practice outlawed in 1572 but not deterred.[90] In one instance a merchant schemed to be named *teniente* (the immediate subordinate of an *alcalde mayor*), presumably for the commercial advantages the position entailed, for officials commonly forced the Indians to sell their goods to them at lower prices.[91]

From at least 1575 licenses to engage in trading were granted to individual Indians,[92] the basic purpose being to afford protection from official harassment.[93] Such harassment was not restricted to provincial areas, but occurred in Mexico City as well.[94] Opposition to Indian traders came from the vested interests of local traders, but many of the regulatory requirements were an effort to retain local production, whereas the viceroy sought to encourage the free flow of goods, which redounded to the benefit of Mexico City. As early as 1561, Indians were required to cultivate 50 *brazas* square (1 *braza* = 2 varas, or 1.68 meters) of fields.[95] Long-distance trade offered an attractive alternative livelihood to Indian farmers caught in the squeeze resulting from price regulations.

After 1580, Spanish participation in the marketplace increased, and the regulation of markets tightened. A city official was charged with overseeing market regulations and assigning places for both Spaniards and Indians so that types of merchandise would not be mixed.[96] The division of the market into areas of specific goods persisted throughout the sixteenth century and was officially sanctioned. Since it was a custom "from time immemorial," preference was given to Indians in their placement within the markets, and Spaniards were kept from encroaching on these assigned places.[97] Market days were regulated, and the Sunday and fiesta-day restrictions were nominally continued.[98] The attempts to eliminate *regatones* apparently failed; in 1599 one Gómez de Cervantes complained that *regatones* were making profits of 400 percent and more.[99]

THE *ALHÓNDIGA*

The attempt to maintain an adequate supply of grain to feed Mexico City available at a reasonable price though cabildo regulations of markets met with little success. In a further attempt to remedy the situation, Mexico City established a public granary: the *pósito* and *alhóndiga*, the former to store grain and the latter to oversee its sale. By buying grain at low prices in times of abundance and storing it until times of scarcity, these institutions sought to remedy periodic grain scarcity and moderate price fluctuations.

Pestilence and the heavy rains of 1577 led to a crop failure that year.[100] The *pósito* and *alhóndiga* were apparently founded as a direct result of the famine of 1578–80,[101] in response to the inadequacy of grain regulations. The *pósito* purchased grain (wheat, maize, flour, and barley)[102] with its own capital and stored it during normal years to be used in times of scarcity or high prices. The *alhóndiga* regulated the sale of stored grain under the guidance of the cabildo. The *alhóndiga* and *pósito* were complementary rather than competing institutions whose purpose was to eliminate the middleman in grain transactions.[103]

In preparation for establishing the *alhóndiga* and *pósito,* in December 1578 the Mexico City cabildo asked for and received permission to take the royal-tribute maize and wheat from within 14 leagues of the city. Shortly thereafter the Audiencia granted further permission to the cabildo to control private-tribute maize. On 7 February 1579 two-thirds of all private-tribute grain within 14 leagues was confiscated for the *alhóndiga* and *pósito* at the 1576 base price.[104] Other supply strategies were also employed, as in 1578, when each Spanish farmer around Mexico City was required to bring 16 fanegas of wheat to the public granary in Mexico City or risk having his Indian labor supply withheld. In contrast, Indian producers were ostensibly free to sell their grain without control.[105] Although private sale of grains was prohibited in times of scarcity, Indians far from the city were allowed to buy grain for their sustenance from other villages rather than from the *alhóndiga.*[106]

The *alhóndiga* was apparently successful during the seventeenth century, when prices remained around 10 reales per fanega from 1610 to the end of the century, except for the years 1624 and 1692.[107] One seventeenth-century source stated that more than 3,000 mules arrived in Mexico City every day with wheat, corn, sugar, and other goods for the *alhóndiga.*[108] But during its sixteenth-century existence the *alhóndiga* did not succeed in maintaining either constant supplies or stable prices. Part of the price fluctuation was tied to the agricultural cycle: following the harvests in October and November maize prices were at their lowest, whereas from May through September, between planting and harvest, prices gradually rose.[109] Thus, in 1587, maize sold for 10 reales per fanega in November, whereas the previous June it had been officially set at 18 reales per fanega, and the black-market price was between 28 and 32 reales per fanega.[110]

The area from which the *alhóndiga* could acquire grain varied. In 1583 the controlled area was within a radius of 20 leagues of the city.[111] In 1587 the radius was reduced to 14 leagues, extended again to 20 leagues in 1594, and then reduced again to 14 leagues in 1598.[112] Grain was brought into Mexico City from such regions as Chalco, Xochimilco, Mexicalzingo, Coyoacan, Guatitlan, Chiconautla, Tequatlan, and Otumba by persons commissioned for that purpose.[113] Grain also came from Toluca, the Valley of Matlalcingo, Texcoco, San Juan Teotihuacan, Tlaxcala, Tepeaca, Huexotzinco, and the Valley of Atlixco, Tepeapulco, Citlaltepec, Xilotepec, and Tepexi.[114]

Since this grain entered Mexico City by cabildo ordinance and not as tribute carried by the payer or wares brought by *regatones,* provision had to be made for its conveyance. By ordinance, transportation was paid for at the rate of twelve maravedis (34 maravedis = 1 *real*) per fanega per league. Tribute grain was brought into the city by Indians using horses, mules, and wagons, and this labor was also compensated,[115] but there was resistance to this, apparently because of inadequate compensation. While the *alhóndiga* and *pósito* aimed at maintaining a supply of grain at stable prices so that the poor would not be harmed by famine or high prices, another effect of the *alhóndiga* was to limit the possibilities of the rural farmers in favor of the urban population.[116]

Official control of grain prices further depressed production, and seizures of goods from Indians by Spaniards, blacks, mestizos, and mulattos increased.[117] Indians, too, victimized other Indians,[118] and the prohibition on black marketeering was restated,[119] indicating its occurrence.

Because Indians continued to abandon farming in favor of trading, the amount of land they were required to cultivate as a prerequisite of trading increased. Before they could engage in trading, Indians were required to establish that they had, in fact, made the fields required by ordinance.[120] The requirement that certain lands must be cultivated was ignored in many places, and so many people abandoned their fields that the order was reemphasized in Tacuba: all Indians were required to make a 50-*braza* field; 40 *brazas* for himself and 10 for the community.[121] These orders applied primarily to merchants, particularly those who used beasts of burden in their trade, requiring not only 40 *brazas* of maize for themselves and 10 for their communities, but an additional 20 *brazas* for each animal.[122] The aim of this regulation was to alleviate the grain shortage caused by the many merchants who did not raise maize yet consumed it along with their beasts, thus raising both demand and prices. Licenses were similarly granted to Indian merchants to own beasts of burden for use in their trade.[123] The requirement that Indians must have licenses to trade or have beasts of burden (up to six) was repealed in 1597, provided they cultivated their maize fields as required.[124] During these years Indian merchants were no longer primary purveyors of elite goods but filled an intermediate role, engaging extensively in the trade of such goods as salt and cotton. Thus references can be found to salt merchants at Yetecomac, Tulnacuchtla, and Tezcatepec, copper merchants at Pochutla and Tetiquipa, and cotton merchants at Tonameca,[125] although not in proportion to their economic significance, as may be judged from indirect references in the *Relaciones geográficas* of 1578–81.[126]

Indians began selling minor Spanish wares during this period, and by 1590 they were selling Spanish goods in quantity.[127] Many of the Indian merchants were local traders dealing in produce who competed directly with Spanish traders in the same trading circuits and with the same commodities.[128] The opposition of *corregidores, alcaldes mayores,* and their *tenientes, justicias,* and *alguaciles* toward Indian traders continued,[129] aimed not only at local Indians but at Indian traders from other pueblos and regions as well.[130]

The history of market control in Mexico is one of continual price regulation and continual failure. Grain regulations, even those not applying directly to Indians, depressed grain prices and removed the incentive to produce, particularly since the official lower prices worked to the advantage of the urban consumer over the rural producer and of the wealthy, who could purchase in advance and in quantity, over the poor. Illegal sales and massive seizures of grain from Indians demonstrate the inadequacy of the regulations in maintaining adequate, low-priced supplies. Depopulation further reduced grain supplies below demand and spurred a viceregal attempt to channel more goods into the city by eliminating competing markets. The competing grain sales to mines as distant as Zacatecas testifies to the inadequacy of price incentives in the Mexico City region.

Increasingly, Indian producers could no longer prosper as farmers, and many of them moved into trade. Initially opposed to this defection from the land, the colonial government relented with the proviso that traders must also produce enough grain to pay their community taxes and support themselves. Traders were licensed by the viceroy in the face of local opposition, as the new traders not only competed with local traders but drained goods from these areas into Mexico City. Indian traders gradually expanded their role in the economy, dealing in Spanish goods and using mules and horses, which primarily benefited lower-cost trade by reducing transport costs. Not only did this trade benefit Mexico City, but by circumscribing the area within which purchase of goods for resale was prohibited, the cabildo guaranteed that whatever flow of goods was generated came from an area not previously supplying the city. The *alhóndiga* and *pósito* were aimed at further curtailing abuses by systematically securing grain at lower prices for resale to retard price increases during periods of scarcity. But again, during the sixteenth century at least, low official grain prices and low transportation wages restricted the quantities available and fueled the black market. Sixteenth-century grain legislation systematically disadvantaged the rural and the poor to the benefit of the urban and the wealthy, resulting in wholesale defections of the poor from the ranks of the producers and causing further grain shortages.

THE URBAN SUPPORT AREA

One would expect the economic hinterland of Mexico City to expand with the introduction of superior Spanish technology. Much of the failure of Mexico City's economic hinterland to expand to its fullest was due to the continued reliance on pre-Conquest patterns of tribute and transportation. But it was also restricted by the price controls imposed by the government. The pressure to maintain provisions for Mexico City was lessened by the Conquest and the plagues of 1520–21, which reduced the city's population. This lessened the supply problems for Mexico City, which had prompted the elaborate Aztec trade, tribute, and agricultural systems. This left the survivors with a better man-to-land ratio, and the land that was cultivated would have been generally better. Thus, per capita, agricultural productivity probably increased following depopulation. The Spaniards did not react to the population decline of 1520–21 since, for them, that population level was the demographic baseline, the population size with which they were familiar. It was only from the perspective of the Indians that this was a population drop similar to those of 1545–48 and 1576–81. Nevertheless, Mexico City and the Valley of Mexico as a whole still required great quantities of foodstuffs for their sustenance. Production in the valley continued, but not as intensively as before.

The combination of a smaller population in the Valley of Mexico, greater per capita productivity, the introduction of livestock, and the availability of Spanish systems of transport enabled Mexico City to draw on productive areas beyond the range of its pre-Columbian economic hinterland.[131] Consequently while the total area from which Mexico City drew its subsistence goods was smaller than the tribute area of Tenochtitlan, greater emphasis was laid on markets and less on political extraction.

In theory the supply problems of Mexico City were resolvable entirely by remunerative rather than coercive means, given the decline in indigenous population and the feasibility of an expanded economic hinterland based on Spanish transportation. But in practice they were not so resolved because the Spaniards continued to rely on indigenous transport and because the existing patterns of supply conflicted with the theoretically feasible expansion of Mexico City's economic hinterland.

Spaniards used tlamemes because the Indians could be forced to act as bearers as part of their encomienda obligations and were thus "cheaper" than mules and wagons to the encomendero, if not to the society as a whole. The continued use of tlamemes perpetuated Spanish reliance on the system and deterred the construction of extensive road systems to accommodate *recuas* and wagons. Even if the Spaniards had been willing to implement their own transportation systems immediately, the more distant areas within Mexico City's expanded economic hinterland were in no position to supply the capital. They were already engaged in supplying existing centers of population in whose original economic hinterlands they were, such as Toluca, Cholula, and Texcoco.

While Tenochtitlan's nontribute maize supply came

from within the Valley of Mexico, by the end of the sixteenth century Mexico City's supply area extended far beyond the Valley of Mexico into the Toluca, Atlixco, and Puebla valleys. The productive areas around pre-Columbian cities were determined by transportation distance from the center. This distance changed after the Conquest, but the productive patterns did not immediately expand to reflect the altered distance. Other centers whose economic hinterlands had been distinct now competed with Mexico City for the production from their areas. Though their populations were smaller than Mexico City's and their market prices were lower, they competed effectively owing to the advantage of proximity to the producing areas and consequent lower transport costs. To overcome this competition, the officially established prices for grain were generally higher in Mexico City than elsewhere, and Mexico City exercised its considerable political power to restructure the economic landscape, first by altering the tribute system, then by restructuring competing markets and commodity egress, and finally by instituting the *pósito* and *alhóndiga* to control the grain supply. These were not merely economic measures but political strategies to allow Mexico City to appropriate food from more distant zones. By the end of the sixteenth century the restructuring of Mexico City's economic hinterland had been largely completed.[132]

At the end of the sixteenth century the Valley of Mexico was still a maize-producing area, particularly in the south, as well as in the province of Xaltocan on the north. The Valley of Cuauhtitlan was a major wheat producer, while other northern Valley of Mexico areas raised livestock.[133] The Atlixco, Puebla, and Tlaxcala valleys on east were major suppliers of wheat for Mexico City, as was Tacuba (Tlacopan), the Valley of Toluca on the west, Guanajuato, and even Querétero on the north, although the last was primarily a cattle-raising area.[134] Some livestock production was scattered throughout the Valley of Mexico, but the major expansion was to the north[135] as haciendas transformed previously unsettled areas. These areas, all far beyond Tenochtitlan's economic hinterland, had now become major suppliers of grain to Mexico City. This grain trade was important to Mexico City, but it had become crucial to the economic well-being of the producing areas.

The alteration of Mexico City's economic hinterland, brought about through lower transportation costs, had another effect: it reduced or eliminated the types of food shortages Tenochtitlan had experienced before the Conquest. In the early 1450s and early 1500s, Tenochtitlan suffered from famines. No famine is strictly ecological, resulting from naturally induced crop failure; social factors also play a role.[136] But the pre-Columbian famines in the Valley of Mexico were largely ecological.[137] The indigenous transportation system was sufficiently flexible that foodstuffs could be drawn from virtually all areas within a restricted radius around Tenochtitlan, if they were available. However, the inefficiency of the system meant that ecological misfortunes, such as drought, frost, and insect infestation, affected the entire area from which foodstuffs could be regularly and economically drawn. Consequently, compared with civilizations in other parts of the world, the Aztecs were extremely vulnerable to such agricultural disasters.

The introduction of wheels and draft animals altered this situation. By reducing the cost of mass conveyance of goods, Mexico City could now draw on a much larger area for its foodstuffs, greatly reducing or eliminating the likelihood of an ecological setback affecting the entire expanded hinterland. The elimination of this risk was not an unalloyed benefit, however. Expansion of the roads to accommodate wheeled vehicles and beasts of burden was costly and, while offering less expensive transport, less flexible than the indigenous system, in which porters could travel virtually everywhere. The Spanish system was tied to roads, which were few and vulnerable to destructive climatic conditions and neglect. Not only was this flow of foodstuffs from distant areas of production vulnerable to transport disruption, but Mexico City found itself in direct competition with new consuming areas, such as the silver-mining communities in the north.[138] Moreover, since shipments of food tended to be larger and fewer under the Spanish transportation system, their flow could be more easily controlled and supplies could be manipulated through the city's political control of the *alhóndiga.* Thus the shortages that now occurred were social in origin and lacked a primarily ecological cause.[139] For example, in 1624 the viceroy (the count of Gélves) joined with a wealthy gentleman, Don Pedro Mejía,

in monopolizing all the Indian maize and wheat about the country. Don Pedro Mejía bought from the Indians their maize at the price he listed, and the wheat of the Spaniards he bought according to that price at which it was taxed by the law of that land to be sold at in time of famine. This is at fourteen reals a bushel (which is not much there considering the abundance of gold and silver), at which price the farmers and husbandmen, knowing it to be a plentiful year, were glad and willing to sell unto him their wheat, not knowing what the end would be. Others, fearing to gainsay him, whom they knew to be the Viceroy's favorite, did the same.

Thus Don Pedro Mejía filled all the barns which he had hired about the country, and himself and the Viceroy became owners of all the wheat. He had officers appointed to bring it into the markets upon his warning, and that was when some small remnants that had escaped his fingers were sold, and the prices raised. Then he hoisted his price, and doubled it above what it had cost him. The poor began to complain, the rich to murmur, the tax of the law was moved in the Court of Chancery before the Viceroy. But he, being privy to the monopoly, expounded the law to be understood in time of famine, and that he was informed that it was as plentiful a year as ever had been, and plenty enough for Mexico and all the country. Thus was the law slighted, the rich mocked, the poor oppressed, and none sold wheat but Don Pedro Mejía's officers for himself and the Viceroy.[140]

Although tlamemes could still be called on, to some extent, to transport foodstuffs from the traditional economic hinterlands, production in these areas was much lower after the Conquest. Much of the land that had formerly been cultivated simply went out of production.[141] Herding had the dual effect of taking considerable land out of cultivation to be used for grazing and degrading these lands.[142] Both bare cropping of the land by Spanish herds and deep tillage caused soil erosion. Of even greater consequence were the combined effects of the loss of ground cover and the rapid deforestation that followed the Conquest.[143] Topsoil was washed away, leaving gulleys and slopes that were no longer capable of being cultivated.[144] In addition to these losses in productive lands much of the previously cultivated land had been rendered marginal.

Marginality of lands is not an inherent quality of land and its productive capacity. Rather, since the profitability of cultivating land depends on a combination of transport costs and labor investment in relation to market price, under conditions of severe transportation constraint lands relatively near the urban center could be profitably cultivated, even when the land was of poor agricultural potential. During the pre-Hispanic period the demand for food had been so great that *tepetate* (Nahuatl, *tepetatl,* "stone mat," from *tetl,* "stone," and *petatl,* "mat"), a caliche soil requiring extensive preparation for modest agricultural return, had been farmed in the Valley of Mexico.[145]

Hill-slope farming between 800 and 200 B.C. exposed large areas of *tepetate,* but reclamation of it did not start until A.D. 600, when terracing began. Reclamation and cultivation of *tepetate* was carried on from 600 (from 1000 in the northern portion of the valley) to 1519, but after the Conquest, *tepetate* areas in the valley were abandoned, the result, in part, of depopulation. But with the advent of more efficient transportation systems, the advantage in lower transportation costs enjoyed by such lands decreases until they can no longer compete with more distant, more productive lands having direct access to the more efficient transportation system. Thus the original economic hinterland of the city is considerably distorted by transportation improvements. Less productive lands off the main transportation lines pass out of production, while more distant areas served by the new transportation network come into production, owing to the higher labor costs of the former lands, coupled with their transportation costs, when compared to the lower labor costs per yield of the latter, coupled with their cheaper transportation costs.

As transportation efficiency increases, agricultural practices conform more closely to the physical variation in the land.[146] The total producing area increases, but the regions nearer the city but not directly served by it enjoy little benefit from the more efficient transportation system. After the Conquest, however, not only did population within the valley decline, but more efficient Spanish systems of transportation allowed the economic hinterland of Mexico City to expand far beyond its pre-Hispanic confines. As a result, new, more distant productive areas could be profitably cultivated to supply the city, and the *tepetate* areas that the combination of proximity and demand had previously made profitable became less so. It was more profitable to cultivate very productive distant areas and pay for transport than to farm closer but less productive areas. What constituted marginal land had changed.

CHAPTER 12

The Economic Reorganization of Central Mexico

DURING the century of the Conquest the status of the various cities in the Valley of Mexico underwent a profound shift. This was a consequence of changing economic relations within the valley, shifts in the relative political power of the towns, the relation of the Valley of Mexico to the world economy, and ecological alterations in the valley itself.

THE CITIES OF THE VALLEY OF MEXICO

The single most important physical change in the Valley of Mexico involved the lake system. As early as 1543 the permanent separation of Lakes Zumpango and Xaltocan from Lake Texcoco not only cut off the northern-lake towns from canoe communication with Mexico City but allowed land transport from the eastern to the western sides of the lake by way of Chiconauhtla and Ecatepec. The effect of this was twofold: first, the northern cities were no longer within the lacustrine economic hinterland of Mexico City, and, second, goods flowing into the valley from the northeast—from the direction of Pánuco and from the Teotihuacan Valley—and bound for Mexico City no longer shifted from land transport to canoes at one of the eastern-shore docks, most prominently Texcoco. These goods continued by *recua* or wagon across the new strait directly into the city. Lake Texcoco itself also suffered some changes, receding from its former shores, especially around Mexico City.

Tied to these physical changes within the Valley of

Mexico was the shift in important routes. The Texcoco-Mexico City canoe route was soon reduced to local transit. Routes north to the mines, west to Michoacán, and south to Cuernavaca and Acapulco were linked directly to Mexico City by land. The routes south to Oaxaca and east to Puebla and Veracruz entered the Valley of Mexico at the southeastern end, where goods were loaded into canoes. The docks of Tetelco, Ayotzingo, and Chalco flourished during the sixteenth century, offering inexpensive year-round shipping into Mexico City. Goods arriving in the Valley of Mexico by the routes from the northeast and east from Veracruz had previously entered Texcoco for transshipment. Now, however, these goods either went south to the Lake Chalco docks or continued directly into Mexico City by land. The previous position of the lakeshore towns as gateway cities had vanished, victims of Mexico City's expanded economic hinterland and the loss of their special break-in-bulk lakeshore locations. While the pre-Conquest economic integration of the region was shattered by changes in topographical features and means of transportation, these changes and new areas of productive significance gave rise to a new pattern of economic integration. The later growth of wagon and mule haulage, particularly in conjunction with the northern mines, reintegrated the northern area into Mexico City's economic orbit, but transporting goods from this area was more expensive by mule than it had been by canoe. The types of goods originating there shifted from the intensive-maize and market-garden varieties to the mixed-grain-and-livestock type sustainable under conditions of more costly transport.

The flow from Veracruz was particularly important as New Spain became tied to Spain's economy. The quantities of goods traversing this route increased, but they were destined for consumption by the new elites, the Spaniards, residing primarily in Mexico City, and they entered the valley skirting Texcoco.

Mexico City became the dominant city in New Spain,

seat of the colonial government and wielder of political power without peer in Mexico. Before the Conquest tribute-paying cities sent goods to the cities that had conquered them, notably imperial capitals, such as those of the Triple Alliance. After the Conquest tribute was royal or local, but local tribute was paid by encomienda Indians to encomenderos. Thus cities such as Texcoco, which had previously enjoyed tribute as conquerors, no longer did so. Royal tribute was due Mexico City alone. Cities that had been independent or semi-independent before the Conquest lost their tribute bases. While each acquired goods from its hinterland on a remunerative basis, the area from which it could require goods through political demands was limited in comparison with Mexico City.

Cattle raising was negligible in the Valley of Mexico, but sheep raising was important in the northern area around Huehuetoca. Agricultural production in the Valley of Mexico also underwent major changes, as land that had become marginal went out of production. The cultivation of grains, maize and wheat, were the important forms of primary production in the valley. A farming belt, chiefly producing wheat and maize, circled Mexico City, including the towns of Texcoco, Chalco, Tlalnepantla, Cuauhtitlan, Tepotzotlan, Huehuetoca, and Tula and extending beyond the valley proper to Toluca. In the northern end of the valley the province of Xaltocan, and particularly the townships of Tecama, Chiconautla, and Ecatepec, were important maize-producing centers. Wheat was produced on the western side of the valley, around Azcapotzalco, Tacuba, Tacubaya, and Coyoacan. This most important irrigation area was given over to wheat production, as was the Valley of Cuauhtitlan on the north. Not only was the area surrounding Mexico City but the entire region surrounding the Valley of Mexico was oriented toward intensive agricultural production for the capital.

The changes in the Valley of Mexico caused major shifts in the relative status of cities. In pre-Columbian times, Tenochtitlan was the largest city in the valley (and, indeed, in all of Mesoamerica), the logical consequence of its role as imperial capital that allowed the expansion of administrative and craft-production functions. After the Conquest, Mexico City continued its dominance of the region, but post-Columbian Mexico City also demonstrated primacy.[1] Primacy is the normal condition for colonial cities because they tend to cluster four main types of town functions and groups (elites, administration, trade, and artisans), whereas they are dispersed in countries with developed economies and long-term urban histories.[2] A colonial city achieves primacy because of its focus as an organizational nexus. Clearly Mexico City was that. It was the elite center, the administrative head of New Spain, the merchant capital, and the artisan center. The importance of Mexico City's primacy, however, was in its effect on the region.

Cities near Tenochtitlan, such as Azcapotzalco and Tlacopan, had already been drawn into a dependent relation to Tenochtitlan before the Conquest, and this subordination proceeded further following the arrival of the Spaniards. The southern-lakes agricultural region continued to supply Mexico City, as did the southwest lakeshore cities. Even Texcoco became a dependent of Mexico City,[3] given over to the production of goods for the center while losing its own market for these commodities. In the early seventeenth century Thomas Gage observed: "Texcoco itself is this day judged to consist only of a hundred Spaniards and three hundred Indian inhabitants, whose chief riches come by gardening and sending daily in their canoes herbs and salads to Mexico."[4] Much of this is explicable in terms of the expanded economic hinterland of Mexico City, based on mule and wagon transport, which, combined with its political power, increased primacy and further subordinated the region. Throughout the sixteenth century Texcoco not only sent goods to Mexico City but also was dependent on the capital for the lawyers, doctors, tailors, and specialized craftsmen it lacked.[5] The absence of such specialists was a feature shared by more distant yet equally subordinated Toluca.[6]

The changes in the importance of the various cities can be seen most clearly in their relative populations. Torquemada listed four orders of cities in immediate post-Conquest Valley of Mexico. Tenochtitlan and Texcoco were first-order cities; Xochimilco and Chalco Atenco were second-order; Otumba, Cuauhtitlan, Azcapotzalco, Tlacopan (Tacuba), Coyoacan, Huitzilopochco, Ixtapalapa, Tlalmanalco, and Amecameca were third-order; and the remaining towns of under 1,000 population were classed as fourth-order. A classification relying on political considerations was the urban status recognized by the Spaniards. Mexico City, Texcoco, Xochimilco, and Tacuba were accorded the highest urban designation, *ciudad* (city) status; Coyoacan and Tacubaya were the next level; villas and all other cities in the Valley of Mexico were pueblos.

Although there was general depopulation through the valley, the decline was not uniform. The relative size of cities changed greatly. All the towns declined in relation to Mexico City, Texcoco most drastically. Their prior importance as independent centers was undermined. They no longer supported their own elites and specialists: they now existed to support Mexico City. They were no longer important in their own right, but only in relation to the capital. Gage observed: "This lake had formerly some fourscore towns, some say more, situated round about it, many of them containing five thousand households, and some ten thousand, yea, and Texcoco (as I have said before) was as big as Mexico. But when I was there, there might be thirty towns and villages about it, and scarce any of above five hundred households between Spaniards and Indians."[7] Although these towns had supplied Tenochtitlan before the Conquest, the pre-Columbian systems of transportation had imposed sufficient distance to allow them a certain degree of autonomy. Each center had possessed its own indigenous elites. After the Conquest the new elites clustered in Mexico City; the social status of the surrounding towns declined as they became tied into a wider consumer-producer hinterland by Spanish systems of transportation.

The general population pattern for the Valley of Mexico was one of decline. Although all cities in the valley declined, the rate was more precipitous for some than for others. During the sixteenth century only Mexico City reversed the trend, because of Spanish, mestizo, and mulatto populations (despite continued Indian decline). The cities around Mexico City faired well, losing their population to the capital much more gradually. Farther away, however, the depopulation was greater except where there was some compensating factor. Thus Xochimilco flourished on intensive cultivation, trade, and lake transport. The eastern-shore cities, however, experienced only decline from their previously favorable positions. The maintenance of a favorable population ratio in the Valley of Mexico depended on providing primary production or serving the trade routes. Tlalmanalco, Xochimilco, Tepotzotlan, and Cuauhtitlan straddled major roads and managed to maintain reasonable populations, while cities no longer on the major routes, such as Texcoco, rapidly lost population. However, there was never any question of competing directly with Mexico City. The towns that became centers of extensive production, such as cattle raising, either lost population or had small populations to begin with, while towns engaged in intensive production needed large populations and experienced relative growth, as in the chinampa town of Xochimilco.

The impact of all these changes is most clearly seen in Texcoco. Formerly the much-vaunted second city of the empire, it fell to lowly status in the sixteenth century. The lowering of the lakes shifted all the important trade around Texcoco. It was no longer a break-in-transit point. Nor could it offer the goods and services sought by the new elites resident in politically dominant Mexico City. It was shorn of its political and economic independence, and the lake that once granted Texcoco insulation from Tenochtitlan's domination now became a barrier, rerouting long-distance traffic and obstructing the remainder.

NEW SPAIN

New Spain's economic situation was reflected not only in changes in the Valley of Mexico but by conditions throughout the country. Crop complexes changed, animal husbandry was introduced, mining was begun on a large scale, and foreign trade was developed. However, interpretations of New Spain's post-1580 economy have been many and varied. In his pioneering work on the subject Borah[8] suggested that New Spain's economy contracted after 1576 because Indian depopulation caused massive loss of labor, particularly in the areas of agriculture and mining. Although the idea that New Spain suffered a depression is not without its supporters,[9] that interpretation has been seriously challenged. Data on agriculture available to the cities appear to support the view of a general economic stagnation,[10] but consumption of goods from Spain, at least until the 1620s, and production of silver[11] throughout the seventeenth century indicate the opposite. Thus the existence of a general depression is belied by the data, but economic indicators show some significant changes that have been variously interpreted as stagnation and as a growth in New Spain's self-sufficiency.[12] Rather than attempting to assess the state of Mexico's economy primarily on the basis of mining and agricultural production rates, other factors need to be considered.

Whatever the state of production, distribution dictates the state of regional economic integration. Transport efficiency determines the distance a commodity can travel and remain commercially viable. Owing to its high cost per ton-mile, the pre-Columbian tlameme system did not, and could not, economically integrate central Mexico in terms of basic commodities, but the greater potential efficiency of *arrieros* and *carreteros* made this feasible. Tlamemes were used by the Spaniards from the outset, but taking advantage of their different strengths, tlamemes were partly and gradually displaced by *arrieros* on improved routes and by both *arrieros* and *carreteros* on the best routes. Yet large areas of New Spain were served more efficiently, or exclusively, by tlamemes, thus facilitating the economic integration of the country by linking many areas without requiring the time-consuming and costly construction of European-style roads.

While roads could have been built early in the sixteenth century, they were not for it was easier to rely on tlamemes. But while there were still millions of Indians, the impact of their ultimate decline was not adequately anticipated and political realities precluded the construction of roads, which were not yet essential, until there were too few Indians to construct and maintain them. Thus the need for adequate roads between all but the most important centers was muted and could be, and was, deferred. But as a consequence, by the end of the sixteenth century, New Spain possessed only a skeletal European transportation network and the tlamemes who had completed the system were vastly reduced. The indigenous system precipitously declined, yet Spanish systems were not sufficiently developed to compensate. The combination of higher-paid Spanish *arrieros* and *carreteros* and poor roads led to an increase in transportation costs, crippling the economic integration of New Spain.[13]

High-value goods, such as silver, continued to move on roads linking the mines, cities and ports, aided by their ability to bear greater transport costs, as did expensive Spanish imports, which found a ready market among the urban colonial elite.[14] Trade constricted everywhere, although to a lesser extent along existing but decaying roads, as cheaper goods unable to bear the increased cost of transport were restricted to smaller and smaller market areas.

The rise of haciendas was not just an economic response to the world economic situation. It was a natural result of the century-long structuring of the regional economy. The hacienda was a logical adaptation to production at a distance from the consuming center. It produced goods on an extensive basis to retain marketability, with the consequence that it had to be largely self-sufficient. It could produce livestock for the Mexico City and export markets cheaply, but as transportation costs rose, it could not be effectively tied into the distant and hence expensive consumer market and consequently became largely self-sufficient.

Thus New Spain's economic unity disintegrated. The changing economic pattern in late-sixteenth- and seventeenth-century New Spain was not primarily the result of declining production. Rather, the rising cost of transportation rendered long-distance trade in cheaper commodities infeasible and gave rise to regional self-sufficiency in basic goods, linking only those areas along the few roads, and then only in the trade for luxuries. The policy of relying on tlameme labor that allowed the early economic integration of New Spain, when relied on overlong, also led to its disintegration.

In short, the economic hinterland of Tenochtitlan had been relatively restricted because of inefficient transport. But once Spanish systems of transportation were available, one would expect that the economic hinterland increased correspondingly. In fact, it did not. Despite the improved transport, Mexico City was not free to exploit all areas that should have been economically viable, because competing centers existed in this expanded area. These centers had been established before the Conquest and had occupied discrete hinterlands. But after the Conquest economic hinterlands were redefined, and they were placed in conflict with Mexico City. The capital exercised its political power by regulating prices and controlling grain sales. Over the course of the century the previously competing centers had been converted from competitors of the capital to its suppliers.

CHAPTER 13

Comparisons and Conclusions

MANY of the developments in pre-Columbian Mexico were constrained by transportation. The low efficiency of tlamemes limited the support areas of urban centers, resulting in small cities that were closely packed on the landscape. In contrast to the rest of Mesoamerica, the Valley of Mexico enjoyed an additional transportation system, highly efficient canoes, that allowed Tenochtitlan to exploit a productive area much larger than that available to other Mesoamerican cities. This expanded support area permitted a larger population in Tenochtitlan and served as the basis for its political dominance.

The Aztec elites of Tenochtitlan had largely pursued remunerative strategies to generate foodstuffs within the Valley of Mexico, resulting in a highly efficient agricultural system that ranged from intensive chinampa cultivation through more extensive forms of production. In addition to the remunerative transport of high-bulk–low-value foodstuffs, the Aztecs employed a coercive tribute system. Their imperial strategy was, in large measure, to incorporate tributary areas that could supply Tenochtitlan with goods, including foodstuffs. Most of the tributary provinces were beyond the transportationally circumscribed economic support area of Tenochtitlan, and goods from them flowed into the center on a noneconomic basis. The tribute system was Tenochtitlan's means of artificially expanding its economic hinterland: it overcame the transportational constraints of the tlameme system by placing the cost of transportation outside its own polity onto the shoulders of the tribute-paying populations. It also allowed manufacturing in the Valley of Mexico to be undermined by providing goods at or below production prices, thus making surrounding cities dependent on Tenochtitlan.

Transportation constraints had further effects on the pattern of Aztec polity and economy. The Aztec empire, based on hegemony, was uniquely adapted to the situation in Mesoamerica. Rather than pursuing a course of territorial incorporation with all the responsibilities that entails, the hegemonic empire was tailored to generate resources from the broadest base possible at minimal cost to the polity.

Pochtecah traders, too, were constrained by transport considerations. One of the principal reasons the pochtecah engaged in the continual expansion of the Aztec empire was not to fuel the coffers of Tenochtitlan with free tribute goods in lieu of pochtecah trade items but to create a larger, safer, and more efficiently organized trading area within the empire. This was made possible by imperial demands for tlameme carriers to feed interregional trade. The pochtecah also gave Tenochtitlan a monopoly on goods available beyond the empire and thus bolstered the city's craft manufacturing.

Through its political control of trade and tribute Tenochtitlan converted the Valley of Mexico from a fragmented collection of economically and politically autonomous or semiautonomous city-states into a unified system. Tenochtitlan, the core, supplied secondary goods, and the remaining cities, the periphery, bought and consumed these in exchange for primary agricultural goods.

The advent of the Spaniards changed the indigenous urban-support system. The colonial government placed more emphasis on remunerative compliance in supporting its cities and less on overtly coercive means, although coercion initially played a central role. Spanish systems of transportation augmented and partly displaced indigenous forms of transport. Despite the initial reliance by Spaniards on tlamemes, trade with Spain fostered the development of *arrieros* and particularly *carreteros* in New Spain. While the emerging Atlantic trade consisted largely of exotics capable of bearing the high cost of tlameme transport, climatological conditions and political events in Europe combined to channel the flow of overseas goods, shifting from a low-volume, irregular flow to a high-volume flow concentrated in a few weeks' time. The enormous increase in porter demand during peak periods could not be met by the existing tlamemes, particularly given the drastic depopulation. Moreover, expansion of the tlameme system was highly inelastic, any increase in load-hauling capacity being tied directly to increased manpower. Spanish transportation systems, however, could much more easily expand since their crucial elements were wagons and beasts of burden rather than manpower. Thus tlamemes were relegated to a secondary role in transporting the major flow of goods in New Spain, although they continued to be used in conjunction with *arrieros* and *carreteros,* as well as in areas of difficult terrain and for other portage services. Perhaps their greatest use in the latter half of the sixteenth century was not as professional organized porters but as casual coerced labor seized in villages en route.

Both *arrieros* and *carreteros* were more efficient than tlamemes. Thus they offered the prospect of expanding economic hinterlands to sizes heretofore impossible. This expansion was not, however, uniform. The new systems of transportation were tied to supporting facilities, primarily roads, to a degree unprecedented in Mexico. Consequently, the economic hinterland was not a uniformly expanding circular area around the city. While the Aztecs had expanded their economic hinterlands in a roughly circular fashion, the Spaniards did not. Under the Aztecs' transportation constraints the more proximate the area the city drew on, the more fully exploited that area was. With the advent of the more efficient Spanish transport systems, however, the proximity of the economic hinterland became less crucial. Areas of agricultural exploitation developed with more concern for favorable production than for transportation ease. While depopulation reduced the foodstuffs needed in the capital, the Spanish transport systems greatly expanded the area within which this production could take place. Once initiated, however, the pattern of areal exploitation achieved a certain inertia, funneling further traffic along the routes initially established. Being dependent on roads, these transportation systems linked distant, major producing areas as roads developed, that is, unevenly. In seeming contradiction, the very development of such regional linkages fostered continued reliance on the earlier tlameme system, for linking certain areas by the roads joining each to Mexico City left other areas served inadequately or not at all. Thus tlamemes, less hindered by terrain and less dependent on roads, served these areas. In large part the three land-transport systems—tlamemes, *arrieros,* and *carreteros*—served complementary areas, varying by terrain and degree of road improvement.

The tlameme system was undermined by two important developments: indigenous population decline and rise of competing Spanish systems of transportation. Depopulation decreased the numbers of Indians available to serve, and potential tlamemes were siphoned off into other occupations, being no longer constrained by the Aztec hereditary occupation system.

In the Valley of Mexico the canoe system, on which Tenochtitlan depended for its pre-Columbian dominance, was undergoing changes as well. Not only did the more efficient Spanish systems of transportation reduce the disparity between lake and land transport, but, in addition, deforestation, overgrazing, and erosion combined to alter the lakes themselves, reducing their area of usefulness to the two southern lakes serving Mexico City. Much of the economic reorientation within the Valley of Mexico revolved around the changes in the lake system. Lake desiccation reoriented much of the trade away from previously important centers, such as Texcoco, both by reducing the effectiveness of the lake as a conduit and by presenting opportunities to continue the Spanish systems of transport directly into Mexico City, thus removing the lakeshore cities as break-in-bulk points and denying them their earlier gateway-city status. Thus the transport grid of central Mexico and the Valley of Mexico was radically altered, with important consequences for Mexico City's economic hinterland.

Mexico City had less need than Tenochtitlan to rely on coercive factors to maintain its supplies of foodstuffs. The combination of a larger economic hinterland and the effective loss of revenue entailed in transporting tribute goods to Mexico City led to the curtailment of the tribute system. Tribute goods continued to be required, but not portage to the capital. Monetary tribute or local sale of tribute in kind did away with the large expense of portage: money was substituted and used in part to purchase foodstuffs from areas nearer Mexico City. Thus the Spaniards engaged in intensive production in areas that were adjacent to the Valley of Mexico albeit more distant than could have feasibly supplied the city in pre-Columbian times, by using efficient wagon transportation to link the major producing areas to the capital.

However, Mesoamerica was not a tabula rasa upon which Spanish transportation systems could construct logical and efficient hinterlands. Mexico City found itself in competition with urban centers that had previously dominated their own economic hinterlands. The potential expansion of economic hinterlands, born of increased transport efficiency, now threw into conflict cities that had previously drawn on discrete economic hinterlands. As a consequence, Mexico City did not rely solely on its remunerative appeal but attempted to secure goods through coercive means.

Grain regulations and market control were instituted over the surrounding areas with the avowed purpose of securing and guaranteeing the flow of foodstuffs into Mexico City. The effect of these regulations, however, was to decrease the amount of grain being produced, since it was now inadequately compensated, and many people moved into secondary production occupations.

This exercise of coercion by Mexico City was less

blatant than that of the Aztecs, and it was less effective, at least initially. It resulted in a reduced grain flow, but by the end of the sixteenth century political control of markets and production had restricted competing centers, restructured the economic hinterlands of central Mexico, and funneled into the capital goods that had previously gone to other cities.

However, the economic situation of the country as a whole was less integrated. Although limited areas, such as Mexico City and its environs, could succeed in restructuring their surroundings to promote their maintenance and growth, economic integration of large areas was dependent on transportation efficiency. But as transportation faltered and fragmented, the diverse regions of New Spain were left only tenuously linked by inadequate roads, permitting economic interaction only at the level of elite goods and reducing the countryside to relatively isolated and necessarily self-sufficient regions.

Appendices

APPENDEX A

Agriculture in the Valley of Mexico

CHARLTON lists modern yields in the Teotihuacan Valley, a subsystem of the Valley of Mexico, but these cover only a few years.[1] Sanders estimates the modern-day average annual yield to be 1,000 kilograms per hectare in the alluvial plain of the middle valley, 1,400 kilograms per hectare (kg/ha) in the lower valley and delta, and 600 kg/ha on sloping terrain lacking adequate floodwater irrigation.[2] In an earlier study Sanders listed the modern-day production levels through both annual and twenty-four-year cycles, contrasting highland and lowland (see table A.1).[3]

Sanders also estimates the cultivation of the Texcoco region before the Conquest (see table A.2.).[4]

Table A.1. Agricultural Productivity Under Various Conditions

Community	Land type
Highlands:	
San Pablo Izquitlan	Irrigated
San Francisco Mazapan	Temporal
Santiago Atlatongo	Irrigated
Calvario Acolman	Irrigated
San Gregorio	Chinampa
	Fertilized
	Unfertilized
	Fertilized hillside
Eloxochitlan	Barbecho (fallowing)
	Calmil ("household" lots)
Tecomatepec	Irrigated
Panajachel	Delta
	Hillside
Lowlands:	
Chicoacan	Forested hills
Tierra Nueva	Flat forested
El Puente	Floodplain
Pisté	Scrub forest
Tajín	Forest (two harvests)

*Unless otherwise noted, amounts are in tons.
Source: Sanders 1957:330–31.

Production*	
Annual	Per 24-Year Cycle
Maize, 1.2	28.8
Year 1: maize, 0.5	6
Year 2: barley, 0.5	6
Year 1: maize, 2	24
wheat, 2	24
Year 2: barley, 1.4	16.8
Year 1: maize, 1.35	16.2
wheat, 1.1	13.2
Year 2: barley, 0.9	10.8
Maize, 4	96
Maize, 3	72
Maize, 1.5	36
Year 1: maize, 2.25	18
Year 2: amaranth, 15 cargas	120 cargas
Year 3: chili, 1	8
Maize, 1.5	18
Maize, 3	72
Maize, 3.75	90
Maize, 2	48
Maize, 1.2	17
Maize, 1	6
Year 1: maize, 2.5	12
Year 2: maize, 1	
Year 1: maize, 4.3	17.4
Year 2: maize, 1.5	
Maize, 0.8	3.2
Maize, 3	6–9

Table A.2. Agricultural Productivity in Pre-Conquest Texcoco

Cultivation	Average Yield of Cropped Fields (Kilograms per Hectare per Year)	Average Yield of Agricultural Lands (Kilograms per Hectare per Year)
Calmil ("household" lots)	1,400	1,400
Alluvial plain (permanent irrigation)	1,400	1,400
Piedmont (permanent irrigation)	1,000	1,000
Alluvial plain (floodwater irrigation)	1,000	1,000
Piedmont (floodwater terraces)	800	800
Riverine floodplain	1,200	1,200
Naturally humid land	1,400	700
Chinampa	3,000	3,000
Pseudo-chinampa	2,000	2,000
Temporal (alluvial plain)	1,000	500
Temporal (piedmont)	400–800	200–400
Bush fallowing	1,400	280

Source: Sanders 176a:144.

It is on the basis of these kinds of data that valley-wide extrapolations are made.

Sanders collected chinampa productivity data in the Valley of Mexico during the early 1950s.[5] Maize is sown in rows about 0.5 meter apart with plants in each row about 0.5 meter apart, four to five seeds per hole. Approximately 1 *cuartillo* (1.2 to 1.5 kilograms) of seed is used per 0.1 hectare, or 10 *cuartillos* per hectare (see table A.3).

Table A.3. Productivity of Chinampa Cultivation

Chinampa size (Hectare)	1.2–1.5 Kilograms of Seed per Hectare	Production (Kilograms per Hectare)
Tlahuac, predrought:		
0.32	3,700	5,550
0.10	2,500–3,000	3,750–4,500
0.16	3,100–3,700	4,650–5,500
0.10	2,500–3,000	3,750–4,500
0.16	3,100	4,650
0.16	4,650	6,300
Tlahuac, dessicated chinampas:		
2.00	2,000	3,000
0.36	3,000–3,300	4,500–4,950
0.40	3,300–4,000	4,950–6,000
0.26	1,600–1,700	2,400–2,550
San Gregorio Atlapulco:		
0.21	2,500–3,000	3,750–4,500
0.21	2,400–2,900	3,600–4,350
0.10	2,500–3,000	3,750–4,500
0.12	3,300	4,950

Source: Sanders 1957:84.

APPENDIX B

The Aztec Tribute System

TRIBUTE data are scattered throughout a large number of materials, the three primary sources being the *Matrícula de tributos,* the *Codex Mendoza,* and the *Información de 1554.*[1] The *Matrícula de tributos* consists of sixteen leaves of native *amatl* (paper) with pictographic representations of towns and tribute assessments[2] dating from between 1511[3] and the 1540s.[4] Bound in European fashion, it bears no evidence of having once been cut and bound as an indigenous screenfold. Thus whether it is pre- or post-Columbian is problematic, but from a study of the layout of typical pages Robertson (1959:75) suggests that it could be a reworking of a prototype in another format. Since it retains the indigenous style, Berdan assumes that it also retains the indigenous content.[5] The *Codex Mendoza,* although pictographic, was ordered painted for the king of Spain by Viceroy Mendoza between 1541 and 1550. It consists of three sections, the middle one dealing with tribute "most probably copied with some changes from the Matrícula de Tributos."[6] The *Codex Mendoza* has Spanish glosses that are more than literal translations of the pictorial content, containing information not included pictographically: "The Spanish written commentary is given first place and the native pictorial matter second for most of the manuscript."[7] The *Codex Mendoza* lists tribute from thirty-eight provinces, four more than the *Matrícula,* though they were presumably on two missing leaves of the latter. The provinces are listed in the same order in both, but the *Codex Mendoza* differs from the *Matrícula* in two basic ways. First, it annotates cloth and clothing as loads or cargas rather than as items, resulting in a twentyfold increase. Second, it indicates that manufactured items, exclusive of various costumes and shields, were due semiannually.[8] The *Información de 1554* resulted from a royal *cédula* of 20 December, 1553 seeking information concerning, among other things, the pre-Conquest tribute system.[9] This document is based on the testimony of thirteen witnesses, all Indian nobles from fifty to more than seventy years of age. The *Información* follows the same order in listing provinces as do the *Matrícula* and *Codex Mendoza* but omits three provinces, while adding one, Apan, not included in either of the others.[10]

Despite the relatedness of the *Matrícula* and the *Codex Mendoza,* Borah and Cook point out differences between them that are not explained as errors in recording.[11] Thus they suggest another record, which they call prototype A, as the source from which both were drawn, and a prototype B, on which the *Información* was based. In any case, the three basic sources were recorded in the following chronological sequence: *Matrícula, Codex Mendoza, Información.* But each differs in content in ways not patently derivable from its immediate predecessor. So while they may be compared for some purposes, the sources cannot be evaluated for accuracy by so doing.

Reconciliation of differences among sources when one is derived from others is relatively simple, but reconciliation of differences among sources derived from an unknown third source is a difficult and uncertain process if one desires to go beyond the minimum common elements. Thus in analyzing tribute based on these documents, three major issues arise: (1) What provinces were paying tribute? (2) What was the frequency of tribute payment? and (3) What were the quantities of tribute paid? The provinces to be included in the Aztec tribute system are a simple matter. Additions of provinces in some sources do not require complementary deletions from others, and other sources, such as the *Relaciones geográficas,* tend to confirm maximal inclusion. Periodicity of payment does require exclusionary choice. Three payment periods are mentioned in the sources: yearly, twice yearly, and every 80 days. The *Matrícula* mentions all three periods, but the semiannual period applies only to Xoconochco (Soconusco) and is represented by glyphs. For all other provinces only annual periods (usually shown by warriors' costumes and shields) and 80-day periods are listed in the annotations.[12] The *Codex Mendoza,* however, indicates in the annotations annual and semiannual payments, with occasional 80-day assessments. The *Información* lists annual and 80-day assessments. The problems raised by these conflicts are (1) Which of these periods were used? and (2) What was their significance? There is little disagreement concerning annual assessments. The problem is the 80-day and semiannual assessments. Although the semiannual sequence has been accepted by some authorities,[13] Berdan[14] favors the 80-day sequence for three reasons. First, she places stress on the temporal priority of the *Matrícula* over the *Codex Mendoza.* Second, she believes that the semiannual periods were not viable units in the Aztec calendar. Third, the frequency of the 80-day period in other matters and in colonial tribute assessments argue for its indigenous use, despite its awkward fit with the European calendar. As Borah and Cook point out, the disagreement is basically between the Spanish annotations and text of the *Codex Mendoza* (favoring semiannual) on the one hand and the annotations of the *Matrícula* and the text of the *Información* (favoring 80 days) on the other.[15] The semiannual glyphs for Xoconochco's tribute can be used both to argue for semiannual assessments, since this is clear evidence of their existence, and to argue against them, since the very use of the glyphs indicates the peculiarity of such an assessment. Despite its inconclusiveness, the weight of evidence is on the side of the 80-day assessments, but there is also debate over the significance of an 80-day payment. It has been suggested[16] that, although the 80-day period was frequently reported throughout the sixteenth century,[17] it was keyed to four festivals and followed a sequence of 80-100-80-100 days, plus 5 days which rounded out the year to 365 and were considered "dead." This interpretation also has explicit supporting statements from the sixteenth century.[18] But again the evidence favors the 80-day period, or 4.5 assessments a year. Much evidence favors annual and 80-day tribute payments, except in the case of Xoconochco, but there is sufficient countervailing evidence to prevent it from being conclusive. Furthermore, there is conflict over the application of the annual and 80-day figures. Documentary evidence, Nahuatl and Spanish notations of the *Matrícula,* and the logic of annual harvests argue for annual grain assessments.[19] However, Berdan states that, since annotations of the *Matrícula* for tribute periods are mentioned at the beginning of the text, they are to be construed as applying to all the tribute on the page, including foodstuffs. The issue of periodicity and application of those periods is inconclusively argued.[20]

The third major difficulty concerns the quantities assessed. Again, the discrepancy is between the *Matrícula* and the *Codex Mendoza.* In reference to mantas (blankets), the former refers to "mantas" whereas the latter refers to "loads of mantas." Berdan argues that "loads" was a later addition to the Spanish annotations and that the Nahuatl numerical classifier *-quimilli* is used to specify twenty in two instances in the *Matrícula* when particularly small amounts are given, and not otherwise.[21] Likewise, *Codex Mendoza* adds "bunches" to the *Matrícula's* "feathers." Borah and Cook agree that "mantas" rather than "loads of mantas" are indicated, since single mantas, rather than loads, to which numerical quantities are designated are pictorially represented.[22] However, on the same logical basis, they accept "bunches of feathers," as does Berdan, rather than "feathers," when the *Matrícula* depicts groups of feathers with quantities numerically indicated.[23] It is evident that there is some vacillation in the credence given to the two pictorial sources and their respective Spanish and Nahuatl glosses and pictographic representations. But most important for my interests here, quantities of food are in issue. The *Codex Mendoza* and the *Información de*

1554 mention four staple foods, maize, beans, chia, and *huauhtli,* although the *Matrícula* lists only maize and beans.[24] Furthermore, where single bins are depicted in the *Matrícula,* two bins are depicted in the *Codex Mendoza,* and textual annotations double these. In short, the matter of tribute is a complicated one. A seemingly simple formula of "number of goods times period of payment" becomes "number of goods (times single or multiple units) times 1, 2, 4, or 4.5 times per year" depending on the interpretation placed on the various sources.

APPENDIX C

Mule Transport

Conditions of mule transport established for the U.S. Army in 1917 present a good picture of organized pack-train portage.[1] In a packtrain of 50 mules, there should be one pack master, one assistant pack master, ten packers, one blacksmith, and one cook, as well as 14 riding mules. Thus there was a packer for every 5 mules on the trail.

The mules used in the U.S. Army were between 14.1 and 15.1 hands (1.45 to 1.55 meters) high, weighed 950 to 1,100 pounds (432 to 500 kilograms), and were between four and six years old (although mules can work for many years, there is a two-year period of peak efficiency). This accords with eighteenth-century Mexican records that state the working life of mules in *recuas* to be about two years.[2] Ordinarily, a pack mule carries 250 pounds (113 kilograms) plus pack frame, and travels 20 to 25 miles (32 to 40 kilometers) a day at the rate of 4.5 to 5 miles (7 to 8 kilometers) per hour on level terrain, and in rough or mountainous terrain they carry the same load 10 to 15 miles (16 to 24 kilometers) a day. Mules require occasional days of rest. In warm climates marches should be avoided during the heat of the day, as should two marches a day.[3] The incidence of animal loss is difficult to estimate. During ten months and twenty days in the field in Mexico, the U.S. Army lost 16 percent of its mules (36 of 224), none owing to combat. In Spain during the eighteenth and nineteenth centuries each *arriero* had an average of three pack animals.[4] Loads, distance, and *arriero*-to-mule ratios conform to the general standards recorded for the U.S. Army.

The speed at which mules travel is related to the

number of days traveled and the load, as well as to terrain and weather, and a simple statement fails to cover the variables adequately. Daly,[5] however, presents an admirable summary (see table C.1).

In the mid-nineteenth century one *jornada* (daily distance) was 12 to 15 miles with loaded mules.[6]

The efforts required in mule raising appear to be more than rewarded. Mules are the premier pack animals, owing to their surefootedness; they are resistant to disease and heat, they are long-lived, and they can furnish transport in areas unsuited for horses.[7] Mules eat slightly less than

Table C.1. Mule Transport Efficiency

Weight of Load, Pounds (Kilograms)	Rate of Travel per Hour, Miles (Kilometers)	Rate of Travel per Day, Miles (Kilometers)	Days of Travel
200 (91)	8 (13)	25 (40)	7
200 (91)	7 (11)	40 (65)	10
200 (91)	6 (10)	50 (81)	7
200 (91)	6 (10)	100 (161)	3
200 (91)	5 (8)	25 (40)	365
250 (114)	8 (13)	25 (40)	3
250 (114)	7 (11)	40 (65)	7
250 (114)	6 (10)	100 (161)	1
250 (114)	6 (10)	50 (81)	5
250 (114)	6 (10)	25 (40)	30
250 (114)	6 (10)	20 (32)	60
250 (114)	5 (8)	100 (161)	2
250 (114)	5 (8)	50 (81)	10
250 (114)	5 (8)	25 (40)	60
250 (114)	5 (8)	20 (32)	90
300 (136)	5 (8)	75 (121)	1
300 (136)	5 (8)	50 (81)	7
300 (136)	5 (8)	25 (40)	30
300 (136)	5 (8)	20 (32)	60
350 (159)	4 (6)	20 (32)	30
400 (182)	4 (6)	15 (24)	30

Source: U.S. Army 1917:145.

horses in proportion to their body weight, 0.94 pounds per hundredweight versus 1.07 pounds per hundredweight for horses.[8] In 1900 U.S. Army standards set the daily forage ration for a horse at 12 pounds of oats, corn, or barley and only 9 pounds for a mule. Both animals also received 14 pounds of hay a day plus two ounces of salt a week.[9] Mules also adapt to a maize diet when it is balanced with adequate forage, and they can subsist on grasses for extended periods.[10] The mule reputedly thrives on coarse fodder that horses cannot utilize.[11]

The hauling capacity of mules varies widely under different conditions. In the tropical jungles of Yucatán, Morley recorded the average packtrain speed as slightly less than 4 kilometers per hour, with daily journeys ranging from 20 to 32 kilometers.[12] During the rainy season, however, speed was reduced to 8 to 10 kilometers on a good day. Stephens described the difficulty of traveling with mules, even half-loaded, during the rainy season.[13] During the U.S. Army campaign against Geronimo of 1885–86, the daily rate of travel was 30 miles (48 kilometers) a day, except in mountainous terrain, where it fell to about 15 miles (24 kilometers).[14]

ABBREVIATIONS USED IN NOTES

ARCHIVES

AA	Archivo Antiguo de Ayuntamiento, Mexico
-Co	Compendio
-D	Desagüe
-O	Ordenanzas
AGN	Archivo General de la Nación, Mexico
-C	Civil
-Con	Consulado
-GP	General de Parte
-I	Indios
-M	Mercedes
-O	Ordenanzas
-RCD	Reales Cédulas Duplicadas
AHN	Archivo Histórico de Notarias, Mexico

PUBLISHED SOURCES

AC	*Actas de cabildo de la Ciudad de México.* Ignacio Bejarano, Comp 54 vols. Mexico, 1889-1916.
CI	*Cedulario indiano.* 4 vols. Madrid: Ediciones Cultura Hispánica, 1945–46.
DCLI	*Disposiciones complementárias de las leyes de Indias.* 3 vols. Madrid.
DIHC	*Documentos inéditos relativos a Hernán Cortés y su familia.* Mexico, 1935.
DII	*Colección de documentos inéditos relativos al descubrimiento, conquista y organización de las antiguas posesiones españolas de América y Oceania.* 41 vols. Madrid, 1864–84.
DIU	*Colección de documentos inéditos relativos al descubrimiento, conquista y organización de las antiguas posesiones españolas de ultramar.* 25 vols. Madrid, 1885–1932.
ENE	*Epistolario de Nueva España.* Francisco del Paso y Troncoso, ed. 16 vols. Mexico: José Porrúa e Hijos.
FHT	*Fuentes para la historia del trabajo en Nueva España.* Silvio Zavala and María Castelo, eds. 8 vols. Mexico: Fondo de Cultura Económica, 1939–46.
IE	*Indice y extractos de los protocolos de la notaria de Cholula (1590-1600).* Cayetano Reyes García, ed. Mexico: Sepinah, 1973.
IEPAN	*Indice y extractos de los protocolos del archivo de notarias de México, df (1524-1528).* A. Millares Carlo and J. I. Mantecón, eds. Mexico: El Colegio de México, 1945.
NEW LAWS	*The New Laws for the Government of the Indies and for the Preservation of the Indians, 1542-1543.* New York: AMS Press, 1971.
PNE	*Papeles de Nueva España.* Francisco del Paso y Troncoso, ed. 9 vols. Madrid and Mexico.
RDI	*Recopilación de leyes de los reynos de las Indias.* 4 vols. Madrid: Ediciones Cultura Híspánica, 1973.
RMEH	*Revista mexicana de estudios históricos.*
VEA	*Los virreyes españoles en América durante el gobierno de la Casa de Austria.* Lewis Hanke, ed. 5 vols. Madrid: Ediciones Atlas, 1976–78.

Notes

CHAPTER 1

1. Cortés 1971:102–108. See also Aguilar 1977:74–79, 101–102; Anonymous Conqueror 1917:55, 61–75; Díaz del Castillo 1974:160 [chap. 88].
2. Durán 1967.
3. Davies 1977a:xv–xvi.
4. R. M. Adams 1979; Blouet 1972; Davis 1973; M. Hammond 1972; Hauser 1965; Price 1978a,b; Schaedel 1978; Sjoberg 1965; Trigger 1972; Wheatley 1972.
5. Eighmy 1972:299.
6. Jones 1966b:10, 18.
7. Borah 1980.
8. E.g., Parsons 1971; Blanton 1972; Brumfiel 1976.

CHAPTER 2

1. Sanders and Price (1968:104) distinguish three zones by altitude and subdivide each by amounts of rainfall, yielding the following:

1. *Tierra caliente* (0 to 1,000 m)
   a. Arid (below 800 mm annual precipitation)
   b. Subhumid (800 to 1,200 mm)
   c. Humid (over 1,200 mm)
2. *Tierra templada* (1,000 to 2,000 m)
   a. Arid (below 500 mm)
   b. Subhumid (500 to 1,000 mm)
   c. Humid (over 1,000 mm)
3. *Tierra fría* (2,000 to 2,800 m)
   a. Arid (below 500 mm)
   b. Subhumid (500 to 1,000 mm)
   c. Humid (over 1,000 mm)

Other divisions by altitude have been used (0 to 2,000 ft., 2,000 to 6,000 ft, above 6,000 ft [Poole 1951:28]; 0 to 800 m, 800 to 1,600 m, 1,600 to 2,800 m [Sanders 1957:5], but the Sanders and Price divisions are useful and probably have the greatest currency. Sanders and Price have correlated altitude divisions with temperature tolerance of plants (e.g., cacao does not flourish above 1,000 m, maguey is found primarily above 2,000 m, and the growing season for maize above 2,000 m is restricted to six to seven months). Including both indigenous and introduced plants and combining the data of Sanders (1957:5) and Moreno Toscano (1968:43–46), reveal the following productive zones: *tierra caliente* produces cacao, bananas, sugarcane, zapote, tobacco, and cotton; *tierra templada* produces coffee, citrus fruits, maize, beans, and squash; *tierra fría,* which includes the Valley of Mexico, produces mainly grains—wheat, barley, and maize. Sixteen hundred meters is the approximate altitude below which year-round cropping is possible and above which frosts occur, limiting the agricultural season for most crops to approximately seven months (Sanders 1957:276).

2. Emmart 1940:37; Guerra 1969:39; Sahagún 1963:251–56 [bk. 11, chap. 12]; Williams 1972:619–20.

3. Sahagún 1963:283–84 [bk. 11, Chap. 13].

4. Sanders and Price 1968:145.

5. Palerm 1955:28–29.

6. Boserup 1973.

7. Bray 1972a:910; Palerm 1961:240; Sanders and Price 1968:123.

8. Palerm 1961:242–67.

9. Offner 1980.

10. Callen 1973. By the Conquest not only did cultivated plants constitute the major part of the indigenous diet, but there had been a shift away from earlier cultivated plants such as cactus, agave, roots, and herbs in favor of greater proportions of maize, beans, squash, and chili. Even a cursory examination of the *Relaciones geográficas* of 1579–80 reveals an overwhelming reliance on grains.

11. López A. and Serrano S. 1974:144.

12. Benedict and Steggerda 1937:157–88; Bray 1972a:921; Charlton 1970:320; Kirkby 1973:127; Sanders 1957:304, 1970b:440.

13. Jaén Esquivel and López Alonso 1974:129-30; Stewart 1973:48–49.

14. Borah and Cook (1963) use the 4.5-per-family estimate to reflect a slightly growing population. While it may be low, I shall nevertheless use it since there is no strong basis for selecting another figure, and I am primarily concerned with per capita consumption, not household size.

15. Cuevas 1975:52–53.

16. Mexico, Archivo General de la Nación 1940, 11:16.

17. AGN-RCD 3-17-9, 1587.

18. Cook and Borah's (1963) estimates apparently assume a consumption rate for women and children two-thirds that of the adult male, approximately five fanegas a year, or 2,533 calories a day.

19. Establishing pre-Columbian agricultural productivity is a

very uncertain undertaking, particularly when one is discussing crops drawn from a considerable area, as was the case in the tribute system. As a tentative basis for assessing the land area required per family (of 4.5 persons), I have used the agricultural production figures for 1970 for Mexico, aggregated by state (Mexico, Dirección General de Estadística 1975), making the assumption that modern production is on a par with that of the pre-Columbian era, since Palerm (1961) has shown that irrigation agriculture existed in virtually all areas tributary to Tenochtitlan. I assume that the intensively worked *coa* agriculture was as productive as modern agriculture, and where the former was more productive, modern improvements in crops and cultivation techniques should more than offset the advantage. Consequently, I feel the modern estimates to be a fair sample for *coa* cultivation or, at worst, conservative. From calculations of maize production per hectare (the cob corn being reduced to achieve a shelled-corn estimate [Cowgill 1962:277], the number of hectares required to support a family per year are as follows: México, 1.686; Guerrero, 1.434; Hidalgo, 1.374; Tamaulipas, 1.622; San Luis Potosi, 1.370; Veracruz, 1.737; Puebla, 1.516; Morelos, 1.957; Oaxaca, 1.333.

These figures thus provide a basis for calculating not only how much land was required per family but also the population totals in a given area. These totals are, of course, skewed by such social factors as the requirement to bring food into densely populated areas such as Tenochtitlan. However, hunting and fishing also supplemented the Aztec diet (Linné 1937, 1940), and agriculture was not solely responsible for supporting the population.

20. Thünen 1966.

21. Boserup 1973.

22. Thünen 1966.

23. Ibid., pp. 12–14.

24. Ekholm 1946.

25. There are two likely explanations for the use of *t* rather than *tl* in the word *tameme*. The first is that the Spaniards found the *tl* phoneme difficult to pronounce and thus altered it, as they did with many other Nahuatl words: *ocelotl › ocelote, tomatl › tomate, coyotl › coyote.* The second is that, along the Gulf Coast, where Cortés began his inland trek, there were many Nahuat speakers. Although similar to Nahuatl, Nahuat lacks the *tl* phoneme, using *t* instead. Thus the *tla* prefix would be *ta,* yielding *tameme.* Adding further to the second hypothesis is the selection of *memeh* over *mamah. Memeh* and *mamah* are spatially distinguished, the latter being used in central Mexico, and the former elsewhere. Thus, the Nahuat version, *tameme,* could have entered Spanish common usage as a consequence of the original invasion route.

I have chosen to use the Anglicized plural of *tlameme,* spelled without the glottal *h,* as being more convenient for the readers. Most Nahuatl words, especially those used infrequently, have been used with Nahuatl singular and pluralization.

26. Clavijero 1974:239 [bk. 7, chap. 40]; Sahagún 1957:60 [bk. 4, chap. 16], 88 [bk. 4, chap. 25], 1969:239 [bk. 6, chap. 42].

27. Clavijero 1974:238 [bk. 7, chap. 40]; Castillo Farreras 1972:113; M. Moreno 1971:67–68.

28. México, Secretaria de Hacienda y Crédito Público 1965, 1:122–23.

29. Sahagún 1953:3 [bk. 7, chap. 2], 1957:7–8 [bk. 4, chap. 2], 1969:132 [bk. 6, chap. 23], 258 [bk. 6, chap. 43].

30. Sahagún 1957:5 [bk. 4, chap. 2], 1970:11 [bk. 1, chap. 6].

31. M. Moreno 1971:67–68; Castillo Farreras 1972:113.

32. Durán 1967, 2:158 [chap. 19].

33. Castillo Farreras 1972:111–12.

34. Sahagún 1963:269 [bk. 11, chap. 12]. *Tequatoc (tēcuahtoc),* literally, "it lies eating people."

35. Castillo Farreras 1969:181–83.

36. *ENE* 16:16–17, 1531.

37. Rees 1971:21–22; Rojas Rabiela 1977; Gibson 1964b.

38. The issue of league distance in New Spain is not simple. Much of the confusion arises from the tendency of chroniclers and records to use the term *legua* uncritically. Chardon (1980) states that, in fact, two different measures of *legua* were in use. The *legua legal,* or statute league, was 4.19 km and was intended to be used for legal linear and areal measures while the *legua común,* or common league, was 5.572 km and was used for itinerary measures by travelers. Some sixteenth-century accounts do distinguish between a short league and a long league, presumably based on the above types of leagues. Nevertheless, where no distinction is drawn, a range of distance must be used.

39. Torquemada 1975–79, 4:320–21 [bk. 14, chap. 1]; Clavijero 1974:212 [bk. 7, chap. 12].

40. Rees 1971:34.

41. Díaz del Castillo 1974:99 [chap. 59].

42. To appreciate more fully what was entailed in a tlameme journey, modern data elaborate on the probable tlameme practice. Bunzel (1959:30) states for present-day Guatemala: "If Europeans hire bearers through special channels, they set 80 pounds as a limit, but Indians on their own business sometimes carry as much as 150 pounds, or more. A day's journey on mountain trails, with burdens, is reckoned at 6–7 leagues."

N. Hammond (1978) recorded the trip of modern peddlars in the Guatemala-Belize border area on a trip in which they traveled 43, 34, 20, 32, 32, and 32 km a day (there is confusion about the actual distance covered during the sixth day of the journey, and I have accordingly deleted it), an average of 32 km (20 miles) a day. They began their trek with 45-kg packs (99 pounds) at Cobán, Guatemala, and by the time they reached San Antonio and San Pedro, Belize, they had little left, so the load factor was a declining one. The trip was normally completed in three weeks rather than one, the peddlars sleeping in almost every village en route. The three-week version would result in daily trips averaging about 10 km each.

R. E. W. Adams (1978), also working in Guatemala, estimates the maximum rate for porters at 3 km/hr in mountainous terrain, which approaches the rate of an unladen person. He states that 31 to 35 km can be covered in 10 hours if one urges the party on, but in more difficult terrain the rate falls to 2.2 km/hr. He records a trek undertaken by A. L. Smith over a four-day period, averaging 32 km/day.

Morley (1937,2:233–34) estimated that his carriers in Yucatán averaged approximately 4.5 kilometers per hour, even allowing for rest at least once an hour, and stated: "To secure really good results it is recommended that the individual packs be limited to a maximum of 35 kilograms, and 25-kilogram cargoes give much better results both in time made and in satisfaction among the carriers."

Stephens (1969, 1848) presents more detailed information concerning the carrying of people in chairs and *"coches"* (hammocks are also recorded as having been used in the seventeenth century to transport people [Morley 1937, 1:56]). *Coches* were used when Stephens was too ill to travel by horseback (1848, 1:258–59, 340–42). The exact nature of a *coche* is not given, but it appears to have been a rigid structure (1848, 1:328) carried by means of poles on the shoulders of bearers (1848, 1:340–41), presumably a sedan chair. One-man chairs, or *sillas,* were used to cross mountains: ". . . here it was customary for those who intended to cross the mountains to take hammacas or sillas; the former being a cushioned chair, with a long pole at each end, to be borne by four Indians before and behind, the traveller sitting with his face to the side, and, as the justitia told us, only used by very heavy men and padres; and the latter an armchair to be carried on the back of an Indian" (1969, 2:269). When chairs were used, relief carriers were employed (1969,2:274), three reliefs (plus carrier) per chair in the one instance recorded, the porters carrying it in relays (1969, 1:51).

43. Anonymous Conqueror 1917:55–56; Cortés 1971:84; Díaz del Castillo 1974:128 [chap. 74]; Oviedo y Valdés 1979:142 [chap. 10]; Tapia 1963:44.

44. Gibson 1964a:34–36.

45. In sixteenth-century usage a cabecera was the capital town of a local Indian ruler who bore the title tlahtoani. But since the criterion for cabecera status was based on caciques rather than on tlahtohqueh it was uncertain. Before the Conquest tlahtohqueh had been promoted or suppressed for political reasons, leaving a certain ambiguity about who was a legitimate tlahtoani. As the century wore on, the overlap of subimperial or preimperial tlahtohqueh communities and post-Conquest cabeceras was not absolute (Gibson 1964a:34–37).

46. Gibson 1964a:34.

47. Díaz del Castillo 1974:99 [chap. 59]; *FHT* 3:144, 1591.
48. Díaz del Castillo 1974:99 [chap. 59]; Gómara 1965–66, 2:216.
49. *CI* 4:309–10, 1549; Sahagún 1959:14 [bk. 9, chap. 3]; Clavijero 1974:238 [bk. 7, chap. 40].
50. Gibson 1967:177; Peterson 1962:172.
51. Scholes and Adams 1938, 2:107.
52. *FHT* 1:87–88, 1576; 1:134, 1576; 2:290–92, 1580.
53. *FHT* 3:144, 1591.
54. Gómara 1965–66, 2:127.
55. Morley 1937, 1:58.
56. Gómara 1965–66, 2:232.
57. Durán 1967, 2:158 [chap. 18].
58. Rees 1971:26–30.
59. Caso 1928a:146.
60. Barlow 1949a:37.
61. *RDI* 6-12-13.
62. Sanders and Price 1968:152.
63. Late-medieval Europe does not appear to have achieved large urban concentrations (Pounds 1976:348–55) despite the potential to do so (Imperial Rome's population may have been around one million inhabitants [Pounds 1976:112]). In contrast to this situation of unexercised possibilities, pre-Columbian central Mexico lacked the potential owing to transportation constraints.

CHAPTER 3

1. The Valley of Mexico was, in the sixteenth century, an internally draining basin, but the term "valley" has been applied so long and so frequently that I shall use it when referring to the Valley of Mexico proper.
2. Kovar 1970:15. The area of the Valley of Mexico is given as 9,600 km² (México, Departmento del Distrito Federal 1975, 1:43), including the following:

State	Area, Square Kilometers	Percent of Total Area
Mexico	4,800	50.00
Hidalgo	2,540	26.46
Tlaxcala	840	8.75
Puebla	100	1.04
Federal District	1,320	13.75
Total	9,600 km²	100.00

However, this area includes land that drains not into the Valley of Mexico but into separate basins, such as Apam and Tecocomulco. Kovar (1970:15) estimates the basin proper to have 7,853 km²; 1,330 km² in the Federal District, 4,800 km² in the state of Mexico, and 1,723 km² in the state of Hidalgo, thus excluding all those portions of Tlaxcala and Puebla as well as some 800 km² in Hidalgo. For purposes of this discussion I shall adopt the sizes given by Kovar, with two exceptions. In the Federal District I shall use the 1,320 km² figure; I do this because I am not in a position to resolve the discrepancy, the 10 km² involved is not a significant amount, and most of my statistics derive from a source using the smaller figure. There is a discrepancy of 100 km² between Kovar's figures and those of México, Departmento del Distrito Federal (1975), in zones defined by altitude. Since Kovar's figures exceed the total cited by Mexico. Departmento del Distrito Federal (1975) for the area in question, I am accordingly adopting the latter and reducing Kovar's estimates by 100 km² in Hidalgo as well as in the total. Thus, I shall use 100 percent of the Federal District (1,320 km²), 100 percent of Mexico (4,800 km²), and approximately 60 percent of Hidalgo (1,623 km²), totaling 7,753 km².

3. México, Departmento del Distrito Federal 1975:44; Blanton 1972:23; Kovar 1970:15–16.

4. Sanders 1970a:72–73.

5. R. Moreno 1977:275–77; Palerm 1973:235.

6. Blanton 1972:23; Moriarty 1968:463; Palerm 1973:17; 230–34; Sanders 1970a:71. While México, Departmento del Distrito Federal (1975, 1:32) places the lake size at 600 km², this conflicts with the geological map in the *Atlas* (4, *tomo* 1, *plano* 1) in which lacustrine deposits corresponding to the sixteenth-century lake area as defined by town locations, cover approximately 1,000 km².

7. Ecatepec, Tulpetlac, Coatitlan, Xalostoc, Atzacoalco, Tenayuca, cercanías de Tlalnepantla, Azcapotzalco, Tlacopan, Popotla, Atlacuihuayan, Mixcoac, Coyohuacan, Churubusco, Tepepan, Xochimilco, Tulyehualco, Ixtayopa, Tetelco, Tezompa, Ayotzinco, Chalco, Iztapaluca, Ayotla, Tlaltenango, Culhuacan, Mexicaltzingo, Iztapalapan, Chimalhuacan, *Aledaños* de Texcoco, Atenco, Nexquipaya, Iztapan, Totolcingo, and Chiconauhtla (México, Departmento del Distrito Federal 1975, 2:78). However, Armillas (1971:659–60) bases his lacustrine study on test pits at Tlahuac (ancient Cuitlahuac) and places the permissible extremes at 2,238 and 2,240 m. He claims that above 2,240 m the lake would have flooded the entire plain and below 2,238 m the lake would have been reduced to discrete lagoons and scattered pools. The level of the floor of the lowest building in Aztec times was 2,238 m but the latest precolonial building was 2,240.2 m.

8. Sanders 1970a:81; Kovar 1970:18; México. Departmento del Distrito Federal 1975, 2:14.

9. Kirkby 1973:73; O. Lewis 1963.

10. Sanders 1976a:143. Buck (1964:258) estimates the annual night-

soil production per adult male at 992 pounds, an estimate based on data from China. In her study of agriculture in Oaxaca, Kirkby (1973:119–20) assumes the adult female's nightsoil production at 0.7 of an adult male's, and children under fourteen at 0.5, yielding an eight-member family production total of 1.5 kg/day (a cow produces 3 kg/day, or 1 ton a year), or one-half ton a year. One such family's production would be sufficient to intensively fertilize 0.04 hectares a year.

11. Coe 1964:93.

12. Coe 1964:93; Humboldt 1814, 2:75; Clavijero 1974:229 [bk. 7, chap. 27]; Sanders 1957:77.

13. Ciudad Real 1976, 1:108 [chap. 14]; Coe 1964:93; Sanders 1957:80.

14. Sanders 1957:72; Price 1971:22.

15. Coe 1974:93–94; Sanders 1957:88; Armillas 1971:654; Ciudad Real 1976, 1:108 [chap. 14]; Early 1977:70–71; Moriarty 1968:474.

16. Clavijero 1974:229 [bk. 7, chap. 27]; Sanders 1957:89; Early 1977:73.

17. Palerm 1973:182, 235; Calnek 1972:112–14.

18. Sanders 1957:76, 349; Moriarty 1968:469; Palerm 1973:237.

19. Armillas 1971:660; J. R. Parsons 1976:243. Sanders (1957:350) estimates the southern chinampa area at 10,000 hectares and postulates a minimum valley total of 10 to 15,000 hectares. In all these estimates there is a false precision, and it is perhaps best to leave them as gross approximations.

20. Estimates are ventured by Armillas (1971:660), Calnek (1972:111), and J. R. Parsons (1976:242–43), but they all derive from a common source, Sanders (1957).

21. J. R. Parsons 1976:245.

22. Sanders 1957:80–85, 331.

23. Bray 1972a:911; Coe 1964:95.

24. Armillas 1971:657; Price 1971:23; J. R. Parsons 1976:237; Blanton 1972:1325.

25. Palerm 1973:18.

26. Calnek 1975:45; Palerm 1973:72.

27. Lameiras 1974.

28. As reconstructed by Palerm (1973:182, 238).

29. Armillas 1971:660; J. R. Parsons 1976:248–49.

30. Canoe (Sp., *canoa*) is probably an Arawak word, brought from the West Indies by the Spaniards, and replaced the Nahuatl term *acalli* (<*atl*, "water" + *calli*, "house").

31. Gibson 1964a:362; Leshikar 1982:61–66.

32. Doran 1971:129; Paulsen 1977:41–160; Sabloff 1977:67–88; Núñez Ortega 1878:49–50, 52, 56.

33. Torquemada 1975–79, 1:409–10 [bk. 3, chap. 26]; Hakluyt 1914, 9:380; Cortés 1971:108; Motolinia 1973:142 [*trat.* 3, chap. 6]; Ciudad Real 1976, 1:107 [chap. 14]; Murillo Velarde 1752, 9:74.

34. Tezozomoc 1975:234 [chap. 4].
35. Calnek, in Bray 1972a:167.
36. Chimalpahin 1965:94 [*rel.* 3].
37. Calnek 1972:114.
38. Calnek 1975; Durán 1967, 1:66–67 [chap. 6].
39. According to Palerm (1973:73–74).
40. Durán 1967, 1:22 [chap. 2], 78 [chap. 7].
41. Hardoy (1973:36–37, 164, 168) based his conclusions about Tenochtitlan's urban pattern on the Maguey Map (for an earlier discussion of the Maguey Map and a reproduction, see Robertson 1959:77–83, pl. 17–19). Although Calnek (1973) has shown this map to be of a nearby chinampa settlement northwest of the city and not of Tenochtitlan, Hardoy's general statements are still applicable to Tenochtitlan.
42. *AC* 9:56, 1573; Torquemada 1975–79, 4:346–47 [bk. 14, chap. 13].
43. Calnek 1975:46. See also Hassig 1981.
44. Military use of canoes illustrates the capability of the Aztecs to organize and coordinate canoe transport, as when the Aztecs sent 20,000 soldiers against Chalco in 2,000 canoes (Díaz del Castillo 1974:308 [chap. 142]) and 1,000 canoes against Cuitlahuac (Durán 1967, 2:119–20 [chap. 14]).
45. Clavijero 1974:238 [bk. 7, chap. 39]; Torquemada 1975–79, 4:346–47 [bk. 14, chap. 13]; Peter Martyr 1912, 2:109; García Icazbalceta 1971, 1:359.
46. Peter Martyr 1912, 2:109.
47. García Icazbalceta 1891, 3:3.
48. AGN-M 2-325-129, 1543.
49. AA-D 1-1-11, 1785; AGN-I 2-76-18v, 1582.
50. Armillas 1964:321; Hardoy 1973:140.
51. Ciudad Real 1976, 1:110 [chap. 15]; Cortés 1971:102; Aguilar 1977:80; Motolinía 1973:151 [*trat.* 3, chap. 8].
52. AGN-I 2-76-18v, 1582; 2-972-224, 1583; AA-D 1-1-11, 1785; Clavijero 1974:238 [bk. 7, chap. 39]; *FHT* 7:13–15, 1633; 7:3–4, 1633; Ciudad Real 1976, 1:121 [chap. 17]; Cortés 1971:128; Gibson 1964a:364.
53. AGN-M 2-309-122v, 1543.
54. AGN-I 2-972-224, 1583.
55. Sahagún 1957:99 [bk. 4, chap. 30].
56. AGN-I 2-76-18v, 1582.
57. Gómara 1965–66, 2:150; García Icazbalceta 1971:359; Casas 1967, 1:368 [bk. 3, chap. 70]; PNE 6:194.
58. Gibson 1964a:364.
59. Gibson 1964a:362.
60. According to Gibson (1964a:571n.184); Clavijero 1974:238 [bk 7, chap. 39]; Cobo 1964:469.
61. Ojea 1897:3.
62. Sanders 1957:445.
63. *FHT* 3:44–45, 1587; 7:3–4, 1633; Vázquez de Espinoza 1942:156;

Clavijero 1974:238 [bk. 7, chap. 39]. AGN-GP 3-2-1, 1587; 3-247-110, 1587.

64. Humboldt 1814, 2:131; AA-D 1-1-11, 1785. Gibson (1964a:362) calculates the maximum load at several tons. He estimates the normal maize load as 70 fanegas and, calculating 84 pounds per fanega, arrives at a transport capacity of 3 tons (1964a:571–72n.184). My own conclusions favor 46-kg per fanega (Borah and Cook 1958:10), which would be a capacity of 3.5 tons.

65. Torquemada 1975–79, 2:164 [bk. 4, chap. 51]; Herrera 1725–26, 2:205; Casas 1967, 1:368 [bk. 3, chap. 70].

66. Gibson 1964a:571–72n.184.

67. *ENE* 7:260, 1554; R. E. W. Adams 1978:34.

68. Gibson 1964a:362, 364. For the early 1950s, Sanders (1957:445) records the following trips and times of travel: Tlahuac (Cuitlahuac)–Mexico City, 6 hr; Tlahuac-Chalco, 4 hr; Tlahuac-Xochimilco, 3 hr; Atlapulco–Mexico City, 6 hr.

69. *ENE* 7:260, 1554.

70. To describe the Valley of Mexico in conventional central-place patterns (e.g., see M. Smith 1979) is to ignore the role played by transport in defining support areas and results in a meaningless preoccupation with hexagonal patterns devoid of function. The actual hinterland of Tenochtitlan-Tlatelolco, which is very irregular in shape owing to topographical features and differential transport, must first be defined, and then the hinterlands of its trading partners can be better understood. The foregoing does not mean that Tenochtitlan actually drew resources from the total area, but it describes the maximum area of transportable commodities.

CHAPTER 4

1. Clavijero 1974:385 [bk. 7, chap. 35]; Ixtlilxochitl 1975–77, 2:93 [chap. 36]; Hicks, n.d.

2. Durán 1967, 1:65 [chap. 6]; Clavijero 1974:237 [bk. 7, chap. 37]; Feldman 1978.

3. Clavijero 1974:386–87 [bk. 7, chap. 36].

4. Durán 1967, 1:177–79 [chap. 20].

5. C. A. Smith 1976a:26.

6. Christaller 1972:608; C. A. Smith 1976a:19–20, 34–36.

7. Skinner 1964–65; C. A. Smith 1976a:15–18.

8. *PNE* 6:62, 77, 85, 176, 218, 225, 230, 236; Pomar 1975:67–68; Sanders, Parsons, and Santley 1979:172–76; Gibson 1964a:335–36.

9. Durán 1967, 2:180 [chap. 21]; Motolinia 1971:375–78 [2, chap. 23]; Torquemada 1975–79, 4:349–51 [bk. 4, chap. 14].

10. Brumfiel 1976:200–207.

11. C. A. Smith 1976a:36–39.

12. C. A. Smith 1974:181–86; 1976a:15–18.

13. For a fuller explanation of Aztec market periodicity than that given here, see Hassig 1982.

14. Bromley, Symanski, and Good 1975:531.

15. Carrasco 1978:55; Casas 1967, 1:366 [bk. 3, chap. 70]; Gibson 1964a:352; Gómara 1965–66, 2:151; Motolinia 1973:30 [*trat.* 1, chap. 5], 1971:375 [2, chap. 23]; Torquemada 1975–79, 4:350 [bk. 4, chap. 14].

16. Bromley 1974:7; Gibson 1964a:357; Kurtz 1974:690.

17. The discussion of the calendar is based loosely on Caso 1971 for simplicity.

18. See Caso 1971 and Cline 1973 for opposing positions.

19. Serna 1892:313.

20. Serna 1892:345.

21. E.g., *PNE* 7:27.

22. Sahagún 1957:138–39 [bk. 4, app.].

23. Motolinia 1973:110–11 [*trat.* 2, chap. 10].

24. Torquemada 1975–79, 4:350 [bk. 4, chap. 14]; Bromley, Symanski, and Good 1975:536–37.

25. Ixtlilxochitl 1975–77, 1:283 [1, *Historia de los señores toltecas,* 5].

26. Caso 1967, 1968; Kirchhoff 1968.

27. Broda 1969:33.

28. Bromley, Symanski, and Good 1975:534.

29. Motolinia 1973:25 [*trat.* 1, chap. 4]; Durán 1967, 2:225 [chap. 28].; Sahagún 1974:25; Torquemada 1975–79, 3:429 [bk. 10, chap. 36]. See also the interpretation of the Tovar calendar by Kubler and Gibson 1951:44.

30. Caso 1971:345; Goubaud Carrera 1935:46.

31. Torquemada 1975–79, 4:350 [bk. 4, chap. 14]; Motolinia 1971:375. [2, chap. 23]; Gómara 1965–66, 2:151; Casas 1967, 1:366 [bk. 3, chap. 70].

32. Anderson, Berdan, and Lockhart 1976:123.

33. Clavijero 1974:235 [bk. 7, chap. 35].

34. Durán 1967, 1:83 [chap. 8], 126 [chap. 13].

35. Durán 1967, 1:233–34 [chap. 3].

36. Durán 1967, 1:32 [chap. 3], 72 [chap. 7], 125 [chap. 13], 189 [chap. 21], 207 [chap. 23].

37. Gibson 1964a:357; Vaillant 1966:84.

CHAPTER 5

1. Skinner and Winckler 1969.

2. Berdan 1975:272–79.

3. Katz 1972:151; Berdan 1975:238–39; Gibson 1971:378–80; Holt 1979.

4. Davies 1977a: 157.

5. Clausewitz 1943:3–24.

6. Finer 1975:85–86; Tilly 1975a:73.

7. Gorenstein 1966:60–63.

8. Bosch Gimpera 1966:14; Gibson 1971:392; Gorenstein 1966:46.

9. Gorenstein 1966:53–55.

10. Aztec garrisons are mentioned at Oztuma (*PNE* 6:105, 149), Alahuiztlan (*PNE* 6:123), Asuchitlan (Vargas Rea 1944–46, 7/5:26), Chinantla (*PNE* 4:61–62), Oaxaca (*PNE* 4:120, 194), Cuestlahuaca (*PNE*-4:165–66), the Mixteca (*PNE* 4:185), Acatlan (*PNE* 5:113), Teozacualco (Gómez de Orozco 1927:175), Ayusuchiquilazala (Caso 1928a:147–48), Xilotepec (Frías y Frías 1906:21), Cotastla and Otopo (Ramírez Cabañas 1943:24), and Tepecuacuilco. Tarascan garrisons are mentioned at Taymeo (Vargas Rea 1944–46, 7/1:104), Sirandaro and Guayameo (Vargas Rea 1944–46, 7/8:20–21), and Metztitlan had a garrison on their frontier with the Aztecs (*DII* 4:532). Since garrisons imply a standing force, this concept has been the subject of reconsideration. For Gorenstein the fates of a standing army, garrisons, and specialized fortifications are interwoven. If any exist, the others may exist, but if none are supposed to exist, as her perspective demands (Gorenstein 1963:125, 138, 148, 161–62, 167, 168, 178), the admission of any is detrimental. Davies (1972: 219) likewise contests the existence of garrisons, but the consequences of error are not as telling on his general view. Gorenstein states (1966:56), and Davies concurs (1972:219), that the original meaning of the *guarnición* was not that now assigned to it. Referring to the Spanish term *guarnición*, Gorenstein says, "A 17th century dictionary (Covarrubias 1943:665) defines it as 'soldiers guarding or protecting a place where they were,' not troops *stationed* at a fortification." She takes *guarnición* to refer to transient troops without reference to a location, which could easily exist without a standing army. In short, Gorenstein would dismantle the Aztec military *qua* military, by beginning with the recorded political fragility of the empire and then explaining it as the result of martial inadequacy.

11. Skinner 1977b:308–45.

12. Bernal 1966; Borgonio Gaspar 1954–55; Bosch Gimpera 1966; Caso 1966; Corona Núñez 1966; Davies 1972, 1977a; Gorenstein 1963, 1966; Jiménez Moreno 1966; Paddock 1966a, 1966b, 1966c; Palerm 1956; Phillips 1979.

13. Luttwak 1976.

14. Luttwak 1976:19.

15. Gibson 1971:378–80; Holt 1979.

16. Davies 1972:213.

17. Davies 1972:214; Gorenstein 1966:57–58; Borgonio Gaspar 1954–55:383; Anonymous Conqueror 1917:69.

18. Piho 1972, 1974; Borgonio Gaspar 1954–55:383; Stenzel 1976:180.

19. Armillas 1948, 1951.

20. See, for instance, Hardoy (1973:91) on Xochicalco, and Armillas (1942–44:165) and Gorenstein (1966:55) for opposing interpretations of Oztuma.

21. Caso 1928b:170.

22. *PNE* 6:105, 147; Ramírez Cabañas 1943:24; Frías y Frías 1906:21.

23. *PNE* 4:61–62.

24. Armillas 1942–44; *PNE* 6:105, 110, 123, 147, 257, 4:61–62, 165–66; Ramírez Cabañas 1943:24.

25. *PNE* 4:85.

26. *PNE* 6:116, 257.

27. *PNE* 5:113.

28. Caso 1928a:147–48; Toussaint 1931:223; *PNE* 4:61–62, 165–66, 185; 6:110, 147.

29. Davies 1977b:299; Gorenstein 1966:58.

30. Hernández Xolocotzin 1949:160–63; Zorita 1971:192–93.

31. Caso 1963:869; *PNE* 4:90, 5:70, 74, 76.

32. Barlow 1947:264; Caso 1928b:170; 1963:869; *PNE* 4:165–66, 194, 6:149.

33. *PNE* 6:70, 196, 213; Durán 1967, 2:319 [chap. 41].

34. *PNE* 4:61–62, 111, 117; 5:70, 86, 178; 6:8, 102, 133, 206, 235, 286; 7:11.

35. *PNE* 4:84; 6:116, 147.

36. Durán 1967, 2:351–55 [chap. 45].

37. *PNE* 4:61–62; 6:105.

38. Davies 1972:215–17.

39. Davies 1972:217, 220; Gorenstein 1966:60–63.

40. Davies 1977b:342.

41. Stanislawski 1947; Davies 1972:217.

42. See Skinner and Winckler 1969.

43. The opposite was true in imperial China, where revenue and defense were inversely related in space, with most emphasis on defense at the periphery of the empire and more on revenue at the center (Skinner 1977b:308–36). This is not the case in the Aztec empire. The inverse relationship between defense and revenue demonstrated in the case of imperial China does not hold for Mesoamerica owing to the differences in imperial structures. In a territorial empire, such as China, the threat to centralized control is greatest at the periphery of the system, since areas could more easily break away from the central polity to become autonomous or align themselves with competing powers, while the likelihood of a successful revolt in the heart of the empire is much diminished owing to the absence of either outside support or the possibility of refuge and to the effectiveness of the political structure, which should be most effective at the center.

44. Holt 1976:61.

45. Berdan 1975:80; Pershits 1979. Carneiro (1978:210) views the imposition of tribute as a somewhat transitional form of political domination in which the conquered groups lose only part of their autonomy.

46. E.g., Barlow 1949b; Litvak King 1971.

47. Gibson 1971:392; Berdan 1975:272–75; Carrasco 1978:3.

48. Berdan 1975:265; 1974:131.

49. *PNE* 4:127, 133; 5:2, 78, 87; 6:52, 123, 134, 140, 143, 234, 276; 7:21.

50. Caso 1954.
51. Barlow 1949b.
52. Hicks 1977.
53. Berdan 1976:132.
54. Motolinia 1971:359 [2, chap. 17].
55. Borah and Cook 1963:8–10.
56. Hicks 1976.
57. Miranda 1952:25.
58. Gibson 1971:388.
59. Borah and Cook 1963:17.
60. Zorita 1971:192–93; Durán 1967, 2:241–42 [chap. 30]; Clavijero 1974:215 [bk. 7, chap. 15].
61. Anderson and Barlow 1943:416.
62. Hernández Xolocotzin (1949:159–63) has identified four types of imperial granaries.
63. Sahagún 1954:44 [bk. 8, chap. 14].
64. Berdan 1975:245–52.
65. Berdan 1975:112; Broda 1978:118–21.
66. *PNE* 6:16–17; Bernal 1962:5–6.
67. Zorita 1971:188; Durán 1967, 2:347 [chap. 44].
68. Berdan 1975:247; Borah and Cook 1963:61; Holt 1976:53.
69. Borah and Cook 1963:60.
70. Miranda 1952:33.
71. Borah and Cook 1963:14–15; Broda 1978:129, 136; *PNE* 6:116, 257.
72. Viraphol 1977:149–50.
73. Durán 1967, 2:295–98 [chap. 39].
74. Broda (1978:129–36) maintains that the tributaries that did not give warriors' costumes were distant or gave war captives or feathers instead. However, the correlation does not hold up. Even such common items as loincloths and women's *naguas* ("skirts") did not depend on proximity to either Tenochtitlan or cotton supplies (Rodríguez Vallejo 1976:58–61). Nor did the demand for gold objects correspond with areas of indigenous gold production (León-Portilla 1978:18).
75. Litvak King (1971:99–112) has estimated the partial costs of tribute for the provinces of Cihuatlan and Tepecuacuilco in terms of agricultural production. He does so by estimating the area one family could cultivate annually and subtracting the amount needed for their subsistence, thus arriving at the family surplus per hectare. This process allows the calculation of the number of people and the number of hectares necessary to produce the tribute demanded. In addition to the base tribute amount, however, is added the cost of transporting it from the provincial centers to Tenochtitlan. By multiplying the number of days required for a round trip by the daily food requirements of a tlameme, the costs can be figured for each 23-kg load of tribute. This additional food requirement must be added to the base tribute demand to reach the actual cost of tribute. From this figure the numbers of people

and hectares required may be calculated. Litvak King used the following estimates: Cihuatlan: 722 kg of cotton per hectare, 213 kg of cacao per hectare; Tepecuacuilco: 816.4 kg of frijoles per hectare; annual family (5.8) consumption of 2,909 kg; average tlameme load of 23 kg, tlameme travel per day, 5 hr at 6 km/hr = 30 km/day. My calculations are based on my own estimates of tlameme loads (23 kg), distances per day (5 leagues, or 21 to 28 km) and consumption (since tlamemes were professionals, consumption alone was a minimum expense, not their total cost). Furthermore, there are two estimates: consumption per tlameme and consumption per tlameme plus his dependent family (3,150 g/day). Thus, considering the basic cost of the tribute goods, and the cost of transport, the general picture of the tributary provinces is of permanently deprived economic zones with a consequently reduced standard of living (Litvak King 1971:111–12).

76. One issue in urban studies as yet unaddressed is whether or not Tenochtitlan can be regarded as a parasitic city. Wrigley (1978: 296–97) states: "The archetypical parasitic city is often said to be one in which the power of a ruling group enables them to levy from the dwellers in the countryside a tribute in money or in kind which is consumed in the cities." He concludes by distinguishing between cities that merely divide the current flow of goods and cities that create circumstances that increase the volume of goods, the former being parasitic and the latter not. Tenochtitlan fits into both categories, depending on the area considered. Within the Valley of Mexico, Tenochtitlan both stimulated local production, encouraging specialization, and imported goods from the outside, enriching the area and lowering the price of such goods below local production costs. Beyond the Valley of Mexico, however, the return for paying tribute was minimal. Tenochtitlan was clearly parasitic in relation to these towns. It siphoned off much of the local production and the benefits of better tlameme organization were small recompense. Nor can Pax Azteca be considered beneficial, since both supplying and augmenting Aztec troops were common obligations. Furthermore, the Aztecs seem to have permitted local conflicts, and even encouraged them to acquire captives for tribute. Thus the issue of parasitism is a problem of focus.

77. Torquemada 1975–79, 4:349–51 [bk. 4, chap. 14]; Motolinia 1971:375–78 [2, chap. 23]; Durán 1967, 1:180 [chap. 20].

78. Durán 1967, 1:64 [chap. 6], 133 [chap. 13], 180 [chap. 20].

79. Torquemada 1975–79, 4:349-51 [bk. 4, chap. 14].

80. Carrasco 1980:256; Kirchhoff, Odena Güemes, and Reyes García 1976:226.

81. *Códice Chimalpopoca* 1975:43; Davies 1977a:72.

82. Durán 1967, 1:180 [chap. 20].

83. Chimalpahin 1965:204 [*rel.* 7].

84. Durán 1967, 1:64 [chap. 6].

85. Motolinia 1971:373 [2, chap. 22]. See also the market descrip-

tions of Tenochtitlan-Tlatelolco of Durand-Forest 1971 and Feldman 1978.

86. Motolinia 1971:378 [2, chap. 22].

87. Sahagún 1959 [bk. 9]. A certain amount of caution should be exercised in accepting the pochtecah materials at face value, since Sahagún collected the data in Tlatelolco, where the pochtecah were particularly important, and thus their place in society may have been somewhat exaggerated (Edmonson 1974b:4–69).

88. Simons and Sullivan 1972:203.

89. A mural in Teotihuacan depicts Yahcateuctli (Miller 1973, fig. 206).

90. Parsons and Price 1971:182; Chapman 1971a:204.

91. Acosta Saignes 1945.

92. Sahagún 1959:1–2 [bk. 9, chap. 1]; Berlin and Barlow 1948:5, 84.

93. Weigand, Harbottle, and Sayre 1977; Reyman 1978.

94. Rojas González 1945:127; Zantwijk 1970:4.

95. Torquemada 1975–79, 4:383 [bk. 14, chap. 27].

96. Clavijero 1974:238 [bk. 7, chap. 39]; Dillon 1975:94; Sahagún 1959:48–49 [bk. 9, chap. 10].

97. Chapman 1971b:115.

98. Sahagún 1959 [bk. 9].

99. Berdan 1975:1; 1977a:92; 1978a:78; Parsons and Price 1971:170; Chapman 1971a:200; 1971b: 115; Dillon 1975:85.

100. Carrasco 1978; Hicks n.d.

101. Calnek 1978a; Offner 1981; Hicks n.d.

102. Sahagún 1959:7 [bk. 9, chap. 2].

103. Durán 1967, 1:179 [chap. 20], 276 [chap. 24].

104. Calnek 1978a:106; Sahagún 1961:60–94 [bk. 10, chap. 16–26].

105. Simons and Sullivan 1972:204; Dillon 1975:90; Acosta Saignes 1945:13; Berdan 1975:151.

106. Simons and Sullivan 1972:204.

107. Acosta Saignes 1945:25–32; Chapman 1971a:207; Sahagún 1959:23 [bk. 9, chap. 5].

108. Berdan 1975:148; Simons and Sullivan 1972:204. For a more extensive account of pochtecah customs, rituals, dress, and other matters not directly relevant here, see Sahagún 1959 [bk. 9].

109. Calnek 1978a:106.

110. Durán 1967, 1:68 [chap. 6].

111. Chapman 1971b:122.

112. Durán 1967, 2:351 [chap. 45]; Sahagún 1959:1 [bk. 9, chap. 1], 8 [bk. 9, chap. 2], 21 [bk. 9, chap. 5].

113. Calnek 1978a:105.

114. Sahagún 1959:88 [bk. 9, chap. 19].

115. Berdan 1975:1; 1977:92; 1978:78; Parsons and Price 1971:170; Chapman 1971a:200; 1971b:115; Dillon 1975:85.

116. Durán 1967, 2:86 [chap. 10], 163 [chap. 19], 185 [chap. 22], 479

[chap. 65]; Zorita 1971:134.

117. Simons and Sullivan 1972:205.

118. Sahagún 1959:7 [bk. 9, chap. 2], 17 [bk. 9, chap. 4], 21–25 [bk. 9, chap. 5].

119. Sahagún 1959:17 [bk. 9, chap. 4].

120. Berdan 1975:147–48.

121. Acosta Saignes 1945, map facing 40.

122. Simons and Sullivan 1972:204.

123. Polanyi 1971:262.

124. Chapman 1971b:115; Simons and Sullivan 1972: 205; Carrasco 1978:63; Berdan 1978:87–88.

125. Calnek 1978a:107.

126. Sahagún 1959:7–8 [bk. 9, chap. 2].

127. Berdan 1975:275; 1977a:98.

128. Chapman 1971b:116; Simons and Sullivan 1972:204; Berdan 1978:93; Parsons and Price 1971:173.

129. Sahagún 1959:18 [bk. 9, chap. 4], 22 [bk. 9, chap. 5].

130. Chapman 1971b:122.

131. Calnek 1978a:108.

CHAPTER 6

1. Davies 1977a:46, 78–79.
2. Davies 1977a:78–79; Rounds 1979:79–81.
3. Barlow 1949a.
4. Bray 1972b:921.
5. Bray 1972b:921.
6. Acona 1933; Farrar 1966; Furst 1978; Pirie 1975a; Santley and Rose 1979.
7. Palerm 1973:237.
8. Gibson 1964a:9–20.
9. *ENE* 4:169–70.
10. Brumfiel 1980.
11. Gibson 1971:383.
12. Berdan 1975:112.
13. Carrasco 1978:90.
14. Berdan 1975:293–94, 300.
15. Litvak King 1971:118–19.
16. Brumfiel 1980.
17. Berdan 1975:147–48; Sahagún 1959:17 [bk. 9, chap. 4].
18. Zantwijk 1970:4.
19. Calnek 1978a:316; Sahagún 1959:80–83 [bk. 9, chaps. 17–18].
20. Calnek 1978b:105.
21. Calnek 1975:51, 59.
22. Sanders 1957:445.

23. C. A. Smith 1976a:5.
24. García Icazbalceta 1891, 3:3.
25. Blanton 1972:1325; J. R. Parsons 1971:208; Sanders, Parsons, and Santley 1979:155.
26. C. A. Smith 1976a:34.
27. Burghardt 1971:269–70.
28. More 1969:67.
29. México, Departmento del Distrito Federal 1975, 1:32; Kovar 1970:24.
30. México, Departmento del Distrito Federal 1975, 1:49.
31. Durán 1967, 2:370 [chap. 48]; Palerm 1973:234; Sanders 1970a:71 1976c:60. For a longer discussion of the lake environment, see Deevey 1957.
32. Sanders 1957:445.
33. *PNE* 6:66–67, 77. That winds might sink canoes on the lake was a recognized danger, especially during the north winds (Sahagún 1953:12 [bk. 7, chap. 3]). In the mid-nineteenth century, Tylor (1970:134) also commented on the extreme peril experienced by the blunt-bowed keelless vessels in Lake Texcoco during storms.
34. J. R. Parsons 1971:208.

CHAPTER 9

1. McNeill 1977:1–4.
2. Cook and Borah's (1971:80–82) estimates have been the object of many criticisms, both factual (Denevan 1976b) and methodological (Bath 1978; Zambardino 1980). Sanders's estimate (Denevan 1976b:291), corrected for an area equivalent to that of Cook and Borah, is about half as large for the Conquest period but agreement is more general that there was a population decline from a high in 1521 to approximately one million by the close of the century.
3. Gibson 1964a:448–49.
4. Cook and Borah 1971:115.
5. Burnet and White 1972:13; McNeill 1977:55.
6. S. F. Cook 1946:335.
7. Buikstra 1981; Marks and Beatty 1976:149; S. F. Cook 1946:335.
8. Bruce-Chwatt 1965:376; Joralemon 1982; McNeill 1977:183–88. Despite general consensus on the relatively disease-free condition of the pre-Hispanic New World, a minority opinion holds that some of the diseases were pre-Columbian; see Guerra 1964:41, 1966:330; Shimkin 1973:283–84.
9. McNeill 1977:177–78.
10. Crosby 1973:35–63.
11. Sanders estimated the urban-to-rural population ratio for the Valley of Mexico to be 1 to 2 (1970b:449–50), but changed that estimate

to 1 to 1 (1976b:150) in a later publication of essentially the same article by raising his population estimate for Tenochtitlan from 80,000 to 150,000–200,000. For the Gulf Coast city-state of Cempoala, Cook and Borah (1971:9–10) estimate the urban-to-rural ratio to be 2 to 3.

12. Curtin 1968:200; Marks and Beatty 1976:172.

13. May 1961. The origin of malaria has been extensively debated, but Stewart (1973:38–40) convincingly argues for its Old World origin, citing the "cold filter" of the Bering Strait migration and the small numbers of suitable nonhuman hosts in the Americas.

14. Curtin 1968; Hunter, Swartzwelder, and Clyde 1976:369.

CHAPTER 10

1. Wallerstein 1974:68.
2. Wallerstein 1974:329.
3. Edwards 1972.
4. Jones 1966a:217.
5. Haring 1918; Usher 1932; Parry 1970.
6. Frank 1979:16–17.
7. Gage 1969:65.
8. Haring 1918:136.
9. Parry 1970:123; Usher 1932:206; Benzoni 1970:116.
10. Parry 1970:123–24.
11. Haring 1918:222; Chaunu and Chaunu 1955–59, 7:28–29.
12. Rees 1971:128; Chaunu and Chaunu 1955–59, 7:30–31.
13. Haring 1918:227; Chaunu and Chaunu 1955–59, 7:28–29.
14. Chaunu and Chaunu 1955–59, 7:30–31. In 1525, Oviedo y Valdés (1979:81–83 [chap. 1] said that the journey of 1,500 leagues from Spain to the islands of the Indies required 35 to 40 days and for the return about 50 days.
15. Haring 1918:208.
16. Haring 1918:201–205; Schurz 1939:404.
17. Haring 1918:226–27.
18. Borah 1954:8, 73, 80–81, 88–92.
19. Borah 1954:29–31.
20. Borah 1954:23–24.
21. Gerhard 1960:32.
22. Borah 1954:116.
23. Haring 1918:144; Chaunu 1974:232.
24. Schurz 1939:275.
25. Gerhard 1960:36–38.
26. Haring 1918:146.
27. Gerhard 1960:89–92.
28. Schurz 1939:216, 279–81; Parry 1970:132.
29. Schurz 1939:263–64; Parry 1970:132.

30. Haring 1918:146.

31. Castillo Farreras 1969:183.

32. *ENE* 16:16–17, 1531.

33. In the early nineteenth century von Humboldt (1814, 3:492) listed the most traveled and commercially important roads as (1) Mexico City to Veracruz by way of Puebla and Xalapa, (2) Mexico City to Acapulco by way of Chilpanzingo, (3) Mexico City to Guatemala by way of Oaxaca and (4) Mexico City to Durango and Santa Fe, New Mexico.

34. Rees 1971:71–72.

35. Gibson 1964b; *AC* 2:125, 1531.

36. *AC* 3:8, 1532.

37. Kubler 1948, 1:162; Rees 1971:74.

38. Rees 1971:75.

39. *RDI* 6-3-26, 1528; 6-3-25, 1563.

40. *ENE* 16:14, 1531.

41. Gage 1969:45.

42. Oviedo y Valdés 1959, 4:244.

43. Rees 1971:78–80.

44. Rees 1971:88–90, 110–11.

45. Borah 1954:26–29; Chance 1978:54.

46. Borah 1954:28; Chance 1978:54.

47. Borah 1954:28–29; Chance 1978:54.

48. García Icazbalceta 1971, 2:72–140.

49. Borah 1954:29; Gage 1969:112.

50. Powell 1952:4–7.

51. Powell 1952:18–19.

52. Schurz 1939:384–86.

53. *AC* 8:180–81, 1564; AGN-GP 3-403-188, 1587; *AC* 12:65–66, 1591.

54. Gage 1969:32.

55. Hakluyt 1914, 9:355, 1555; 9:361, 1568; Parry 1970:129.

56. Carrera Stampa 1952–53:320; Gage 1969:35–36.

57. R. Smith 1940:67, 72; Foster 1960:107–108; Carrera Stampa 1952–53:321, 329–30; Wilson 1855:135.

58. Parry 1970:129; Gerhard 1960:39; Carrera Stampa 1952-53: 329–30.

59. Gibson 1966:49–65, 143–46.

60. Gibson 1966:63.

61. In the absence of good data, or even consensual population estimates, I attempted to reconstruct an ideal population. In so doing, I followed the approach and model (the "west" stable population model at level 3 [Coale and Demeny 1966]) employed by N. D. Cook (1981). Cook's focus is on the aboriginal population of sixteenth-century Peru; thus it approximates that of central Mexico more closely than any other population in terms of social organization, density, level of medical expertise (both native and Spanish), and epidemiological vulnerability. Nevertheless, population pyramids calculated for the sixteenth century

failed to fit the modern population reconstructions. While it may be possible to tailor various population models to yield an approximation of some of the sixteenth-century population estimates, to do so would undermine the predictive value of the model and be of questionable utility.

62. Wrigley 1969:113–15; Bongaarts and Cain 1982.

63. Cox 1978:213–15.

64. Dixon 1962:321–22.

65. Comprehensive data on this subject are not available since many social and nutritional factors affect mortality rates, and, with the recent eradication of smallpox, they are unlikely to be. However, available data for unvaccinated populations (albeit Western populations) indicate a high mortality for those 0–10 years of age and lower for 10–20. Dixon (1962:326) records nineteenth-century mortality at ranges of 42 to 60 percent for 0–4, declining up through 30 years of age, then increasing until mortality matches the high in the 50s and 60s. The rate for 1960, however, is somewhat lower in the 0–4 age group. Razzell (1977:126–27) records nineteenth-century mortality rates at 40 percent for those 0–10, 12 to 27 percent from 10–40, and 39 percent thereafter for Berlin, and for London, 60+ percent for 0–3, declining to 23 percent for 10–15, climbing to 40+ percent thereafter. Virtually everyone (97.5 percent) exposed to smallpox contracts the disease (Dixon 1962:318). Mortality among pregnant women is 50 percent (Dixon 1962:326).

66. Imperato 1974:589; Wisseman 1981:536; Hoeprich 1977:777; Zdrodovskii and Golinevich 1960:224; Wolbach, Todd, and Palfrey 1922:32.

67. N. D. Cook 1981:65.

68. For differential sex mortality see Coale and Demeny 1966.

69. *RDI* 6-12-14, 1538.

70. Wrigley (1969:102), on whom I have drawn, makes a similar argument for Europe following the Black Plague, although the differential mortality rate between upper and lower classes in Europe is less clear than it was in New Spain, where disparate population and epidemiological characteristics of the classes highlight their different survival rates.

71. Boyd-Bowman 1976:582–83.

72. E. S. Lee 1966:56–57.

73. Boyd-Bowman 1976:601; 1973:53.

74. Hackett 1923:128–29, 132–33.

75. Jones 1966a:216; Vidal de la Blache 1926:349–75.

76. Foster 1960:104; Taafe and Gauthier 1973:34.

77. Santa Cruz 1918:535. See also Foster 1960:104.

78. Matesanz 1965:540–43.

79. Dusenberry 1963:26–30.

80. *DIU* 1:28, 1511; *DIU* 1:36–37, 1512.

81. Mendieta 1971:472. [bk. 4, chap. 29].
82. *RDI* 6-12-6, 1528, 1549, 1601, 1609; Simpson 1938:67.
83. Vásquez 1940:143, 1528.
84. Warren 1974:95.
85. Mendieta 1971:472. [bk. 4, chap. 29].
86. AGN-I 4-649-185, 1590; AGN-M 2-452-182, 1543; AGN-M 2-738-321v, 1543.
87. Simpson 1938:67–68.
88. *ENE* 2:114.
89. *DCLI* 1:161-62, 1533.
90. *DIHC* 23, 1532.
91. Warren 1974:95–125, 1532.
92. Sahagún 1952:35 [bk. 3, chap. 14].
93. AGN-I 4-649-185, 1590; AGN-I 2-973-224v, 1583; 6-1a-656-175v, 1593.
94. AGN-GP 2-79-39, 1579; 2-920-216, 1580; Cuevas 1975:161–67, 1550.
95. *DII* 6:484-515, 1550; *DII* 41:149-60, 1537.
96. AGN-GP 2-79-39, 1579; *RDI* 6-1-13, 1541.
97. AGN-GP 2-79-39, 1579; 4-289-81v, 1591.
98. *VEA* 1:29, 1535.
99. *DII* 41:149–60, 1537.
100. *ENE* 16:30–34, 1537.
101. *ENE* 16:30-34, 1537.
102. *AC* 4:134, 1538.
103. *RDI* 6-12-14, 1538.
104. Warren 1974:95–99, 1532; AGN-M 1-131-65r–v, 1542; 1-381-176v, 1542; 1-430-202v, 1542; *AC* 4:134, 1538.
105. *New Laws* 1971:xiii, 1542; Simpson 1938:68.
106. *RDI* 6-12-6, 1528, 1549, 1601, 1609; *CI* 4:304-306, 1549.
107. Puga 1945:200v–201v, 1549.
108. *ENE* 16:30–34, 1537.
109. Hackett 1923:124–45.
110. Bancroft 1883–88, 2:527, 565.
111. AGN-M 1-131-65, 1542.
112. DII 41:149–60, 1537; *AC* 4:134, 1538.
113. Hackett 1923:134–35.
114. IEPAN 2-454v-455v, 1527.
115. *ENE* 16:30-34, 1537.
116. *AC* 2:83–85, 1531.
117. Kubler 1948, 1:162.
118. *ENE* 16:30–34, 1537.
119. AGN-M 1-256-121, 1542; AGN-GP 4-289-81v, 1591; AGN-RCD 3-76-47, 1589; AGN-GP 5-876-184v, 1600; 5-885-185, 1600; AGN-RCD 3-76-47, 1589.
120. AGN-M 1-256-121, 1542.

121. *IEPAN* passim, *IE* passim, Barrett 1970:132.
122. Boyd-Bowman 1969:137.
123. Gage 1969:200.
124. *IEPAN* 3-697r–v, 1528.
125. AA-Co 1-14v-15r, 1526.
126. AHN 553, 1576.
127. Humboldt 1814, 2:131.
128. Webster 1956:130.
129. Leighton 1967:45.
130. *AC* 1:71–72, 12 January 1526.
131. Hassig 1980.
132. Ciudad Real 1976, 1:111 [chap. 15]; Scholes and Adams 1961:60, 1564; Gómez de Cervantes 1944:111–14; Barrio Lorenzot 1920:261; 1587.
133. Grigg 1977:30–31.
134. *IEPAN* 2-454v–455v, 1527; ENE 16:30–34, 1537. Motolinia (1973: 142 [*trat.* 3, chap. 6]) placed the number of mule trains between Veracruz and Mexico City at 100.
135. *AC* 2:83–85, 1531.
136. Childe 1958:718. In 1823, however, Bullock (1971:250) described the nightly unloading of wagons in Mexico, a task requiring up to two hours.
137. Rees 1971:74; Kubler 1948, 1:162.
138. Ringrose 1970a:33–34.
139. Ringrose 1970a:38.
140. Kubler 1948, 1:162.
141. Rees 1971:75–78.
142. *ENE* 16:30–34, 1537.
143. Powell 1950:241.
144. García Icazbalceta 1971, 2:77.
145. Gerhard 1960:38.
146. AGN-M 2-384-161, 1543; *AC* 4:221–23, 1540.
147. *AC* 4:248, 1541. In 1625 there were over 15,000 *coches* in Mexico City (Gage 1969:67).
148. Matesanz 1965:539–43.
149. *VEA* 1:135, 1550; Bancroft 1883–88, 2:565.
150. *VEA* 1:191, 1568; 1:232, 1580.
151. Cuevas 1975:249, 1561.
152. *CI* 4:296, 310–11, 1552; Cuevas 1975:183–218, 1554.
153. AGN-GP 1-235-47v, 1575; 1-732-142, 1576; 1-49-198, 1576.
154. Gage 1969; 114.
155. AGN-GP 2-920-216, 1580; *ENE* 8:116, 1556; AGN-I 2-685-157v, 1580; 3-416-96, 1591; 5-6-71, 1590; 6-2a-645-146, 1592.
156. *FHT* 2:247–48, 1580.
157. *RDI* 6-12-10, 1549, 1579; 3-3-63, 1595, 1628.
158. AGN-I 2-685-157v, 1580; 3-416-96, 1591; 5-6-71, 1590; 6-2a-645-146, 1592.

159. AGN-GP 1-800-148v, 1576; AGN-GP 1-1049-198, 1576.

160. *FHT* 1:87-88, 1576; 1:134, 1576; 2:290-92, 1580; DII 6:490-91, 1550.

161. AGN-I 5-1117-353, 1591; FHT 1:87-88, 1576; 1:134, 1576; 2:290–92, 1580; García 1907, 15:122–24, 1558; García and Pereyra 1905–11, 15:122–24, 1558; AGN-I 2-685-157v, 1580.

162. *DII* 6:490–91, 1550.

163. *VEA* 1:42, 1550 or 1551.

164. García and Pereyra 1905–11, 15:122–24, 1558.

165. *VEA* 1:136, 1550.

166. *FHT* 2:322–23, 1580.

167. AGN-RCD 3-56-30, 1580.

168. AGN-GP 2-616-145v, 1580; Ruiz de Alarcón 1892:156–57.

169. Gage 1969:219; *ENE* 16:31, 1537.

170. Gage 1969:219. In a footnote to his edition of Gage's *Travels,* Thompson (Gage 1969:219n.1) states: "There is an exaggeration here. The Indians still carry very heavy loads by a tumpline across the forehead, but I have never seen or heard of foreheads bleeding as a result." Nevertheless, this was a common allegation in the sixteenth century, and certainly the conditions of transport then differed substantially from those of the present day.

171. AGN-M 6-243, 1563.

172. Díaz del Castillo 1974:582 [chap. 209].

173. *PNE* 6:250.

174. Cuevas 1975:197, 1554; AA-O 3-181v-182r, 1562.

175. Bakewell 1971:20.

176. Powell 1950:25, 241.

177. Ringrose 1970a:37, 39.

178. Bakewell 1971:20. Since the types of wagons commonly employed throughout the sixteenth century have long since been superseded, no adequate contemporary comparison is available, similar to that of the U.S. Army for *arrieros.* However, U.S. Army standards for turn-of-the-century wagons indicate a considerable superiority in loads pulled in wagons over those packed on muleback (U.S. Army 1900: 92–93, 135; U.S. Army 1904:186), although travel distance per day was less. A six-mule team in the U.S. Army normally pulled a 1,950-lb (886-kg) wagon with a load of 3,500 lb (1,591 kg), while a four-mule team pulled a 1,550-lb (704-kg) wagon with a load of 2,500 lb (1,136 kg). Thus the load pulled per mule was 908.3 lb (413 kg) (583.3-lb [265-kg] load plus 325-lb [148-kg] wagon) and 1,012.5 lb (460 kg) 625 lb ([284 kg] load, plus 387.5 lb [176 kg] wagon), respectively. However, these standards are for normal conditions and level terrain and are roughly double the hauling capacity of the ox-drawn *carretas* of Spain. It is probable that the cargo load per mule decreases as the wagon increases in size and percentage of the overall load.

In the nineteenth century Tylor (1970:84) stated that mules hauling wagons were four to five times as efficient as mules alone, but presumably this refers to total amounts hauled rather than considering the comparative time-distance factor. In Spain during the eighteenth and nineteenth centuries, *carreteros* had an average of three and a half carts each (Ringrose 1970b:90).

179. Chevalier 1970:14; Mecham 1927:99.

180. Powell 1952:24.

181. Hakluyt 1914, 9:378–79, 1572; AGN-O 1-45-41, 1580.

182. Zavala 1947:235, 248–49, 1580.

183. Boyd-Bowman 1969:137.

184. Hakluyt 1914, 9:378–79, 1572; AGN-O 1-45-41, 1580; Benzoni 1970:85.

185. García Pimentel 1897:267.

186. Zavala 1947:235, 1580.

187. Zavala 1947:235, 248–49. This prohibition was lifted in 1616, and presumably grain or fodder either was being shipped into the area or was being produced locally.

188. Zavala 1947:236, 1580; 237, 1602; 238–39, 1604.

189. AA-O 3-181v–182r, 1562.

190. Powell 1950:240.

191. *CI* 4:310–11, 1552; Cuevas 1975:197–99, 1554.

192. García Pimentel 1897:53; *AC* 8:199, 1564; 8:180–81, 1564.

193. Borah 1954:28–29.

194. AGN-I 3-560-133v, 1591; 4-840-228v 1590; 6-2a-645-146, 1592; AGN-GP 2-616-145v, 1580; 5-876-184v, 1600; 5-885-185, 1600; AA-O 1-156-184, 1613; AGN-I 6-2a-645-146, 1592; 6-2a-45-12v, 1591; AGN-RCD 3-31-15, 1587.

195. *VEA* 1:255, 1585; 2:133, 1596.

196. AGN-I 2-11-2v, 1582; 2-62-15, 1582; 2-230-58v, 1582; 2-973-224v, 1583; 3-112-26v, 1590; 4-649-185, 1590; 4-704-198, 1590; 4-859-232v, 1590; 5-52bis-85, 1590; 5-629-242v, 1591; 6-1a-213-55v, 1592; 6-1a-1130-310, 1596; AGN-GP 2-572-136, 1580; 2-743-174v, 1580; 2-754-177, 1580; 3-266-188v, 1587.

197. AGN-I 6-1a-656-175v, 1593; 6-1a-1039-281, 1591.

198. Barlow 1949:37.

199. AGN-I 2-11-2v, 1582; 5-629-242v, 1591; AGN-GP 2-754-177, 1590.

200. AGN-RCD 3-56-30, 1588.

201. Ringrose 1970a:47–48.

202. AGN-GP 4-289-81v, 1591; 5-876-184v, 1600; 5-885-185, 1600; AGN-RCD 3-76-47, 1589; *IE* 1299:18-38v–39r, 1596; 1590:28–53r, 1598; 1420:23–39v, 1598; AGN-I 3-560-133v, 1591.

203. AGN-RCD 3-56-30, 1588.

204. Scholes and Adams 1956:60–61, 1595; *FHT* 4:426, 1600.

205. AGN-GP 3-86-39v, 1587; *AC* 12:180–81, 1593; 12:65–66, 1591.

206. *AC* 12:105–106, 1591; 12:113, 1591.

207. Ciudad Real 1976, 1:86 [chap. 12]; *IE* 123, 1590; 605, 1591; 155

1591; 479, 1592; 838, 1593.

208. Kubler 1948, 1:162.

209. Ringrose 1970a:47–48.

210. Rees 1971:211–12.

211. *RDI* 6-12-9, 1609.

212. AGN-O 1-156-184, 1613.

213. AGN-O 1-158-186, 1613.

214. *RDI* 3-3-63, 1595, 1628; 6-12-6, 1528, 1549, 1601; Vásquez 1940: 283, 1609.

215. *FHT* 7:283, 1617; 7:143–44, 1639.

216. AGN-M 2-309-122v, 1543. Apparently, the two northern lakes, Zumpango and Xaltocan, were already drying up at Conquest (Tamayo and West 1964:111).

217. Boyer 1973:1; Gibson 1964a:303-306.

218. AA-D 1-7, 1750; Humboldt 1814, 2:27.

219. Ciudad Real 1976, 1:111 [chap. 15]; Motolinia 1973:151. [*trat.* 3, chap. 8].

220. Gemelli Careri 1976:81 [bk. 1, chap. 9]; Hoberman 1974:212.

221. AGN-GP 3-86-39v, 1587; Ciudad Real 1976, 1:110–12 [chap. 15].

222. García Icazbalceta 1891, 3:3.

223. AA-D 1-1-11, 1785; Gibson 1964a:362.

224. Vázquez de Espinoza 1942:118.

225. Gage 1969:56.

226. AA-D 3-89, 1856; 1-1-11, 1785; AGN-I 2-76-18v, 1582; 2-972-224, 1583; Clavijero 1974:238 [bk. 7, chap. 389]; *PNE* 6:194.

227. Boyer 1973:2; Vásquez de Espinoza 1942:138.

228. México, Departmento de Distrito Federal 1975, 2:65–113; Hoberman 1974.

229. Gibson 1964a:364–65; AGN-I 2-972-224, 1583; AGN-GP 3-247-110, 1587.

230. Gardiner 1956:130–32.

231. Parry 1974:16–17.

232. *DII* 6:493, 1550; Gibson 1964a:364.

233. Peter Martyr 1912, 2:108 [*dec.* 5, bk. 3]; AGN-O 1-31v-22, 1579.

234. AGN-I 2-76-18v, 1582; AGN-GP 2-938-222, 1580; AGN-I 2-972-224, 1583.

235. AGN-I 6-1a-1130-310, 1596.

236. Barrett 1970:132.

237. *DII* 26:170–73, 1525.

238. AA-Co 1-6r, 1525.

239. *IEPAN* 3-372v, 1528.

240. *AC* 2:83–85, 1531.

241. *ENE* 16:30–34, 1537.

242. AGN-RCD 3-16-9, 1587.

243. *IE* 1265, 1594.

244. Cuevas 1975:199, 1554.

245. Gibson 1964a:364–65.
246. *FHT* 7:3–4.
247. AGN-I 6-1a-1130-310, 1596.
248. Humboldt 1814, 2:131.
249. AA-D 1-1-11, 1785.
250. Data from Taiwan indicate that porters are four times as costly as rafts, and oxcarts are about equal to rafts, but only over short distances (Deglopper 1980:161). In Spain in 1773 the government paid 15 to 20 maravedis per fanega per league for transport by pack animals versus 10 to 15 maravedis per fanega for carting (Ringrose 1970b:46). Wagons were thus significantly more efficient than pack animals, although wagons were slower.
251. *IE* 1265, 1594; AGN-RCD 3-16-9, 1587.
252. *IEPAN* 2-454v-455v, 1527; AGN-M 6-243, 1563; Díaz del Castillo 1974:582 [chap. 209]; *IE* 453:5–146r, 1592; 498:5–170v, 1591.
253. AGN-M 1-256-121, 1542; AGN-GP 4-289-81v, 1591; AGN-RCD 3-76-47, 1589; AGN-GP 5-876-184v, 1600; 5-885-185, 1600; AGN-RCD 3-76-47, 1589.
254. AA-D 1-1-11, 1785.

CHAPTER 11

1. Florescano 1965:570.
2. Frank 1979:8–16, 37–38.
3. Ewald 1977:123; Simpson 1952:1.
4. Logan and Sanders 1976:39–41; Morrisey 1957:24, 28.
5. Ewald 1977:125, 129; Kubler 1942:609; Morrisey 1957:24.
6. Ewald 1977:125, 129; Florescano 1965:571; Kubler 1942:609; Morrisey 1957:24, 26; Simpson 1952:24.
7. Moreno Toscano 1968:62.
8. Moreno Toscano 1965:640.
9. Florescano 1965:571.
10. Dusenberry 1963:45.
11. Moreno Toscano 1965:64.
12. Matesanz 1965:539–43.
13. Moreno Toscano 1965:44; Chevalier 1970:98; *AC* 1:79–80, 27 February 1526.
14. Florescano 1965:584; Frank 1979:36.
15. Denhardt 1950:147.
16. Matesanz 1965:539.
17. Chevalier 1970:92-93.
18. Chevalier 1970:92–93; Morrisey 1950:121.
19. Chevalier 1970:110; Dusenberry 1963:112; Gage 1969:111.
20. Gage 1969:109; Moreno Toscano 1965:631–32.

21. Florescano 1965:571.
22. Simpson 1952:24.
23. Guthrie 1941:42; Borah and Cook 1958:19; R. L. Lee 1947: 650–51.
24. Moreno Toscano 1965:634; Florescano 1965:585.
25. Moreno Toscano 1965:637–38; Florescano 1965:584.
26. Gage 1969:111.
27. Gerhard 1972b:63–76; Cline 1972a:21–27. For a fuller treatment of the field administration of New Spain, see Haring 1963.
28. Miranda 1952:81.
29. Miranda 1952:88.
30. Frank 1979:9–10.
31. Florescano 1965:572–73; Borah and Cook 1958:4; Frank 1979:29.
32. Florescano 1965:579.
33. Borah and Cook 1958:4; Florescano 1965:573.
34. Cuevas 1975:243, 1555.
35. Borah and Cook 1958:6; Miranda 1952:138–43.
36. Cortés 1971:323.
37. This can be seen by examining the lists of Díaz del Castillo 1974:171–72 [chap. 92]; Cervantes de Salazar 1953:58–62; and Sahagún 1961:59-94 [bk. 10, chap. 16–26]; and the Coyoacan market records in Anderson, Berdan, and Lockhart 1976:138–49.
38. Gibson 1964a:355.
39. *AC* 1:70, 5 January 1526. Although the Nahuatl word for market was *tianquiztli,* it was Hispanized and a colonial-period market was generally called a *tianguiz* (also spelled *tianguis* and *tiangues*). Accordingly, I have adopted this convention to distinguish Indian markets of the colonial period (the *tianguiz*) from those of the pre-Conquest period (*tianquiztli*).
40. *AC* 3:64, 1533.
41. Oviedo y Valdés 1959, 4:45.
42. AA-Co 1-2v, 26 August 1524; AA-Co 1-83r, 1536.
43. AA-Co 1-31v, 1530; 1-85v, 1537; 1-88r, 1538; 1-84v, 1537.
44. AGN-GP 2-587-139, 1580; AGN-I 2-410-98v, 1583; AGN-I 4-795-218, 1590.
45. AA-Co 1-15v, 1527.
46. Gibson 1964a:357.
47. Anderson, Berdan, and Lockhart 1976:138–49, ca. 1560–70.
48. Casas 1967, 1:366 [bk. 3, chap. 70].
49. AGN-M 1-28-14v, 1542, Cuquila; AGN-I 4-162-52v, 1589, San Juan Acaxucuiches.
50. AGN-I 6-1a-459-122v, 1593.
51. AGN-I 2-172-44, 1582.
52. Torquemada 1975–79, 6:350–51 [bk. 14, chap. 14].
53. Gibson 1964a:356–57.
54. *DII* 26:181, 1525.

55. *PNE* 6:59.
56. AGN-GP 1-243-48v, 1575.
57. AGN-GP 1-355-81, 1575.
58. AGN-GP 2-957-226, 1580.
59. Motolinia 1971:205 [1, chap. 53]; Torquemada 1975–79, 6:346 [bk. 14, chap. 13]; Hakluyt 1914, 9:380.
60. *CI* 310–11, 1552.
61. Torquemada 1975–79, 6:346 [bk. 14, chap. 13]; *AC* 7:15, 1551; AA-Co 1-139v, 1551; Hakluyt 1914, 9:380; AGN-I 6-2a-547-119v, 1592.
62. Clavijero 1974:235. [bk. 7, chap. 35].
63. Anderson, Berdan, and Lockhart 1976:123.
64. AGN-I 2-59-14, 1582.
65. Gerhard 1972a:332.
66. AGN-I 6-1a-1083-296, 1595.
67. Gerhard 1972a:295–300.
68. *AC* 1:43, 1525.
69. *AC* 1:20–22, 1554.
70. *AC* 2:65–66, 1530.
71. *AC* 3:64, 1533.
72. RDI 6-1-25, 1521; AA-Co 1-18r-v, 1527.
73. Florescano 1965:604–11.
74. *AC* 4:39–41, 1536; 4:34–35, 1537; 4:237, 1541.
75. AGN-M 2-380-160, 1543.
76. *AC* 1:168, 1528.
77. AGN-M 2-523-212v, 1543; *AC* 5:61–63, 1544; *AC* 4:113–16, 1538; AA-Co 1-51r, 1531; *AC* 4:113–16, 1538.
78. *AC* 4:134, 1538.
79. AGN-M 1-243-116, 1542; 1-436-205, 1542; 2-674-168v, 1543; Gibson 1964a:452-54.
80. An instance was merchants from Huaquechula who traded in Guatemala, Chiapas, Xicalango, Piastla, Tabasco, Soconusco, Chilatengo, and elsewhere (AGN-M 2-532-215v, 1543).
81. *ENE* 16:30–34, 1537.
82. Gibson 1964a:355.
83. *DCLI* 3:77–78, 1552.
84. *CI* 4:296, 1552.
85. *DCLI* 3:78–79, 1552.
86. AA-O 3:181v–182r, 1562.
87. AGN-M 6-243, 1563; *ENE* 8:102, 1556. Gibson (1964a:358–59) feels that these positions were likely filled by commoners accustomed to long foot journeys.
88. García Pimentel 1897:74.
89. Humboldt 1814, 1:194; RDI 7-8-28, 1579, 1593.
90. RDI 4-10-11, 1572.
91. AGN-GP 2-616-145v, 1580; Cuevas 1975:247, 1561.
92. AGN-GP 1-86-17, 1575; 1-338-78, 1575.

93. AGN-GP 1-3-12, 1575; 2-84-40, 1579; 2-476-116, 1580; 2-1268-292, 1580; AGN-I 2-211-54v, 1582; 2-954-220, 1583; 4-716-210, 1590; 6-2a-132-31v, 1591; 6-1a-410-108, 1592; 6-2a-170-39v, 1591.

94. AGN-GP 1-776-146, 1576; 2-328-90, 1579; 2-838-196v, 1580.

95. Cuevas 1975:249, 1561. Although the document specified 50 *brazas* square, such an amount would be 4.2 hectares, a huge amount of land to cultivate merely as a prerequisite for trading. Cook and Borah (1960:19) put the average yield of such an area at 11.5 fanegas (495.6 kg) of wheat or 16.2 fanegas (695.5 kg) of maize. It is more likely that 50 square *brazas* was intended, or 0.84 hectares, yielding 0.23 fanegas (10.6 kg) of wheat or 0.32 fanegas (14.7 kg) of maize.

96. AGN-I 4-4-1v, 1589; 4-194-60v, 1590.

97. AGN-I 6-1a-173-44, 1592.

98. AGN-I 6-2a-1063-289, 1595.

99. Gómez de Cervantes 1944:100.

100. R. L. Lee 1947:648–50.

101. Florescano 1965:615.

102. RDI 4-14-5, 1583; AGN-GP 3-476-221v, 1587; 3-512-239v, 1587.

103. Vásquez de Warman 1967–68:395; R. L. Lee 1947:647; Florescano 1965:617–18.

104. R. L. Lee 1947:653.

105. Guthrie 1941:38.

106. AGN-RCD 3-13-7, 1587; AGN-I 6-1a-807-215v, 1594.

107. Guthrie 1941:40.

108. Vásquez de Espinoza 1942:118.

109. Florescano 1965:597.

110. AGN-GP 3-457-213, 18 November 1587; AC 11:233-34, 13 November 1587; AGN-RCD 3-13-7, 5 June 1587; 3-16-9, 5 June 1587; 3-16-9, 16 June 1587.

111. *AC* 9:619.

112. AGN-GP 3-44-23; 3-86-39v, 1587; AA-Co 1-396v, 1594; AGN-I 6-2a-1007-266, 1598.

113. AGN-GP 3-268-12, 1587.

114. AGN-GP 3-476-221r, 1587; AGN-GP 3-559-269, 1588.

115. AGN-RCD 3-16-9, 16 June 1587; AGN-GP 3-86-39v, 1587.

116. Florescano 1965:619.

117. AGN-I 2-517-120v, 1583; 6-2a-286-63v, 1591; AGN-C 75-9-6, 1599; AGN-O 2-252v-286, 1580; 1-51-48, 1580; AGN-RCD 3-124-84, 1590; AGN-GP 2-616-145v, 1580.

118. AGN-GP 2-989-232, 1580.

119. AGN-RCD 3-16-9, 1587.

120. AGN-I 4-716-210, 1590.

121. AGN-I 6-2a-848-207, 1594.

122. AGN-RCD 3-49-23, 1588.

123. AGN-GP 1-1284-241, 1576; AGN-I 4-716-210, 1590.

124. AGN-O 2-189v-215, 1607.

125. *PNE* 6:23, 25, 33; *PNE* 4:241, 245; *RMEH* 2:116.

126. See Cline 1972b:183–242.

127. AGN-I 2-723-166, 1583; AGN-I 4-716-210, 1590.

128. AGN-I 6-2a-170-39v, 1591; 2-195-50v, 1582; AGN-GP 2-1128-271v, 1581; AGN-GP 4-289-81v, 1591; 5-1207-250, 1600.

129. AGN-I 3-976-236, 1591; 4-716-210, 1590; 6-2a-36-10v, 1591; 6-2a-671-154, 1592; AGN-GP 4-33-9, 1590.

130. AGN-M 6-243, 1563; AGN-I 2-190-49, 1582; 6-1a-410-108, 1592; 4-537-159v, 1590; 4-538-160, 1590.

131. Leaman and Conkling 1975:431–32.

132. Following von Thünen, Ewald (1977:123) describes the late-sixteenth-century Mexican productive pattern in terms of concentric zones from the center outward, namely: (1) labor-intensive market gardening; fruit growing, and pulque production, (2) forest exploitation, (3) small-scale livestock husbandry and the production of wheat, beans, and sugarcane, and (4) extensive livestock husbandry and the production of such high-value goods as cochineal and woven wares. Of course, this pattern was not merely the pre-Columbian pattern writ large, since new crops, new animals, and different values placed on various products presented different patterns of exploitation, but the same principle of intensive-to-extensive productive zonation applied.

133. Moreno Toscano 1965:637–38.

134. Moreno Toscano 1965:631–35; Ciudad Real 1976, 1:141 [chap. 21]; Chávez Orozco 1965:65–66; Lockhart 1976:109; *AC* 13:12–13, 1594; Super 1976:239; Morrisey 1950:116.

135. Chevalier 1970:110.

136. Dando 1980:11–12.

137. Hassig 1981.

138. AA-O 3:181v–182r, 1562.

139. Florescano and Gil Sánchez 1976:281.

140. Gage 1969:78–79.

141. Donkin 1979:35–38; West 1968:366–68; Williams 1972:622.

142. Sanders, Parsons, and Santley 1979:243; Simpson 1952:1–2, 23.

143. Gibson 1964a:5–6.

144. Donkin 1979:38; West 1968:367; Williams 1972:622, 625.

145. Williams 1972:626.

146. Leaman and Conkling 1975:431.

CHAPTER 12

1. The rank-size rule describes a situation in which the second-largest city of a region has half the first city's population; the third-largest city, a third, and so on, vividly illustrated as a 45-degree line on double-log graph paper (C. D. Harris 1970:129–32). The presence of a normal rank-size distribution suggests an integrated region. Primacy, on the

other hand, exists when there are fewer cities of intermediate sizes than would be expected from the rank-size rule (Berry and Horton 1970:66). One city dominates the region. Berry and Horton (1970:74) associate primacy with economic or political dependence and simplicity and suggest that primate cities arise when the country is small, there is a shorter history of urbanization, and the political and economic life is simple. The opposite conditions give rise to rank-size development. Primacy indicates, as Skinner (1977c:238) states, extraordinary centralization of regional services or a role extending beyond the regional hinterland.

Primacy is associated with imperial capitals (Berry and Horton 1970:74). Tenochtitlan-Tlatelolco was such a capital, and clearly its functions extended beyond its regional hinterland. While Tenochtitlan-Tlatelolco's dominance in the region is reflected in its primacy, Harris (C. D. Harris 1970:138) suggests that the existence of two or more large cities of more nearly equal size indicates residual regionalization or lack of full spatial integration. In 1519 and 1568 there were two equal-size subprimate cities, Texcoco and Xochimilco. While it is tempting to conclude that there was such subregionalization, it was a fleeting phenomenon. Texcoco's population was declining, whereas Xochimilco's was remaining relatively steady. By 1746 although overall urban population had declined, Mexico City's primacy was unquestionable (Villaseñor y Sanchez 1952).

2. Johnston 1977:4–6.
3. L. Lewis 1976:126.
4. Gage 1969:56.
5. L. Lewis 1976:127.
6. Lockhart 1976:113.
7. Gage 1969:62.
8. Borah 1951.
9. E.g., Israel 1974.
10. TePaske and Klein 1981.
11. Bakewell 1971:226, 231; TePaske and Klein 1981:123–29.
12. Bakewell 1971:235; TePaske and Klein 1981:134.
13. E.g., Taaffe and Gauthier 1973:34; Ullman 1954:312.
14. Brading 1971:19; Parry 1970:123–24.

APPENDIX A

1. Charlton 1970:228–91.
2. Sanders 1970b:440–41.
3. Sanders 1967:330–31.
4. Sanders 1976a:144.
5. Sanders 1967:84.

NOTES

APPENDIX B

1. Scholes and Adams 1967.
2. Berdan 1976:132.
3. Anderson and Borah 1943:414.
4. Robertson 1969:73.
5. Berdan 1976:132.
6. Robertson 1969:46.
7. Robertson 1959:94–97, 99.
8. Borah and Cook 1963:32–33.
9. Berdan 1976:134; Borah and Cook 1963:33–34.
10. Borah and Cook 1963:35.
11. Borah and Cook 1963:36–38.
12. Berdan 1976:138; Borah and Cook 1963:45.
13. Barlow 1949b; Molins Fábrega 1954–55.
14. Berdan 1976:138–39.
15. Borah and Cook 1963:47–48.
16. Berdan 1975:107; Borah and Cook 1963:49–51.
17. Cuevas 1975:228; Durán 1967, 2:160 [chap. 18], 182 [chap. 21], 367 [chap. 47]; Scholes and Adams 1957; Zorita 1971:192–93.
18. Borah and Cook 1963:50.
19. Borah and Cook 1963:46.
20. Berdan 1976:138.
21. Berdan 1976:138.
22. Borah and Cook 1963:41–42.
23. Berdan 1976:138.
24. Berdan 1976:137–38.

APPENDIX C

1. U.S. Army 1917:137–48.
2. AA-D 1-1-11, 1785.
3. U.S. Army 1917:162.
4. Ringrose 1970b:90.
5. U.S. Army 1917:145.
6. Ruxton 1848:183.
7. Leighton 1967:51–52.
8. Lamb 1963:28.
9. U.S. Army 1900:78–81.
10. Fraser 1918:358; U.S. Army 1917:18.
11. Leighton 1967:51.
12. Morley 1937, 1:137, 262; 3:378.
13. Stephens 1969, 1:43.
14. U.S. Army 1917:18.

References

See also list of abbreviations of archival sources preceding notes.

Abrams, Philip, and E. A. Wrigley
1978 *Towns in Societies.* Cambridge: Cambridge University Press.

Acona, H. L.
1933 "El ahuautle de Texcoco." *Anales del Instituto de Biología de la Universidad Nacional de México* 4:51–69.

Acosta Saignes, Miguel
1945 "Los pochteca." *Acta Anthropologica* 1:9–54.

Adams, Richard E. W.
1978 "Routes of Communication in Mesoamerica: The Northern Guatemalan Highlands and the Peten." In Lee and Navarrete 1978.

Adams, Robert M.
1979 "The Origin of Cities." In Lamberg-Karlovsky 1979.

Aguilar, Franciso de
1977 *Relación breve de la conquista de la Nueva España.* Mexico: Universidad Nacional Autónoma de México.

Altman, Ida, and James Lockhart
1976 *Provinces of Early Mexico.* Los Angeles: UCLA Latin American Center Publications.

Anderson, Arthur J.O., Frances Berdan, and James Lockhart
1976 *Beyond the Codices.* Berkeley and Los Angeles: University of California Press.

Anderson, Edgar, and R. H. Barlow
1943 "The Maize Tribute of Moctezuma's Empire." *Annals of the Missouri Botonical Garden* 30:413-30.

Andrews, J. Richard
1975 *Introduction to Classical Nahuatl.* Austin: University of Texas Press.

Anonymous Conqueror

1917 *Narrative of Some Things of New Spain and of the Great City of Temestitlan Mexico.* Marshall H. Saville, trans. New York: Cortes Society.

Armillas, Pedro

1942–44 "Oztuma, Gro., fortaleza de los mexicanos en la frontera de Michoacán." *Revista Mexicana de Estudios Antropológicos* 6:165–75.

1948 "Fortalezas mexicanas." *Cuadernos Americanos* 7:5:143–63.

1951 "Mesoamerican Fortifications." *Antiquity* 25:77–86.

1964 "Northern Mesoamerica." In Jennings and Norbeck 1964.

1971 "Gardens on Swamps." *Science* 174:653–61.

Bakewell, P. J.

1971 *Silver Mining and Society in Colonial Mexico, Zacatecas, 1546-1700.* Cambridge: Cambridge University Press.

Ball, Hugh G., and Donald L. Brockington

1978 "Trade and Travel in Prehispanic Oaxaca." In Lee and Navarrete 1978.

Bancroft, Hubert Howe

1883–88 *History of Mexico.* 6 vols. San Francisco: A. L. Bancroft and Co.

Barlow, R. H.

1947 "Relación de Zacatula, 1580." *Tlalocan* 2/3:258–68.

1949a "Relación de Zempoala y su partido, 1580." *Tlalocan* 3:29–41.

1949b "The Extent of the Empire of the Culhua Mexica." *Ibero-Americana* 28.

Barrett, Ward

1970 *The Sugar Hacienda of the Marques del Valle.* Minneapolis: University of Minnesota Press.

Barrio Lorenzot, Francisco del

1920 *Ordenanzas de gremios de la Nueva España.* Mexico: Secretaria de Gobernación.

Bath, B. H. Slicher van

1978 "The Calculation of the Population of New Spain, Especially for the Period Before 1570." *Boletín de Estudios Latinoamericanos y del Caribe* 24:67–95.

Bejarano, Ignacio, comp.

1889–1916 *Actas de cabildo de la Ciudad de México.* 54 vols. Mexico.

Benedict, Francis G., and Morris Steggerda

1937 "The Food of the Present-Day Maya Indians of Yucatan." *Carnegie Institution of Washington Publication* no. 456.

Benson, Elizabeth P.
1977 *The Sea in the Pre-Columbian World.* Washington, D.C. Dumbarton Oaks.
Benzoni, Girolamo
1970 *History of the New World.* W. H. Smith, trans. New York: Burt Franklin.
Berdan, Frances Frei
1975 Trade, Tribute, and Market in the Aztec Empire. Ph.D. diss., University of Texas—Austin. Ann Arbor, Mich: University Microfilm.
1976 "A Comparative Analysis of Aztec Tribute Documents." *Actas del XLI Congresso Internacional de Americanistas, 1974* vol. 2 Mexico.
1977 "Distributive Mechanisms in the Aztec Economy." In Halperin and Dow 1977.
1978 "Tres formas de intercambio en la economía azteca." In Carrasco and Broda 1978.
Berlin, Heinrich, and Robert H. Barlow
1948 *Anales de Tlatelolco.* Mexico: Antigua Librería Robredo, de José Porrúa e Hijos.
Bernal, Ignacio
1962 "Relación de Guautla." *Tlalocan* 4:3–16.
1966 "Teotihuacan, capital de imperio?" *Revista Mexicana de Estudios Antropológicos* 20:95–110.
Berry, Brian J. L., and Frank E. Horton
1970 *Geographic Perspectives on Urban Systems.* Englewood Cliffs, N.J.: Prentice-Hall.
Blanton, Richard Edward
1972 *Prehispanic Settlement Patterns of the Ixtapalapa Peninsula Region, Mexico.* University Park: Pennsylvania State University, Occasional Papers in Anthropology, no. 6.
Blouet, Brian W.
1972 "Factors Influencing the Evolution of Settlement Patterns." In Ucko, Tringham, and Dimbleby 1972.
Bongaarts, John, and Mead Cain
1982 "Demographic Responses to Famine." In Cahill 1982.
Borah, Woodrow
1951 "New Spain's Century of Depression." *Ibero-Americana* 35.
1954 "Early Colonial Trade and Navigation Between Mexico and Peru." *Ibero-Americana* 38.
1980 "Demographic and Physical Aspects of the Transition from the Aboriginal to the Colonial World." *Compara-*

tive Urban Research 8:41–70.

———, and Sherburne F. Cook

1958 "Price Trends of Some Basic Commodities in Central Mexico, 1531–1570." *Ibero-Americana* 40.

1963 "The Aboriginal Population of Central Mexico on the Eve of the Spanish Conquest." *Ibero-Americana* 45.

Borgonio Gaspar, Guadalupe

1954–55 "Organización militar de los tenochca." *Revista Mexicana de Estudios Antropológicos* 14:381–83.

Bosch, Gimpera

1966 "Pueblos e imperios." *Revista Mexicana de Estudios Antropológicos* 20:9–39.

Boserup, Ester

1973 *The Conditions of Agricultural Growth.* Chicago: Aldine.

Boyd-Bowman, Peter

1969 "Negro Slaves in Early Colonial Mexico." *Americas* 26:134–51.

1973 *Patterns of Spanish Emigration to the New World (1493-1580).* Council on International Studies, Special Studies, State University of New York at Buffalo.

1976 "Patterns of Spanish Emigration to the Indies Until 1600." *Hispanic American Historical Review* 56:580–604.

Boyer, Richard Everett

1973 "Mexico City and the Great Flood: Aspects of Life and Society, 1629–1635." Ph.D. diss., University of Connecticut. Ann Arbor, Mich: University Microfilms.

Brading, D. A.

1971 *Miners and Merchants in Bourbon Mexico, 1763-1810.* Cambridge: Cambridge University Press.

Bray, Warwick

1972a "Land-Use, Settlement Pattern and Politics in Prehispanic Middle America: A Review." In Ucko, Tringham, and Dimbleby 1972.

1972b "The City State in Central Mexico at the Time of the Spanish Conquest." *Journal of Latin American Studies* 4:161–85.

Broda, Johanna

1969 "The Mexican Calendar." *Acta Ethnologica et Linguistica* no. 15.

1978 "El tributo en trajes guerreros y la estructura del sistema tributario mexica." In Carrasco and Broda 1978.

Bromley, R.J.

1974 "Marketplace Trade in Latin America." *Latin American Research Review* 9:3–38.

———, Richard Symanski, and Charles M. Good

1975 "The Rationale of Periodic Markets." *Annals of the Association of American Geographers* 65:530-37.

Bruce-Chwatt, L. J.

1965 "Paleogenesis and Paleo-Epidemiology of Primate Malaria," *Bulletin of the World Health Organization* 32:363–87.

Brumfiel, Elizabeth

1976 "Specialization and Exchange at the Late Postclassic (Aztec) Community of Huexotla, Mexico." Ph.D. diss., University of Michigan. Ann Arbor, Mich.: University Microfilms.

1980 "Specialization, Market Exchange, and the Aztec State: A View from Huexotla." *Current Anthropology* 21:459–78.

Buck, John Lossing

1964 *Land Utilization in China.* New York: Paragon.

Buikstra, Jane E.

1981 *Prehistoric Tuberculosis in the Americas.* Evanston, Ill. Northwestern University Archaeological Program.

Bullock, W.

1971 *Six Months' Residence and Travels in Mexico.* Port Washington, N.Y.: Kennikat Press.

Burnet, Macfarlane, and David O. White

1972 *Natural History of Infectious Disease.* Cambridge: Cambridge University Press.

Bunzel, Ruth

1959 *Chichicastenango.* Seattle: University of Washington Press.

Burghardt, A.F.

1971 "A Hypothesis About Gateway Cities." *Annals of the American Association of Geographers* 61:269–85.

Cahill, Kevin M.

1982 *Famine.* Maryknoll, N.Y.: Orbis Books.

Callen, E. O.

1973 "Dietary Patterns in Mexico Between 6500 B.C. and 1580 A.D." In C. E. Smith 1973.

Calnek, Edward F.

1972 "Settlement Pattern and Chinampa Agriculture at Tenochtitlan." *American Antiquity* 37:104–15.

1973 "The Localization of the Sixteenth Century Map Called the Maguey Plan." *American Antiquity* 38:190–95.

1975 "Organización de los sistemas de abastecimiento urbano

de alimentos: el caso de Tenochtitlan." In Hardoy and Schaedel 1975.
1976 "The Internal Structure of Tenochtitlan." In Wolf 1976.
1978a "El sistema de mercados de tenochtitlan." In Carrasco and Broda 1978.
1978b "The Internal Structure of Cities in America: Pre-Columbian Cities: The Case of Tenochtitlan." In Schaedal, Hardoy, and Kinzer 1978.
1978c "The City-State in the Basin of Mexico: Late Pre-Hispanic Period." In Schaedel, Hardoy, and Kinzer 1978.

Carneiro, Robert L.
1978 "Political Expansion as an Expression of the Principle of Competitive Exclusion." In Cohen and Service 1978.

Carrasco, Pedro
1978 "La economía del México prehispánica." In Carrasco and Broda 1978.
1980 "Markets and Merchants in the Aztec Economy." *Journal of the Steward Anthropological Society* 11:249–69.

———, and Johanna Broda
1976 *Estratificación social en la Mesoamérica prehispánica.* Mexico: SEPINAH.
1978 *Economía política e ideología en el México prehispánico.* Mexico: Editorial Nueva Imagen.

Carrera Stampa, Manuel
1952–53 "Las ferias novohispanas." *Historia Mexicana* 2:319–42.

Las Casas, Bartolomé de
1967 *Apologética historia sumaria.* 2 vols. Mexico: Universidad Nacional Autónoma de México.

Caso, Alfonso
1928a "Relación del Mistepeque." *Revista Mexicana de Estudios Historicos* 2:142–46.
1928b "Tehuantepec." *Revista Mexicana de Estudios Históricos* 2:164–75.
1954 "Instituciones indígenas precortesianas." In Caso, Zavala, Miranda, Gonzalez, Aguirre Beltran, and Pozas 1954.
1963 "Land Tenure Among the Ancient Mexicans." *American Anthropologist* 65:863–78.
1966 "La época de los señorios independientes: 1232–1427." *Revista Mexicana de Estudios Antropológicos* 20:147–52.
1967 *Los calendarios prehispánicos.* Mexico: Universidad Nacional Autónoma de México.

1968 "Religión o religiones mesoamericanas?" *Internationalen Amerikanistenkongresses* 38:3:189–200. Stuttgart-München.

1971 "Calendrical Systems of Central Mexico." In Ekholm and Bernal 1971.

Castillo Farreras, Victor M.

1969 "Caminos del mundo nahuatl." *Estudios de Cultura Nahuatl* 8:175–87.

1972 *Estructura económica de la sociedad mexica.* Mexico: Universidad Nacional Autónoma de México.

Cervantes de Salazar, Francisco

1953 *Life in the Imperial and Loyal City of Mexico in New Spain and the Royal and Pontifical University of Mexico as described in the Dialogues for the Study of the Latin Language.* Minnie Lee Barrett Shepard, trans. Austin: University of Texas Press.

Chance, John K.

1978 *Race and Class in Colonial Oaxaca.* Stanford, Calif.: Stanford University Press.

Chapman, Anne M.

1971a "Commentary on: Mesoamerican Trade and its Role in the Emergence of Civilization." *Contributions of the California Archaeological Research Facility* no. 11:196–211.

1971b "Port of Trade Enclaves in Aztec and Maya Civilizations." In Polanyi, Arensberg, and Pearson 1971.

Chardon, Roland

1980 "The Elusive Spanish League: A Problem of Measurement in Sixteenth-Century New Spain." *Hispanic American Historical Review* 60:294–302.

Charlton, Thomas

1970 "Contemporary Agriculture of the Valley." In Sanders, Kovar, Charlton, and Diehl 1970.

Chaunu, Huguette, and Pierre Chaunu

1955–59 *Séville et l'Atlantique (1504-1650).* 8 vols. Paris.

Chaunu, Pierre

1974 *Las Filipinas y el Pacífico de los ibéricos, Siglos XVI, XVII, y XVIII.* Mexico: Instituto Mexicano de Comercio Exterior.

Chávez Orozco, Luis

1965 "El camino de México a Toluca." In Colin 1965.

Chevalier, Francois

1970 *Land and Society in Colonial Mexico: The Great Hacienda.* Berkeley: University of California Press.

Childe, V. Gordon
1958 "Wheeled Vehicles." In Singer, Holmyard, and Hall 1958.

Chimalpahin, Francisco de San Antón Muñón
1965 *Relaciones originales de Chalco Amaquemecan.* Mexico: Fondo de Cultura Económica.

Chorley, Richard J.
1969 *Water, Earth, and Man.* London: Methuen.

Christaller, Walter
1972 "How I Discovered the Theory of Central Places: A Report About the Origin of Central Places." In English and Mayfield 1972.

Ciudad Real, Antonio de
1976 *Tratado curioso y docto de las grandezas de la Nueva España.* 2 vols. Mexico: Universidad Nacional Autónoma de México.

Clausewitz, Karl von
1943 *On War.* O. J. Matthijs Jolles, trans. New York: Random House.

Clavijero, Francisco Javier
1974 *Historia antigua de México.* Mexico: Porrúa.

Cleland, Charles
1976 *Cultural Change and Continuity: Essays in Honor of James Bennett Griffin.* New York: Academic Press.

Cline, Howard F.
1972a "Introductory Notes on Territorial Division of Middle America." In Cline 1972b.
1972b *Guide to Ethnohistorical Sources, Part One. Handbook of Middle American Indians,* vol. 12. Austin: University of Texas Press.
1973 "The Chronology of the Conquest: Synchronologies in Codex Telleriano-Remensis and Sahagún." *Journal de la Société des Américanistes* 62:9–34.
1975 *Guide to Ethnohistorical Sources, Part Four. Handbook of Middle American Indians,* vol. 15. Austin: University of Texas Press.

Coale, Ansley J., and Paul Demeny
1966 *Regional Model Life Tables and Stable Populations.* Princeton, N.J.: Princeton University Press.

Cobo, Bernabé
1964 *Obras.* 2 vols. Madrid: Atlas.

Códice Chimalpopoca

1975 *Códice Chimalpopoca.* Mexico: Universidad Nacional Autonóma de México.

Coe, Michael D.

1964 "The Chinampas of Mexico." *Scientific American* 211:-90–98.

Cohen, Ronald, and Elman R. Service

1978 *Origins of the State.* Philadelphia: ISHI Press.

Colin, Mario

1965 *Toluca: crónicas de una ciudad: antología.* Mexico: Biblioteca Enciclopédica del Estado de México.

Comas, Juan, Samuel Fastlicht, María Teresa Jaén A., Sergio López A., Arturo Romano, Javier Romero, and Carlos Serrano S.

1974 *Antropología Física.* Mexico: Instituto Nacional de Antropología e Historia.

Cook, Noble David

1981 *Demographic Collapse: Indian Peru, 1520-1620.* New York: Cambridge University Press.

Cook, Sherburne F.

1946 "The Incidence and Significance of Disease Among the Aztecs and Related Tribes." *Hispanic American Historical Review* 26:320–35.

———, and Woodrow Borah

1960 "The Indian Population of Central Mexico, 1531–1610." *Ibero-Americana* 44.

1971 *Essays in Population History.* Vol. I. Berkeley and Los Angeles: University of California Press.

Corona Núñez, José

1966 "Los teotihuacanos en el occidente de México." *Revista Mexicana de Estudios Antropológicos* 20:111–16.

Cortés, Hernán

1971 *Hernan Cortes: Letters from Mexico.* A. R. Pagden, trans. New York: Grossman.

Covarrubias, Sebastián de

1943 *Tesoro de la lengua castellana o española.* Barcelona: Horta.

Cowgill, Ursula M.

1962 "An Agricultural Study of the Southern Maya Lowlands." *American Anthropologist* 64:273–86.

Cox, G. W.

1978 "Famine Symposium—The Ecology of Famine: An Overview." *Ecology of Food and Nutrition* 6:207–20.

Crosby, Alfred W., Jr.

1973 *The Columbian Exchange: Biological and Cultural Consequences of 1492.* Westport, Conn.: Greenwood Press.

Cuevas, P. Mariano
1975 *Documentos inéditos del siglo XVI para la historia de México.* Mexico: Porrúa.

Culbert, T. Patrick
1973 *The Classic Maya Collapse.* Albuquerque: University of New Mexico Press.

Curtin, Philip D.
1968 "Epidemiology and the Slave Trade." *Political Science Quarterly* 83:190–216.

Dando, William A.
1980 *The Geography of Famine.* New York: John Wiley & Sons.

Davies, Nigel
1972 "The Military Organization of the Aztec Empire." *Atti del XL Congresso Internazionale Degli Americanisti* 4:213–21.
1977a *The Aztecs.* London: Abacus.
1977b *The Toltecs: Until the Fall of Tula.* Norman: University of Oklahoma Press.

Davis, Kingsley
1973 "The First Cities: How and Why Did They Arise." In Press and Smith 1973.

Deevey, Edward S., Jr.
1957 "Limnologic Studies in Middle America." *Transactions of the Connecticut Academy of Arts and Sciences* 39:213–328.

Deglopper, Donald R.
1980 "Lu-kang: A City and Its Trading System." In Knapp 1980.

Denevan, William M.
1976a *The Native Population of the Americas in 1492.* Madison: University of Wisconsin Press.
1976b "Epilogue." In Denevan 1976a.

Denhardt, Robert M.
1950 "The Horse in New Spain and the Borderlands." *Agricultural History* 24:145–50.

Díaz del Castillo, Bernal
1974 *Historia de la conquista de Nueva España.* Mexico: Porrúa.

Dillon, Brian D.
1975 "Notes on Trade in Ancient Mesoamerica." *Contributions of the University of California Archaeological Research Facility* no. 24:80–135.

Dixon, C. W.

1962 *Smallpox.* London: J. and A. Churchill.

Donkin, R. A.

1979 *Agricultural Terracing in the Aboriginal New World.* Viking Fund Publications in Anthropology no. 56. Tucson: University of Arizona Press.

Doren, Edwin Jr.

1971 "The Sailing Raft as a Great Tradition." In Riley, Kelley, Pennington, and Rands 1971.

Durán, Diego

1967 *Historia de las Indias de Nueva España e islas de la Tierra Firma.* 2 vols. Mexico: Porrúa.

Durand-Forest, Jacqueline de

1971 "Cambios económicos y moneda entre los aztecas." *Estudios de Cultura Nahuatl* 9:105–24.

Dusenberry, William H.

1963 *The Mexican Mesta.* Urbana: University of Illinois Press.

Earle, Timothy K., and Jonathon E. Ericson

1977 *Exchange Systems in Prehistory.* New York: Academic Press.

Early, Daniel

1977 "Amaranth Secrets of the Aztecs." *Organic Gardening and Farming* 24:12:69–73.

Edmonson, Munro S.

1974a *Sixteenth-Century Mexico: The Works of Sahagún.* Albuquerque: University of New Mexico Press.

1974b "Introduction." In Edmonson 1974a.

Edwards, Clinton R.

1972 "Nautical Technology and Maritime Routes in Mesoamerica." *Atti del XL Congresso Internazionale degli Americanisti* 4:199–202.

Eighmy, Thomas H.

1972 "Rural Periodic Markets and the Extension of an Urban System: A Western Nigeria Example." *Economic Geography* 48:299–315.

Ekholm, G. F.

1946 "Wheeled Toys in Mexico." *American Antiquity* 11:223–28.

———, and Ignacio Bernal

1971 *Archaeology of Northern Mesoamerica, Part One. Handbook of Middle American Indians,* vol. 10. Austin: University of Texas Press.

Emmart, Emily Walcott

1940 *The Badianus Manuscript.* Baltimore: Johns Hopkins

Press.

English, Paul Ward, and Robert C. Mayfield
1972 *Man, Space, and Environment.* New York: Oxford University Press.

Etzioni, Amitai
1969 *A Sociological Reader on Complex Organizations.* 2d ed. New York: Holt, Rinehart and Winston.

Ewald, Ursula
1977 "The von Thünen Principle and Agricultural Zonation in Colonial Mexico." *Journal of Historical Geography* 3:123–33.

Farrar, W. V.
1966 "Tecuitlatl; A Glimpse of Aztec Food Technology." *Nature* 211:341–42.

Feldman, Lawrence H.
1978 "Inside a Mexica Market." In Lee and Navarrete 1978.

Finer, Samuel E.
1975 "State- and Nation-building in Europe: The Role of the Military." In Tilly 1975b.

Flannery, Kent V.
1972 "The Cultural Evolution of Civilizations." *Annual Review of Ecology and Systematics* vol. 3.
1976a *The Early Mesoamerican Village.* New York: Academic Press.
1976b "Evolution of Complex Settlement Systems." In Flannery 1976a.

Florescano, Enrique
1965 "El abasto y la legislación de granos en el siglo XVI." *Historia Mexicana* 14:567–630.

———, and Isabel Gil Sánchez
1976 "La época de los reformas borbónicas y el crecimiento económico, 1750–1808." *Historia General de México,* vol. 2 Mexico: El Colegio de México.

Foster, George M.
1960 *Culture and Conquest: America's Spanish Heritage.* Viking Fund Publications in Anthropology, no. 27. New York: Wenner-Gren Foundation.

Frank, Andre Gunder
1979 *Mexican Agriculture, 1521-1630.* Cambridge: Cambridge University Press.

Fraser, Alexander G.
1918 "Draft Mules in the Field in Mexico." *Journal of the*

American Veterinary Medical Association 52:357-61.
Frías y Frías, Valentín
1906 *La conquista de Querétaro.* Querétaro, Mexico.
Fuentes, Patricia de
1963 *The Conquistadors.* New York: Orion Press.
Furst, Peter T.
1978 "Spirulina." *Human Nature* 1:3:60-65.
Gage, Thomas
1969 *Thomas Gage's Travels in the New World.* J. Eric S. Thompson, ed. Norman: University of Oklahoma Press. Originally published 1958.
García, Género
1907 *Documentos inéditos o muy raros para la historia de México.* Mexico.
———, and Carlos Pereyra
1905-11 *Documentos inéditos o muy raros para la historia de México.* 36 vols. Mexico.
García Icazbalceta, Joaquín
1891 *Nueva colección de documentos para la historia de México.* 3 vols. Mexico.
1971 *Colección de documentos para la historia de México.* 2 vols. Mexico: Porrúa.
García Pimentel, Luis
1897 *Descripción del arzobispado de México hecha en 1570 y otros documentos.* Mexico: José Joaquín Terrazas.
Gardiner, C. Harvey
1956 *Naval Power in the Conquest of Mexico.* Austin: University of Texas Press.
Gemelli Careri, Giovanni Francesco
1976 *Viaje a la Nueva España.* Mexico: Universidad Nacional Autónoma de México.
Gerhard, Peter
1960 *Pirates on the West Coast of New Spain, 1575-1742.* Glendale, Calif.: Arthur H. Clark Co.
1972a *A Guide to the Historical Geography of New Spain.* Cambridge: Cambridge University Press.
1972b "Colonial New Spain, 1519-1786: Historical Notes on the Evolution of Minor Political Jurisdictions." In Cline 1972b.
Gibson, Charles
1964a *The Aztecs Under Spanish Rule.* Stanford, Calif.: Stanford University Press.

1964b "The Pre-Conquest Tepanec Zone and the Labor Drafts of the Sixteenth Century." *Revista de Historia de América* 57–58:136–45.

1966 *Spain in America.* New York: Harper and Row.

1967 *Tlaxcala in the Sixteenth Century.* Stanford, Calif.: Stanford University Press.

1971 "Structure of the Aztec Empire." In Ekholm and Bernal 1971.

Gómara, Francisco López de

1965-66 *Historia general de las Indias.* 2 vols. Barcelona: Ibéria.

Gómez de Cervantes, Gonzalo

1944 *La vida económica y social de Nueva España al finalizar el siglo XVI.* Mexico: José Porrúa.

Gómez de Orozco, Frederico

1927 "Descripción de Cholula." *Revista Mexicana de Estudios Históricos* 1:158–70.

Gorenstein, Shirley

1963 "The Differential Development of Military and Political Organization in Prehispanic Peru and Mexico." Ph.D. diss., Columbia University.

1966 "The Differential Development of New World Empires." *Revista Mexicana de Estudios Antropológicos* 20: 41–67.

Goubaud Carrera, A.

1935 "El 'Guajxaquip Bats'—Ceremonia Calendárica Indígena." *Anales Sociedad de Geografía e Historia de Guatemala* 12:39–52.

Grigg, D. B.

1977 *The Agricultural Systems of the World.* Cambridge: Cambridge University Press.

Guerra, Francisco

1964 "Maya Medicine." *Medical History* 8:31–43.

1966 "Aztec Medicine." *Medical History* 10:315–38.

1969 "Aztec Science and Technology." *History of Science* 8:32–52.

Guthrie, Chester L.

1941 "A Seventeenth Century 'Ever-Normal Granary.'" *Agricultural History* 15:37–43.

Hackett, Charles Wilson

1923 *Historical Documents Relating to New Mexico, Nueva Vizcaya, and Approaches Thereto, to 1773.* Collected by Adolph F. A. Bandelier and Fanny R. Bandelier. Vol. 1. Washington, D.C.: Carnegie Institution.

Hakluyt, Richard
1914 *The Principal Navigations, Voyages, Traffiques and Discoveries of the English Nation.* 12 vols. New York: Macmillan Co.

Hammond, Mason
1972 *The City in the Ancient World.* Cambridge, Mass.: Harvard University Press.

Hammond, Norman
1978 "Cacao and Cobaneros: An Overland Trade Route Between the Maya Highlands and Lowlands." In Lee and Navarrete 1978.

Hanke, Lewis
1976-78 *Los virreyes españoles en América durante el gobierno de la Casa de Austria.* 5 vols. Madrid: Ediciones Atlas.

Hardoy, Jorge
1973 *Pre-Columbian Cities.* New York: Walker and Co.

Haring, Clarence Henry
1918 *Trade and Navigation Between Spain and the Indies in the Time of the Hapsburgs.* Cambridge, Mass.: Harvard University Press.
1963 *The Spanish Empire in America.* New York: Harcourt, Brace, and World.

Hassig, Ross
1980 "Commerce or Conquest: the Caballo Ordinance of 1526." *New Mexico Historical Review* 55:331–33.
1981 "The Famine of One Rabbit: Ecological Causes and Social Consequences of a Pre-Columbian Calamity." *Journal of Anthropological Research* 37:171–81.
1982 "Periodic Markets in Pre-Columbian Mexico." *American Antiquity* 47:346–55.

Hauser, Philip M.
1965 "Urbanization: An Overview." In Hauser and Schnore 1965.

——, and Leo F. Schnore
1965 *The Study of Urbanization.* New York: John Wiley & Sons.

Hernández Xolocotzin, Efraim
1949 "Maize Granaries in Mexico." *Botanical Museum Leaflets, Harvard University,* 13:7:153–211.

Herrera, Antonio de
1725–26 *The General History of the Vast Continent and Islands of America, Commonly Called the West Indies.* 6 vols.

London.

Hicks, Frederic

1976 "Mayeque y calpuleque en el sistema de clases del México antiguo." In Carrasco and Broda 1976.

1977 "Social Stratification and the Calpixque of Aztec Mexico." Paper presented at the 76th Convention of the American Anthropological Association, Houston, Texas, 3 December, 1977.

N.d. "Prehispanic Background of Colonial Political and Economic Organization of Central Mexico." *Handbook of Middle American Indians, Colonial Ethnohistory.* Austin: University of Texas Press.

Hoberman, Louisa

1974 "Bureaucracy and Disaster: Mexico City and the Flood of 1629." *Journal of Latin American Studies* 6:211–30.

Hoeprich, Paul D.

1977 *Infectious Diseases.* New York: Harper and Row.

Holt, H. Barry

1976 "The Extent of the Dominance of Tenochtitlan During the Reign of Mocteuczoma Ilhuicamina." *Middle American Research Institute Publication* 22:49–62.

1979 "Mexica-Aztec Warfare: A Developmental and Cultural Analysis." Ph.D. diss., University of Texas—Austin.

Humboldt, Alexander de

1814 *Political Essay on the Kingdom of New Spain.* 4 vols. London.

Hunter, George W., III, J. Clyde Swartzwelder, and David F. Clyde

1976 *Tropical Medicine.* Philadelphia: W. B. Saunders Co.

Imperato, Pascal James

1974 *The Treatment and Control of Infectious Diseases in Man.* Springfield, Ill.: Charles C. Thomas.

Israel, J. I.

1974 "Mexico and the 'General Crisis' of the Seventeenth Century." *Past and Present* 63:33–57.

Ixtlilxochitl, Fernando de Alva

1975–77 *Obras históricas.* 2 vols. Mexico: Universidad Nacional Autónoma de México.

Jaén Esquivel, María Teresa, and Sergio López Alonso

1974 "Algunas características físicas de la población prehispánica de México." In Comas, Fastlicht, Jaén E., López A., Romano, Romero, and Serrano S. 1974.

James, Preston E., and Clarence F. Jones

1954 *American Geography: Inventory and Prospect.* Syracuse, N.Y.: Syracuse University Press.

Jiménez Moreno, Wigberto

1966 "Los Imperios prehispánicos de Mesoamérica." *Revista Mexicana de Estudios Antropológicos* 20:179–95.

Johnston, R. J.

1977 "Regarding Urban Designs, Urbanization and Urban Patterns." *Geography* 62:1–8.

Jones, Emrys

1966a *Human Geography.* New York: Praeger.

1966b *Towns and Cities.* New York: Oxford University Press.

Joralemon, Donald

1982 "New World Population and the Case of Disease." *Journal of Anthropological Research* 38:108–27.

Katz, Friedrich

1972 *The Ancient American Civilization.* New York: Praeger.

Kelly, Isabel, and Angel Palerm

1952 *The Tajín Totonac, Part 1: History, Subsístence, Shelter, and Technology.* Smithsonian Institution, Institute of Social Anthropology, Publication No. 13. Washington, D.C.: U.S. Government Printing Office.

Kirchhoff, Paul

1968 "Las 18 fiestas anuales en Mesoamérica: 6 fiestas sencillas y 6 fiestas dobles." *Internationalen Amerikanistenkongresses* 38:3:207–21. Stuttgart-München.

———, Lina Odena Güemes, and Luis Reyes García

1976 *Historia tolteca-chichimeca.* Mexico: CISINAH.

Kirkby, Anne V. T.

1973 *The Use of Land and Water Resources in the Past and Present Valley of Oaxaca, Mexico.* Memoirs of the Museum of Anthropology, University of Michigan, no. 5.

Knapp, Ronald G.

1980 *China's Island Frontier.* Honolulu: University of Hawaii Press.

Konetzke, Richard, ed.

1953–62 *Collección de documentos para la historia de la formación social de Hispanoamérica, 1493-1810.* 3 vols. Madrid: Consejo Superior de Investigaciones Científicas.

Kovar, Anton

1970 "The Physical and Biological Environment of the Basin of Mexico." In Sanders, Kovar, Charlton, and Diehl 1970.

Kubler, George

1942 "Population Movements in Mexico 1500–1600." *Hispanic American Historical Review* 22:606–43.

1948 *Mexican Architecture of the Sixteenth Century.* 2 vols. New Haven, Conn.: Yale University Press.

———, and Charles Gibson

1951 *The Tovar Calendar.* Memoirs of the Connecticut Academy of Arts and Sciences, vol. 11.

Kurtz, Donald V.

1974 "Peripheral and Transitional Markets: The Aztec Case." *American Ethnologist* 1:685–705.

Lamb, Robert Byron

1963 "The Mule in Southern Agriculture." *University of California Publications in Geography,* vol. 15.

Lamberg-Karlovsky, C. C.

1979 *Hunters, Farmers, and Civilizations: Old World Archaeology.* San Francisco: W. H. Freeman and Co.

Lameiras, Brigitte B. de

1974 *Terminológia agrohidráulica prehispánica nahua.* Mexico: SEPINAH.

Leaman, J. Harold, and E. C. Conkling

1975 "Transport Change and Agricultural Specialization." *Annals of the Association of American Geographers* 65:425–32.

Lee, Everett S.

1966 "A Theory of Migration." *Demography* 3:47–57.

Lee, Raymond L.

1947 "Grain Legislation in Colonial Mexico, 1575–1585." *Hispanic American Historical Review* 27:647–60.

Lee, Thomas A., and Carlos Navarrete

1978 *Mesoamerican Communication Routes and Cultural Contacts.* Papers of the New World Archaeological Foundation, no. 40.

Leighton, Albert C.

1967 "The Mule as a Cultural Invention." *Technology and Culture* 8:45–52.

León-Portilla, Miguel

1978 "Minería y metalurgia en el México antiguo." In León-Portilla, Gurria Lacroix, Moreno, and Madero Bracho 1978.

———, Jorge Gurria Lacroix, Roberto Moreno, and Enrique Madero Bracho

1978 *La minería en México.* Mexico: Universidad Nacional Autónoma de México.

Leshikar, Margaret Elaine
1982 "The Mexica Canoe: An Archaeological and Ethnohistorical Study of Its Design, Uses, and Significance." M.A. thesis, University of Texas—Austin.
Lewis, Leslie
1976 "In Mexico City's Shadow: Some Aspects of Economic Activity and Social Processes in Texcoco, 1570–1620." In Altman and Lockhart 1976.
Lewis, Oscar
1963 *Life in a Mexican Village: Tepoztlan Restudied.* Urbana: University of Illinois Press.
Linné, S.
1937 "Hunting and Fishing in the Valley of Mexico in the Middle of the 16th Century." *Ethnos* 2:56–64.
1940 "Bird-nets of Lake Texcoco, Mexico Valley." *Ethnos* 5:122–30.
Litvak King, Jaime
1971 *Cihuatlan y Tepecoacuilco: províncias tributárias de México en el siglo XVI.* Mexico: Universidad Nacional Autónoma de México.
Lockhart, James
1976 "Capital and Province, Spaniard and Indian: The Example of Late Sixteenth-Century Toluca." In Altman and Lockhart 1976.
Logan, Michael H., and William T. Sanders
1976 "The Valley as an Ecological System: The Model." In Wolf 1976.
López Alonso, Sergio, and Carlos Serrano Sánchez
1974 "La alimentación en el México prehispánico." In Comas, Fastlicht, Jaén E., López A., Romano, Romero, and Serrano S. 1974.
Luttwak, Edward N.
1976 *The Grand Strategy of the Roman Empire.* Baltimore, Md. Johns Hopkins University Press.
McNeill, William H.
1977 *Plagues and Peoples.* Garden City, N.Y.: Anchor Books.
Marks, Geoffrey, and William K. Beatty
1976 *Epidemics.* New York: Charles Scribner's Sons.
Matesanz, José
1965 "Introducción de la ganadería en Nueva España 1521–1535." *Historia Mexicana* 14:533–66.
May, Jacques M.

1961 *Studies in Disease Ecology.* New York: Hafner Publishing Co.

Mayer, Brantz
1844 *Mexico as It Was and as It Is.* New York: J. Winchester, New World Press.

Mecham, J. Lloyd
1927 *Francisco de Ibarra and Nueva Vizcaya.* Durham, N.C.: Duke University Press.

Mendieta, Gerónimo de
1971 *Historia eclesiástica indiana.* Mexico: Porrúa.

México, Archivo General de la Nación
1940 *Boletín.* Mexico.
1952 *El libro de las tasaciones de pueblos de la Nueva España.* Mexico.

———, Departmento del Distrito Federal
1975 *Memoria de las obras del sistema de drenaje profundo del Distrito Federal.* 3 vols. + *Atlas.* Mexico.

———, Dirección General de Estadística
1975 *V censos agrícola-ganadero y ejidal 1970, resumen general.* Mexico.

———, Secretaria de Hacienda y Crédito Público
1965 *Antigüedades de México.* 3 vols. Mexico.

Millares Carlo, A., and J. I. Mantecón, eds.
1945 *Indice y extractos de los protocolos del archivo de notarias de México, df (1525-1528).* Mexico: El Colegio de México.

Miller, Arthur G.
1973 *The Mural Painting of Teotihuacán.* Washington, D.C.: Dumbarton Oaks.

Miranda, José
1952 *El tributo indígena en la Nueva España durante el siglo XVI.* Mexico: El Colégio de México.

Molina, Alonso de
1970 *Vocabulario en lengua castellana y mexicana y mexicana y castellana.* Mexico: Porrúa.

Molins Fábrega, N.
1954–55 "El códice mendocino y la economía de Tenochtitlan." *Revista Mexicana de Estudios Antropológicos* 14:303–35.

More, Rosemary J.
1969 "The Basin Hydrological Cycle." In Chorley 1969.

Moreno, Manual M.
1971 *La organización política y social de los aztecas.* Mexico: Instituto Nacional de Antropología e Historia.

Moreno, Roberto
1977 *Joaquín Velázquez de León y sus trabajos cientifícos sobre el Valle de México.* Mexico: Universidad Nacional Autónoma de México.

Moreno Toscano, Alejandra
1965 "Tres problemas en la geografía de maíz 1600–1624." *Historia Mexicana* 14:631–55.
1968 *Geografía económica de México (siglo XVI).* Mexico: El Colégio de México.

Moriarty, James Robert
1968 "Floating Gardens (Chinampas) Agriculture in the Old Lakes of Mexico." *América Indígena* 28:461–84.

Morley, Sylvanus Griswold
1937 *The Inscriptions of Peten.* 5 vols. Carnegie Institution of Washington publication 437.

Morrisey, Richard J.
1950 "The Northward Expansion of Cattle Ranching in New Spain, 1550–1600." *Agricultural History* 24:115–21.
1957 "Colonial Agriculture in New Spain." *Agricultural History* 31:24–29.

Motolinia (Toribio de Benavente)
1971 *Memoriales o libro de las cosas de Nueva España y de los naturales de ella.* Mexico: Universidad Nacional Autónoma de México.
1973 *Historia de los indios de la Nueva España.* Mexico: Porrúa.

Murillo Velarde, Pedro
1752 *Geographia historica.* Madrid.

Newman, Marshall T.
1976 "Aboriginal New World Epidemiology and Medical Care, and the Impact of Old World Disease Imports." *American Journal of Physical Anthropology* 45:667–72.

Núñez Ortega, A.
1878 "Los navegantes indígenas en la época de la conquista." *Boletín de la Sociedad de Geografía y Estadística de la Republica Mexicana.* Tercera Época 4:47–57.

Offner, Jerome A.
1980 "Archival Reports of Poor Crop Yields in the Early Postconquest Texcocan Heartland and Their Implications for Studies of Aztec Period Population." *American Antiquity* 45:848–56.
1981 "On Carrasco's Use of 'First Principles.' " *American Antiquity* 46:69–74.

Ojea, Hernando
1897 *Libro tercero de la historia religiosa de la provincia de México de la Orden de Sto. Domingo.* Mexico: Museo Nacional de México.
Oviedo y Valdés, Gonzalo Fernández de
1959 *Historia general y natural de las Indias.* 5 vols. Madrid.
1979 *Sumario de la natural historia de las Indias.* Mexico: Fondo de Cultura Económica.
Paddock, John
1966a "El fenómemo imperial: algunas enfoques teóricos." *Revista Mexicana de Estudios Antropológicos* 20:69–81.
1966b "La idea del imperio aplicada a Mesoamérica." *Revista Mexicana de Estudios Antropológicos* 20:83–94.
1966c "Monte Albán: sede de imperio?" *Revista Mexicana de Estudios Antropológicos* 20:117–46.
Palafox y Mendoza, Juan de
1893 *Virtudes del indio.* Madrid.
Palerm, Angel
1955 "The Agricultural Basis of Urban Civilization in Mesoamerica." In Steward 1955.
1956 "Notas sobre las construcciones militares y la guerra en Mesoamérica." *Ciencias Sociales* 7:189–202.
1961 "Aspectos agrícolas del desarrollo de la civilización en Mesoamérica." *Ciencias Sociales* 1:233-41.
1973 *Obras hidráulicas prehispánicas en el sistema lacustre del Valle de México.* Mexico: Instituto Nacional de Antropologia e Historia.
Parry, J. H.
1970 *The Spanish Seaborne Empire.* New York: Alfred A. Knopf.
1974 *The Discovery of the Sea.* New York: Dial Press.
Parsons, Jeffrey R.
1971 *Prehistoric Settlement Patterns in the Texcoco Region, Mexico.* Memoirs of the Museum of Anthropology, University of Michigan, no. 3
1976 "The Role of Chinampa Agriculture in the Food Supply of Aztec Tenochtitlan." In Cleland 1976.
Parsons, Lee A., and Barbara J. Price
1971 "Mesoamerican Trade and Its Role in the Emergence of Civilization." *Contributions of the University of California Archaeological Research Facility,* no. 11.
Paso y Troncoso, Francisco del, ed.
1905–48 *Papeles de Nueva España.* 9 vols. Madrid and Mexico.

1939–42 *Epistolario de Nueva España.* 16 vols. Mexico: José Porrúa e Hijos.

Paulsen, Allison C.

1977 "Patterns of Maritime Trade Between South Coastal Ecuador and Western Mesoamerica, 1500 B.C.–A.D. 600." In Benson 1977.

Pershits, Abraham I.

1979 "Tribute Relations." In Seaton and Claessen 1979.

Peter Martyr

1912 *De Orbe Novo: The Eight Decades of Peter Martyr D'Anghera.* 2 vols. New York: Burt Franklin.

Peterson, Frederick

1962 *Ancient Mexico.* New York: Capricorn Books.

Phillips, David A.

1979 "The Growth and Decline of States in Mesoamerica." *Journal of the Steward Anthropological Society* 10:137–59.

Piho, Virve

1972 "La jerarquía militar azteca." *Atti del XL Congresso Internazionale degli Americanisti* 2:273–88.

1974 "Esquema provisional de la organización militar mexica." *Actas del XLI Congresso Internacional de Americanistas.* 3 vols. 2:169-78.

Pirie, N. W.

1975a "The Spirulina Algae." In Pirie 1975b.

1975b *Food Protein Sources.* New York: Cambridge University Press.

Polanyi, Karl

1971 "The Economy as Instituted Process." In Polanyi, Arensberg, and Pearson 1971.

———, Conrad M. Arensberg, and Harry W. Pearson.

1971 *Trade and Market in the Early Empires.* Chicago: Henry Regnery Co.

Pomar, Juan Bautista

1975 *Relación de Texcoco.* Mexico: Enciclopédia del Estado de México.

Poole, D. M.

1951 "The Spanish Conquest of Mexico: Some Geographical Aspects." *Geographical Journal* 117:27–42.

Pounds, Norman J. G.

1976 *An Historical Geography of Europe, 450 B.C.-A.D. 1330.* Cambridge, Mass.: Cambridge University Press.

Powell, Philip Wayne

1950 "The Forty-Niners of Sixteenth-Century Mexico." *Pacific Historical Review* 19:235–49.
1952 *Soldiers, Indians, and Silver.* Berkeley and Los Angeles: University of California Press.

Press, Irwin, and M. Estellie Smith
1973 *Urban Place and Process.* New York: Macmillan Publishing Co.

Price, Barbara J.
1971 "Prehispanic Irrigation Agriculture in Nuclear America." *Latin American Research Review* 6:3–60.
1978a "Population Composition in Pre-Hispanic Mesoamerican Urban Settlements: A Problem in Archaeological Inference." In Schaedel, Hardoy, and Kinzer 1978.
1978b "Demystification, Enriddlement, and Aztec Cannibalism: A Materialist Rejoinder to Harner." *American Ethnologist* 5:98–115.

Puga, Vasco de
1945 *Provisiones cédulas instrucciones para el gobierno de la Nueva España.* Madrid: Ediciones Cultura Hispánica.

Ramírez Cabañas, Joaquín
1943 *La ciudad de Veracruz en el siglo XVI,* Mexico.

Razzell, Peter
1977 *The Conquest of Smallpox: The Impact of Inoculation on Smallpox Mortality in Eighteenth Century Britain.* Sussex: Caliban Books.

Rees, Peter William
1971 "Route Inertia and Route Competition: An Historical Geography of Transportation Between Mexico City and Vera Cruz." Ph.D. diss., University of California at Berkeley. Ann Arbor, Mich.: University Microfilms.

Reyes García, Cayetano, ed.
1973 *Indice y extractos de los protocolos de la notaria de Cholula (1590-1600).* Mexico: SEPINAH.

Reyman, Jonathan E.
1978 "Pochteca Burials at Anasazi Sites?" In Riley and Hedrick 1978.

Riley, Carroll L., and Basil C. Hedrick
1978 *Across the Chichimec Sea: Papers in Honor of J. Charles Kelley.* Carbondale and Edwardsville: Southern Illinois University Press.

——, J. C. Kelley, C. W. Pennington, and R. L. Rands
1971 *Man Across the Sea: Problems of Pre-Columbian Contacts.*

Austin: University of Texas Press.
Ringrose, David R.
1970a "Carting in the Hispanic World: An Example of Divergent Development." *Hispanic American Historical Review* 50:30–51.
1970b *Transportation and Economic Stagnation in Spain, 1750-1850.* Durham, N.C.: Duke University Press.
Robertson, Donald
1959 *Mexican Manuscript Painting of the Early Colonial Period: The Metropolitan Schools.* New Haven, Conn.: Yale University Press.
Rodríguez Vallejo, José
1976 *Ixcatl, el algodón mexicano.* Mexico: Fondo de Cultura Económica.
Rojas González, Francisco
1945 "El comercio entre los indios de México." *Revista Mexicana de Sociología* 7:123–37.
Rojas Rabiela, Teresa
1977 *La organización del trabajo para las obras públicas: el coatequitl y las cuadrillas de trabajadores.* Mexico: Ediciones de la Casa Chata.
Rounds, J.
1979 "Lineage, Class, and Power in the Aztec State." *American Ethnologist* 6:73–86.
Ruiz de Alarcón, Hernando
1892 "Tratado de las supersticiones y costumbres gentilicas que oy viuen entre los indios naturales desta Nueua España." *Anales del Museo Nacional de México* 6:125–223.
Ruxton, George F.
1848 *Adventures in Mexico and the Rocky Mountains.* New York: Harper and Brothers.
Sabloff, Jeremy A.
1977 "Old Myths, New Myths: The Role of Sea Traders in the Development of Ancient Maya Civilization." In Benson 1977.
Sahagún, Bernardino de
1974 *'Primeros memoriales' de Fray Bernardino de Sahagún.* Wigberto Jiménez Moreno, ed. Mexico: Instituto Nacional de Antropología e Historia.
1950–75 *General History of the Things of New Spain: Florentine Codex.* Arthur J. O. Anderson and Charles E. Dibble, trans. 12 vols. Salt Lake City: University of Utah Press.

1952 *The Origin of the Gods.* Book 3.
1953 *The Sun, Moon, and Stars, and the Binding of the Years.* Book 7.
1954 *Kings and Lords.* Book 8.
1957 *The Soothsayers.* Book 4.
1957 *The Omens.* Book 5.
1959 *The Merchants.* Book 9.
1961 *The People.* Book 10.
1963 *Earthly Things.* Book 11.
1969 *Rhetoric and Moral Philosophy.* Book 6.
1970 *The Gods.* Book 1.

Sanders, William T.
1957 "Tierra y Agua (Soil and Water)." Ph.D. diss., Harvard University.
1970a "The Geography of the Valley of Teotihuacan." In Sanders, Kovar, Charlton, and Diehl 1970.
1970b "The Population of the Teotihuacan Valley, the Basin of Mexico, and the Central Mexican Symbiotic Region in the Sixteenth Century." In Sanders, Kovar, Charlton, and Diehl 1970.
1976a "The Agricultural History of the Basin of Mexico." In Wolf 1976.
1976b "The Population of the Teotihuacan Valley, the Basin of Mexico and the Central Mexican Symbiotic Region in the Sixteenth Century." In Devevan 1976a.
1976c "The Natural Environment of the Basin of Mexico." In Wolf 1976.

———, Anton Kovar, Thomas Charlton, and Richard Diehl
1970 *The Natural Environment, Contemporary Occupation and 16th Century Population of the Valley—The Teotihuacan Valley Project: Final Report.* Volume 1. Pennsylvania State University, Occasional Papers in Anthropology, no. 3.

———, Jeffrey R. Parsons, and Robert S. Santley
1979 *The Basin of Mexico: Ecological Process in the Evolution of a Civilization.* New York: Academic Press.

———, and Barbara J. Price
1968 *Mesoamerica: The Evolution of a Civilization.* New York: Random House.

Santa Cruz, Alonso de
1918 *Islario general de todos las islas del mundo.* Madrid.

Santley, Robert S., and Eric K. Rose
1979 "Diet, Nutrition and Population Dynamics in the Basin

of Mexico." *World Archaeology* 11:185–207.

Schaedel, Richard P.
1978 "The City and the Origin of the State in America." In Schaedel, Hardoy, and Kinzer 1978.

———, Jorge E. Hardoy, and Nora Scott Kinzer
1978 *Urbanization in the Americas from Its Beginnings to the Present.* The Hague: Mouton.

Scholes, France V., and Eleanor B. Adams
1938 *Don Diego Quijada, alcalde mayor de Yucatán, 1561-1565.* 2 vols. Mexico: José Porrúa.
1957 *Información sobre los tributos que los indios pagaban a Moctezuma, año de 1554.* Mexico: José Porrúa.
1961 *Cartas del licenciado Jeronimo Valderrama y otros documentos sobre su visita al gobierno de Nueva España.* Mexico: José Porrúa.

Schurz, William Lytle
1939 *The Manila Galleon.* New York: E. P. Dutton and Co.

Seaton, S. Lee, and Henri J. M. Claessen
1979 *Political Anthropology: The State of the Art.* The Hague: Mouton.

Serna, Jacinto de la
1892 "Manual de ministros de indios para el conocimiento de sus idolatrías y extirpación de ellas." *Anales del Museo Nacional de México* 6:261–475.

Shimkin, Demitri B.
1973 "Models for the Downfall: Some Ecological and Culture-Historical Considerations." In Culbert 1973.

Siegel, Bernard J.
1972 *Annual Review of Anthropology, 1972.* Palo Alto: Annual Reviews.

Simons, Bente Bittmann, and Thelma D. Sullivan
1972 "The Pochteca." *Atti del XL Congresso Internazionale degli Americanisti* 4:203–12.

Simpson, Lesley Byrd
1938 "Studies in the Administration of the Indians of New Spain." *Ibero-Americana* 13.
1952 "Exploitation of Land in Central Mexico in the Sixteenth Century." *Ibero-Americana* 36.

Singer, Charles, E. J. Holmyard, and A. R. Hall
1958 *A History of Technology.* Vol. 1. New York: Oxford University Press.

Sjoberg, Gideon

1965 *The Preindustrial City.* New York: Free Press.
Skinner, G. William
1964–65 "Marketing and Social Structure in Rural China." *Journal of Asian Studies* 24:3–43, 195–228, 363–99.
1977a *The City in Late Imperial China.* Stanford, Calif.: Stanford University Press.
1977b "Cities and the Hierarchy of Local Systems." In Skinner 1977a.
1977c "Regional Urbanization in Nineteenth-Century China." In Skinner 1977a.
——, and Edwin A. Winckler
1969 "Compliance Succession in Rural Communist China: A Cyclical Theory." In Etzioni 1969.
Smith, C. Earle
1973 *Man and His Foods.* University: University of Alabama Press.
Smith, Carol A.
1974 "Economics of Marketing Systems: Models from Economic Geography." In *Annual Review of Anthropology,* vol. 3. Bernard J. Siegel, Alan R. Beals, and Stephen A. Tyler, eds. Palo Alto: Annual Reviews.
1976a "Regional Economic Systems: Linking Geographical Models and Socioeconomic Problems." In Smith, C. A. 1976b.
1976b *Regional Analysis.* Vol. 1, *Economic Systems.* New York: Academic Press.
Smith, Michael
1979 "The Aztec Marketing System and Settlement Pattern in the Valley of Mexico: A Central Place Analysis." *American Antiquity* 44:110–25.
Smith, Robert Sidney
1940 *The Spanish Guild Merchant.* Durham, N.C.: Duke University Press.
Stanislawski, Dan
1947 "Tarascan Political Geography." *American Anthropologist* 49:46–55.
Stenzel, Werner
1976 "The Military and Religious Orders of Ancient Mexico." *Actas del XLI Congresso Internacional de Americanistas* 2:179–87.
Stephens, John L.
1848 *Incidents of Travel in Yucatan.* 2 vols. New York: Harper

and Brothers.
1969 *Incidents of Travel in Central America, Chiapas, and Yucatan.* 2 vols. New York: Dover.

Stewart, T. D.
1973 *The People of America.* New York: Charles Scribner's Sons.

Super, John C.
1976 "The Agricultural Near North: Queretaro in the Seventeenth Century." In Altman and Lockhart 1976.

Taaffe, Edward J., and Howard L. Gauthier, Jr.
1973 *Geography of Transportation.* Englewood Cliffs, N.J.: Prentice-Hall.

Tamayo, Jorge L., and Robert C. West
1964 "The Hydrography of Middle America." In West 1964.

Tapia, Andrés de
1963 "The Chronicle of Andres de Tapia." In Fuentes 1963.

TePaske, John J., and Herbert S. Klein
1981 "The Seventeenth-Century Crisis in New Spain: Myth or Reality?" *Past and Present* 90:116–35.

Tezozómoc, Hernando Alvarado
1975 *Crónica mexicana.* Mexico: Porrúa.

Thünen, Johann Heinrich von
1966 *Von Thünen's Isolated State.* C. M. Wartenberg, trans. Oxford: Pergamon Press.

Tilly, Charles
1975a "Reflections on the History of European State-Making." In Tilly 1975b.
1975b *The Formation of National States in Western Europe.* Princeton, N.M.: Princeton University Press.

Torquemada, Juan de
1975–79 *Monarquía Indiana.* 6 vols. Mexico: Universidad Nacional Autónoma de México.

Toussaint, Manuel
1931 *Tasco: su historia, sus monumentos, características actuales y posibilidades turísticas.* Mexico: Editorial "Cultura."

Trigger, Bruce
1972 "Determinants of Urban Growth in Pre-Industrial Societies." In Ucko, Tringham, and Dimbleby 1972.

Tylor, Edward B.
1970 *Anahuac: Or Mexico and the Mexicans, Ancient and Modern.* New York: Bergman.

Ucko, Peter J., Ruth Tringham, and G. W. Dimbleby

1972 *Man, Settlement and Urbanism.* Cambridge, Mass.: Schenkman Publishing Co.

Ullman, Edward L.

1954 "Transportation Geography." In James and Jones 1954.

U.S. Army, Quartermaster Corps

1900 *Manual of Instruction for Quartermasters Serving in the Field.* Daniel E. McCarthy. Washington, D.C.: U.S. Government Printing Office.

1904 *Manual for the Quartermaster's Department, United States Army, 1904.* Washington, D.C.: U.S. Printing Office.

1917 *Manual of Pack Transportation.* H. W. Daly. Washington, D.C.: U.S. Government Printing Office.

Usher, Abbott Payson

1932 "Spanish Ships and Shipping in the Sixteenth and Seventeenth Centuries." In *Facts and Factors in Economic History: Articles by Former Students of Edwin Francis Gay.* Cambridge, Mass.: Harvard University Press.

Vaillant, George C.

1966 *Aztecs of Mexico.* Baltimore, Md.: Penguin Books.

Vargas Rea, Luis, ed.

1944–46 *Papeles de Nueva España colecionados por Francisco del Paso y Troncoso.* Mexico.

Vásquez, Genaro V.

1940 *Doctrinas y realidades en la legislación para los indios.* Mexico: Departmento de Asuntos Indígenas.

Vásquez de Espinoza, Antonio

1942 *Compendium and Description of the West Indies.* Smithsonian Miscellaneous Collections, vol. 102. Washington, D.C.

Vásquez de Warman, Irene

1967–68 "El pósito y la alhóndiga en la Nueva España." *Historia Mexicana* 17:395–426.

Vidal de la Blache, Paul

1926 *Principles of Human Geography.* New York: Henry Holt and Co.

Villaseñor y Sánchez, Joseph Antonio de

1952 *Theatro americano, descripción general de los reynos y províncias de la Nueva España, y sus jurisdiciones.* Vol. 1. Mexico: Editorial Nacional.

Viraphol, Sarasin

1977 *Tribute and Profit: Sino-Siamese Trade, 1652-1853.* Cambridge, Mass.: Council on East Asian Studies, Harvard

University.

Wallerstein, Immanuel
1974 *The Modern World System.* New York: Academic Press.

Warren, J. Benedict
1974 *The Harkness Collection in the Library of Congress.* Washington, D.C.: U.S. Government Printing Office.

Webster, Gary
1956 "Unsung Empire Builder—The Mule." *Natural History* 65:130–35.

Wehrle, Paul F., and Franklin H. Top
1981 *Communicable and Infectious Diseases.* St. Louis: C. V. Mosby Co.

Weigand, Phil C., Garman Harbottle, and Edward V. Sayre
1977 "Turquoise Sources and Source Analysis: Mesoamerica and the Southwestern U.S.A." In Earle and Ericson 1977

West, Robert C.
1964 *Natural Environment and Early Cultures. Handbook of Middle American Indians,* vol. 1. Austin: University of Texas Press.
1968 "Population Densities and Agricultural Practices in Pre-Columbian Mexico, with Emphasis on Semi-Terracing." *Verhandlungen des XXXVIII Internationalen Amerikanistenkongresses* 2:361–69. *Stuttgart-München.*

———, and Pedro Armillas
1950 "Las chinampas de México." *Cuadernos Americanos* 50:165–82.

Wheatley, Paul
1972 "The Concept of Urbanism." In Ucko, Tringham, and Dimbleby 1972.

Williams, Barbara J.
1972 "Tepetate in the Valley of Mexico." *Association of American Geographers Annals* 62:618–26.

Wilson, Robert A.
1855 *Mexico.* New York: Harper and Brothers.

Wisseman, Charles L., Jr.
1981 "Rickettsial Diseases." In Wehrle and Top 1981.

Wolbach, S. Burt, John L. Todd, and Francis W. Palfrey
1922 *The Etiology and Pathology of Typhus.* Cambridge, Mass.: Harvard University Press.

Wolf, Eric R.
1976 *The Valley of Mexico.* Albuquerque: University of New Mexico Press.

Wrigley, E. W.
1969 *Population and History.* New York: McGraw-Hill Book Co.
1978 "Parasite or Stimulus: The Town in a Pre-Industrial Economy." In Abrams and Wrigley 1978.
Zambardino, Rudolph A.
1980 "Mexico's Population in the Sixteenth Century: Demographic Anomaly or Mathematical Illusion?" *Journal of Interdisciplinary History* 11:1–27.
Zantwijk, Rudolf van
1970 "Las Organizaciones social-económica y religiosa de los mercaderes gemiales aztecas." *Boletín de Estudios Latinoamericanos* 10:1–20.
Zavala, Silvio
1947 *Ordenanzas del trabajo, siglos XVI y XVII.* Mexico Elede.
———, and María Castelo
1939–46 *Fuentes para la historia del trabajo en Nueva España.* 8 vols. Mexico: Fondo de Cultura Económica.
Zdrodovskii, P. F., and H. M. Golinevich
1960 *The Rickettsial Diseases.* New York: Pergamon Press.
Zorita, Alonso de
1971 *Life and Labor in Ancient Mexico.* Benjamin Keen, trans. New Brunswick, N.J.: Rutgers University Press.

Index